COMMERCIAL REMEDIES
CURRENT ISSUES AND PROBLEMS

NORTON ROSE
THE OXFORD LAW COLLOQUIUM

COMMERCIAL REMEDIES
CURRENT ISSUES AND PROBLEMS

Edited by

ANDREW BURROWS

*Norton Rose Professor of Commercial Law, in the University of Oxford; Fellow
of St Hugh's College, Barrister and Honorary Bencher of the Middle Temple*

and

EDWIN PEEL

Fellow and Tutor in Law, Keble College, Oxford; Solicitor

OXFORD
UNIVERSITY PRESS

OXFORD
UNIVERSITY PRESS

Great Clarendon Street, Oxford OX2 6DP

Oxford University Press is a department of the University of Oxford.
It furthers the University's objective of excellence in research, scholarship,
and education by publishing worldwide in

Oxford New York

Auckland Bangkok Buenos Aires Cape Town Chennai
Dar es Salaam Delhi Hong Kong Istanbul Karachi Kolkata
Kuala Lumpur Madrid Melbourne Mexico City Mumbai Nairobi
São Paulo Shanghai Taipei Tokyo Toronto

Oxford is a registered trade mark of Oxford University Press
in the UK and in certain other countries

Published in the United States
by Oxford University Press Inc., New York

British ... Data
Data available
Library of Congress ... ation Data
Data available

1 3 5 7 9 10 8 6 4 2

Typeset by Hope Services (Abingdon) Ltd.
Printed in Great Britain
on ... er by
T. J. International Ltd, Padstow, Cornwall

Foreword

This is a valuable book. It should be compulsory reading for all lawyers concerned with business disputes.

Over the last quarter of a century the field of business disputes has been notable for two trends: the growth in business fraud, especially at the international level, and a rise in the standards expected of those engaged in business. These two contrary trends have led the courts to scrutinize the remedies they afford when conduct falls short of an acceptable standard. A legal right is not more valuable in law than the remedy provided for its breach.

It is of vital importance, therefore, that remedies should match the wrong. The common law duty of care extends more widely now than in the past. It is important that liability should be adequate but should not be imposed for losses outside the scope of the duty. Equitable concepts of trust and fiduciary obligation are invoked more extensively in commercial dealings. The remedies provided by the law for breach must be coherent. Unjust enrichment, moving firmly into the legal mainstream, ought to attract appropriate remedial relief. Restitution, as a remedial response to unjust enrichment and to wrongs, must be available on a principled basis.

These and other developments in the law relating to remedies are still continuing. They are not without their attendant problems. Some of the problems, problems of principle as well as practical problems, have yet to be resolved.

This book highlights these difficulties. It also draws attention to areas, especially relating to conflict of laws, where some radical re-thinking seems to be called for.

The unique format of the book enables the reader to have the benefit of views of legal scholars as well as practitioners. The best way forward is not always clear. But in every instance invaluable aid is given by identifying the problem and discussing its wider implications.

Lord Nicholls of Birkenhead

Preface

The colloquium at which the papers in this book were presented was held at St Hugh's College, Oxford on Friday and Saturday, September 27–28, 2002.

Building on previous Oxford-Norton Rose colloquia (this was the sixth), the purpose of the colloquium was to bring together practitioners (solicitors, barristers, and judges) and academics to examine and discuss an area of commercial law. This was based on the firm belief that, despite advances made in recent years, it is still far too rarely that the academic and practising branches of the profession meet to discuss questions of law. It was thought that a sharing of views on a topic as central as commercial remedies could only work to the mutual advantage of both groups. So it proved; and it is hoped that readers of this book will be equally enriched by the often contrasting insights offered by those whose primary job it is, on the one hand, to write and teach about the law and, on the other hand, to apply and advise on it.

The format of the proceedings was as follows. Eight papers, written by members of the Oxford Law Faculty, were distributed in advance and a paper in reply—from a practitioner's perspective—was given to each paper by a solicitor from Norton Rose. As can be seen, these replies largely took the form of a relatively brief 'comment', although three of the solicitors took the opportunity to write full papers in response. The bulk of the time at the colloquium was devoted to an open discussion of the issues raised by each pair of papers. Rather than writing an introductory chapter, the editors have attempted to capture the unique flavour of the colloquium—and to make the 'hot issues' more readily identifiable and understandable—by writing a short chapter, after each relevant pair of papers, reviewing the discussion that took place.

Thanks are due to Norton Rose for funding this event; and to Lord Nicholls of Birkenhead, Lord Justice Mance, and The Honourable Mr Justice Andrew Smith for their skill, enthusiasm, and good humour in chairing the various sessions. We would further like to thank Lord Nicholls for contributing the Foreword to this book.

Andrew Burrows
Edwin Peel
January 10 2003

Contents

List of Contributors   xi
List of Participants   xii
Tables of Cases   xv
Tables of Legislation   xxxi

PART A COMPENSATION

Chapter 1 Compensatory Damages:
           Some Central Issues of Assessment   1
JOHN CARTWRIGHT

Chapter 2 Compensatory Damages: Comment   21
GABRIELLE HURLEY

Chapter 3 Compensatory Damages: Review of Discussion   25

Chapter 4 Limitations on Compensation   27
ANDREW BURROWS

Chapter 5 Limitations on Compensation: Comment   49
CHRIS RYAN

Chapter 6 Limitations on Compensation: Review of Discussion   53

Chapter 7 *SAAMCO* Revisited   55
EDWIN PEEL

Chapter 8 *SAAMCO* in Practice   71
RICHARD BUTLER

Chapter 9 *SAAMCO*: Review of Discussion   89

PART B RESTITUTION AND PUNISHMENT

Chapter 10 Breach of Contract, Restitution for Wrongs,
            and Punishment   93
EWAN MCKENDRICK

Chapter 11　Breach of Contract, Restitution for Wrongs
　　　　　　　and Punishment: Comment　　　　　　　　125
SAM EASTWOOD

Chapter 12　Breach of Contract, Restitution for Wrongs,
　　　　　　　and Punishment: Review of Discussion　　129

Chapter 13　Restitution of Unjust Enrichment　　　　　131
PETER BIRKS

Chapter 14　Proprietary Remedies for Unjust Enrichment　　171
RICHARD CALNAN

Chapter 15　Restitution of Unjust Enrichment: Review of Discussion　185

PART C AGREED REMEDIES, HUMAN RIGHTS, AND CONFLICT OF LAWS

Chapter 16　Agreed Remedies　　　　　　　　　　191
LOUISE GULLIFER

Chapter 17　Agreed Remedies: Comment　　　　　　221
JOHN SHELTON

Chapter 18　Agreed Remedies: Review of Discussion　　225

Chapter 19　Private Law Remedies and the Human Rights Act 1998:
　　　　　　　An Overview .　　　　　　　　　　　227
NICHOLAS BAMFORTH

Chapter 20　Private Law Remedies and the Human Rights Act 1998:
　　　　　　　Defining the Limits of Interpretation　　257
ANDREW HENDERSON

Chapter 21　Private Law Remedies and the Human Rights Act 1998:
　　　　　　　Review of Discussion　　　　　　　　269

Chapter 22　Conflict of Laws and Commercial Remedies　　271
ADRIAN BRIGGS

Chapter 23　Conflict of Laws and Commercial Remedies: Comment　287
PHILIP REED

Chapter 24　Conflict of Laws and Commercial Remedies: Review of
　　　　　　　Discussion　　　　　　　　　　　　291

List of Contributors

NICHOLAS BAMFORTH, Fellow and Tutor in Law, The Queen's College, Oxford

PETER BIRKS, Regius Professor of Civil Law in the University of Oxford; Fellow of All Souls

ADRIAN BRIGGS, Fellow and Tutor in Law, St Edmund Hall, Oxford

ANDREW BURROWS, Norton Rose Professor of Commercial Law in the University of Oxford; Fellow of St Hugh's College

RICHARD BUTLER, Head of Research and Training, Commercial Litigation, Norton Rose

RICHARD CALNAN, Partner, Norton Rose

JOHN CARTWRIGHT, Tutor in Law, Christ Church, Oxford

SAM EASTWOOD, Partner, Norton Rose

LOUISE GULLIFER, Fellow and Tutor in Law, Harris Manchester College, Oxford

ANDREW HENDERSON, Associate Solicitor, Norton Rose

GABRIELLE HURLEY, Partner, Norton Rose

EWAN McKENDRICK, Professor of English Private Law in the University of Oxford; Fellow of Lady Margaret Hall

EDWIN PEEL, Fellow and Tutor in Law, Keble College, Oxford

PHILIP REED, Partner, Norton Rose

CHRIS RYAN, Partner, Norton Rose

JOHN SHELTON, Partner, Norton Rose

List of Participants at the Colloquium

Chairmen
Lord Nicholls of Birkenhead
Lord Justice Mance
The Honourable Mr Justice Andrew Smith

Oxford Law Faculty

Clare Ambrose	Somerville
Emily Baldock	Trinity
Nicholas Bamforth*	Queens
Peter Birks*	All Souls
Adrian Briggs*	St Edmund Hall
Andrew Burrows*	St Hugh's
John Cartwright*	Christ Church
Mindy Chen-Wishart	Merton
Stefan Enchelmaier	Wadham
Joshua Getzler	St Hugh's
Louise Gullifer*	Harris Manchester
Michael Hall	St Hilda's
Laura Hoyano	Wadham
Ewan McKendrick*	Lady Margaret Hall
Donal Nolan	Worcester
Edwin Peel*	Keble
Arianna Pretto	Brasenose
Robert Stevens	Lady Margaret Hall
Jessica Wells	Keble

Norton Rose

Steve Abraham	Sam Eastwood*
Helen Ashenden	Charles Evans
Nadja Atkins	Bernice Farah
Chris Bates	Patrick Farrell
Patrick Bourke	Peter Hall
Robin Brooks	Ann Halpern
Richard Butler*	Andrew Henderson*
Richard Calnan*	Gabrielle Hurley*
David Crane	Anna Iversen
Jonathan Dickman	Catherine Johnson
Michele Dykes	Rina Kaur

Adam Kirby   Polly Salter
Harriet Levy   John Shelton*
David Lewis   Garfield Smith
Mark Lewis   Loraine Watson
Philip Reed*   Mark Lloyd Williams
Chris Ryan*   Simon Williams

Guests
Michael Bridge   University College, London
Michael Furmston   University of Bristol
Richard Hooley   Fitzwilliam, Cambridge
Michael Lerego   Fountain Court Chambers
Bridget Lucas   Fountain Court Chambers
Hector MacQueen   University of Edinburgh
Harvey McGregor   4 Paper Buildings
Gerard McMeel   University of Bristol
Stephen Moriarty   Fountain Court Chambers
Francis Rose   University of Bristol
Chris Rycroft   Oxford University Press
Marcus Smith   Fountain Court Chambers
Nicholas Underhill   Fountain Court Chambers
Graham Virgo   Downing College, Cambridge
David Waksman   Fountain Court Chambers
Philip Wood   Allen & Overy
Sarah Worthington   London School of Economics

* Speaker

Table of Cases

UNITED KINGDOM

A *v* B plc [2002] 3 WLR 542, [2002] 2 All ER 545 ....237, 239, 242–4, 258

A *v* Bottrill [2002] UKPC 44, [2002] 3 WLR 1406 122

AB Corp *v* CD Co (*The 'Sine Nomine'*) [2002] 1 Lloyd's Rep 805,
noted Beatson (2002) 118 LQR 377 ....95, 108–9

A-G *v* Blake (Jonathan Cape Ltd, Third Party) [1997] Ch 84, [1998]
Ch 439, CA, [2001] 1 AC 268, HL....................7, 93–8, 100–1, 103, 107–16,
118, 120, 122–3, 125–7, 129–30, 133, 192, 269

A-G *v* Guardian Newspapers Ltd (No 2) [1990] 1 AC 109 100

A-G for Hong Kong *v* Reid [1994] 1 AC 324, PC................174, 182, 156, 158

Addis *v* Gramophone Co Ltd [1909] AC 488......................................119, 121

Aiken *v* Short (1856) 1 H&N 210, 25 LJ Ex 321, 156 ER 1180 141

Air Jamaica Ltd *v* Charlton [1999] 1 WLR 1399, PC..................................162

Airbus Industrie GIE *v* Patel [1999] 1 AC 119 ....279, 282, 291

Albazero (The) [1977] AC 774, HL..14

Alcoa Minerals of Jamaica Inc *v* Broderick [2000] 3 WLR 23, PC 28

Alder *v* Moore [1961] 2 QB 57 ....198, 203

Alfred McAlpine Construction Ltd *v* Panatown Ltd [2001]
1 AC 518, HL 12–13, 15–19, 23–5, 95, 192

Alphacell Ltd *v* Woodward [1972] AC 824 74

Aluminium Industrie Vaasen *v* Romalpa Aluminium [1976]
1 WLR 676, CA 182

Amec Developments Ltd *v* Jury's Hotel Management (UK)
Ltd [2001] EGLR 81...95

Aneco Reinsurance Underwriting Ltd *v* Johnson & Higgins Ltd
[2000] Lloyd's Rep IR 12, CA, [2002] 1 Lloyd's Rep 157,
HL 57, 60–2, 70–1, 76, 81, 83–6, 89

Anglia Television Ltd *v* Reed [1972] 1 QB 60, CA..8

Apex Supply Co Ltd, Re [1942] CH 108 201

Arab Monetary Fund *v* Hashim, *The Times*, 11 October 1994..................281

Archer *v* Brown [1985] 1 QB 401..6

Associated Distributors Ltd *v* Hall [1938] 2 KB 83.............................198, 201

Associated Japanese Bank *v* Credit du Nord [1989] 1 WLR 255..............172

Attica Sea Carriers Corp *v* Ferrostaal Poseidon Bulk Reederei
GmbH (*The Puerto Buitrago*) [1976] 1 Lloyd's Rep 250 106

Avon County Council *v* Howlett [1983] 1 WLR 605, CA......................137–8

B *v* Secretary of State for the Home Dept [2000] 2 CMLR 1086 251

Bairstow *v* Queen's Moat Houses plc [2001] 2 BCLC 531, CA..................46

Ball *v* Banner [2000] EGCS 36..79
Bankers' Trust International plc *v* PT Dharmala Sakti Sejahtera
  [1996] CLC 252 284
Banque Bruxelles Lambert SA *v* Eagle Star Insurance Co Ltd *see* South
  Australia Asset Managemenr Corp *v* York Montague Ltd
Barclays Bank Ltd *v* Quistclose Investments Ltd [1970] AC 567,
  HL 162
Barclays Bank Ltd *v* WJ Simms & Son (Southern) Ltd [1980]
  QB 677...135, 141, 172
Barclays Bank plc *v* Fairclough Building Ltd [1994] 3 WLR 1057..............39
Barclays Bank plc *v* Fairclough Building Ltd (No 2) (1995)
  44 Con LR 35, CA..39
Barclays Bank plc *v* O'Brien [1994] 1 AC 180, HL.....................................132
Barrett *v* Enfield LBC [2001] 2 AC 550...227
Barton Thompson & Co *v* Stapling Machines Co [1966]
  Ch 499...215
BCCI *v* Price Waterhouse (No 3), *The Times*, 2 April 1998 66
BCCI *v* Prince Fahd Bin Salaman Abdul Aziz Al-Saud [1997]
  BCC 63...113
Bell *v* Lever Bros [1932] AC 161, HL...146
Berrington *v* Evans (1839) 3 Y & C Ex 384..177
BHP Petroleum *v* British Steel plc [1999] 2 All ER (Comm) 544 ....32, 51
BICC *v* Burndy [1985] 1 Ch 232 212–13
Bishopsgate Investment Management *v* Homan [1995] Ch 211,
  CA 183
Boardman *v* Phipps [1967] 2 AC 46...100, 113
Bock *v* Gorrissen (1860) 2 De G F & J 434..178
Boys *v* Chaplin [1971] AC 356..271, 292
Bradford *v* Robinson Rentals Ltd [1967] 1 WLR 337 36
Bridge *v* Campbell Finance Ltd [1962] AC 600...........194, 198–201, 203, 225
Bristol & West Building Society *v* Fancy & Jackson
  [1997] 4 All ER 582...81
Bristol & West Building Society *v* Mothew [1996]
  4 All ER 698, [1998] Ch 1..45–6, 86, 160
British Sugar plc *v* NEI Power Projects Ltd (1997) 87 BLR 42,
  CA 32, 50–1
Brooks *v* Beirnstein [1909] 1 KB 98..206
Brown *v* KMR Services Ltd [1995] 4 All ER 598 ....29, 34–6, 48, 53
Brown *v* Stott [2001] 2 WLR 817 ....229, 248–9, 251
Brown and Davis *v* Galbraith [1972] 1 WLR 997, CA................................143
Bumper Development Corp *v* Metropolitan Police Commissioner
  [1991] 1 WLR 1362, CA 274
Burdett *v* Willett (1708) 2 Vern 638 173

Caledonia North Sea Ltd *v* British Telecommunications plc [2002]
1 Lloyd's Rep 553...32, 53
Cambridge Water Co Ltd *v* Eastern Counties Leather plc [1994]
2 AC 264, HL 7
Campbell *v* MGN Ltd, *The Times*, 29 March 2002 ....258, 266
Caparo Industries plc *v* Dickman [1990] 2 AC 605 ....56, 79, 83
Car & Universal Finance Co Ltd *v* Caldwell [1965] 1 QB 525, CA 160
Carr-Saunders *v* Dick McNeill Associates Ltd [1986] 1 WLR 922 100
Cave *v* Cave (1880) 15 ChD 639 166
CCC Films (London) Ltd *v* Impact Quadrant Films Ltd [1985]
QB 16...8
Cenargo Ltd *v* Izar Construcciones Navales SA [2002] EWCA
Civ 524...198
Chase Manhattan Bank NA Ltd *v* Israel-British Bank (London)
Ltd [1981] Ch 105 ....160, 173, 179, 186
Chatterton *v* Maclean [1951] 1 All ER 761 206
Chesworth *v* Farrar [1967] 1 QB 407 100
Clea Shipping Corporation *v* Bulk Oil International Ltd (*The
Alaskan Trader*) [1984] 1 All ER 129...106
Clough Mill *v* Martin [1985] 1 WLR 111...206, 214
Clydebank Engineering and Shipbuilding Co Ltd *v* Don Jose
Ramos Yzquierdo y Castenceda [1905] AC 6 194–5
CMS Dolphin Ltd *v* Simonet [2001] 2 BCLC 704..................................95, 105
Colin Bishop case *see* Bristol & West Building Society *v* Fancy
& Jackson
Commercial Banking Co of Sydney Ltd *v* Mann [1961] AC 1,
PC, approved [1991] 2 AC 548, HL 149
Commissioner of Public Works *v* Hills [1906] AC 368................194, 209–10
Coneco Ltd *v* Foxboro Great Britain Ltd (CA,
24 February 1992)..203
Cooden Engineering Co Ltd *v* Stanford [1953] 1 QB 86...........................200
Cook *v* Lewis [1952] 1 DLR 1 90
Credit Suisse Fides Trust SA *v* Cuoghi [1998] QB 818, CA 282, 289
Crittall Windows Ltd *v* Stormseal (UPVC) Window Systems
Ltd [1991] RPC 265 191
Croudace Construction Ltd *v* Cawoods Concrete Products Ltd
[1978] 2 Lloyd's Rep 55, CA 32, 49–51
Curtain Dream plc, Re [1990] BCLC 921 216

D and F Estates Ltd *v* Church Commrs for England [1989]
AC 177, HL 16
Deepak Fertilisers & Petrochemicals Ltd *v* Davy McKee (London) Ltd
[1999] 1 All ER (Comm) 69, CA 32

Dept of the Environment *v* Thomas Bates and Sons Ltd [1991]
  1 AC 499, HL 16
Dewar *v* Mintoft [1912] 2 KB 373..205
Dextra Bank & Trust Co Ltd *v* Bank of Jamaica [2002] 1 All ER Com
  193, PC, noted McInnes (2002) 119 LQR 208....................................138–40
Dies *v* British and International Mining and Finance Corp [1939]
  1 KB 724..205, 208
Diplock, Re [1948] Ch 465, CA..181, 186
DnB Mortgages *v* Bullock & Lees [2000] Lloyd's Rep PN 290 77
Douglas and Zeta-Jones *v* Hello! Ltd [2001]
  QB 697..237–8, 241–3, 258
Downs *v* Chappell [1997] 1 WLR 426 58
Doyle *v* Olby (Ironmongers) Ltd [1969] 2 QB 158, CA...............................36
Dunlop Pneumatic Tyre Co *v* New Garage & Motor Co [1915]
  AC 79 ....194–6, 225

ECGD *v* Universal Oil Products [1983] 1 Lloyd's Rep 448, CA,
  [1983] 1 WLR 399, HL..204
Else (1982) Ltd *v* Parkland Holdings Ltd [1994] 1 BCLC 130.............209–12
Esso Petroleum Co *v* Mardon [1976] QB 801, CA 8
Esso Petroleum Co Ltd *v* Niad Ltd (unreported, ChD,
  22 November 2001).........................95, 103, 108–10, 112, 118–19, 125–7, 130
Exports Credit Guarantee Dept *v* Universal Oil Products Co
  [1983] 1 WLR 399 198

Fairchild *v* Glenhaven Funeral Services Ltd [2002] ICR 412,
  [2002] 3 WLR 89, HL...66–70, 73–5, 90, 271
Farley *v* Skinner [2001] UKHL 49, [2002] 2 AC 732
  at [21] 6, 13, 17, 19, 28, 192
FC Jones (Trustee in Bankruptcy) *v* Jones [1997] Ch 159, CA 117, 155
Fibrosa Spolka Akcyjna *v* Fairbairn Lawson Combe Barbour
  [1943] AC 32, HL...145
Financing Ltd *v* Baldock [1963] 2 QB 104..201
Forsikringsaktieselskapet Vesta *v* Butcher [1989] AC 852, CA,
  affd [1989] AC 880, HL...5, 38
Foskett *v* McKeown [2001] 1 AC 102, [2000] 2 WLR 1299,
  HL 153–6, 159, 166, 174, 182

Galbraith *v* Mitchenall Estates Ltd [1965] 2 QB 473....................................209
Galoo Ltd *v* Bright Grahame Murray [1994] 1 WLR 1360, CA..................66
George Inglefield Ltd, Re [1933] Ch 1...216
Gillingham Bus Disaster Fund, Re [1958] Ch 300, affd [1959]
  Ch 62, CA 163

Glencore International AG *v* Metro Trading International Inc
  [2002] EWCA Civ 524; [2002] CLC 1090 (18 April 2002).......................284
Godfrey *v* Furzo (1733) 3 P Wms 185...173
Goker *v* NWS Bank plc (CA, 1 August 1990)....................................191, 214
Goldcorp Exchange Ltd, Re [1995] 1 AC 74, PC............162, 165–6, 173, 176
Goss *v* Chilcott [1996] AC 788..206
Graham *v* JA Pye (Oxford) Ltd [2001] Ch 804 ....229, 234
Gray's Truck Centre Ltd *v* Olaf L Johnson Ltd (CA,
  25 January 1990)...143
Great Peace Shipping Ltd *v* Tsavliris Salvage (International)
  Ltd (2001) 151 NLJ 1696, QBD Comm Ct, affd [2002]
  EWCA Civ 1407 160
Gregg *v* Scott [2002] EWCA Civ 1471, CA 70
Grupo Torras SA *v* Al Sabah [2001] CLC 221, CA 281, 291
Guinness Mahon & Co Ltd *v* Kensington and Chelsea Royal
  London BC [1999] QB 215, CA...165
Guinness plc *v* Saunders [1990] 2 AC 663 113
GUS Property Management Ltd *v* Littlewoods Mail Order Stores Ltd
  1982 SLT 533, HL 16

H Parsons (Livestock) Ltd *v* Uttley Ingham & Co Ltd
  [1978] QB 791, CA...6, 30, 34–5
Hadley *v* Baxendale (1854) 9 Exch 341 ....29–34, 49, 51, 191
Halifax Building Society *v* Thomas [1996] Ch 217 100
Hallett's Estate, Re (1880) 13 ChD 696, CA...174, 182
Hancock *v* Tucker [1999] Lloyd's Rep PN 814 81
Harris *v* Wyre Forest DC [1990] 1 AC 831...83
Harrods (Buenos Aires) Ltd, Re [1992] Ch 72, CA......................................272
Hedley Byrne & Co *v* Heller & Partners [1964] AC 465.........................83, 87
Henderson *v* Jaouen [2002] 1 WLR 2971, CA 275
Henderson *v* Merrett Syndicates Ltd [1994] 3 WLR 761,
  [1995] 2 AC 145, HL...4, 8, 35, 39, 41, 86–7
Hill *v* Perrott (1810) 3 Taunt 274...100
Hodgson *v* Marks [1971] Ch 892, CA...162
Holmes *v* Bangladesh Biman Corp [1989] AC 1112...................273, 287, 292
Holroyd *v* Marshall (1862) 10 HLC 191, HL 177
Holtby *v* Brigham & Cowan (Hull) Ltd [2000] 3 All ER 421 68
Home Office *v* Wainwright [2001] EWCA Civ 2081...............................238–9
Hotel Services Ltd *v* Hilton International Hotels (UK) Ltd
  [2000] 1 All ER (Comm) 750, CA 32
Hotson *v* East Berkshire Area Health Authority [1987]
  AC 570 ....69, 90
Howe *v* Smith (1881) 27 ChD 89...207

Hyundai Heavy Industries Co Ltd *v* Papadopoulos [1980]
    1 WLR 1129 205–7

Imutran Ltd *v* Uncaged Campaigns Ltd [2001] 2 All ER 385 244
Interfoto Picture Library Ltd *v* Stiletto Visual Programmes Ltd
    [1989] QB 433 ....193, 199
International Mineral and Chemical Corp *v* Carl O'Helm AG
    [1986] 1 Lloyd's Rep 81 31

JA Pye (Oxford) Ltd *v* Graham [2002] 3 WLR 221, HL 229–30
Jackson *v* Horizon Holidays Ltd [1975] 1 WLR 1468, CA 12
Jarvis *v* Swans Tours Ltd [1973] QB 233, CA 12
Jervis *v* Harris [1996] Ch 195 198
Jobson *v* Johnson [1989] 1 All ER 621 ....192, 195, 213
Johnson *v* Gore Wood & Co [2002] 1 AC 1, HL 13
Jones *v* Waring & Gillow [1926] AC 670, HL 140

Kamouh *v* Associated Electrical Industries International Ltd
    [1980] QB 199 274
Kayford, Re [1975] 1 WLR 279 180
Kelly *v* Cooper [1993] Ac 205, PC 86–7
Kelly *v* Solari (1841) 9 M&W 54, [1835–1842] All ER Rep 320,
    152 ER 24 134
Kemble *v* Farren (1829) 6 Bing 141, 130 ER 1234 195
Kent & Sussex Sawmills Ltd, Re [1947] Ch 177 177
Kleinwort Benson *v* Lincoln City Council [1999] 2 AC 349,
    HL 145, 165, 172
Kleinwort Benson Ltd *v* Birmingham City Council [1997]
    QB 380, CA 148
Kleinwort Benson Ltd *v* Sandwell BC [1994] 4 All ER 890,
    [1994] 4 All ER 957, CA 164–5
Kleinwort Benson Ltd *v* South Tyneside MBC [1994] 2 All
    ER 972 148
Koufos *v* C Czarnikow Ltd (*The Heron II*) [1969] 1 AC 350,
    HL 7, 30, 32, 35
Kpohraror *v* Woolwich Building Society [1996] 4 All ER 119 31
Kuddus *v* Chief Constable of Leicestershire Constabulary [2002]
    2 AC 122, [2001] UKHL 29, [2001] 1 WLR 1789 ....7, 93–5, 99,
                                                  119–20, 122–3, 127, 130, 267
Kuwait Airways Corp *v* Iraqi Airways Co (Nos 4 and 5) [2002]
    UKHL 19, [2002] 2 WLR 1353, [2002] 1 All ER
    (Comm) 843 ....53–4, 95, 118
Kuwait Oil Tanker SAK *v* Al Bader [2000] 2 All ER (Comm) 271, CA ...281

Lamb *v* Camden LBC [1981] Q 625 ....59–60, 63
Lamine *v* Dorrell (1701) 2 Ld Raym 1216 100
Laverack *v* Woods of Colchester [1976] 1 QB 278 28
Liesbosch (The) [1933] AC 449, HL 28
Linden Gardens Trust Ltd *v* Lenesta Sludge Disposals Ltd [1994]
    1 AC 85, HL 14, 26
Lion Nathan Ltd *v* CC Bottlers Ltd [1996] 1 WLR 1438 56
Lipkin Gorman *v* Karpnale Ltd [1991] 2 AC 548,
    HL 137–8, 148–53, 166, 173, 179
Livingstone *v* Rawyards (1880) 5 App Cas 25, HL 4, 56
Lloyds Bank plc *v* Independent Insurance Co Ltd [1999]
    2 WLR 986, CA 140–3, 150
Lombard North Central *v* Butterworth [1987] 2 WLR 6,
    [1987] QB 527 ....192, 198, 200, 202–3, 214
London, Chatham & Dover Rwy *v* South Eastern Rwy [1893]
    AC 429 28
Lonrho plc *v* Fayed [1992] 1 WLR 1 160
Lord Elphinstone Monkland Iron and Coal Co Ltd (1886)
    11 App Cas 332..195
Lord Napier and Ettrick *v* Hunter [1993] AC 713, HL 157
Lordsvale Finance plc *v* Bank of Zambia [1996] 3 WLR 688,
    [1996] 3 All ER 156..191, 195, 198
Lubbe *v* Cape [2000] 1 WLR 1545 292
Lunn *v* Thornton (1845) 1 CB 379 176
Lysaght *v* Edwards (1876) 2 ChD 499 177

McCartan Turkington Breen *v* Times Newspapers Ltd [2000]
    4 All ER 913..229
McGhee *v* National Coal Board [1973] 1 WLR 1 ....68–9, 75, 90
Mackreth *v* Symmons (1808) 15 Ves 329 178
McMillan Inc *v* Bishopsgate Investment Trust plc (No 3) [1996]
    1 WLR 387 291
Maharaj *v* A-G of Trinidad and Tobago (No 2) [1979] AC 385 237
Marcic *v* Thames Water Utilities Ltd [2002] QB 929, CA, [2002]
    EWCA Civ 64 ....235, 258–9, 264–6
Marcic *v* Thames Water Utilities Ltd (No 2) [2002]
    QB 1003...235, 260, 269–70
Mayson *v* Clouet [1924] AC 980 208
Miliangos *v* George Frank (Textiles) Ltd [1976] AC 443 274
Millar's Machinery Company Ltd *v* David Way & Son (1934)
    40 Com Cas 204 49
Ministry of Defence *v* Ashman [1993] 2 EGLR 102....................................100
Ministry of Defence *v* Thompson [1993] 2 EGLR 107................................100

Monarch SS Co *v* A/B Karlshamns Oljefabriker [1949] AC 196 31
Morgan Guaranty Trust Co of New York *v* Lothian Regional
   Council 1995 SC 151, Ct of Sess 134
Mornington *v* Keane (1858) 2 De G & J 292 177
Moss' Empires Ltd *v* Olympia (Liverpool) Ltd [1939] AC 544 199
Motorola Credit Corp *v* Uzan [2002] EWCA Civ 989, *The Times*,
   10 July 2002 254
Murphy *v* Brentwood DC [1991] 1 AC 398, HL 16
Mussen *v* Van Diemen's Land Co [1938] Ch 253 212

National Westminster Bank *v* Morgan [1985] AC 686............................199
National Westminster Bank plc *v* Somer International (UK) Ltd
   [2001] EWCA Civ 970, [2002] 3 WLR 64, CA 137
Naughton *v* O'Callaghan [1990] 3 All ER 191 58
Neste Oy *v* Lloyds Bank [1983] 2 Lloyd's Rep 658............................162, 164
Nocton *v* Lord Ashburton [1914] AC 932..86–7
North and South Trust Co *v* Berkeley [1971] 1 WLR 470...........................86
Nutting *v* Baldwin [1995] 1 WLR 201 ....191, 198–9
Nykredit Mortgage Bank plc *v* Edward Erdman Group Ltd
   (No 2) [1997] 1 WLR 1627, HL 58, 73, 76–8

Omega Group Holdings Ltd *v* Kozeny [2002] CLC 132............................284
On Demand Information plc *v* Michael Gerson (Finance) plc [2002]
   2 WLR 919, HL, [2000] 4 All ER 734, CA 202, 212, 214–15, 219, 226
Orion Finance Ltd *v* Crown Financial Management Ltd [1996]
   2 BCLC 78...216
Orphanos *v* Queen Mary College [1985] AC 761, HL 147
Oughton *v* Seepings (1830) 1 B & Ad 241..100

Palmer *v* Carey [1926] AC 703, PC 180
Penarth Dock Engineering Co Ltd *v* Pounds [1963] 1 Lloyd's
   Rep 359 100
Pepper *v* Hart [1993] AC 593..265
Peter Pan Manufacturing Corp *v* Corsets Silhouette Ltd [1964]
   1 WLR 96..100
Phillips Hong Kong *v* The A-G of Hong Kong (1993) 61 Building
   Law Reports 49...196, 204, 225
Phrantzes *v* Argenti [1960] 2 QB 19..275
Platform Home Loans Ltd *v* Oyston Shipways Ltd [2000]
   2 AC 190...63–5, 67, 71, 79–80, 89
Polly Peck International plc, Re [1998] 3 All ER 812, CA..........................173
Poplar Housing Association *v* Donoghue [2002] QB 48.....................229–33
Portman Building Society *v* Bevan Ashford [2000] PNLR 344, CA.....81, 83

President of India *v* La Pintada Compania Navigacion SA
[1985] AC 104 31
Pye *v* British Automobile Commercial Syndicate Ltd [1906]
1 KB 425..209
Python (Monty) Pictures Ltd *v* Paragon Entertainment Corp
[1998] EMLR 697 ....191, 212

Quinn *v* Burch Brothers (Builders) Ltd [1966] 2 QB 370, CA 42

R *v* A [2002] 1 AC 45..230–3, 249, 251
R *v* DPP, ex p Kebilene [2000] 2 AC 326 ....245, 250, 253
R *v* Kansal [2002] 2 AC 69..230
R *v* Knuller (Publishing, Printing and Promotions) Ltd
[1973] AC 435 257
R *v* Lambert [2001] 3 WLR 206, HL......................................230, 232, 249, 257
R *v* Secretary of State for the Home Dept, ex p Isiko [2001]
1 FCR 633 251
R (Alconbury) *v* Secretary of State for the Environment, Transport
and the Regions [2001] 2 WLR 1389..249
R (on the application of International Transport Roth GmbH) *v*
Secretary of State for the Home Dept [2002] EWCA Civ 158 251
Raflatac Ltd *v* Eade [1999] 1 Lloyd's Rep 506 39
Raiffeisen Zentralbank Oesterreich AG *v* Five Star General
Trading LLC [2001] QB 825, CA 276
Reed, Re, ex p Barnett (1876) 3 ChD 123 179
Reeves *v* Commissioner of Police for the Metropolis [2000]
1 AC 360 ....66, 75, 89
Regal (Hastings) Ltd *v* Gulliver [1942] 1 All ER 378....................................100
Reid-Newfoundland Co *v* Anglo-American Telegraph Co
Ltd [1912] AC 555 104
Robinson *v* Harman (1848) 1 Ex 850 4
Robophone Facilities Ltd *v* Blank [1966] 1 WLR 1428 ....30, 191, 195, 225
Roerig *v* Valiant Trawlers Ltd [2002] 1 WLR 2304, CA 272, 276
Rookes *v* Barnard [1964] AC 1129 ....93, 119–20, 122
Rowland *v* Divall [1923] 2 KB 500 206
Royal Bank of Scotland *v* Etridge (No 2) [2001] UKHL 44,
[2001] 3 WLR 1021, HL..132
Royal Brunei Airlines *v* Tan [1995] 2 AC 378...43
Royscot Trust Ltd *v* Rogerson [1991] 2 QB 297, CA 36
Rugg *v* Minett (1809) 11 East 211, 103 ER 985..206
Ruxley Electronics & Construction Ltd *v* Forsyth [1996] 1 AC 344,
HL, [1994] 1 WLR 650, CA..................7, 9–12, 17, 19, 23, 25, 195, 269
Ryan *v* Friction Dynamics Ltd, *The Times*, 14 June 2000 284

Rylands *v* Fletcher (1868) LR 3 HL 330 ....7, 259

SAAMCO *see* South Australia Asset Management Corporation *v* York
Montague Ltd
St Martins Property Corp Ltd *v* Sir Robert McAlpine Ltd [1994]
1 AC 85, HL 14–17
Satef-Huttenes Albertus SpA *v* Paloma Tercera Shipping Co SA
(*The Pegase*) [1981] 1 Lloyd's Rep 175..30
Scandinavian Trading Tanker Co AB *v* Flota Petrolera Ecuatoriana
(*The Scaptrade*) [1983] 2 AC 694 ....191, 212, 214–15
Schering Agrochemicals *v* Resibel NV SA noted Burrows
(1993) 109 LQR 175 42
Schuler AG *v* Wickman Machine Tool Sales [1974] AC 235 84
Scottish Equitable plc *v* Derby [2001] 3 All ER 818, CA 134–8, 186–7
Services Europe Atlantique Sud *v* Stockholms Rederiaktiebolag
Svea (*The Despina R*) [1979] AC 685..274
Shiloh Spinners *v* Harding [1973] AC 691...................................212–13, 215
Sinclair *v* Brougham [1914] AC 348, HL...165, 181
Slipper *v* BBC [1991] 1 QB 283, CA 7
Smith *v* Eric S Bush [1990] 1 AC 831 83
Smith *v* Leech Brain & Co Ltd [1962] 2 QB 405 69
Smith *v* Littlewoods Organisation [1987] AC 241 60
Smith New Court Securities Ltd *v* Scrimgeour Vickers (Asset
Management) Ltd [1997] AC 254, HL...6–7, 36, 58
South Australia Asset Management Corporation *v* York
Montague Ltd (SAAMCO) [1997] AC 191, HL, [1995]
QB 375, CA...5–6, 29, 55–67, 70–2, 76, 78–86, 89
South Carolina Insurance Co *v* Assutantie Maatschappij 'De Zeven
Provincien' NV [1999] 1 AC 119 283
South Tyneside MBC *v* Svenska International [1995] 1 All ER 545.........138
Sport International Bussum BV *v* Inter-Footwear Ltd [1984]
2 All ER 321..212, 214
Spurling *v* Bradshaw [1956] 1 WLR 461 193
Standard Chartered Bank *v* Pakistan National Shipping Co
(No 2) [2002] UKHL 43, [2002] 3 WLR 1547, HL 37
Standard Chartered Bank *v* Pakistan National Shipping Co
(No 4) [2001] QB 167, CA...5
State of Brunei Darussalam *v* Bolkiah, *The Times*,
5 September 2001 284
Steedman *v* Drinkle [1916] 1 AC 275 ....212, 215
Steggles & Palmer case *see* Bristol & West Building Society *v* Fancy
& Jackson
Stockloser *v* Johnson [1954] 1 QB 476 209–12

Stocznia Gdanska SA *v* Latvian Shipping Co [1998]
  1 WLR 574 ....205–7, 211
Stovin *v* Wise [1996] AC 92 259
Strand Electric and Engineering Co Ltd *v* Brisford Entertainments Ltd
  [1952] 2 QB 246 100
Surrey CC *v* Bredero Homes Ltd [1993] 1 WLR 1361 ....103, 129
Swiss Bank Corp *v* Lloyds Bank [1979] 1 Ch 548, [1982] AC 584,
  CA & HL 177, 180

Tailby *v* Official Receiver (1888) 13 App Cas 523, HL 177
Tang Man Sit *v* Capacious Investments Ltd [1996] AC 514 118
Tappenden *v* Artus [1964] 2 QB 185, CA 178
Target Holdings Ltd *v* Redfern [1996] AC 421 ....43–4, 46–7
Teacher *v* Calder (1899) 1 F (HL) 39, [1899] AC 451 116
Tinsley *v* Milligan [1994] 1 AC 340, HL..162
Transag Haulage Ltd *v* Leyland DAF Finance Co [1994]
  2 BCLC 88..198, 201–3, 212–14
Trego *v* Hunt [1896] AC 7..110
Tremain *v* Pike [1969] 1 WLR 1556..36
Triffit Nurseries *v* Salads Etcetera Ltd [2000] 1 All ER
  (Comm) 737, CA 164
Turner *v* Grovit [2002] 1 WLR 104, HL..284
Twinsectra Ltd *v* Yardley [1999] Lloyd's Rep Banking 348, CA, affd
  on other grounds [2002] UKHL 12, [2002] 2 WLR 802, HL 160, 162–3

UCB Bank plc *v* Hepherd Winstanley and Pugh, *The Times*,
  25 August 1999, CA 38
Union Bank of Australia Ltd *v* McClintock [1922] 1 AC 240, PC 149
Union Eagle Ltd *v* Golden Achievement Ltd [1997] AC 514............191, 213
United Australia Ltd *v* Barclays Bank Ltd [1941] AC 1.............................100
United Bank of Kuwait plc *v* Prudential Property Services Ltd 57, 76
United Dominions Trust (Commercial) Ltd *v* Ennis [1968] 1 QB 54 201
United Scientific Holdings Ltd *v* Burnley BC [1978] AC 904 45
Universal Corp *v* Five Ways Properties Ltd [1979] 1 All ER 552 209
University of Nottingham *v* Fishel [2000] ICR 1462 ....95, 104

Vandervell *v* IRC [1967] 2 AC 291, HL 161
Venables and Thompson *v* News Group Newspapers Ltd
  [2001] 2 WLR 1038 ....237–8, 241, 258
Victoria Laundry (Windsor) Ltd *v* Newman Industries Ltd
  [1949] 2 KB 528 ....29–30, 33–5, 53

Wadsworth *v* Lydall [1981] 1 WLR 598 195

Wagon Mound (No 1) [1961] AC 388, PC 7, 33, 36
Wagon Mound (No 2) [1967] 1 AC 617, PC 7
Wait, Re [1927] 1 Ch 606 177
Wallis *v* Smith (1879) 21 C D 243..209
Watford Electronics Ltd *v* Sanderson CFL Ltd [2001] 1 All ER
    (Comm) 696 32
Watts *v* Morrow [1991] 1 WLR 1421, CA 13, 28
Welsh Development Agency *v* Export Finance Co Ltd [1992]
    BCLC 148...216
Westdeutsche Landesbank Girozentrale *v* Islington LBC [1996]
    AC 669, HL 145, 159–60, 163–6, 168, 181
White & Carter (Councils) Ltd *v* McGregor [1962] AC 413 105
Whitecomb *v* Jacob (1710) 1 Salk 161 173
Widnes Foundry (1925) Ltd *v* Cellulose Acetate Silk Co [1931]
    2 KB 393..192
Wilsher *v* Essex Area Health Authority [1988] AC 1074.......................69, 90
Wilson *v* First County Trust (No 1) [2001] QB 407 252
Wilson *v* First County Trust (No 2) [2002] QB 74 ......232–4, 236, 251–4, 270
Windsor Securities Ltd *v* Loreldale Ltd, *The Times*,
    10 September 1975 209
Workers Trust & Merchant Bank Ltd *v* Dojap Investments
    Ltd [1993] AC 532 209–10
Wroth *v* Tyler [1974] Ch 30...34
Wrotham Park Estate Co Ltd *v* Parkside Homes Ltd [1974]
    1 WLR 798 ....114–15, 129
WWF – World Wide Fund for Nature *v* World Wrestling Federation
    Entertainment Inc [2002] FSR 32, [2002] EWCA Civ 196,
    [2002] FSR 33, CA 95, 104, 106–7

AUSTRALIA

Allstate Life Insurance Co *v* ANZ Banking Group Ltd (1996)
    64 FLR 61, Aust Fed Ct..283
AMEV – UDC Finance Ltd *v* Austin (1986) 162 CLR 170 ....199, 201–2
Astley *v* Austrust Ltd (1999) 161 ALR 155 37

Commissioner of State Revenue *v* Royal Insurance Australia Ltd
    (1994) 182 CLR 51, HCA 148

David Securities Pty Ltd *v* Commonwealth Bank of Australia
    (1992) 175 CLR 353, HCA 145, 147
Digital Pulse Pty Ltd *v* Christopher Harris [2002]
    NSWSC 33...120

Gray *v* Motor Accident Commission (1998) 196 CLR 1 121

Ha *v* New South Wales (1999) 187 CLR 465, HCA 144
Hospitality Group Pty Ltd *v* Australian Rugby Union [2001]
  FCA 1040, (2001) ATPR 43...95

John Pfeiffer Pty Ltd *v* Rogerson (2000) 203 CLR 503 277

Kenny & Good Property Ltd *v* MGICA (1992) Ltd (1999) 163 ALR 611...81

Legione v Hateley (1983) 152 Commonwealth Law Reports 406............213

McDonald *v* Dennys Lascalles (1933) 48 CLR 457 207
Majeauw Carrying Co *v* Coastal Rutile [1973] 129 CLR 58, HCA 178
Mason *v* New South Wales (1959) 102 CLR 108, HCA...............................148

National Australia Bank *v* Idoport [2002] NSWSC 623.............................283

O'Dea *v* Allstates Leasing System (WA) Pty Ltd (1983)
  152 CLR 359 201

Paramasivam *v* Flynn (1998–9) 160 ALR 203................................279–80, 289
Pilmer *v* The Duke Group Ltd [2001] HCA 31 45

Regie Nationale des Usines Renault SA *v* Zhang (2002)
  187 ALR 1...277, 284
Roxborough *v* Rothmans of Pall Mall (Australia) Ltd [2001] HCA 68,
  (2001) 185 ALR 355, HCA, noted Beatson and Virgo (2002) 118 LQR
  352–8, Birks (2002) Oxford U Commonwealth LJ 1 ....132, 143–8

Stern *v* McArthur (1988) 165 CLR 489 ....209, 214
Stevens *v* Head (1993) 176 CLR 433 277

US Surgical Corp *v* Hospital Products International Pty Ltd [1982] 2
  NSWLR 766, NSW SC, affd [1983] 2 NSWLR 157, NSW CA, revd on
  different grounds (1984) 156 CLR 41 280

Wimbourne *v* National Commercial Bank (1978) 5 BPR 11958,
  NSW SC..280

CANADA
Air Canada *v* British Columbia [1989] 1 SCR 1161, 59 DLR
  (4th) 161, SCC 147

Canson Enterprises *v* Boughton (1991) 85 DLR (4th) 129 44–5

Elsey *v* JG Collins Insurance Agencies Ltd (1978)
  83 DLR 1 ....197, 204

Performance Industries Ltd *v* Sylvan Lake Golf & Tennis Club
  Ltd [2002] SCC 19 121

Royal Bank of Canada *v* W Got & Associates Electric Ltd (2000)
  178 DLR (4th) 385...121

Whiten *v* Pilot Insurance Co [2002] SCC 18.................................121

IRELAND
ffrench's Estate, Re (1887) 21 LR Ir 283, Ir CA 166

MALAYSIA
Linggi Plantations Ltd *v* Jagatheeson [1972] 1 Malaysian Law
  Journal 89 ....209, 211

NEW ZEALAND
Bank of New Zealand *v* New Zealand Guardian Trust Ltd [1999]
  1 NZLR 664 45

Day *v* Mead [1987] 2 NZLR 443...45

Her Majesty's A-G for England and Wales *v* R [2002] 2 NZLR 91,
  NZCA, (29 November 2001)...279

Simpson *v* A-G (Baigent's Case) [1994] 3 NZLR 667 237

SOUTH AFRICA
S *v* Mhlungu and ors 1996 (3) SA 867, CC....................................266

Willis Faber Enthoven Pty Ltd *v* Receiver of Revenue (1992) (4)
  SA 202 (AC), Supreme Ct of South Africa, App Div)............................134

UNITED STATES
Bank Worms *v* Bankamerica International 77 NY 2d 362,
  570 NE 2d 189 (1991) 142

Dow Corning Corp, Re 192 BR 428 (Bankr E D Much 1996) resisted
  in A Kull 72 American Bankruptcy J 265 (1998)....................................160

Edwards *v* Lee's Administrators (Kentucky Cave Case)
  96 SW 2d 1028 (1936)..155

Federal Sugar Refining Co *v* The United States Equalisation
  Board 268 F 575 (1920)...100

Omegas Group, Re 16 F 3d 1443 (6ᵗʰ Cir 1994)..........................160

Shield Benefit Administrators *v* University of Michigan
  225 Mich App 467, 571 NW 2d 556 (1997)..............................142

Tennessee Trailways Inc *v* Ervin 438 SW 2d 733 Tenn (1969)........59–60, 73

European Court of Human Rights

Baggs *v* UK (1985) 9 EHRR 235..260
Beyeler *v* Italy (Application 33202/96)....................................247–8

Chappell *v* UK (1990) 12 EHRR 1 ....254, 258

Dudgeon *v* UK (1981) 4 EHRR 149......................................247, 250

Guerra *v* Italy (1998) 26 EHRR 357...260

Handyside *v* UK (1976) 1 EHRR 737................................246–7, 250
Holy Monasteries *v* Greece (1995) 20 EHRR 1...........................248

James *v* UK (1986) 8 EHRR 123...248

Lithgow *v* UK (1986) 8 EHRR 329 248
Lopez Ostra *v* Spain (1994) 20 EHRR 277............................260, 263

Observer (The) and Guardian *v* UK (1992) 14 EHRR 153.........258
Osman *v* UK (1999) 29 EHRR 245..227

Pizetti *v* Italy (1993) Series A No 257-C....................................265

S *v* France (1990) 65 DR 250...260
Silver *v* UK (1983) 5 EHRR 347 265
Smith *v* UK (2000) 29 EHRR 493.......................................247–8, 250
Sporrong *v* Sweden (1983) 5 EHRR 35.......................................247
Sunday Times *v* UK (1979) 2 EHRR 245 ....246–7, 250

Z *v* UK (Case 29392/95)..227

Table of Legislation

UK Statutes

Civil Jurisdiction and Judgments Act 1982
 s 25 274
Companies Act 1985
 s 151 270
 ss 395–6..216
Consumer Credit Act 1974 ....200, 233, 251
 s 61(1)(a) 252
 s 65(1)..252
 s 127 252
   (3) 232, 251–3
Contracts (Applicable Law) Act 1990
 Sch 1...271, 275
Contracts (Rights of Third Parties) Act 1999 ....17, 24, 26

Data Protection Act 1998 267

Financial Services and Markets Act 2000...258
Foreign Limitation Periods Act 1984 276

Human Rights Act 1998...227–8, 234, 237, 241,
                                             250, 255, 257–64, 266–7, 269–70
 s 2 ....239, 254, 266
 s 3 ....227–35, 238, 244, 253–4, 265
   (1)...228, 232–3, 263–6
   (2)(b) 228–9
 s 4 ....229, 231–3, 253, 258
   (2), (6) 228
 s 6 ....228, 233–41, 242, 244, 251, 258, 260–1, 265–6, 269–70
   (1)...234–7, 241–2, 264, 266
   (3)(a) 234–6
   (6)..260
 s 7 ....261, 269
   (1)...241, 261
     (a), (b) 261
   (5)..261
 s 8 ....238–9, 264–5
   (1)..241

(3) 263
s 10 258
s 12 ....228, 238–41, 243–4
s 19 258
Sch 1 ....259, 265–6

Insolvency Act 1986
s 107 173
s 328 173
s 329 173
Insurance Brokers (Registration) Act 1977 86

Law of Property Act 1925
s 49(2) 209
Law Reform (Contributory Negligence) Act 1945 ....37, 39–40, 80
s 1(1) 37, 63, 65, 81
s 4 37–8
Law Reform (Frustrated Contracts) Act 1943 206
Leasehold Reform Act 1967 248
Limitation Act 1980 234–5
Lord Cairn's Act 114

Misrepresentation Act 1967
s 2(1) 36
Misuse of Drugs Act 1971
s 5 230
s 28 230

Private International Law (Miscellaneous Provisions) Act 1995 276
s 12(1) 288
s 14 271
Pt III 276

Sale of Goods Act 1979 176
s 15A 214
s 53(3) 10
Statute of 8 & 9 Will 3, Ch 11
s VIII 194
Statute of Frauds 1677 270
Supply of Goods and Services Act 1982
s 13 8
Supreme Court Act 1981 254
s 50 ....44, 260

Unfair Contract Terms Act 1977 196

Water Act 1989 259
Water Industry Act 1991 ....259, 261, 263–5
    s 18(8) 263
    s 94 259

Youth Justice and Criminal Evidence Act 1999
    s 41 230

UK Statutory Instruments

Insolvency Rules 1986, SI 1986 No 1925
    r 4.181(1) 173

Unfair Terms in Consumer Contracts Regulations 1999,
    SI 1999 No 2083 ....193, 196, 203, 214, 225
    reg 3(1) 193
    reg 5(1) 196
    reg 6(2) 199, 218
    Sch 2 ....193, 203
        para 1
            (d) 193, 218
            (e) 203, 218
            (f) 193, 203

National Legislation

AUSTRALIA
Trade Practices Act 1974 275

FRANCE
Code Civil
    arts 1150, 1151 18
    art 1152 202

GERMANY
Civil Code (BGB)
    § 343 202

NEW ZEALAND
Personal Property Security Act 1999
s 133 217

SOUTH AFRICA
Constitution
s 39(1)...266

UNITED STATES
Restatement of Restitution 138, 143
s 14(1)...142
s 55 142
s 163 160
s 166 160

Uniform Commercial Code
s 4-407 142

EU Legislation

Council Directive (EC) 1999/44 on Certain Aspects of the Sale of
    Consumer Goods and Associated Guarantees [1999] OJ L171/12........94

Council Regulation (EC) 44/2001 on the Jurisdiction and the
    Recognition and Enforcement of Judgments in Civil and
    Commercial Matters [2001] OJ L12/1..283
    art 31 289

Rome Convention on the Law Applicable to Contractual Obligations
    1980...275
    art 2 277
    art 10 ....271, 276
        (1) 288

International Conventions

European Convention on Human Rights....................................227, 229, 231,
                                                    233–7, 242, 246, 255, 257–8, 267
    art 6 ....227, 244–5, 248–9, 252–5, 264–5
        (1)..248–9, 265

art 8 ....227, 238–41, 243–8, 254, 259–60, 264, 266–7, 269
   (1)..239
   (2)..239, 245
art 10 ....227, 238–9, 240–1, 243–7
   (2)..243, 245
art 13 ....259, 265–6
First Protocol, art 1 ....227, 244, 246–8, 252–3, 259–60, 264, 269

Brussels Convention on Jurisdiction and the Enforcement of
  Judgments in Civil and Commercial Matters 1968.................................283
  art 24 289

Lugano Convention on Jurisdiction and the Enforcement of Judgments
  in Civil and Commercial Matters 1988...283

Vienna Convention on Contracts for the International Sale of Goods 94

Warsaw Convention 1929...287

Principles

Principles of European Contract Law
  art 9.504 41
  art 9.509 ....196–7, 202

UNIDROIT Principles of International Commercial Contracts
  art 7.4.7 41–2
  art 7.4.13 196–7

PART A

Compensation

1

Compensatory Damages: Some Central Issues of Assessment

JOHN CARTWRIGHT[1]

This paper discusses some of the central issues relating to the loss which can be compensated in contract. The core question is: in making an award of damages in contract, *what are we compensating for?* In recent years the courts (and, in particular, the House of Lords) have re-thought some aspects of this question, and have opened some new paths of enquiry in the assessment of compensatory damages.

However, in considering the assessment of loss recoverable in a claim in contact—and therefore to enable the claimant's adviser to see how best to frame the claim—it is useful to bear in mind a number of contrasts: the contrast between damages recoverable in contract and damages recoverable in tort; the contrast between different measures recoverable in contract depending on the content of the contractual obligation broken; and contrasts between different basic measures of damages recoverable in contract depending on how the claimant's loss can be proved, and how it should properly be characterized.

1. THE CONTRAST BETWEEN CONTRACT AND TORT

It is commonly said[2] that the difference between damages in contract and damages in tort is that contract damages are designed to protect the claimant's 'expectation', whereas tort damages are designed to protect his 'reliance', or his 'out-of-pocket' losses. There is truth in this, but it can be too simple, and more detail is necessary to see how the claimant should in practice choose between different causes of action.

(a) The basic measure of damages in contract and tort: the choice between contract and tort claims

The underlying purpose of an award of compensatory damages, whether the claim is brought in contract or tort, is the same: by means of an award

---

[1] Tutor in Law, Christ Church, Oxford.
[2] For criticism of the terminology, however, see D Friedmann, 'The Performance Interest in Contract Damages' (1995) 111 LQR 628.

of money, to place the claimant as far as possible in the position that he would have been in if the wrong had not been committed:[3]

> where any injury is to be compensated by damages, in settling the sum of money to be given for reparation of damages you should as nearly as possible get at that sum of money which will put the party who has been injured, or who has suffered, in the same position as he would have been in if he had not sustained the wrong for which he is now getting his compensation or reparation.

In contract, this means that damages are to put the claimant into the position that he would have been in if the contract had not been broken;[4] in tort, damages are awarded to put the claimant into the position that he would have been in if the tort had not been committed. Sometimes a claimant can have concurrent claims in contract and tort[5] and therefore the choice between the contract measure and the tort measure is crucial. To take a simple example:[6]

> the claimant buys a car, and the seller falsely misrepresents to him (and warrants in the contract) that the car is only two years old, but in fact it is five years old. The claimant pays £5,000; the market value of a two year-old car (but with the other characteristics—apart from the age—of the car the claimant buys) is £5,500; but the value of the car he actually receives (given its real age) is £3,500.

If the purchaser brings a claim for damages in tort for the misrepresentation, the question will be how much worse off is he now than if the misrepresentation had not been made?

Originally he had	£5,000
Now he has	£3,500 worth of car
Loss:	£1,500

But if the purchaser brings a claim for damages for breach of the contractual warranty as to the age of the car, the question is how much better off he should have been if the statement had been true:

He was promised	£5,500 worth of car
He actually has	£3,500 worth of car
Loss:	£2,000

So in such a case the claimant's choice is likely to be in favour of the contract remedy, because the bargain was a good one: the contract measure is higher because, if he had received what he was promised, the claimant

---

[3] *Livingstone v Rawyards* (1880) 5 App Cas 25, 39, HL.

[4] Normally (but see p 8 below) the 'expectation' measure: *Robinson v Harman* (1848) 1 Ex 850 at 855.

[5] Concurrence of claims was expressly permitted (and even encouraged?) by the House of Lords in *Henderson v Merrett Syndicates Ltd* [1995] 2 AC 145.

[6] Taken from J Cartwright, *Misrepresentation* (Sweet & Maxwell Contract Law Library, 2002) 1.12.

would have made an overall profit by paying less than the (promised) car's market value. And in the case of the reverse—a bad bargain—the measure of damages in tort will generally be higher.

But this is too simple. Beyond the basic measure, there are also questions of whether the particular losses suffered by the claimant are recoverable in contract and/or tort: the rules for the kinds of recoverable loss, remoteness of damage, and the precise method of calculating the 'expectation' or 'reliance' will vary between contract and tort, and even within torts; and the choice between contract and tort, or between torts, will affect the range of consequential losses the claimant can recover, and such things as whether he can recover intangible as well as tangible losses.

(b) The rules for assessment: differences between contract and tort, and within tort

The rules for assessment of recoverable loss differ depending on the basis of the claim, whether contract or tort; and in particular within tort there are some marked differences between intentional torts (such as deceit) and torts that do not require proof of intention (such as negligence). For example:[7]

(i) The kinds and scope of recoverable loss

In *contract*, the obligation defines the scope of recoverable loss in the event of breach.[8] In *tort*, the kinds and scope of recoverable loss vary from one tort to another. In negligence the duty of care itself often defines the scope of recoverable loss: the test for the duty of care defines whether the particular duty undertaken by the defendant extends to economic loss or only physical damage; and the extent of recoverable loss may also be defined by the scope of duty.[9] But in deceit the courts are reluctant to limit

---

[7] In addition to the calculation of damages other factors may point the claimant towards the contract or the tort claim, such as different defences to which his claim might be subject. Since contributory negligence is not a defence to the tort of deceit (*Standard Chartered Bank v Pakistan National Shipping Co (Nos 2 and 4)* [2002] UKHL 43; [2002] 3 WLR 1547, HL a claimant who might be met with that defence will seek to avoid it by claiming in deceit rather than negligence if the case so permits. Similarly, he will seek to avoid the defence in a contract claim by alleging a breach of a strict contractual obligation, since contributory negligence is available as a defence only where the claim in contract is based on an act or omission which comprises a contractual duty concurrent with, and of content equivalent to, a duty in the tort of negligence: *Forsikringsaktieselskapet Vesta v Butcher* [1989] AC 852, CA, discussed by Andrew Burrows below, pp 37–43.

[8] See below, pp 8–9.

[9] *South Australia Asset Management Corporation v York Montague Ltd* [1997] AC 191, HL, discussed in detail by Edwin Peel below, in Chapter 7.

the claimant's recovery. If the defendant intended to cause harm to the claimant by his fraudulent statement, he should pay the whole loss flowing from the claimant's reliance.[10] And there appears to be a greater willingness to allow recovery of damages for intangible losses, such as inconvenience and disappointment, in deceit[11] than in negligence or even than in contract.[12] So tort takes into account in the assessment of damages the defendant's culpability, and sanctions an intentional tort more harshly than a non-intentional tort. Contract draws no such distinction, and focuses only on the obligation in the contract, not whether the breach was deliberate.

(ii) Remoteness of damage

Similarly, there is a difference in the range of recoverable consequential losses in contract and tort. In contract, the defendant is liable only for the losses of a kind which were, or ought to have been, in the contemplation of the parties at the time of the contract. The circumstances of the breach (what the defendant can *then* foresee as the likely consequences of his breach, and whether the breach is deliberate or not) are irrelevant. But again, in tort, the test is different and can lead to a wider range of recovery than in contract.[13] In negligence the defendant is liable only for loss which is within the scope of the duty he owed and broke, and which is of

---

[10] *Smith New Court Securities Ltd v Scrimgeour Vickers (Asset Management) Ltd* [1997] AC 254, HL (purchaser induced by vendor's fraudulent misrepresentation to purchase shares in a company on which it was later discovered that a major fraud had been committed, and which resulted in a catastrophic reduction in the market value of the shares. Although the vendor's fraudulent misrepresentation was not about a fact which had any bearing on the reason for the later reduction in the value of the shares in the company, the purchaser was held entitled to recover from the representor in deceit the whole of its loss on later sale of the shares: the causative influence of the fraud was not significantly attenuated or diluted by other causative factors acting simultaneously with or subsequent to the fraud.) So in a case of deceit, where the representee's reliance consists in his entering into a contract, he will recover the losses which he suffers as a result of entering into that contract; the recoverable loss is not limited to that part of the loss which flows from the fact that the statement was false. But in negligence where the defendant's duty is limited to taking reasonable care in providing accurate information, damages for breach of that duty cover only the consequences for the representee of the statement being inaccurate: *South Australia Asset Management Corp v York Montague Ltd* [1997] AC 191, HL (at 216–17 Lord Hoffmann made clear that he did not intend his statements about this principle to extend to the tort of deceit).

[11] *Archer v Brown* [1985] 1 QB 401.

[12] Cases have awarded damages in claims in negligence for physical inconvenience (not simply disappointment) flowing from the breach of duty, by analogy with the cases in contract (on which see now *Farley v Skinner*, p 13 below).

[13] However, in cases of concurrent liability, the courts are reluctant to find that on the facts the scope of recoverable consequential losses differs according to whether the claim is pursued in contract or in tort: *H Parsons (Livestock) Ltd v Uttley Ingham & Co Ltd* [1978] QB 791, CA. For further discussion, see J Cartwright, 'Remoteness of Damage in Contract and Tort: A Reconsideration' [1996] CLJ 488.

a kind that he could reasonably have foreseen: *Wagon Mound (No 1)*.[14] But in deceit the defendant is liable for all the loss which flows from his wrongful act, whether or not he could reasonably have foreseen it: the test is causation not foreseeability.[15] It is the intentional nature of the wrong that brings this more extensive test. Other non-intentional torts also tend to follow the *Wagon Mound* rule and so limit the defendant's liability to what he could have foreseen, such as nuisance,[16] the rule in *Rylands v Fletcher*[17] and defamation.[18]

(iii) Punitive (exemplary) damages

It is outside the scope of this paper to discuss non-compensatory damages, but it should be noted that punitive (exemplary) damages may be awarded in tort; but more easily in the case of an intentional tort (such as deceit) than in negligence.[19] And because in contract the question is only compensation of the claimant's losses, not taking account of the defendant's culpability, punitive damages are not in principle recoverable.[20]

2. DAMAGES IN CONTRACT: THE CONTENT OF THE CONTRACTUAL OBLIGATION BROKEN

Since damages in contract are calculated so as to put the claimant into the position that he would have been in if the contract had not been broken, it is crucial to identify the content of the contractual obligation. Where the obligation was a strict obligation which promised a result, then the damages should reflect the lost value of that promised result. But where the obligation was a contractual duty of care, the contract does not promise a result and so the measure of damages will be calculated to put the claimant only into the position he would have been in had the defendant

---

[14] [1961] AC 388, PC. This opens a wider potential liability than contract because (1) the test of 'reasonable foreseeability' is wider than the contract test: *The Heron II* [1969] 1 AC 350, HL; and (2) the time at which the test is applied is the time at which the negligent act is done.

[15] *Smith New Court Securities Ltd v Scrimgeour Vickers (Asset Management) Ltd* [1997] AC 254, HL.

[16] *Wagon Mound (No 2)* [1967] 1 AC 617, PC.

[17] *Cambridge Water Co Ltd v Eastern Counties Leather plc* [1994] 2 AC 264, HL.

[18] *Slipper v BBC* [1991] 1 QB 283, CA. See now, however, *McManus v Beckham* [2002] EWCA Civ 939, [2002] 1 WLR 2982.

[19] *Kuddus v Chief Constable of Leicestershire Constabulary* [2001] UKHL 29, [2002] AC 122, discussed by Ewan McKendrick in Chapter 10.

[20] *Ruxley Electronics & Construction Ltd v Forsyth* [1996] AC 344 at 353, HL (Lord Bridge, quoted below at 4(a)). However, the *effect* of an award of damages calculated to deprive the defendant of a profit from his breach of contract (*A-G v Blake* [2001] 1 AC 268, decided by the House of Lords after the *Ruxley* case) may be punitive.

taken care. In practice, this measure (although it is damages in contract) is calculated on the same 'out of pocket' measure as a tort claim.[21] This will be the normal measure of damages in cases of breach of a duty of care under a contract to provide services, such as a professional who generally undertakes a contractual obligation of reasonable care and skill[22] concurrently with an identical obligation in the tort of negligence.[23]

3. DAMAGES IN CONTRACT: THE CLAIM FOR 'WASTED EXPENDITURE'

Sometimes a claimant will be allowed to recover for breach of contract not his 'expectation', but his out-of-pocket losses: his actual expenditure (including even pre-contract expenditure) which has been wasted as a consequence of the defendant's breach.[24] However, such an award will only be made where the court does not have evidence of the proper valuation of the 'expectation': so it is only available where the claimant cannot prove his expectation or, at least, where if he claims the wasted expenditure, the *defendant* cannot show that he is claiming more than his expectation.[25] In effect, therefore, the wasted expenditure claim is only a substitute for the expectation, and is used to give the claimant the benefit of the doubt that the contract would at least have broken even (that is, he would at least have recouped his expenditure). But if the court knows that the expenditure was higher than the return the claimant would have made from the contract, he will not be allowed to use this claim to escape a bad bargain.

4. DAMAGES IN CONTRACT: CHARACTERIZING THE LOSS

Even where the contract promised a result, and therefore the claim is based on the defendant's failure to confer the benefit for which the claimant contracted, there can still be more than one way of calculating the claimant's loss. This involves a careful analysis of both the defendant's contractual obligation and the claimant's loss, to answer the question: how

---

[21] *Esso Petroleum Co Ltd v Mardon* [1976] QB 801, CA.
[22] Supply of Goods and Services Act 1982, s 13.
[23] *Henderson v Merrett Syndicates Ltd* [1995] 2 AC 145, HL. The concurrence of these obligations generally results in there being no advantage to a claimant in the *measure* of damages, when choosing between the contract claim and the tort claim. But there can be other advantages, such as the limitation period which may sometimes be longer in the tort claim—although the reform of the rules governing limitation periods, proposed by the Law Commission (Law Com No 270, 2001) and now accepted in principle by the Government, will remove this advantage.
[24] *Anglia Television Ltd v Reed* [1972] 1 QB 60, CA.
[25] *CCC Films (London) Ltd v Impact Quadrant Films Ltd* [1985] QB 16.

can the recoverable loss properly be characterized? In recent years this question has been subject to detailed discussion by the courts, and in particular by the House of Lords, and it can be seen that the courts now look more carefully (and, it must be said, more inventively) at the issue. Three areas have been subject to analysis in the recent cases:

- whether best to compensate the claimant's loss by providing damages to enable him to remedy the defect of performance ('cost of cure') or by simply assessing his market value loss ('difference in value'), or by some other measure;
- how far it is possible and appropriate to award damages to compensate the claimant for intangible benefits (such as 'amenity') he has lost by reason of the breach; and
- how far it is possible to allow the claimant to recover losses which in substance are suffered by a third party.

(a) 'Cost of cure' and 'difference in value'

Damages for the *cost of curing* the defective performance will entitle the claimant to obtain the *factual* equivalent of the defendant's promise by allowing him to pay for substitute performance by a third party;[26] damages for the *difference in value* between the promised performance and the defective performance will enable him to have a *financial* equivalent, whilst not necessarily enabling him to pay for the factual equivalent. The House of Lords' decision in *Ruxley Electronics & Construction Ltd v Forsyth*[27] is very significant in indicating not only the circumstances in which a claimant may be able to recover contract damages calculated as the 'cost of cure' of the defective performance, but also the general approach to be taken to quantifying loss in a claim for breach of contract.

Ruxley involved a (counter)claim by the landowner (Mr Forsyth) against a builder (Ruxley) who, in breach of contract, constructed a swimming pool to a depth (at the point of diving) of six feet instead of seven feet six inches. Mr Forsyth claimed damages to cover the cost of demolition and reconstruction of the pool to the contracted specification, which amounted to £21,560, nearly £4,000 more than the original contract price. Ruxley resisted this, and claimed that it was liable only for the difference in value between the pool as promised and as delivered (which was nil, since the

---

[26] Not, of course, ordering the defendant to procure the third-party performance, nor even requiring the claimant to spend the damages on substitute performance. English law knows no contractual remedy similar to the French remedy under which a court authorizes the claimant to have the defendant's obligation performed by a third party, at the defendant's expense: C civ art 1144.

[27] [1996] AC 344.

trial judge held that the pool was perfectly serviceable for the purposes which Mr Forsyth actually intended). The case therefore raised in sharp focus the question of how to value the claimant's loss. There was no doubt that, as a matter of law, Ruxley had failed to provide the benefit for which Mr Forsyth had contracted: the pool was not built to the contractual specification. But, as Lord Bridge said:[28]

> damages for breach of contract must reflect, as accurately as the circumstances allow, the loss which the claimant has sustained because he did not get what he bargained for. There is no question of punishing the contract breaker. Given this basic principle, the court, in assessing the measure of the claimant's loss has ultimately to determine a question of fact, although the law has of course developed detailed criteria which are to be applied in ascertaining the appropriate measure of loss in a wide variety of commonly occurring situations. Since the law relating to damages for breach of contract has developed almost exclusively in a commercial context, these criteria normally proceed on the assumption that each contracting party's interest in the bargain was purely commercial and that the loss resulting from a breach of contract is measurable in purely economic terms. But this assumption may not always be appropriate.

The trial judge had refused to award the cost of cure, on the basis that in the circumstances it would be unreasonable to incur the rebuilding cost.[29] The Court of Appeal disagreed, and by a majority awarded the cost of cure as being the only way of giving Mr Forsyth what he had bargained for.[30] The House of Lords reversed the Court of Appeal, and restored the trial judge's award.

The speeches show that the key issue is to characterize the loss suffered by the claimant. In the case of building contracts, the courts will generally lean in favour of awarding 'cost of cure' damages.[31] But they will not make such an award where it is not in the circumstances reasonable; and the courts will take into account the reasonableness of the expenditure necessary to cure the defective performance as part of the assessment of the true nature of the loss. Where it is unreasonable to spend money (or so much money) curing the defect,[32] or where the claimant does not intend to cure

---

[28] [1996] AC 344, 353.

[29] [1996] AC 344, 359 (Lord Jauncey). However, the judge awarded £2,500 general damages for 'loss of amenity': see 4(b) below.

[30] [1994] 1 WLR 650, 659 (Staughton LJ), 660 (Mann LJ). Dillon LJ dissented.

[31] [1996] AC 344, 355–6 (Lord Jauncey), 366 (Lord Lloyd); Treitel, *The Law of Contract* (10th edn, 1999) 881. By contrast, a buyer of defective goods can normally claim against the seller only damages for the difference in value between the goods as delivered and the goods as promised: Sale of Goods Act 1979, s 53(3). But this too is only a prima facie rule and the cost of remedying the defect might sometimes be the appropriate measure: Treitel 880.

[32] [1996] AC 344, 359 (Lord Jauncey: 'the trial judge found that it would be unreasonable to incur the cost of demolishing the existing pool and building a new and deeper one. In so doing he implicitly recognised that the respondent's loss did not extend to the cost of reinstatement'), 367 (Lord Lloyd).

the defect even if 'cost of cure' damages are awarded,[33] it might be more appropriate to characterize the claimant's loss as the difference in value between the works properly performed and the defective works.

(b) 'Loss of amenity' damages; damages for distress and disappointment

The *Ruxley* case goes beyond this, however, and shows that it might even be appropriate sometimes to focus on a different characterization of the loss: the intangible benefits which the claimant has lost as a result of the defective performance. The trial judge had refused to award 'cost of cure' damages, but he had awarded Mr Forsyth £2,500 as damages for 'loss of pleasurable amenity', which he identified as the proper loss rather than the cost of demolishing and reconstructing the swimming pool. This award was reinstated by the House of Lords. Lord Mustill's approach was particularly instructive:[34]

> There are not two alternative measures of damage, at opposite poles, but only one; namely, the loss truly suffered by the promisee. In some cases the loss cannot be fairly measured except by reference to the full cost of repairing the deficiency in performance. In others, and in particular those where the contract is designed to fulfil a purely commercial purpose, the loss will very often consist only of the monetary detriment brought about by the breach of contract. But these remedies are not exhaustive, for the law must cater for those occasions where the value of the promise to the promisee exceeds the financial enhancement of his position which full performance will secure. This excess, often referred to in the literature as the 'consumer surplus' (see for example the valuable discussion by Harris, Ogus and Phillips (1979) 95 LQR 581) is usually incapable of precise valuation in terms of money, exactly because it represents a personal, subjective and non-monetary gain. Nevertheless where it exists the law should recognise it and compensate the promisee if the misperformance takes it away. The lurid bathroom tiles, or the grotesque folly instanced in argument by my noble and learned friend, Lord Keith of Kinkel, may be so discordant with general taste that in purely economic terms the builder may be said to do the employer a favour by failing to install them. But this is too narrow and materialistic a view of the transaction. Neither the contractor nor the court has the right to substitute for the employer's individual expectation of performance a criterion derived from what ordinary people would regard as sensible. As my Lords have shown, the test of reasonableness plays a central part in determining the basis of recovery, and will indeed be decisive in a case such as the present

---

[33] [1996] AC 344, 373 (Lord Lloyd: 'if, as the judge found, Mr Forsyth had no intention of rebuilding the pool, he has lost nothing except the difference in value, if any'). However, the speeches emphasized that this does not mean that, except for the purposes of characterizing the claimant's true loss, the court is concerned with the use to which he will put his damages: [1996] AC 344, 359 (Lord Jauncey).

[34] [1996] AC 344, 360–1.

when the cost of reinstatement would be wholly disproportionate to the non-monetary loss suffered by the employer. But it would be equally unreasonable to deny all recovery for such a loss. The amount may be small, and since it cannot be quantified directly there may be room for difference of opinion about what it should be. But in several fields the judges are well accustomed to putting figures to intangibles, and I see no reason why the imprecision of the exercise should be a barrier, if that is what fairness demands.

This is admitting that, if the claimant bargains for something which has a *particular value for him*, even though it may have no real value to another person, then the law can include that in its assessment of damages, although it cannot be valued on a scientific basis given that it is an intangible loss which has to be translated into economic terms for the purposes of an award of damages. It is not entirely clear how innovative this is in the *Ruxley* case. Lord Lloyd looked at the question in a more traditional way: that the judge's award of £2,500 was justifiable on the basis that it fell within the established exceptions to the rule that injured feelings are not compensated in contract, since it was in essence a contract which involved the provision of a pleasurable amenity.[35] But Lord Mustill's statement is not put in those terms; and in particular his linking of it to the definition of 'consumer surplus' in the article by Harris, Ogus and Phillips[36] points to his thinking that the compensation is not for the 'distress' involved in not receiving the swimming pool to its full depth, but for the personal value the claimant attaches to the performance for which he bargained. That is a quite different thing.[37] The basis and evaluation[38] of such an award was not fully argued by counsel before the House of Lords in the *Ruxley* case, and there is no discussion in any of the speeches of the differences between the approaches of Lord Mustill and Lord Lloyd.[39] It has since been said in the House of Lords that their decision can be taken as

---

[35] [1996] AC 344, 373–4: it therefore fell within the line of cases, such as *Jarvis v Swans Tours Ltd* [1973] QB 233, CA, and *Jackson v Horizon Holidays Ltd* [1975] 1 WLR 1468, CA (holiday contracts), where damages have been awarded for the breach of a contract of which the object was to provide pleasure.

[36] 'Consumer Remedies and the Consumer Surplus' (1979) 95 LQR 581: see at 582, where the 'consumer surplus' is defined as 'the excess utility or subjective value obtained from a "good" over and above the utility associated with its market price.' At 585 the authors say that, although the 'consumer surplus' is a subjective notion, the 'assessment must proceed on some objective basis (eg how would the reasonable man, in the plaintiff's position, have valued the benefit of performance?)'. But the idea is certainly not that compensation is for the *distress* in not receiving the promised performance.

[37] See the discussion of 'performance interest' in *Alfred Mc Alpine Construction Ltd v Panatown Ltd*, below, at 4(c).

[38] Lord Lloyd at 374 thought that Mr Forsyth was lucky to have obtained so large an award for his disappointed expectations.

[39] [1996] AC 344, 354, 359, 373. Lord Bridge agreed with Lord Mustill on this point, and Lord Keith agreed generally with Lord Mustill and Lord Lloyd. Lord Jauncey preferred not to express an opinion.

having authoritatively established the principles allowing an award of damages for failure to provide a pleasurable amenity,[40] although it is suggested below that there is more to be made of Lord Mustill's approach in the light of the minority speeches in *Alfred McAlpine Construction Ltd v Panatown Ltd*.[41]

The courts have been reluctant to award damages in contract to compensate for the claimant's distress in not receiving the promised performance: contract has been seen as an economic vehicle, and so protecting primarily (if not exclusively) economic interests. Recently the House of Lords has re-affirmed that, in general, damages are not recoverable for mental distress and anxiety.[42] This has for some time been subject to an exception that 'where the very object of a contract is to provide pleasure, relaxation, peace of mind or freedom from molestation, damages will be awarded if the fruit of the contract is not provided or if the contrary result is procured instead',[43] but the House of Lords has now developed this in *Farley v Skinner*[44] to cover the case not only where 'the very object' of the contract is to provide pleasure, etc, but also where that is *an important object* of the contract.

In *Farley v Skinner* a surveyor was employed by a potential purchaser to investigate whether a property was seriously affected by aircraft noise, and failed in his duty of care. The purchaser had no financial loss, since the price he paid for the property corresponded to the open market value after taking into account aircraft noise. But although he decided not to sell the house (having spent a considerable sum on it after purchase) he was held to be entitled still to compensation for the lack of peace and tranquillity. The House of Lords held that, in general, compensation is awarded in contract only for financial loss resulting from the breach, but where a major or important object of the contract is to give pleasure, relaxation or peace of mind, damages can be awarded for that non-financial loss. That was so here: the surveyor was retained not simply on the usual basis but with the specific additional obligation to investigate the noise to which the property was subject. In the alternative, it was held that the judge's award could be upheld as being an award not for the failure to provide an object of the contract, but as being recoverable consequential loss–and an award for consequential loss can include damages for inconvenience and discomfort (but not just for disappointment). In any case, however, such an award must be moderate. The judge's award (of £10,000) was allowed to stand, on the basis that although it was 'at the very top end of what could

---

[40] *Farley v Skinner* [2001] UKHL 49, [2002] 2 AC 732 at [21].
[41] Below, at 4(c).   [42] *Johnson v Gore Wood & Co* [2002] 2 AC 1, HL.
[43] *Watts v Morrow* [1991] 1 WLR 1421, 1445, CA.
[44] [2001] UKHL 49, [2002] 2 AC 732.

possibly be regarded as appropriate damages'[45] it was not so excessive that it should be overturned on appeal.

(c) Damages for losses suffered by a third party

The normal rule is that a contracting party can sue only for his own loss; but the decision of the House of Lords in *Linden Gardens Trust Ltd v Lenesta Sludge Disposals Ltd* (consolidated with *St Martins Property Corp Ltd v Sir Robert McAlpine Ltd*, and generally known as '*St Martins*')[46] showed that sometimes a party can recover substantial damages for losses which are suffered by a third party to the contract. In effect, this decision created a special rule for building contracts: where the purchaser/tenant of a building on which work has been carried out has no direct claim against the building contractor, the original contracting party—the employer under the building contract—can sue for damages to cover the purchaser/ tenant's loss. In later cases this is referred to as the 'narrower ground' of decision in *St Martins*.

Lord Griffiths, however, used an alternative method of analysis which has become significant in the later cases, the 'wider ground' of decision. His approach was to say that the contractor owed a contractual duty to the original employer, and the employer could recover damages to remedy the defect in the building caused by the contractor's breach of duty: this was so whether or not the employer owned (or still owned) the building, or whether it was he or a third party who would in fact pay for the repairs to remedy the defect. The contracting party suffers a loss because he does not receive the bargain for which he contracted, and the measure of loss is the cost of securing the performance of the bargain. Lord Griffiths' analysis was not adopted by the majority. And it is significantly different from the approach taken in Lord Browne-Wilkinson's speech, which was the principal majority speech. Lord Browne-Wilkinson assumed that the contracting party recovers the loss suffered by the third party. So, presumably, a claim can include consequential losses suffered by the third party (such as business disturbance during the period the repairs are carried out). But Lord Griffiths assumed that the loss is the *contracting party's* loss. The cost of remedying the defect can be included here, but surely not the third party's consequential losses. And the majority approach creates a specific rule for building contracts which does not necessarily go beyond that context,[47]

---

[45] [2001] UKHL 49, [2002] 2 AC 732 at [28] (Lord Steyn).   [46] [1994] 1 AC 85, HL.

[47] The rule was an extension into building contracts of a similar rule devised (in *The Albazero* [1977] AC 774, HL) for contracts for carriage of goods by sea. But it is still set out in Lord Browne-Wilkinson's speech as a particular rule for this (new) context, not a general rule for contracts for the benefit of third parties, or contracts where a third party later has consequential losses.

whereas the wider ground appears to be a general principle which could be applied in other contexts, for example, in the case of warranties given on a sale of a business but the business has later been sold on in whole or in part before the claim is made under the warranties.[48]

In *Alfred McAlpine Construction Ltd v Panatown Ltd*[49] the House of Lords has further developed the *St Martins* principles: and has clarified some issues arising from *St Martins* but has left some key issues unresolved.

Panatown contracted for McAlpine to undertake building work on land owned by UIPL. Panatown and UIPL were associated companies, but the transaction was so structured for tax purposes. And McAlpine also entered into direct warranties with UIPL. There were therefore two key differences from the facts of *St Martins*: the third party was not a successor in title to the original contracting party, but was present in the commercial structure from the very beginning. And there was no gap in the legal claims available to the third party since UIPL had its own direct actions against McAlpine under the warranties. But the issue was whether, in spite of this, Panatown could use its own direct contractual rights against McAlpine to sue for losses suffered by UIPL.

In some respects, the decision simply confirms the existing line of authority. The general rule remains that a claimant in an action for breach of contract can recover damages only for his own loss.[50] But the 'narrower' ground of decision in Lord Browne-Wilkinson's speech in *St Martins* was confirmed as an exception to the general rule, and so where A contracts for work to be done by B [the building contractor] but the cost of remedying B's defective work is borne by C [the building owner], A may recover from B damages which are calculated to compensate the losses suffered by C; and A has an obligation to pass the damages, when recovered, over to C. This applies not only where (as in *St Martins* itself) A was originally the owner of the property but the property was later transferred to C, but also where (as in the *Panatown* case) C owned the property from the beginning.[51] But the development made in the *Panatown* case is that the '*St Martins* exception' does not apply where C has a direct right of action against B to recover C's own losses, for example where (as in the *Panatown* case) C has the benefit of a collateral warranty, even where the scope of the obligation it contains is not identical to the obligation undertaken by B in

---

[48] For further discussion of this area, before the decision of the House of Lords in the *Panatown* case, below, see J Cartwright, 'Damages, Third Parties and Common Sense' (1996) 10 JCL 244. Note, however, that in the *Panatown* case Lord Millett preferred to restrict the 'wider ground' for the moment to building contracts and other contracts for the supply of work and materials where the claim is in respect of defective or incomplete work or delay in completing it: [2001] 1 AC 518, 591.

[49] [2001] 1 AC 518, HL.

[50] Lord Goff, however, was sceptical about this: [2001] 1 AC 518, 544.

[51] Lord Goff and Lord Millett rejected this extension.

favour of A under the main contract. The '*St Martins* exception' was designed to fill a gap (a 'black hole')[52] where there was no satisfactory remedy: where A has the claim in contract but no loss to attach to it, and C has loss but no claim. Where C has a claim, the rationale for the exception disappears.

However, for the present purposes the more significant issue is the discussion in the *Panatown* case of the 'wider ground' in Lord Griffiths' speech in *St Martins*: that a contracting party might be able to claim as its own loss the value of its interest in the contractor's performance. That is, the fact that the party does not receive the benefit of having the contract performed may be itself a loss in the claimant's hands, even though the performance was in fact being done for the benefit of a third party, and even though the contracting party may not himself incur the cost of remedying the defect in performance. Lord Goff[53] and Lord Millett[54] used this as part of their reasoning. Lord Browne-Wilkinson 'assumed' that it is correct,[55] but decided that the claim under the wider ground was defeated on the facts by the existence of the collateral warranty in favour of the third-party owner (which therefore means that Panatown suffered no damage to its performance interest since the third-party owner would have a good direct remedy for the relevant loss). Lord Clyde and Lord Jauncey rejected the 'performance interest' analysis.

The 'performance interest' analysis[56] was not part of the ratio of the *Panatown* case which was that, on the facts, Panatown could not recover for the losses suffered by UIPL as the third-party owner of the property: the '*St Martins* exception' did not apply because of the collateral warranty in favour of UIPL;[57] and Panatown could not claim as its own loss the loss that was in fact suffered by UIPL.[58] But of much greater *potential*

---

[52] *St Martins Property Corp Ltd v Sir Robert McAlpine Ltd* [1994] 1 AC 85, 109, HL (Lord Browne-Wilkinson, quoting Lord Keith of Kinkel in *GUS Property Management Ltd v Littlewoods Mail Order Stores Ltd* 1982 SLT 533, 538, HL).

[53] [2001] 1 AC 518, 546ff.   [54] [2001] 1 AC 518, 587–8.   [55] [2001] 1 AC 518, 577.

[56] See also B Coote, 'Contract Damages, *Ruxley* and the Performance Interest' [1997] CLJ 537 written before the decision of the House of Lords in the *Panatown* case, and cited with approval by Lord Goff and Lord Millett, but with less enthusiasm by Lord Clyde.

[57] Lord Clyde, Lord Jauncey and Lord Browne-Wilkinson.

[58] But for varying reasons: Lord Clyde did not accept the formulation which extended to the 'performance interest' at 535; Lord Jauncey at 574 and Lord Browne-Wilkinson at 577–8 both thought that the 'broader ground' did not apply because of the collateral warranty. The scope for the application of the *St Martins* exception may now be more limited, however, since it was created by the House of Lords in 1993 to fill a gap in the remedies for third-party losses, in the particular context of defective buildings. That gap arose in part because of the removal in the late 1980s of the remedies in tort for defects in buildings (see *D and F Estates Ltd v Church Comrs for England* [1989] AC 177, HL, *Murphy v Brentwood D C* [1991] 1 AC 398, HL, and *Dept of the Environment v Thomas Bates and Sons Ltd* [1991] 1 AC 499, HL). Most of the cases which will come through the courts now will be those in which the transaction was put in place after that tort development, and so normally collateral warranties will have been put in place. In such cases, the decision in the *Panatown* case now shows that the *St Martins* exception will not

significance is the fact that the House of Lords has opened the door to argument that the original contracting party suffers a loss by virtue of not receiving the promised performance, even where the actual cost of remedying that loss will be borne by another party (such as the building owner). Lord Millett stated the principle as follows:[59]

> Lord Griffiths [in St Martins] was not proposing to depart from the general rule that a plaintiff can only recover compensatory damages for breach of contract in respect of a loss which he has himself sustained. He was insisting that, in certain kinds of contract at least, the right to performance has a value which is capable of being measured by the cost of obtaining it from a third party. . . .
>
> There has for some time been a growing consensus among academic writers that English law adopts an unduly narrow approach to the concept of loss, and that it ought to recognise that the performance of a contractual obligation may have an economic value of its own which is capable of sounding in damages. Such damages may be measured by the cost of obtaining alternative performance, but they may also take account of loss from delay and other consequential loss.

This is another example of the House of Lords' willingness to re-think what exactly constitutes the loss suffered by a contracting party, and therefore how to characterize his claim to damages. The fact that two members of the House of Lords would have rested their decision on this analysis, and a third was prepared to assume it was correct, means that it has been given a life which can surely now be explored further in the cases. On one view it might be thought regrettable that such a wide-ranging potential reassessment of the nature of contractual loss should be raised inconclusively in the House of Lords, opening up the real possibility of litigation on this issue in the lower courts which can ultimately be resolved only by a further decision in the House of Lords. But it is important to see the 'performance interest' analysis in the *Panatown* case as part of a wider exploration being undertaken by the courts, and especially by the House of Lords in such cases as *Ruxley v Forsyth* and *Farley v Skinner*, about the nature of contractual loss.

normally apply. Moreover, for the future, in order to ensure that future owners and occupiers have appropriate rights to sue in the event of defects being found in the building, there is now a choice between collateral warranties and the creation of a direct right under the Contracts (Rights of Third Parties) Act 1999 and, for the same reason as in the *Panatown* case, if the original contract gives direct rights to a third party under the 1999 Act, the *St Martins* exception will not apply. The safest position for the lawyer involved in drafting the documents for transactions is not to rely on the cases of *St Martins*, *Panatown*, tort liability, or any other uncertain exception to the basic and well-established rules of contract: better to draft the contracts carefully to ensure that the intended rights are properly conferred under the established rules of contract.

[59] [2001] 1 AC 518, 587. However, he would restrict the 'wider ground' for the moment to building contracts and other contracts for the supply of work and materials where the claim is in respect of defective or incomplete work or delay in completing it: at 591.

5. CONCLUSIONS

English law approaches the question of damages in contract from the point of view of seeking to compensate the claimant's loss. It does not aim to punish the defendant,[60] nor even does it generally take account of the manner in which the breach was committed in deciding the extent of compensation to which the claimant is entitled.[61] But a key question is how to convert the defendant's breach into money. The courts have continued to re-think this question, and in recent years the House of Lords have again revisited it and have become more open to admitting that the claimant's loss may sometimes be characterized in more than a straightforward loss of financial expectation. This approach involves a careful analysis of the nature of the contractual obligation which has been broken: the starting point to decide what the claimant has lost is to ask what it was that the defendant promised. But, beyond that, the courts are prepared to consider—perhaps in a more creative fashion than in the past—what is the most appropriate way to characterize the loss in the claimant's hands, and so how best to put a figure on it for the calculation of damages. The *Ruxley* case showed that the courts do not simply ask what was the promised performance, and make an award of damages calculated to secure substitute performance.[62] The distinction between damages calculated as the 'cost of cure' and damages based on the 'difference in value' of the thing as provided and the thing as promised, was not new. But the way in which the question was tackled in the House of Lords was a more open discussion of the need to find, for the particular case in hand, the true nature of the claimant's loss. And the House went further than that, and accepted that sometimes a particular claimant will be able to show that he had a more personal loss which should be reflected in damages. The notion of the 'consumer surplus' which appears to have been accepted there by Lord Mustill is different from, but is similar in its underlying approach to, the 'performance interest' discussed in the *Panatown* case. There too, but in a very different context and as a response to a very different problem,

---

[60] Above, at 1(*b*)(*iii*).

[61] So, for example, a deliberate breach does not attract a different measure of recovery, or even any different rule for the extent of recoverable losses: it is tort, not contract, that draws such distinctions: above, at 1(*b*). Other legal systems take different approaches: eg French law, which gives a greater significance to the *performance* obligation, sees deliberate non-performance as more culpable and therefore attracting less favourable (for the defendant) rules in the quantification of recoverable loss. An example of this approach is the rule for remoteness of damage, which is based on foreseeability for non-deliberate failure of performance, but all direct losses are recoverable for deliberate non-performance: C civ art 1150, 1151.

[62] That was—on the facts, at least—close to the approach of the Court of Appeal, but was rejected by the House of Lords: above, at 4(*a*).

members of the House of Lords have shown that they are open to re-thinking the question of how to compensate for breach of contract. And in *Farley v Skinner* the House developed (albeit in a relatively small way) the rules relating to damages for intangible loss, but again by reference to the questions: what was it that the defendant promised? And how can the failure to provide that benefit best be reflected in the assessment of damages?

There is a tendency in the common law to think of the contractual obligation in financial terms: and therefore to think of the failure of performance of the obligation only in economic terms. The strongest statement of this was Holmes' assertion that the nature of a contractual obligation is to either to perform or to pay;[63] but even without taking that extreme approach the starting point is to convert the obligation into money as soon as it is broken. After all, damages are the primary remedy. But if there is a lesson to be learnt from the recent cases discussed in this paper, it is that we should not expect in all cases to make a simple conversion of the obligation into money as if there were just a single advertised exchange rate. The conversion should be delayed until after the question has been asked: what was it that the claimant was entitled to expect of the defendant, and how has the failure to receive it, as a matter of fact, affected him? Only then can a figure be put on the loss, to become the damages awarded in the action.

This is not to say, though, that there needs to be a major re-thinking of the practical consequences of breach of contract in most cases, and certainly not generally in the commercial context. The recent House of Lords cases discussed in this paper arose in unusual contexts: *Ruxley* and *Farley* were both consumer cases where the personal preferences of the claimant take a different complexion from the interests of a party to a commercial contract; and *Panatown*, although a commercial case, was dealing with a particular difficulty[64] of assessment of damages where the loss was suffered by a third party. Usually, in a commercial context, the claimant's interest in the contractual performance is purely financial and the well-established principles for the assessment of loss will be perfectly adequate.[65] But the general approach to the assessment of compensatory damages shown by these recent decisions means that, even in the commercial context, it is necessary always to make a close analysis of the real nature of the claimant's loss flowing from the breach of contract, and then to ask how best to characterize it in financial terms for the purposes of an award of damages.

---

[63] OW Holmes, 'The Path of the Law' (1896) 10 Harv LR 457 at 462.

[64] Although the context of the *Panatown* case is very common in the construction industry, the solutions which are now available, without having to develop the 'performance interest' analysis of damages in order to obtain a remedy, may remove much of the potential litigation: above, n 58.

[65] As pointed out by Lord Bridge in the *Ruxley* case: quoted above, at 4(*a*).

2
Compensatory Damages: Comment

GABRIELLE HURLEY[1]

This comment on some of the issues raised in John Cartwright's paper (Chapter 1) is written from the perspective of the construction and engineering group at Norton Rose.

In general, the contracts which we draft, or on which we advise, aim to cover all possible eventualities and to set out exhaustively the entire agreement between the parties. They accordingly typically contain clauses which aim to exclude or limit (to the extent permitted by law) any tortious liability and remedies which may otherwise exist between the contracting parties. The rationale for this approach is that clients seek certainty, both in terms of the obligations which they owe to their contracting counterparty and in terms of the remedies which can be pursued against them in the event of their poor performance. Given the continuous development of tort and its tendency to arise in unexpected ways or with unanticipated consequences, there is a perception amongst clients and lawyers alike that claims in tort would introduce an undesirable degree of uncertainty into an otherwise transparent agreement. The desire of the parties (and therefore the intention of the lawyers) is to draft a 'one stop shop' which allows the parties to understand their rights, obligations, liabilities and, most of all, exposure to risk. This is also required if adequate and comprehensive insurance is to be obtained at viable rates.

Our approach can often change, however, once a contractual relationship has broken down and we act for the claimant. We can find ourselves seeking ways to bring claims outside the contract and specifically arguing that the contract fails properly to exclude all tortious claims. Claims in tort may be attractive where they allow a party to circumvent contractual exclusions or limitations of liability and accordingly recover substantial damages. We also find ourselves on the receiving end of such an approach. For example, we are currently advising a defendant client in a case in which the claimant has alleged fraudulent misrepresentation in order to avoid caps on liability which would otherwise apply and which would limit liability on a claim for £80m to approximately £6m.

Other reasons why we may attempt to pursue a tortious claim are fairly obvious:

[1] Partner, Norton Rose. I would like to thank Guy Foster, Jo Clarke, Steve Abraham and Annie Sturge for their assistance in preparing this comment.

(a) Limitation of actions: in both tort and contract the limitation period 'starts running' from the date when the cause of action accrues. In contract, this is generally the date of the breach. In a claim in tort for negligence however, time runs from the date of damage, which may be latent.

(b) Latent damage: limitation is of particular concern where the damage is latent and does not manifest itself until after the expiration of the limitation period applicable to a claim for breach of the contract. In these circumstances the possibility of arguing a later accrual of the cause of action in tort will present a real advantage over a claim for breach of the contract, particularly in view of the Latent Damage Act 1986.

(c) Remoteness of damage: in the tort of negligence, the claimant recovers losses that the defendant might reasonably have foreseen as at the date of the negligent act. The contract rule differs in that the defendant's contemplation is assessed as at the date of the contract rather than of the breach.

Depending on the facts of a particular case, these distinctions may make a difference.

An issue which frequently arises in practice is the situation where one party to a contract intentionally breaches the contract or is guilty of wilful default. Clients, if they are on the receiving end of such default, understandably find it extremely frustrating and generally assume that caps on liability will not apply in these circumstances. However, English law, in terms of assessing damages, does not differentiate between 'deliberate', 'serious' or 'normal' breaches of contract, so caps will continue to apply. In practice, the contract is often drafted to take account of this issue. This is generally not done by altering what in principle is recoverable in damages for such a breach but by disapplying limitations or exclusions of liability, or by allowing the innocent party to terminate the contract and recover its consequential losses, in the case of 'wilful default'. Care must be taken, however, in defining what will amount to 'wilful default'.

As regards the issue of whether the courts should award 'cost of cure' or 'difference in value', some clients enter into contracts where certain benefits of the bargain are intangible. In such circumstances, where the contract is breached so that such benefits are not realized, the client can be left without a remedy. An example is a shopping centre developer client who entered into a contract for the construction of a shopping centre with 'the best car park in Europe'. When built, the car park was patently not as desired and contracted for. The only satisfactory remedy in the client's view was to return to the drawing board and redesign. However, the car park was probably fully fit for purpose. In essence the defect was cosmetic or aesthetic. The cost of repair was out of all proportion to the diminution in value and therefore seemed to be irrecoverable under the principle in the *Ruxley* case.

Particularly where there is no diminution in value caused by a contractor's breach and either the building owner decides not to carry out rectification works or the costs are disproportionate to the nature of the loss, then there are strong arguments to support the building owner being able to recover some monetary remedy for not obtaining what was contracted for rather than being awarded merely nominal damages.

For example, public policy should require the enforcement of the bargain promised so that building standards are maintained and builders are prevented from seeking to obtain a windfall by reduced performance which is still fit for purpose. The builder in the *Ruxley* case may have made a saving (or additional profit) by not having purchased the additional tiles required for the deeper pool and not employing as much manpower as would have been required to construct the deeper pool. The amount of saving may not have been great, taking account of the fairly small difference in the size of the pool contracted for and that built. However it could be much more significant in the context of a multi-million pound construction or engineering project which might comprise millions of components. This must raise public policy issues because a saving by the contractor in this way will result in overpayment by the employer.

From a practical perspective, the possible lacuna which the employer currently faces in gaining a substantial remedy where the contractor fails to perform to specification is, in our area of practice, more usually than not filled in by the insertion of appropriately worded defects liability provisions. These oblige the contractor—if it wishes to be paid the remaining part of the contract price—to return to site and rectify any 'defect' (ie any failure to meet specification) within a defined period, which often extends over several years. One problem with this approach is that the contractor may argue that matters do not amount to defects if they are fit for purpose, even though not up to specification. This problem can be overcome with appropriate contract wording.

Turning to the *Panatown* case, it is not clear whether or not the wider ground referred to can be relied upon where the contractor has given a collateral warranty. In our view, the existence of a warranty should be irrelevant to the application of the wider ground as the wider ground allows the loss of the original contracting party to be compensated. The collateral warranty is concerned to ensure that the *third party* can recover its loss and is therefore more relevant to the narrow ground. As to whether the existence of the collateral warranty *should* defeat the narrow ground, this is more logical than it defeating the application of the wider ground. It does, however, mean that collateral warranties will have to be drafted very carefully to ensure that the third party will be able to recover on its own behalf (pursuant to the warranty) all of the third party losses which the employer would have been able to recover pursuant to the narrow ground.

That said, all of this may be much less relevant now than it was during the *Panatown* litigation because of the Contracts (Rights of Third Parties) Act 1999. It is not clear to us whether the respective scopes of the narrow ground and the Act are exactly the same. The question therefore arises whether a claim under the narrow ground can succeed even where the contract between the litigating parties has excluded the Act.

3

Compensatory Damages: Review of Discussion

Much discussion centred on the 'loss of amenity' award in the *Ruxley* case.[1] There was a split of views between those who thought it was genuinely compensatory—albeit compensating a non-financial loss—and those who regarded it as a symbolic award based simply on there having been a breach of contract which would otherwise unacceptably not attract a substantial award. Those taking the former view regarded 'loss of amenity' as an accurate description and tied it to other examples of damages for disappointment, ie Mr Forsyth had lost the pleasure of diving into a deep pool rather than merely diving into a safe pool. Like the holiday cases, this was a contract where the predominant object of the contract was mental pleasure. Those taking the latter view stressed that there appeared to be no finding that Mr Forsyth would find swimming or diving less pleasurable in the pool as was, rather than the pool as it should have been.[2] This split of views was thought to reflect the somewhat differing reasoning of Lord Lloyd and Lord Mustill respectively.

Linked to this was an issue raised directly by the example in Gabrielle Hurley's comment of the supermarket car park. Can a company be awarded 'loss of amenity' damages? For example, had the contract been concluded with a company run by Mr Forsyth rather than with Mr Forsyth himself, could that company have been awarded 'loss of amenity' damages? On the face of it, if one is concerned with compensating non-financial loss, this cannot be suffered by a non-human. A company does not itself have feelings. So that unless one takes the symbolic view above— or unless, more tortuously, one regards a company as recovering for the disappointment suffered by its members—a company should not be able to recover damages for a 'loss of amenity'. This may the thought to tie in with the Lords' emphasis on the 'consumer surplus' which, of course, is geared towards human consumers and not business entities.

In relation to the *Panatown* case,[3] questions were similarly raised as to whether the 'wider ground' reflects a genuine loss. If a contracting party has not effected repairs, and does not intend to do so, how can it be said that the cost of repairs reflects a true loss? On the other hand, it was pointed out that, irrespective of the buyer's intended use of goods, the buyer in a contract for the sale of goods is entitled to damages if there is a

---

[1] [1996] AC 344.

[2] But while this is not made clear in the House of Lords, Staughton LJ's judgment in the Court of Appeal does refer to the judge's indication that Mr Forsyth's pleasure in diving was affected: see [1994] 1 WLR 650, 654.

[3] [2001] 1 AC 518, HL.

defect or shortfall in the goods on the basis that it has 'paid too much' for the goods. Indeed there is the self-help remedy of diminution or extinction of the price. Analogously it was thought that a buyer who has bought goods as a gift for a third party is entitled to damages for having 'paid too much' if the goods are defective.

The consensus of opinion was that the exclusion of the Contracts (Rights of Third Parties) Act 1999—so that the third party has been given no right to sue—does not preclude the contracting party being given a right to recover a third party's loss (under the *Linden Gardens*[4] exception to a contracting party being able to recover its own loss only). That that should be so is borne out by the facts of the *Linden Gardens* case itself. There was there a clause preventing assignment to a third party. But this did not preclude the employer recovering damages for the loss suffered by the third-party purchaser. Moreover, if one regards the 1999 Act and the *Linden Gardens* exception as underpinned by a desire to effect the contracting parties' intentions, it is clear that the contracting parties may intend that the contracting party shall have the right to recover the third party's loss without necessarily intending that the third party shall have a right to sue.

It was also pointed out that the policy referred to in Gabrielle Hurley's comment (in Chapter 2) of preventing the contractor saving expense by breaking the contract is to switch to a restitutionary principle (designed to remove a gain from the contract-breaker) and away from compensating the claimant.

---

[4] [1994] 1 AC 85, HL.

4

Limitations on Compensation

ANDREW BURROWS[1]

1. INTRODUCTION

In assessing compensatory damages for torts and breach of contract, one must first decide what the aim of those damages is. This aim can be expressed in general terms for all civil wrongs as being to put the claimant into as good a position as if no wrong had been committed. However, in applying that general compensatory aim, very different results may ensue depending on whether the duty broken was a positive or a negative one. Hence the distinction between compensatory damages for breach of positive contractual obligations where the aim is to put the claimant into as good a position as if the contract had been performed (often termed the protection of the 'expectation' or 'performance' interest);[2] and compensatory damages for breach of the negative obligations typically imposed by torts where the aim is to put the claimant into as good a position as if the tort had not been committed (often termed the protection of the 'reliance' interest). So, for example, the tort of deceit or negligent misrepresentation imposes a negative obligation not to make a false statement. Compensatory damages for a misrepresentation inducing a contract therefore aim to put the claimant into as good a position as if no statement had been made which, in this context, means as if no contract had been entered into. This may therefore yield a different measure of compensatory damages—depending on whether the contractual bargain was a good or bad one—than those awarded for breach of contract aimed at putting the claimant into as good a position as if the contract had been performed.

But the complexity and interest of the law on compensatory damages is generated not only by the application of the above general aim but also, and perhaps primarily, by the numerous limitations on compensatory damages that the law has developed. These limitations mean that the courts are concerned to some extent only, and not fully, to put the claimant into as good a position as if no wrong had been committed. The claimant will be left to bear some of its loss even though factually consequent on the wrong.

---

[1] Norton Rose Professor of Commercial Law in the Unversity of Oxford; Fellow of St Hugh's College.

[2] The terms 'expectation' and 'reliance interest' were coined by Fuller and Perdue, 'The Reliance Interest in Contract Damages' (1936–37) 46 Yale LJ 52 and 373. The term 'performance interest' was coined by Friedmann, 'The Performance Interest in Contract Damages' (1995) 111 LQR 628.

The general limitations on compensatory damages can be listed as follows: remoteness, intervening cause, the duty to mitigate, contributory negligence (although, as we shall see, the application of this to breach of contract is restricted), and, although it is doubtful whether this survives as a limitation, impecuniosity.[3] There are also some limitations that are essentially specific to compensatory damages for breach of contract and do not apply to torts: for example, the restrictions on the availability of damages for mental distress;[4] and that damages (as opposed to statutory interest) cannot be awarded for the general loss of the use of money payable by the defendant to the claimant.[5]

Also important in assessing compensatory damages—although not a limitation as such—is that advantages that have accrued to the claimant as a result of the wrong need to be deducted provided they are direct, and not 'collateral' or 'remote', benefits.[6]

It might be expected that similar limitations would apply if one switches one's attention from compensatory damages for breach of contract and torts to equitable compensation for equitable wrongs, such as breach of fiduciary duty, breach of confidence, and dishonest assistance. However, as we shall see, there is an ongoing debate as to whether limitations like remoteness and contributory negligence do apply to equitable compensation.

In this paper I want to confine my examination of limitations on compensation to three main areas: remoteness in contract; contributory negligence in contract; and equitable compensation for equitable wrongs. In a book designed to consider the views of both academics and practitioners, these three areas have been chosen not merely because they are topical but also because they will enable us to see the different perspectives, if any, of academics and practitioners on three significantly different sets of legal issues. The first comprises a very well-known and basic area of the law. In relation to the second, the burning issue is whether, as a matter of policy, there should be statutory reform of the present law. The third area is one where English law is, as yet, relatively undeveloped and unclear.

2. REMOTENESS IN CONTRACT

In looking at the law of remoteness in contract, academic lawyers have spent much time agonizing about the precise test to be applied and how it

---

[3] *The Liesbosch* [1933] AC 449, HL, technically remains good law. But it has generally been distinguished or ignored. See, most recently, *Alcoa Minerals of Jamaica Inc v Broderick* [2000] 3 WLR 23, PC. See generally Coote, 'Damages, *The Liesbosch* and Impecuniosity' [2001] CLJ 511.

[4] See, eg, *Watts v Morrow* [1991] 1 WLR 1421, CA; *Farley v Skinner* [2001] 3 WLR 899, HL.

[5] *London, Chatham & Dover Rwy v South Eastern Rwy* [1893] AC 429.

[6] See, eg, *Laverack v Woods of Colchester* [1976] 1 QB 278.

compares with the remoteness test in tort. Attention has been focused on issues such as the degree of likelihood of loss occurring that needs to be contemplated or foreseen; on the time at which the foresight or contemplation is to be judged; and on how far it is the type of loss rather than the actual loss that is important. It may be that practitioners tend to adopt a more broad-brush approach to remoteness according to which such points of detail are rarely considered and where all that one generally needs to know is that, as established in *Hadley v Baxendale*,[7] loss is too remote in contract if it was not within the reasonable contemplation of the parties. Such a broad-brush approach may explain why *Hadley v Baxendale* remains such a prominently cited case, despite the fact that subsequent cases have significantly refined its approach. It may also explain why relatively little attention has been devoted to what appears to be the most significant remoteness case in the last decade—on the assumption that we put to one side *South Australia Asset Management Corp v York Montague Ltd (SAAMCO)*[8] as not being a remoteness case—which is the Court of Appeal's decision in *Brown v KMR Services Ltd*.[9]

In order to see the significance of the *Brown* case, it may be helpful to remind ourselves briefly of the four leading cases on remoteness in contract.

I have assumed that it is unnecessary to recap on the facts of *Hadley v Baxendale* which is probably the most famous contract case in the common law world. But it is important to set out verbatim the two rules laid down by Alderson B. He said:

> Where two parties have made a contract which one of them has broken, the damages which the other party ought to receive in respect of such breach of contact, should be such as may fairly and reasonably be considered, either arising naturally, ie according to the usual course of things from such breach of contract itself, or such as may reasonably be supposed to have been in the contemplation of both parties, at the time they made the contract as the probable result of the breach of it.[10]

In *Victoria Laundry (Windsor) Ltd v Newman Industries Ltd*[11] the claimants, launderers and dyers, decided to extend their business and contracted to buy a boiler from the defendant. The defendant knew that the claimants wanted the boiler for immediate use in their business but, in breach of contract, delivered the boiler five months late. The claimants claimed damages for the ordinary loss of profits that would have resulted from using the boiler during those months plus damages for the exceptional loss of profits that they would have been able to gain from contracts with the Ministry of Supply. The Court of Appeal held that, applying

---

[7] (1854) 9 Exch 341.   [8] [1997] AC 191, HL.   [9] [1995] 4 All ER 598.
[10] (1854) 9 Exch 341, 354.   [11] [1949] 2 KB 528.

Hadley v Baxendale, damages for the ordinary loss of profits but not for the exceptional loss of profits should be given. The exceptional profits were too remote because they did not arise naturally and were not in the contemplation of the parties at the time of contracting because the defendants knew nothing about the Ministry of Supply contracts.

Asquith LJ, giving the Court of Appeal's judgment, correctly reasoned that the two rules of *Hadley v Baxendale* could be regarded as comprising a single rule, centring on reasonable contemplation or, as he preferred, reasonable foreseeability. If in applying the second rule one includes as important what the defendant should have reasonably contemplated or foreseen if he had thought about the breach at the time of contracting, then it can swallow up the first rule—for something arising naturally is something that should have been reasonably contemplated by the defendant if he had thought about the breach.

Since the *Victoria Laundry* case, while the courts have sometimes continued to talk of two rules of remoteness, they have tended, like Asquith LJ, to think in terms of one rather than two rules.[12] Indeed Lord Reid in *Heron II* specifically said, 'I do not think that it was intended that there were to be two rules or that two different standards or tests were to be applied.'[13] And in *The Pegase*[14] Robert Goff J said,

> *Hadley v Baxendale* is now no longer stated in terms of two rules, but rather in terms of a single principle—though it is recognised that the application of the principle may depend on the degree of relevant knowledge held by the defendant at the time of the contract in a particular case. This approach accords to what actually happens in practice; the courts have not been over-ready to pigeon-hole the cases under one or other of the so-called rules in *Hadley v Baxendale*, but rather to decide each case on the basis of the relevant knowledge of the defendant.

It is hard to see that anything of substance should turn on whether one formulates the test in two rules or one; and some of the leading contract texts do provide illustrations of the two rules taken separately.[15] In particular, where one is talking about special circumstances that must have been communicated to the defendant in order for particular loss to be non-remote, it can be convenient to say that one is talking about the second rule in *Hadley v Baxendale*.

---

[12] See, for example, Lord Denning in *Robophone Facilties Ltd v Blank* [1966] 1 WLR 1428; *Parsons v Uttley Ingham* [1978] QB 791.

[13] *Koufos v C Czarnikow Ltd, The Heron II* [1969] 1 AC 350, 385.

[14] *Satef-Huttenes Albertus SpA v Paloma Tercera Shipping Co SA, Ther Pegase* [1981] 1 Lloyd's Rep 175, 182.

[15] See, for example, Beatson, *Anson's Law of Contract* (28th edn, 2002) 605–9; McKendrick, *Contract Law* (4th edn, 2000) 416–18.

But what is incorrect is to treat the two rules as providing mutually exclusive, rather than overlapping, tests. This is not least because what occurs naturally will almost always be within the contemplation of the parties. Yet some courts have approached the rules as if they were mutually exclusive so that the first gives the remoteness test for 'general damages' and the second gives the remoteness test for 'special damages'.[16] This requires one to embark initially on an unnecessary, unhelpful and largely circular categorization of loss as being either general or special. In truth, one shades into the other.

This was expressly emphasized by the Court of Appeal in *Kpohraror v Woolwich Building Society*.[17] The case was concerned with what damages were recoverable for the wrongful dishonour of a cheque where the defendant bank's error had been corrected, and the claimant informed that the cheque would be honoured, later the same day. The claimant sought compensation for the damage to his credit and his reputation and for the trading loss caused by being unable, as a consequence of the breach, to pay for and hence resell a particular shipment of goods. The Court of Appeal upheld the master's judgment awarding £5,500 for the injury to the claimant's credit and reputation but refusing damages for the particular trading loss. The reasoning was that there was no 'traders only' rule denying the claimant damages for the injury to his credit and reputation and that loss was not too remote. In contrast, the specific trading loss was too remote because the defendant bank had not been informed, and did not know, that a short delay in payment would cause the loss of a transaction. In particular, the bank had not been given notice of the need for immediate clearance.

The important point for us here is that in respect of remoteness the case had been argued by making a rigid distinction between the general damage to the claimant's credit and reputation which was presented as being entirely a matter for the first rule in *Hadley v Baxendale*; and the specific trading loss which had been presented as being entirely a matter for the second rule in *Hadley v Baxendale*. As the Court of Appeal clarified, the correct approach should have been to apply both rules to both types of loss. Evans LJ, with whom Waite LJ and Sir John May agreed, said:

> The contentions for both parties were presented as if in a straightjacket imposed by the strict application of the rule in *Hadley v Baxendale* so as to require the separate consideration of each of the two limbs . . . I would prefer that the starting point for any application of *Hadley v Baxendale* is the extent of the shared

---

[16] See, for example, *Monarch SS Co v A/B Karlshamns Oljefabriker* [1949] AC 196, 221 (*per* Lord Wright); *President of India v La Pintada Compania Navigacion SA* [1985] AC 104.

[17] [1996] 4 All ER 119. See also *International Mineral and Chemical Corp v Carl O'Helm AG* [1986] 1 Lloyds Rep 81 (*per* Hobhouse J).

knowledge of both parties when the contract was made (. . . including the possibility that knowledge of the defendant alone is enough). When that is established, it may often be the case that the first and the second parts of the rule overlap, or at least that it is unnecessary to draw a clear line of demarcation between them.[18]

It is also perhaps worth interjecting here that, although not mentioned in any of the student texts on contract, a rigid distinction has been drawn between the two rules in *Hadley v Baxendale* for the rather different purpose of defining 'consequential or indirect loss' in exclusion clauses. That is, in a number of decisions concerned with the construction of clauses excluding liability for 'indirect or consequential loss' the courts have laid down that the line between direct and indirect or consequential loss is drawn along the boundary between the first and second rules in *Hadley v Baxendale*.[19] Direct loss is treated as loss that follows naturally from the breach within the first rule, while indirect or consequential loss falls within the second rule and is loss that is legally recoverable only if special circumstances were brought to the defendant's attention. Construing exclusion clauses is, of course, a different matter from deciding when losses are, and are not, too remote and one should not reason back from these cases to say that, for the purposes of remoteness, there is a sharp line between the two rules in *Hadley v Baxendale*. As Sedley LJ said in *Hotel Services Ltd v Hilton International Hotels (UK) Ltd*,[20] having referred to the rules in *Hadley v Baxendale*:

> This is not a dichotomous but a continuous classification, bringing into the region of recoverability all loss which the parties must in the nature of things or for known reasons have anticipated. It is the framing of exclusion clauses which has made it necessary to divide up its elements . . .'

Returning to our quartet of leading cases, in *Heron II*[21] the House of Lords was concerned with the degree of likelihood of the loss occurring that needs to be reasonably contemplatable by the defendant in order for the loss to be non-remote. The claim was being brought by charterers of a ship against the defendant shipowner for delivering sugar at Basrah, nine days late. During those nine days, 8,000 tonnes of sugar had arrived at Basrah with the result that the market price for sugar at Basrah had fallen.

---

[18] ibid at 127–8.

[19] eg *Croudace Construction Ltd v Cawoods Concrete Products Ltd* [1978] 2 Lloyd's Rep 55, CA; *British Sugar plc v Projects Ltd* (1997) 87 BLR 42, CA; *Deepak Fertilisers & Petrochemicals Ltd v Davy McKee (London) Ltd* [1999] 1 All ER (Comm) 69, CA; *BHP Petroleum Ltd v British Steel plc* [1999] 2 All ER (Comm) 544, Rix J; *Hotel Services Ltd v Hilton International Hotels (UK) Ltd* [2000] 1 All ER (Comm) 750, CA; *Watford Electronics Ltd v Sanderson CFL Ltd* [2001] 1 All ER (Comm) 696. cf *Caledonia North Sea Ltd v British Telecommunications plc* [2002] 1 Lloyd's Rep 553, 572 (*per* Lord Hoffmann).

[20] [2000] 1 All ER (Comm) 750, 755, CA.   [21] [1969] 1 AC 350, HL.

The shipowner had not known that the charterer intended to sell the sugar as soon as it reached Basrah but had known that there was a market for sugar at Basrah. The House of Lords held that, applying *Hadley v Baxendale*, as refined by the *Victoria Laundry* case, the loss of profit from the fall in the market was not too remote and was recoverable. The argument that the remoteness test for carriage of goods by sea was more restricted than that of *Hadley v Baxendale* was rejected. The Law Lords agreed that a higher degree of likelihood of the loss occurring was required in contract than under the tort remoteness test of reasonable forseeability laid down in the *Wagon Mound* case[22] so that losses may be too remote in contract that would not be too remote in tort. Unfortunately, there was no clear consensus as to how the degree of likelihood required in contract should be expressed. The various expressions used, and the lack of clarity in their Lordships' reasoning, has been castigated by the well-known American commentators Dawson and Harvey. In their student case-book[23] they write:

> Five Law Lords gave speeches which restated each others' views at great length in a stunning display of prolixity. . . . Without distinguishing between which or what issues they were addressing, the learned Lords spent much time discussing the phrases proposed by Asquith LJ in *Victoria Laundry*. In choosing the words to describe how probable the loss must appear to be at the time of the contract, the vote of the noble lords was in favour of 'a real danger' (3 to 1), and 'a serious possibility' (3 to 1), but against 'odds on' (4 to 0). The vote was 5 to 0 against 'on the cards' and some severe disapproval of this phrase was expressed. For as Lord Reid said, in an unshuffled pack of cards the probability that the top card will be a diamond is 1 in 4 (apparently this would be a high enough probability for him) but the chance that it will be the 9 of diamonds is 1 in 52—not nearly high enough though it would clearly be 'on the cards.' For most of the learned lords 'not unlikely' seemed to be acceptable. Some thought that Asquith's 'liable to result', though somewhat indeterminate, could not after all be improved upon. We have had to read this case. There is no reason why you should!

Putting to one side Dawson and Harvey's exasperation, perhaps the clearest way of expressing the essence of their Lordships' reasoning is that, while a slight possibility of the loss occurring is required in tort, a serious possibility of the loss occurring is required in contract. So, on the facts, the loss of profit from the market fall was not too remote because the defendant could have reasonably contemplated that loss as a serious possibility had it thought about the breach at the time the contract was made.

In some subsequent cases, additional complexity has been caused by the necessity for the courts to analyse in greater detail the 'fit' between the

---

[22] [1961] AC 388, PC.   [23] *Contracts: Cases and Comment* (3rd edn, 1977) 70–1.

remoteness tests in tort and contract. The best known is the fourth of our quartet of leading cases, *Parsons v Uttley Ingham & Co Ltd*.[24] The question at issue was whether the supplier of a defective pig hopper was liable in contract for the loss of 254 pigs that had died from a rare intestinal disease after eating nuts that had gone mouldy in the hopper. The Court of Appeal decided that the loss of the pigs was not too remote but the judges found this difficult to reconcile with the traditional *Hadley v Baxendale* approach. Lord Denning MR took an unconventional view according to which there are two tests for remoteness in contract: one deals with physical damage, where the contract and tort remoteness tests are the same; and the other deals with loss of profit, where the tests differ. The majority, Scarman and Orr LJJ, preferred to say that the crucial question was whether the type of loss, not the precise loss suffered, was reasonably contemplatable: as illness of pigs and death of pigs were both the same type of loss and, as the former was reasonably contemplatable, the death of the 254 pigs was not too remote. The majority judges also went out of their way to try to equate the remoteness tests in contract and tort. In a passage that has become a favourite of contract law examiners, Scarman LJ said, '. . . The law must be such that in the factual situation where all had the same actual or imputed knowledge . . . the amount of damages recoverable does not depend on whether, as a matter of legal classification, the plaintiff's cause of action is breach of contract or tort.'[25]

The *Parsons* case left the law in an unclear position. The majority's emphasis on the type of loss had not figured prominently in the earlier leading cases;[26] and Lord Denning's bifurcation between loss of profit and physical damage was both novel and problematic.

Hence the scene was set for *Brown v KMR Services Ltd* where one question, in claims by Lloyd's Names against their members' agents for breach of contract and the tort of negligence, was whether the loss was too remote. The defendants' argument was that the magnitude of the financial disasters that had struck, and the consequent scale of the loss, was unforeseeable and could not have been contemplated. No-one would have predicted such a run of major catastrophes as had occurred in the relevant years (1988–90).

The Court of Appeal held that the loss was not too remote because it was the type and not the extent of the loss that needed to be foreseen or contemplated: the majority's approach in *Parsons v Uttley Ingham* was approved; and the decision in *Victoria Laundry (Windsor) Ltd v Newham Industries Ltd* was distinguished. Hobhouse LJ, with whom Peter Gibson LJ agreed, said that the only type of loss in question was that suffered by being a member of a high risk syndicate. Stuart-Smith LJ similarly

---

[24] [1978] QB 791, CA.   [25] ibid, at 807.   [26] But see *Wroth v Tyler* [1974] Ch 30.

regarded there as being only one type of loss in issue although he described that as underwriting loss. He distinguished the *Victoria Laundry* case saying:

> I accept that difficulty in practice may arise in categorisation of loss into types or kinds, especially where financial loss is involved. But I do not see any difficulty in holding that loss of ordinary business profits is different in kind from that flowing from a particular contract which gives rise to very high profits, the existence of which is unknown to the other contracting party who therefore does not accept the risk of such loss occurring.[27]

There are three main points to emerge from this important case. First, it clearly establishes that the majority view in the *Parsons* case was correct; applying the contract test, even for economic loss, it is the type of loss and not the precise loss that needs to be reasonably in contemplation or foreseeable. Secondly, it appears that the contract test was applied even in relation to the concurrent claim in the tort of negligence.[28] This must be correct. Where there is a contractual relationship between the parties and the claim is brought in both contract and tort it would be very odd to have a different remoteness test in contract and tort. If we think about the policy behind having different tests, this rests on there being an opportunity for a contracting party to inform the other party of unusual risks. That other party can then exclude or limit its liability or can negotiate a higher price. This is not an opportunity that a party suing in tort normally has because the claimant prior to the commission of the tort is a stranger.[29] But where the claim is being brought in tort in the context of a contractual relationship the parties are not strangers and plainly the claimant has had the same opportunity to inform the defendant of risks *vis-à-vis* the tort claim as he has had *vis-à-vis* the contract claim. Thirdly, the way in which the *Victoria Laundry* case was distinguished shows that there is a wide degree

---

[27] [1995] 4 All ER 598, 621.

[28] Admittedly both Gatehouse J and the Court of Appeal used only the language of breach of contract in expressing their conclusions; and at the time of Gatehouse J's judgment the House of Lords' decision in *Henderson v Merrett Syndicates Ltd* [1994] 3 WLR 761 authoritatively accepting concurrent liability had not yet been laid down. But the claims in the *Brown* case were for both breach of contract and the tort of negligence and the appeal in the *Brown* case was heard, and the judgment of the Court of Appeal was given, almost a year after *Henderson v Merrett*.

[29] In *Heron II* [1969] 1 AC 350, 385–6, Lord Reid said, 'In contract, if one party wishes to protect himself against a risk which to the other party would appear unusual, he can direct the other party's attention to it before the contract is made, and I need not stop to consider in what circumstances the other party will then be held to have accepted responsibility in that event. In tort however, there is no opportunity for the injured party to protect himself in that way and the tortfeasor cannot reasonably complain if he has to pay for some very unusual but nevertheless foreseeable damage which results from his wrongdoing.' Similarly it has been argued that it is economically efficient to encourage the disclosure of information regarding unusual potential losses so that the defendant with full knowledge of the risks involved can plan and act rationally: see, eg, Posner, *Economic Analysis of Law* (5th edn).

of discretion open to the courts in deciding how to divide up types of loss. It is mirrored in well-known tort remoteness cases on personal injury.[30] This discretionary flexibility is obviously achieved at the expense of a degree of certainty.

It would seem therefore that, despite little attention being devoted to it, the *Brown* decision provides the final major piece in the remoteness jigsaw. After it, we can describe the law, in a way that is relatively clear and based on sound policy, in the following three points. First, there is a single contract test of remoteness which lays down that losses are too remote if at the time the contract was made the defendant did not contemplate and could not reasonably have contemplated that type of loss as a serious possibility. Secondly, the normal tort test, applicable in standard tort claims where the parties are not in a contractual relationship, is that losses are too remote if at the time of the breach of duty the defendant did not foresee and could not reasonably have foreseen that type of loss as a slight possibility. Thirdly, where the parties are in a contractual relationship, the above contract test applies even where the claim is being brought in tort because of the equal opportunity that the claimant has had to inform the other party of unusual risks.[31]

It is finally important to add that, while the *Wagon Mound* remoteness test applies to unintentional torts, in particular negligence and nuisance, the courts have applied a wider remoteness test of 'direct consequence' to the tort of deceit.[32] The explanation for this is that the wrong requires proof of dishonesty and the courts are less willing to cut back a dishonest, as opposed to a negligent, wrongdoer's liability by treating loss as remote. Although the point has not been tested it may be that the same applies to other intentional torts, for example the economic torts.

---

[30] *Bradford v Robinson Rentals Ltd* [1967] 1 WLR 337; *Tremain v Pike* [1969] 1 WLR 1556.

[31] One can strongly argue that, wherever there is a pre-existing relationship, even if non-contractual between the parties, the 'contract' test should apply even where the claim is being brought in tort because the claimant has had the opportunity, and should be encouraged, to inform the other party of unusual risks. Admittedly the scope for the defendant to deal with that information is more restricted than where there is a contractual relationship: in particular there is no price to modify. But the defendant can exclude or limit his tortious liability (eg for negligent advice) by a non-contractual disclaimer.

[32] *Doyle v Olby (Ironmongers) Ltd* [1969] 2 QB 158, CA; *Smith New Court Securities Ltd v Scrimgeour Vickers (Asset Mangement) Ltd* [1997] AC 254, HL. In *Royscot Trust Ltd v Rogerson* [1991] 2 QB 297, CA, it was held that the wider remoteness test for deceit also applied to damages under s 2(1) of the Misrepresentation Act 1967 which uses the language of fraud. This seems wrong in terms of policy and in *Smith New Court* it was left open whether *Royscot* was correctly decided on this point: [1997] AC 254, 267, 283.

3. CONTRIBUTORY NEGLIGENCE IN CONTRACT

Contributory negligence as a defence to breach of contract has for many years been a highly controversial issue.[33] If it applies, contributory negligence operates to reduce the damages that the claimant would be entitled to for the defendant's breach of contract proportionate to the relative blameworthiness and causal potency of the parties' conduct. While the claimant's fault is indisputably relevant to the duty to mitigate, or may alternatively mean that the causal link between the defendant's breach of contract and the claimant's loss is broken through the concept of intervening causation, those two limitations apply in an all or nothing fashion. They mean that the claimant recovers 100 per cent or nothing of the loss in question. In contrast, contributory negligence, in its modern form, is a proportionate defence.[34]

The defence is now entirely contained in the Law Reform (Contributory Negligence) Act 1945. Section 1(1) provides as follows:

> Where any person suffers damage as a result partly of his own fault and partly of the fault of any other person or persons, a claim in respect of that damage shall not be defeated by reason of the fault of the person suffering the damage, but the damages recoverable in respect thereof shall be reduced to such extent as the court thinks just and equitable having regard to the claimant's share in the responsibility for the damage.'

Particularly important in working out the scope of contributory negligence is the definition of 'fault' in section 1(1). By section 4, 'fault' is defined to mean 'negligence, breach of statutory duty or other act or omission which gives rise to liability in tort or would, apart from this Act, give rise to the defence of contributory negligence.'

It is clear from that definition that the defence applies to torts,[35] including torts of strict liability, but it is far from clear that it applies to breach of contract. For if one divides section 4 into two parts with the first ('negligence, breach of statutory duty or act or omission which gives rise to a liability in tort') referring to the defendant's fault and the second (any act or omission which 'would apart from this Act, give rise to the defence of

---

[33] In Australia enormous controversy was recently created by *Astley v Austrust Ltd* (1999) 161 ALR 155 in which the High Court of Australia decided that contributory negligence is never a defence to breach of contract. In most (all?) of the states and territories the decision has subsequently been legislatively overruled so that contributory negligence applies in what English law, as we shall see, calls a category three case.

[34] It operated in an all or nothing way and was therefore merely an aspect of legal causation at common law.

[35] An exception is the tort of deceit: *Standard Chartered Bank v Pakistan National Shipping Co (No 2)* [2002] UKHL 43, [2002] 3 WLR 1547, HL.

contributory negligence') referring to the claimant's fault, the first part on its most natural interpretation does not apply to breach of contract.

The correct approach to construing section 4 of the 1945 Act in relation to breach of contract was first put forward as late as 1989 in obiter dicta of the Court of Appeal, confirming Hobhouse J's reasoning, in *Forsikrings-aktieselskapet Vesta v Butcher*.[36] According to this, contract cases should be divided into three categories. A category one case is where the defendant has been in breach of a strict contractual duty. A category two case is where the defendant has been in breach of a contractual duty of care. A category three case is where the defendant has been in breach of a contractual duty of care and is also liable in the tort of negligence. According to the Court of Appeal, it is in a category three case only that section 4 of the 1945 Act allows contributory negligence to be a defence to breach of contract. This is because, as a matter of statutory interpretation, 'negligence . . . which gives rise to a liability in tort' is satisfied where the defendant is liable for breach of a contractual duty of care which also renders the defendant liable in the tort of negligence. *Vesta v Butcher* was itself a category three case: the allegation was that re-insurers, in breach of their contractual duty of care to the claimants, had failed to ensure the deletion of a term in the re-insurance contract contrary to the instructions of the claimant. While the claim was framed in contract, the defendants would also have been liable in the tort of negligence.

The leading case on category three is now the unreported decision in *UCB Bank plc v Hepherd Winstanley and Pugh*[37] in which, confirming the obiter dicta in *Vesta v Butcher*, the Court of Appeal applied contributory negligence to reduce damages. The claimant bank sought damages from its solicitors in relation to loans made by the bank. It was held that the solicitors had been negligent and in breach of their contractual duty of care in failing, contrary to the wishes of the bank, to ensure that full collateral security for the loans was obtained. As a consequence, when the borrower defaulted and the security was enforced, the bank received £107,151 less than it would have done had it had full collateral security. The Court of Appeal nevertheless reduced the damages by 25 per cent because of the bank's own fault constituted by the failure of its relevant employee to read properly the letter sent by the solicitors. Chadwick LJ said:

> Properly understood this is a category (3) case within [the] classification in *Vesta v Butcher*. Accordingly the damages which UCB may recover in respect of HWP's breach of duty must be reduced to such extent as the court thinks just and equitable having regard to UCB's own share in the responsibility for its loss. In my view, the appropriate reduction in the present case is 25%.

---

[36] [1989] AC 852, CA; affd on a different point [1989] AC 880, HL.
[37] The Times, 25 August 1999, CA.

In contrast, contributory negligence was held to be inapplicable by the Court of Appeal in *Barclays Bank plc v Fairclough Building Ltd*[38] because this was a category one case. The defendant had been in breach of contract in cleaning the roofs of the claimant bank's storage warehouse. The roofs were made of asbestos cement sheeting and the result of the defendant's cleaning, without proper precautions being taken, was that the warehouse was contaminated with asbestos fibres and dust requiring remedial work of £4m. The defendants alleged that the claimant bank was partly responsible, through its property division, for proper precautions not having been taken and that therefore there should be a reduction for contributory negligence. It was held that contributory negligence could not here apply so that full damages were awarded. This was because the facts fell within category one. The claimant's loss followed from the breach of the defendant's strict obligations to carry out the work in accordance with the specifications and to achieve the standard specified. The breach was not merely one of a duty of care. While the Court of Appeal accepted that contributory negligence could apply in a category three case, it was emphatically laid down that it should not apply in a category one case. Indeed Nourse LJ went so far as to say the following:

> It ought to be a cause of general concern that the law should have got into such a state that a contractor who was in breach of two of the main obligations expressly undertaken by him in a standard form building contract was able to persuade the judge in the court below that the building owner's damages should be reduced by 40% because of its own negligence in not preventing the contractor from committing the breaches. In circumstances such as these release, waiver, forbearance or the like are the only defences available to a party to a contract who wishes to assert that the other party's right to recover damages for its breach has been lost or diminished. It ought to have been perfectly obvious that the Law Reform (Contributory Negligence) Act 1945 was never intended to obtrude the defence of contributory negligence into an area of the law where it has no business to be.[39]

Since the House of Lords' acceptance of concurrent liability in *Henderson v Merrett Syndicates Ltd*[40] it will be very rare to find a case that falls within category two but outside category three. *Raflatac Ltd v Eade*[41] is such a rare case. Here the defendant head-contractor had broken its contractual duty of

---

[38] [1994] 3 WLR 1057.

[39] [1994] 3 WLR 1057, 1073–4. In third and fourth party proceedings in *Barclays Bank plc v Fairclough Building Ltd (No 2)* (1995) 44 Con LR 35, CA, the sub-sub-contractors, who had actually carried out the cleaning work, were held liable for breach of a contractual duty of care to the sub-contractors. Ironically there was a 50 per cent reduction because of the sub-contractor's contributory negligence, this being a category three case. *Vesta v Butcher* was applied.

[40] [1994] 3 WLR 761.   [41] [1999] 1 Lloyd's Rep 506.

care as regards acts of a sub-contractor in negligently damaging the claimant's property. Although the defendant head-contractor was in breach of its contractual duty of care it was held that it had no personal or vicarious liability in tort for those acts of the sub-contractor. This was therefore a category two case and contributory negligence was held to be inapplicable.

The picture of the law that the courts have arrived at in construing the 1945 Act is therefore now clear and straightforward. Contributory negligence applies as a defence to breach of contract in category three but not in categories one and two.

But while the law is clear, one can raise doubts as to how satisfactory it is. Prior to my term of office at the Law Commission, the Commission had carried out a project on contributory negligence in contract. In its Working Paper it had provisionally recommended that the 1945 Act should be reformed so that contributory negligence would apply to all three categories of case.[42] However, in its report it instead recommended (contrary to the views of the majority of its consultees who supported its wider provisional recommendation) that contributory negligence should be extended only to category two and not also to category one.[43] What primarily worried the Law Commission in back-tracking from its provisional recommendation—and was stressed to it by some consultees—was the uncertainty that contributory negligence would cause.[44] The fear is that what are at present straightforward damages claims for breach of contract would become complex disputes as to comparative blameworthiness. This would potentially increase litigation and hamper out-of-court settlements. The recommendation to move the law marginally forward to include category two as well as category three was a pragmatic compromise which would not significantly increase uncertainty in commercial litigation.[45]

---

[42] *Contributory Negligence as a Defence in Contract*, Law Commission Working Paper No 114 (1990).

[43] *Contributory Negligence as a Defence in Contract*, Law Com 219 (1993).

[44] ibid at paras 3.39–40, 4.6.

[45] The Law Commission also expressed concerns that extending contributory negligence to category one might operate to the disadvantage of consumers and others in weaker bargaining positions: ibid, paras 3.39–40, 4.6. But this argument was effectively repudiated in the Working Paper No 114, para 4.45(e) (eg 'apportionment will improve the position of the consumer whose conduct, under the present law, is held to break the chain of causation and so results in no recovery'). The Report, paras 4.2–5, also relies on what was termed a reason of principle, namely that a claimant should be able to rely on the defendant fulfilling a strict obligation and should not have to take precautions against the possibility that a breach might occur. But that argument had been comprehensively answered in the Working Paper No 114, Part II by clarifying that, in deciding whether the claimant has been at fault, one must take into account the contractual context. In particular the Working Paper stressed that normally a claimant should not be regarded as being at fault in relying on the defendant to perform his (strict or reasonable care) contractual obligation and by not checking up that he has done so. For instance, if C takes a car to a garage for work to be done on the brakes, C should not be regarded as being at fault if he fails to check that the work has been properly done and as a consequence has an accident.

At the time when the Law Commission was reporting it may not have been as obvious as it now is, subsequent to *Henderson v Merrett*, that in practice there will be very few cases that fall within category two and not category three. On my arrival at the Law Commission, when the Lord Chancellor's Department was deciding what should happen to the recommendation in Report No 219, we were asked what the impact of that recommendation would be. The truth was that, after *Henderson v Merrett*, the impact would be negligible. The Lord Chancellor's Department took the view that, as there was no pressing need for legislation, the recommendation for reform should be rejected. Had the answer been that the effect of the reform would be very significant, the Lord Chancellor's Department would no doubt have decided that too much of a change could not be justified either and that for that reason the reform should not be implemented. Such are the problematic parameters within which the Law Commission has to work!

However, I continue to have doubts as to whether the present law is satisfactory and as to whether the Law Commission was right to abandon its provisional recommendation. Certainly there can be no objection in principle to contributory negligence applying where a defendant has been held strictly liable because this is something that is permitted in relation to strict liability torts, such as breach of statutory duty and *Rylands v Fletcher* liability. Moreover, it seems wrong in terms of policy for the law to be that a claimant may be wholly barred from receiving damages because of the claimant's own fault, through the application of the duty to mitigate or intervening cause, while there is no mid-position where damages may be merely reduced. The denial of contributory negligence unsatisfactorily forces the courts to choose between the blameworthy claimant recovering 100 per cent damages or no damages for the particular loss in question.

With the increased interest in a European Contract Code, it is noteworthy that in the *Principles of European Contract Law*,[46] edited by Lando and Beale, contributory negligence is applicable to all three categories. Article 9:504 reads as follows: 'The non-performing party is not liable for loss suffered by the aggrieved party to the extent that the aggrieved party contributed to the non-performance or its effects.' One of the main illustrations given is a category one case.[47] Similarly Article 7.4.7 of the UNIDROIT Principles of International Commercial Contracts reads:

[46] Kluwer Law International (2000).

[47] 'A leases a computer which under the terms of the contract is to be ready for use in England where the voltage is 240v. The computer supplied is capable of operating on various voltages and, in breach of contract, is actually set for 110v. A prominent sign pasted on the screen warns the user to check the voltage setting before use. A ignores this and switches on without checking the setting. The computer is extensively damaged and repairs will cost A £1,500. The court may take the view that the loss was at least half A's fault and award only £750 damages.'

'Where harm is due in part to an act or omission of the aggrieved party or to another event as to which that party bears the risk, the amount of damages shall be reduced to the extent that these factors have contributed to the harm, having regard to the conduct of the parties.'

We can refer to other illustrations to test whether the present law produces acceptable results. In its working paper, the Law Commission gave the following example. 'A customer, P, buys an iron from retailer, D. When taking it out of the package, he notices that the heat dial has fallen off and that it is defective in several other ways. Nevertheless he uses it and ruins a shirt. Assuming no negligence on D's part, P sues D for breach of his strict contractual obligations that the iron will be of satisfactory quality and reasonably fit for its purpose.'[48] At that stage in its thinking, the Law Commission thought that the law was unnecessarily inflexible in dictating that P would recover either in full for the shirt or not at all.

Again in *Quinn v Burch Brothers (Builders) Ltd*,[49] which is a leading case on intervening causation in contract, the defendants in breach of contract failed to supply a step-ladder to the claimant, a sub-contractor. The claimant injured himself when he fell from an unfooted trestle which he had made use of in the absence of a step-ladder. The Court of Appeal held that the defendants were not liable for the claimant's injuries because the claimant's actions broke the chain of causation from the defendants' breach of contract. One can strongly argue that, instead of denying all damages for the injury on the ground of intervening cause, it would have been preferable to have said that, while the causal chain was not broken, damages should be reduced for the claimant's contributory negligence.

A further excellent example of the potential harshness of the present law is provided by the unreported decision in *Schering Agrochemicals v Resibel NV SA*.[50] The claimants manufactured and bottled inflammable chemicals. The defendants supplied them with equipment that heat-sealed caps onto bottles. The equipment had a safety alarm system so that the heat-sealer would be switched off if the bottle was stationary for too long and exposed to excessive heat. Unfortunately, the equipment was defective so that the alarm system did not always work properly. As a result there was a fire seriously damaging the claimants' premises. It was clear that the defendants were in breach of a strict contractual duty in supplying the defective equipment. The important complication was that three weeks before the fire, the safety system had not switched off properly and there had been a small explosion and an orange flash observed by the claimants. Nevertheless the claimants had carried on using the equipment. The Court of Appeal held that the effect of the claimants' conduct was that they

---

[48] Working Paper No 114, paras 2.9, 5.2. [49] [1966] 2 QB 370, CA.
[50] Noted Burrows (1993) 109 LQR 175.

should recover no damages at all for the fire damage: the claimants' conduct had broken the chain of causation or meant that the claimants had failed in their duty to mitigate the loss. This seems a harsh result, which could have been avoided had the Court been able to award damages reduced for the claimants' contributory negligence.

Naturally one must be sensitive to the concerns that the introduction of contributory negligence in category one cases would increase litigation and hamper settlements. However, one would have thought that this would only be a major problem if the courts were called upon to fine-tune the degree of contributory negligence in play. If instead the courts were encouraged to apply broad bands of contributory negligence (eg 25 per cent, 50 per cent or 75 per cent) it is hard to believe that this would produce the significant increase in litigation that the Law Commission feared.

4. LIMITATIONS ON EQUITABLE COMPENSATION FOR EQUITABLE WRONGS

At this point we shift from common law wrongs, that is torts and breach and contract, where the standard remedy is compensatory damages, to equitable wrongs where the equivalent remedy, albeit that this has only been appreciated relatively recently, is equitable compensation.

There has been considerable academic debate in recent years about what counts as an equitable wrong but for the purposes of this paper it is sufficient to say that equitable wrongs include breach of fiduciary duty, breach of confidence, and the wrong that used to be called 'knowing assistance' but after *Royal Brunei Airlines v Tan*[51] is now labelled 'dishonest assistance.' Of these equitable wrongs, the most wide-ranging is breach of fiduciary duty which spans a very large area extending well beyond trustees. In Australia, New Zealand, and Canada, claims for breach of fiduciary duty have for many years been commonplace. In England it is only relatively recently that the potential of breach of fiduciary duty has been realized: it has therefore been something of a new departure for claims for 'professional negligence' against, for example, solicitors to be pleaded not only in contract and tort but also for breach of fiduciary duty.

That equitable compensation is a remedy available for breach of fiduciary duty has now been clearly established. The same can also be said in relation to dishonest assistance. Confusion has sometimes been caused by alternative labels that have been used to describe this remedy, in particular accounting for loss. But subject to an argument that we will consider below in relation to *Target Holdings Ltd v Redfern*,[52] it is submitted

---

[51] [1995] 2 AC 378. [52] [1996] AC 421. See below pp 46–7.

that these different labels are in fact describing the same remedy. Peculiarly, there has been no case in which equitable compensation has been awarded for breach of confidence. Instead, the courts have tended to think of equitable damages, awarded in addition to or in substitution for an injunction under the Supreme Court Act 1981, s 50. But if the standard remedy for breach of fiduciary duty is equitable compensation, the same should apply to breach of confidence.

The primary question that I here want to raise is whether the same limitations that apply to compensatory damages also apply to equitable compensation. In other words do limitations such as remoteness, intervening cause, and contributory negligence apply to equitable compensation? The practical importance of this is that where a claimant has a choice of causes of action, so that the claimant may choose to sue for breach of contract, tort, or an equitable wrong, it may be advantageous to found the claim on the equitable wrong if the limitations that would apply to compensatory damages do not apply (or apply in a less restrictive way) to equitable compensation.

Examination of the cases in the common law world on this question reveals that there is a fundamental conflict of opinion. On the one hand, there are those judges who consider that the limitations on common law compensatory damages, such as remoteness, intervening cause and contributory negligence, do not apply to equitable compensation. This was the opinion of Lord Browne-Wilkinson, giving the leading speech, in *Target Holdings Ltd v Redfern*. In emphasizing that a trustee would be liable for breach of trust even if the immediate cause of the loss was a third party, his Lordship said, 'Thus the common law rules of remoteness of damage and causation do not apply.'[53] This was also the approach of the minority, led by McLachlin J in the influential Canadian case of *Canson Enterprises v Boughton*.[54] Here a claim for equitable compensation was brought against a solicitor for breach of fiduciary duty in relation to the claimant's purchase of land. While all the judges in the Supreme Court of Canada concurred in the result, namely that the solicitor was liable for the claimant's loss but only until the intervention of third parties which in effect broke the chain of causation, the minority and majority disagreed in their reasoning. McLachlin J for the minority said,

> [This case] raises the question of whether the plaintiff can hold the solicitor liable for loss suffered by the plaintiff due to the negligence of architects and engineers in subsequent construction on the land. I agree with La Forest J. that the solicitor's liability does not extend this far . . . I base this result, however, in equity. I cannot concur in the suggestion in my colleague's reasons that . . . damages for breach of fiduciary duty should be measured by analogy to tort and contract.[55]

---

[53] [1996] AC 421, 434.   [54] (1991) 85 DLR (4th) 129.
[55] (1991) 85 DLR (4th) 129, 154.

So the argument of the minority was that common law limitations were not directly applicable to equitable compensation and that no analogy should be drawn with contact and tort. In other words, common law and equity are here different and should remain so.

This is also the view in Australia. In the most recent decision of *Pilmer v The Duke Group Ltd*[56] the High Court, in obiter dicta, said that contributory negligence was inapplicable to equitable compensation for breach of fiduciary duty. In a joint judgment, McHugh, Gummow, Hayne and Callinan JJ. said, '[I]n Australia, the measure of compensation in respect of losses sustained by reason of breach of duty by a trustee or other fiduciary is determined by equitable principles and these do not necessarily reflect the rules for assessment of damages in tort or contract.'[57]

Taking the opposing view—that common law restrictions on compensatory damages should apply also to equitable compensation—are, for example, the majority in the *Canson Enterprises* case, led by La Forest J; the New Zealand Court of Appeal in *Day v Mead*[58] and *Bank of New Zealand v New Zealand Guardian Trust Ltd*;[59] and as regards equitable compensation for breach of a fiduciary duty comprising a failure to use care and skill, Millett LJ in *Bristol & West Building Society v Mothew*.[60]

In *Day v Mead*, where contributory negligence was applied to equitable compensation for breach of fiduciary duty by a solicitor, Cooke P said:[61]

As Lord Diplock put it (in *United Scientific Holdings Ltd v Burnley BC*)[62] law and equity have mingled now; the [Judicature] Acts did not bring to a sudden halt the whole process of development of the common law of England that had been so notable a feature of the preceding decades; the legislation placed no ban upon further development of substantive rules by judicial decision. . . . Whether or not there are reported cases in which compensation for breach of fiduciary obligation has been assessed on the footing that the plaintiff should accept some share of the responsibility, there appears to be no solid reason for denying jurisdiction to follow that obviously just course, especially now that law and equity have mingled or are interacting. It is an opportunity for equity to show that it has not petrified and to live up to the spirit of is maxims.

And Millett LJ in *Bristol & West Building Society v Mothew* said:[63]

Although the remedy which equity makes available for breach of the equitable duty of skill and care is equitable compensation rather than damages, this is merely the product of history and in this context it is in my opinion a distinction without a difference. Equitable compensation for breach of the duty of skill and care resembles common law damages in that it is awarded by way of compensation to the plaintiff for his loss. There is no reason in principle why the

---

[56] [2001] HCA 31 (31 May 2001).   [57] ibid, at para [85].   [58] [1987] 2 NZLR 443.
[59] [1999] 1 NZLR 664.   [60] [1996] 4 All ER 698.   [61] [1987] 2 NZLR 443, 451.
[62] [1978] AC 904, 924–5.   [63] [1996] 4 All ER 698, 711.

common law rules of causation, remoteness of damage and measure of damages should not be applied by analogy in such a case.

I have elsewhere argued in depth[64] that the second view is to be preferred: given the discretion open at common law in applying limitations, and the different approach to limitations that has been taken in respect of, for example, the tort of deceit, there is no good reason for equitable compensation somehow going its own separate way from compensatory damages. On the contrary, compensatory damages and equitable compensation should be regarded as identical in aim—compensation—and identical in relation to the application of limitations.

I do however wish to use this opportunity to clarify briefly that the remedy of equitable compensation seems to have been assimilated with and to be indistinguishable from the remedy of accounting (for loss).[65] The argument has been put that the latter remedy may operate differently as a remedy against a trustee than equitable compensation because it is concerned to restore a trust fund rather than to compensate. The account remedy is therefore analogous to an action in debt (or specific performance) in contrast to equitable compensation which is analogous to an action for compensatory damages. Put another way, the account remedy, unlike equitable compensation, responds to a trustee's primary obligation rather than being a remedy for the trustee's wrong in breaching its primary obligation. That there is this type of difference has been argued by, for example, Peter Birks,[66] Lord Millett[67] and more recently, in rigorous detail, by Steven Elliott in his Oxford D Phil thesis.[68] If correct, it outflanks or cuts across the central reasoning in *Target Holdings Ltd v Redfern*.

In that case the defendants were solicitors who were acting for mortgagees (the claimants) in relation to the purchase of property by C Ltd. In breach of trust the defendants paid over the loaned money (£1,525,000) from the claimants to the vendors prior to completion of the sale and charge. That was a breach of trust albeit that a few days afterwards the completion of the sale and charge did take place. Subsequently C Ltd

---

[64] 'Fusing Common Law and Equity: Remedies, Restitution and Reform' *Hochelaga Lecture* 2001, 6–14; 'We Do This at Common Law but That in Equity' (2002) 22 OJLS 1, 9–12. See similarly Elliott, 'Remoteness Criteria in Equity' (2002) 65 MLR 588.

[65] I put to one side here the clearly different remedy of accounting for profits which is concerned to effect restitution/disgorgement and not compensation.

[66] 'Equity in the Modern Law: an Exercise in Taxonomy' (1996) 26 Univ of Western Aus LR 1, 46–7.

[67] Millett, 'Equity's Place in the Law of Commerce' (1998) 114 LQR 214, 225–7; see also Millett LJ's judgment in *Bristol and West Building Society v Mothew* [1996] 4 All ER 698, 711. cf Parker and Mellows, *The Modern Law of Trusts* (ed Oakley) (7th edn, 1998) 679–83. See also *Bairstow v Queen's Moat Houses plc* [2001] 2 BCLC 531, CA.

[68] Awarded in Trinity Term 2002. For the barest of outlines of his central argument, see Elliott, 'Remoteness Criteria in Equity' (2002) 65 MLR 588, 590.

became insolvent and the claimants repossessed the property selling it for £500,000. The defendants argued that their breach of trust was technical only because the claimants had subsequently obtained the charge to which they were entitled. The breach of trust had not caused the claimants the loss they had suffered which was rather caused by the property having been overvalued so that the claimants' security was inadequate. The House of Lords agreed and held that there can be no equitable compensation and, although this is implied rather than expressly stated, *no account remedy* where, as on these facts, the loss would have been suffered even if there had been no breach of duty.[69]

However, applying the argument of Birks, Millett and Elliott, the House of Lords should have taken a different approach to the account remedy than to equitable compensation (even if ultimately the same result might have been reached on the facts) precisely because, like specific relief, the account remedy does not require loss to have been caused by the breach of fiduciary duty: the fact that the beneficiaries would have suffered the loss in question irrespective of the breach of fiduciary duty is irrelevant.

While historically this argument has much to commend it, it is hard to see why in terms of policy one would wish to retain a distinctive remedy of that type. A trustee does not contract to pay a particular sum to the beneficiaries and, if the beneficiaries would have suffered the loss even if the trustee had performed its fiduciary duties, it is hard to see why, as a matter of policy, they should have redress against the trustee for that loss. Put another way, to regard the trustees as being liable to a distinct account remedy appears to impose on them an unwarranted absolute duty to pay back into the trust fund the value of moneys that, in breach of trust, have been paid out from it and not recovered. *Target Holdings v Redfern*, which is most naturally interpreted as having impliedly laid down that loss must have been factually caused in respect of the remedy of accounting (for loss), should be applauded in terms of policy for (impliedly) rejecting older cases that may have supported the view that the accounting remedy can operate differently from the remedy of equitable compensation.

---

[69] It seems far-fetched to argue (but see Parker and Mellows, *The Modern Law of Trusts* (ed Oakley) (7th edn, 1998) 683) that the account remedy was erroneously forgotten about by counsel and their Lordships and that therefore the decision has no relevance to that remedy. Having said that, it would clearly have been preferable for their Lordships to have expressly mentioned the account remedy and to have expressly anticipated the type of argument made by Birks, Millett, and Elliott.

5. CONCLUSION

A very different range of issues—on which practitioners and academics may have rather different views—is raised by the three areas that have been examined in this paper. Remoteness in contract is well-worked and well-known although the impact of the *Brown* case seems to have been underplayed. Contributory negligence in contract is statute-based and improvements to the law—which, it has been suggested are required—must involve statutory law reform. Finally, equitable compensation is a relatively unexplored and developing remedy which, it has been urged, the courts should tie in with compensatory damages by applying to the equitable remedy the same limitations as apply at common law.

5

Limitations on Compensation: Comment

CHRIS RYAN[1]

In one paragraph of his paper (see Chapter 4)[2] Andrew Burrows points out that the two rules of *Hadley v Baxendale* have been regarded as important in some recent Court of Appeal cases in construing what is meant by 'consequential or indirect loss' in exclusion or limitation clauses. This question of what is meant by 'consequential or indirect loss' in such clauses is very important in practice.

Certainly it is not surprising that there may be differences (for instance, as regards whether the two rules are seen as mutually exclusive or not) between the approach adopted to 'pure' damage assessment and as applied in determining whether an exclusion of liability applies. This is because the two exercises are different. Construing what the contract draftsman meant is not the same exercise as deciding what the law regards as a fair cut-off point for liability.

In understanding the present approach of the courts—and in seeing that a contrary interpretation of 'consequential and indirect loss' has been advocated in the leading textbook, *McGregor on Damages*[3]—it is helpful to refer in more detail to two of the recent cases.

In *Croudace Construction Ltd v Cawoods Concrete Products Ltd*[4] Cawoods contracted to supply materials to Croudace for use on a particular construction site but the deliveries were delayed. The contract included a provision that Cawoods would 'not under any circumstances . . . be liable for any consequential loss or damage caused or arising by reason of late supply'. This was relied on to resist a claim for the costs thrown away in having workmen on site with no work to do due to the absence of necessary materials. The Court of Appeal rejected that argument (without even calling upon Croudace's counsel) by simply saying that *Millar's Machinery Company Ltd v David Way & Son*[5] was a decision, the ratio decidendi of which was directly applicable and, having stood for 40 years, bound the Court. As a result it concluded that 'consequential' did not cover any loss which 'directly and naturally results in the ordinary course of events from late delivery'. That language is very similar to that describing the first rule in *Hadley v Baxendale* and, although the Court of Appeal did not refer to that case, Parker J at first instance had done so.

[1] Partner, Norton Rose. [2] At p 32 above. [3] Now in its 16th edn (1997).
[4] [1978] 2 Lloyd's Rep 55. [5] (1934) 40 Com Cas 204.

In reaching its decision the Court expressly rejected an argument that went as follows:

(a) Consequential loss was all loss that was not the normal or ordinary damage, which is recoverable in the case of delay in delivery.
(b) For this purpose normal or ordinary loss is the difference in the value of the goods between the date when the goods should have been delivered and the date when they were in fact delivered.
(c) The costs wasted by having a workforce standing idle did not come within this meaning and were therefore consequential.

Although the report in the *Croudace* case does not clarify the basis of the argument summarized above it may be that the argument was founded in part on certain statements found in *McGregor on Damages*.[6] The Court of Appeal report certainly mentions that Cawood's counsel relied on passages from textbooks but does not identify them.

An analysis set out in *McGregor on Damages*,[7] that is precisely in line with the argument summarized in (a)–(c) above, was argued for in the second of the cases that I wish to look at. In *British Sugar plc v NEI Power Projects Ltd*[8] electrical equipment supplied by NEI did not function properly and caused breakdowns in the power supply to the British Sugar's plant. This lead to increased production costs and loss of profit. NEI relied on a provision that was deemed to be included in the parties' contract and which read:

> the Seller will be liable for any loss, damage, cost or expense incurred by the Purchaser arising from the supply by the Seller of any such faulty goods or materials or any goods or materials not being suitable for the purpose for which they are acquired save that the Seller's liability for consequential loss is limited to the value of the contract.

The waste of production costs and loss of profits would therefore be limited if they were found to be 'consequential', but unlimited if they were regarded as basic or normal types of damage recoverable for a breach of contract. It was argued for NEI that the test of what was normal in this respect was the reasonable expectation of a businessman in the context of the particular contract under review. It was suggested, by reference to the analysis in *McGregor on Damages*, that in contract the normal loss would be the difference between the value of what was provided and the market value of what should have been provided.

The present (16th) edition of *McGregor on Damages*,[9] explains the distinction between 'normal' loss and 'consequential' loss in the following words:

---

[6] Then in its 13th edn (1972).   [7] Then in its 15th edn (1988).   [8] (1997) 87 BLR 42.
[9] The 16th edn published in 1997, stating the law as at the end of 1996.

In contract the normal loss can generally be stated as the market value of the property, money or services that the plaintiff should have received under the contract, less the market value of what he does receive. . . . Consequential losses are anything beyond this normal measure, such as profits lost or expenses incurred through the breach . . .

McGregor on Damages goes on to say that the distinction is *not* the same as that between the first and second rules in *Hadley v Baxendale* and explains that, in the author's view, the distinction arises from the provisions of the Sale of Goods Act legislation and that the views to the contrary expressed in, for example, the *Croudace* case were obiter.

But the wider meaning of consequential loss advocated in *McGregor on Damages*[10] was dismissed by the Court of Appeal in *British Sugar* without even calling on opposing counsel. The Court concluded that it should only depart from the guidance provided to it in *Croudace* if the circumstances or the language of the clause in question were materially different. In its view there was no material difference in the case before it. The Court then went on to say that a further reason for following the earlier cases was that once a phrase had been authoritatively construed, a reasonable businessman is more likely to intend the same phrase to have the same meaning when he includes it in a future contract. Provided you interpret the 'reasonable businessman' to mean a reasonably up-to-date draftsman that may be right. Waller LJ, giving the leading judgment of the Court of Appeal, expressly treated the meaning of 'consequential loss' as referring to losses recoverable under the second limb in *Hadley v Baxendale*. He said:[11]

On a proper reading of that clause, an obligation was being placed on the defendants to pay such damages as flowed naturally and directly from any supply by the defendants of faulty goods or materials, with the limitation being imposed in relation to some other type of loss which did not flow so directly, for example, damage which might flow from special circumstances and come within the second limb in *Hadley v Baxendale*.

It was particularly in the light of those two decisions that Rix J in *BHP Petroleum Ltd v British Steel plc*[12] concluded that, '[T]he parties are correct to agree that authority dictates that the line between direct and indirect or consequential losses is drawn along the boundary between the first and second limbs of *Hadley v Baxendale* . . .'

It is interesting to note that the latest supplement to *McGregor on Damages*[13] updates the earlier text by reference to *British Sugar* and subsequent cases and concedes that the issue is now clearly decided. The author

---

[10] 16th edn (1997).   [11] ibid, at 51.   [12] [1999] 2 All ER (Comm) 544, 565.
[13] Fourth Supplement (2002), p 7.

then displays admirable resistance in the face of the contrary forces ranged against him by adding:[14]

> Nevertheless, despite the mounting authority against, the argument as to the . . . proper meaning [of the term 'consequential loss'] is still adhered to and retained generally in the text, providing, as it does, a useful and valuable analysis of the damage recoverable; after all the analysis makes no practical difference to the recovery of damages outside the exclusion clause context. What is proposed is that the term 'consequential loss' should be construed narrowly where exclusion clauses are concerned by resort to the *contra proferentem* rule and widely in all other cases.

On the face of it, therefore, the contract draftsman will not be excluding much if he simply excludes 'consequential or indirect loss'. There seems little alternative, in the face of the present construction adopted by the courts, than to include a lengthy list of individual, and sometimes eccentric, heads of damage that are to be expressly excluded.

[14] ibid.

6
Limitations on Compensation: Review of Discussion

It was agreed that, in the light of the recent decisions[1] on the meaning of 'consequential or indirect loss' a prudent contract draftsman would seek to list specifically what is excluded. Indeed there is a hint in Lord Hoffmann's speech in *Caledonia North Sea Ltd v British Telecommunications plc*[2] that the House of Lords may be willing to reopen the Court of Appeal cases on what is meant by 'consequential or indirect loss'. Such uncertainty strengthens the case for spelling out expressly in the contract what is meant.

It was suggested that *Brown v KMR Services*[3] had not been given the recognition that it may merit because of the difficulty in reconciling it with *Victoria Laundry*.[4] Moreover, the judgments had referred only to the cases on the contract remoteness test and their language was confined to the cause of action in contract and did not expressly mention the concurrent claim in the tort of negligence.

It was further suggested that, in line with footnote 31 of Andrew Burrows' paper (Chapter 4), the crucial point justifying a stricter remoteness test is not so much that the parties were in a contractual relationship but that the parties were in a prior relationship where one could inform the other of risks. Moreover, a view was expressed that, although this would further complicate the law, even where there is a contractual relationship, the stricter test should only apply where the risks are such that one could sensibly expect one contracting party to inform the other about them. The example was given of a house-owner who is having an extension built to his home by builders. Freak weather conditions mean that masonry collapses onto the house-owner's car and also onto his neighbour's car. It was argued that the neighbour's cause of action against the builders in the tort of negligence and the house-owner's cause of action against the builders in contract should have the same test of remoteness applied to them because the risk of freak weather conditions is outside the realm of risk of which the house-owner has particular knowledge. That is, the fact that the house-owner is in a contractual relationship with the builders may be thought to be irrelevant in relation to risks of freak weather.

Reference was also made to the remoteness test for the tort of deceit. In the light of Lord Nicholls' statements in *Kuwait Airways Corp v Iraqi*

[1] Above p 32 n 19.
[2] [2002] 1 Lloyd's Rep 553, 572.
[3] [1995] 4 ALL ER 598.
[4] [1949] 2 KB 528.

Airways Co[5] the consensus view appeared to be that where a tort was committed dishonestly the wider 'direct consequence' remoteness test should apply even if the tort was one of strict liability (as is the tort of conversion).

Questions were asked as to the relationship between contributory negligence as a defence to a breach of contract, the duty to mitigate, and the claimant's conduct breaking the chain of causation. The essential distinction was thought to be that the latter two concepts are all-or-nothing and result in no damages being awarded for the loss in question; whereas contributory negligence is a proportionate defence which would lead to some damages being awarded for the loss in question. So in relation to the defective iron example,[6] the consumer is plainly able to recover damages for the defect in the iron (whether assessed according to the cost of repair or difference in value). There is no contributory negligence in relation to that loss. The question at issue relates to the ruined shirt. It is in relation to that loss that the consumer has been contributorily negligent. Under the present law, the consumer would recover all or nothing for the loss of the shirt. If contributory negligence were extended to category one cases, the consumer and the retailer would share that loss proportionate to their respective fault and causal responsibility.

It was also clarified that, as under the present law (and as recommended by the Law Commission),[7] the parties would be free to exclude the operation of contributory negligence if its ambit were extended (subject to normal controls on unfair terms).

In relation to breach of fiduciary duty, it was argued that it would enhance understanding if that were seen as an umbrella heading which includes obligations imposed through the tort of negligence on fiduciaries as well as distinct obligations that have no parallel in tort, in particular the obligation of loyalty. Doubts were expressed as to whether contributory negligence should ever apply to the obligation of loyalty. An alternative view is that contributory negligence should always be a potential defence but that in a particular context[8] one would not regard a claimant who relied on the defendant to perform its duty as contributorily negligent.

The idea that equitable compensation is more discretionary than compensatory damages was challenged by pointing to the large element of discretion in assessing damages, for example in relation to remoteness, intervening causation and contributory negligence.

---

[5] [2002] 2 AC 883, at paras. [100]–[104].
[6] Above, p 42.
[7] Law Commission Report No 219 (1993) paras 4.23–5.
[8] See n 45 of Andrew Burrows' paper, Chapter 4 above.

7
SAAMCO Revisited

EDWIN PEEL[1]

This paper should, perhaps, begin with an explanation of why it might be thought relevant to a book on 'Commercial Remedies'. The remedy with which it is concerned is damages. It is trite law that the level of damages recoverable for a breach of duty is subject to a number of 'restrictions', such as causation, mitigation, remoteness and contributory negligence.[2] By far the most fundamental restriction, however, is whether the loss for which damages are claimed fell within the scope of the duty which has been breached. It is this simple point which was reaffirmed by Lord Hoffmann in the *SAAMCO* case.[3] The need for such reaffirmation stemmed from the failure of the Court of Appeal[4] to distinguish sufficiently clearly between questions of duty and questions of causation. It is the relationship between, and the effect of, these two 'restrictions' on the recovery of damages which is the principal *focus* of this paper.

In a recent review Lord Justice Buxton observed that while there is 'greatly more to jurisprudence than analysis of the decided law . . . to turn one's back on the cases deprives the legal theorist of proper exposure to an important part of the raw material of his trade.'[5] That is a sentiment which, it is hoped, is reflected in the *content* of this paper. In addition to *SAAMCO*, three subsequent decisions of the House of Lords are also subjected to close scrutiny, if only to illustrate either that the courts may still not always concern themselves with the right question, or that when they do, the right answer is not always guaranteed. It will conclude with some reflection on the potentially wider implications of a clearer division between duty and causation.

---

[1] Fellow and Tutor in Law, Keble College, Oxford.

[2] See further the papers by Andrew Burrows, Chapter 4, above, and John Cartwright, Chapter 1, above.

[3] *Banque Bruxelles Lambert SA v Eagle Star Insurance Co Ltd* [1997] AC 191, also known as *South Australia Asset Management Corp v York Montague Ltd* (hence, '*SAAMCO*').

[4] [1995] QB 375.

[5] Extract from a review of *Relating to Responsibility: Essays for Tony Honore on his Eightieth Birthday* Peter Cane and John Gardner (eds) (Oxford: Hart Publishing, 2001), (2002) 118 LQR 476.

1. SAAMCO

SAAMCO involved three cases, all of which concerned the extent of the liability of valuers for the negligent overvaluation of commercial properties against which loans were advanced. When the borrowers defaulted, the losses suffered by the lenders were greatly increased by a collapse in the property market which took its toll on the security realized.[6] The lenders sued the valuers for recovery of all the losses they had incurred. There was a deceptive simplicity to their claims. The valuers were undoubtedly in breach of their duty to prepare the valuations with reasonable care. Whether analysed in terms of their contractual duty of care, or any concurrent common law duty, the principle upon which damages were to be assessed was to place each lender 'in the same position as he would have been in if he had not sustained the wrong.'[7] In the Court of Appeal, the application of this principle to the facts was seen primarily as a matter of causation: but for the negligence of the valuers, a 'correct'[8] valuation would have been made, on the basis of which the *lenders would not have made the loans in question at all*. There being no further restrictions on the scope of recovery, such as remoteness, the lenders were entitled to recover all of their losses, including those attributable to the fall in the property market.

In the House of Lords, the only reasoned speech was given by Lord Hoffmann. As one might expect, he had no argument with the well-established principle for the assessment of damages quoted above. Where he disagreed with the Court of Appeal was in its description of this principle as the 'necessary point of departure'. Before one could ask what position the lenders would have been in if no wrong had been committed, it was first necessary to determine the nature of the 'wrong'. Insufficient attention had been paid to the breach of duty committed by the valuers; in particular, the scope of that duty.[9] The valuers were required to supply information to the lenders, in the form of their valuation, on the basis of which a decision would be taken about whether to advance a loan, and for how much. That express obligation may have been subject to an implied obligation that it would be carried out with reasonable care and skill, but

---

[6] The relevant events took place in and around 1990–91.

[7] *Livingstone v Rawyards Coal Co* (1880) 5 App Cas 25, 39 (*per* Lord Blackburn).

[8] ie, a valuation within the margins of non-negligent error. The actual valuation as at the relevant date may be taken as representing the mean point in this range. cf *Lion Nathan Ltd v CC Bottlers Ltd* [1996] 1 WLR 1438.

[9] There was no doubt that a duty was owed to the lenders, but in some cases it will first be necessary for the claimant to show that *a* duty was owed *to him*. cf *Caparo Industries plc v Dickman* [1990] 2 AC 605.

that was the full extent of the valuer's duty. It did not include a duty to advise generally on the making of the loan.[10] That was a decision for the lenders to take, not only on the basis of the valuations supplied, but also on the basis of other considerations, such as the ability of the borrower to service the loan and the prospects for the market generally. The effect of the approach adopted by the Court of Appeal was to transfer all of the risk associated with the making of the loans to the valuer. This seems to be quite out of step with the allocation of risk made by the parties themselves, whether expressly, or impliedly.

The mistake made by the Court of Appeal was to make the valuers liable for losses which would not have been incurred *if they had given the correct information*. According to Lord Hoffmann, it is a more accurate and fairer reflection of the scope of the duty of one who provides information on which someone else will decide upon a course of action, if they are responsible only *for the consequences of the information being wrong*.[11] The difference in the two approaches is neatly illustrated by the facts, and result, in one of the three appeals in *SAAMCO*. In *United Bank of Kuwait plc v Prudential Property Services Ltd*, the property in question had been valued at £2.5m, when the correct valuation was £1.8m.[12] The losses incurred by the lenders ran to £1.31m. The Court of Appeal ordered recovery in full. Lord Hoffmann found that the consequence of the incorrect information negligently supplied by the valuer was that the lender had less margin of security than he had been led to believe, ie £700k representing the difference between the valuation supplied and the correct valuation which would have been reached if care had been taken. Any loss over and above this sum would have been incurred by the lender in any event and could not

---

[10] For the sake of convenience, Lord Hoffmann referred to a distinction between the provision of negligent *information* and negligent *advice*, but this has been 'widely misunderstood' (*Aneco Reinsurance Underwriting Ltd v Johnson & Higgins Ltd* [2002] 1 Lloyd's Rep 157, 190 (*per* Lord Millett)). The more accurate, and more helpful, distinction is that between 'a duty to provide particular information or advice on request and a duty to advise generally when it is left to the adviser to decide what matters he should consider', ibid.

[11] Lord Hoffmann observed ([1997] AC 191, at 214) that this was necessary to avoid the paradox that the liability of a person who warranted the accuracy of the information would be less than that of a person who gave no such warranty, but failed to take reasonable care. He has been criticized for this observation on the basis that there is no paradox; a defendant's liability may sometimes be greater under a warranty of care than under a strict warranty of accuracy: J Stapleton, 'Negligent Valuers and Falls in the Property Market' (1997) 113 LQR 1. The confines of space prevent any prolonged consideration of this point. Suffice it to say, it seems certain that Lord Hoffmann would accept that there may be no paradox in some cases, but that this rather begs the question: in the particular case before the courts, should the scope of the duty of care owed be drawn so that it is more or less extensive than a strict warranty?

[12] In fact, the correct valuation was said to be between £1.8m and £1.85m. In the light of the decision made by the House of Lords, the question of the precise figure was one which was remitted to the trial judge in the absence of any agreement between the parties.

be attributed to the valuer's breach of duty. The lender was confined to the recovery of £700k in damages.

It is easy to understand the approach which was taken by the Court of Appeal. It is not disputed that the basic principle for the assessment of damages is to place the claimant in the same position as he would have been in if he had not sustained the wrong. In a case like *SAAMCO*, the more natural interpretation of this principle may have been to ask what position the claimant would be in, if care *had been taken*. But the 'wrong' consisted of the *breach* of the duty to take care in the supply of the valuation, with the consequence that the lender adopted a course of action on the basis of a false premise. It is compensation for the correction of this false premise, caused by the negligence of the valuer, which is consistent with the scope of the duty undertaken. The correctness of this outcome may be tested by contemplating the following imaginary instruction from the lender to the valuer: 'I am considering making an advance to the borrower against the property. I will take the decision whether or not to do so, but first I require confirmation that the property is worth £X.'[13] This would appear fairly to reflect the risks taken by each of the parties. To the extent that the valuer, through his negligence, 'confirms' a level of security which does not exist, he should be liable to the lender, but any further loss is for the lender to bear. In other words, the valuer fulfils his duty either by carefully and correctly providing the required confirmation, or by paying damages which represent the equivalent of having done so.

There are, of course, cases where the defendant should be held responsible for all of the losses incurred by a claimant who enters into a transaction as a consequence of the defendant's breach of duty. In addition to the example given by Lord Hoffmann of a defendant who advises generally on whether to enter into the transaction,[14] there may even be cases where the supplier of incorrect information should also be held so liable, for example in cases of fraudulent misrepresentation.[15] Whether or not

[13] Of course, in reality, the lender will simply ask for a valuation and will then make the decision about the loan, but *ex post facto*, he will act as if he has given, and received a response to, an instruction of the sort suggested in the text.

[14] In the third of the appeals in *SAAMCO* (*Nykredit Mortgage Bank plc v Edward Erdman Group Ltd*), the valuers were also asked to advise on the projected rental value of the completed development and its lettability in the market. However, this additional advice was still directed to the value of the security rather than the viability of the project.

[15] cf *Downs v Chappell* [1997] 1 WLR 426, in which Hobhouse LJ expressed the view that even the fraudulent supplier of information should only be held responsible for the consequences of his information being wrong. In *Smith New Court Securities v Scrimgeour Vickers (Asset Management)* [1997] AC 254, the decision to hold the defendant liable for all of the losses incurred as a result of his fraudulent misrepresentation stemmed from the nature and effect of the misrepresentation which not only induced the claimant to buy shares, but also to retain them for the period during which a fraud on the company was discovered, causing the share price to collapse. See to similar effect *Naughton v O'Callaghan* [1990] 3 All ER 191 (a case of negligent misrepresentation).

this is the case, the point to be stressed is that this is a question of duty and not, or not only, a question of causation.

2. DUTY AND CAUSATION — QUESTIONS OF LAW AND QUESTIONS OF FACT

It was the late Lord Denning who observed in *Lamb v Camden LBC* that 'the three questions, duty, causation and remoteness, run continually into one another' and 'are all devices by which the courts limit the range of liability for negligence.'[16] All are 'useful in their way', but 'ultimately it is a question of policy for the judges to decide.'[17] This begs the question whether or not it matters a great deal if the difference between the decisions in the Court of Appeal and the House of Lords in *SAAMCO* is described in terms of duty or causation. It is submitted that it matters a great deal and this may be illustrated by comparing two examples.

The first is Lord Hoffmann's mountaineering example which has already taken its place as a teaching aid for this particular writer. A mountaineer about to undertake a difficult climb is concerned about the fitness of his knee. He goes to a doctor who negligently pronounces the knee fit. The mountaineer goes on the expedition, which he would not have undertaken if the doctor had told him the true state of his knee. He suffers an injury which is an entirely foreseeable consequence of mountaineering but has nothing to do with his knee. The doctor is not liable because it was no part of his duty to protect the mountaineer from injury which would have, and has, occurred regardless of the fitness of his knee. In Lord Hoffmann's words, there 'seems no reason of policy which requires that the negligence of the doctor should require the transfer to him of all the foreseeable risks of the expedition.'[18] Again, one might wish to argue that there are reasons of 'policy' which require that the doctor should be held liable as if he had advised generally on the wisdom of the venture,[19] but the key point is that such reasons must be considered at the duty stage; if there is no duty in the first place to protect from the loss which has been incurred, there is no question of causation which can, or should, be considered. What role then is there left for causation? This brings us to the second example.

In *Tennessee Trailways Inc v Ervin*[20] the defendant's bus was exceeding the speed limit on a highway when the claimant drove his motorcyle in front of it from an adjoining road and was killed. The Tennessee Supreme Court held that the defendant was not liable for the death of the claimant,

---

[16] [1981] QB 625, 636.   [17] ibid.   [18] [1997] AC 191, at 214.
[19] For example, if the injury was caused by another disability under which the mountaineer was labouring and which the doctor should have detected even though he was not consulted about it specifically by the mountaineer.
[20] 438 SW 2d 733 Tenn (1969).

since his breach of duty was not the cause of the claimant's death; he would have been killed even if the defendant had been driving within the speed limit. It would have been highly unusual if counsel for the defendant had begun his submission to the court by questioning whether one motorist (the defendant) owes a duty to another (the claimant) to take care to prevent the injury or death of the latter. This question of 'policy' has already been settled and it is hard to see the circumstances in which it could now be re-opened. The only issue was whether the defendant's breach of this self-evident duty had caused the death of the claimant. Nevertheless, though it may not have been the subject of any debate, the starting point in *Tennessee Trailways*, as in the mountaineering example and *SAAMCO*, is to ask first whether the defendant owed a duty to the claimant to protect him from the loss which has occurred. In *SAAMCO* and the mountaineering example, the answer to this first question was no, and that was the end of the matter. In *Tennessee Trailways* the answer was yes, but it was still necessary to then determine whether the defendant's breach of duty had, in fact, caused the claimant's death.

In summary, to ask whether the defendant owed a duty to protect the claimant from the loss which has occurred is a *question of law* which must be answered before any question of causation may arise. If, and only if, a duty was owed is it necessary to ask whether, as a *question of fact*, the defendant's breach of duty caused the loss in question. With the greatest of hesitation where the observations of Lord Denning are concerned, it might be said that there is, or should be, no question of 'policy' involved in causation.[21] There is no earth shattering revelation in any of this, but the need to reaffirm both the nature of the questions involved and the order in which they should be considered was apparent from the error into which the Court of Appeal fell in *SAAMCO*. Perhaps more worrying is the prospect that the House of Lords may have subsequently fallen into error in its application of the very principles which it has so recently sought to reaffirm.

3. ANECO REINSURANCE UNDERWRITING LIMITED V JOHNSON & HIGGINS LIMITED[22]

The facts in *Aneco* are a little complex. Given that two of their Lordships thought the central issue was a purely evaluative one involving matters of

---

[21] There is, it is submitted, undoubtedly a question of policy involved in remoteness even if it may be described as a question of fact whether a particular type of loss was reasonably foreseeable, eg the issue in *Lamb v Camden LBC* itself (when a defendant should be liable for damage done by a third party) may be analysed in terms of duty (as in *Smith v Littlewoods Organisation* [1987] AC 241, *per* Lord Goff), or remoteness (as in *Lamb*), but the same question of law or policy is involved, ie the scope of the duty breached by the defendant.

[22] [2002] 1 Lloyd's Rep 157.

fact and degree,[23] there is an obvious danger in any attempt to simplify them for the purposes of this paper. What is certainly crucial to an understanding of the case is that the defendant broker acted in two different capacities. In the first, he acted for four syndicates at Lloyd's in the drafting of a reinsurance treaty known as the Bullen Treaty. Still in that capacity, he approached the claimant as a potential reinsurer of the Bullen Treaty.[24] The claimant expressed an interest, but only on the basis that it could itself secure reinsurance for its share in the Bullen Treaty. The task of obtaining reinsurance for the claimant was entrusted to the defendant who, *at this point*, acted in his second capacity for the claimant. The defendant obtained reinsurance in the sum of $11m and the claimant wrote the Bullen Treaty. The losses subsequently incurred by the claimant under the Bullen Treaty ran to $35m. The claimant's reinsurers were able to repudiate their liability because the defendant had negligently failed properly to present the risk under the Bullen Treaty. The latter had been represented as a quota share treaty when it was in fact a fac/oblig treaty and therefore far less attractive to a reinsurer.[25]

It was not in dispute that the defendant was liable for the losses incurred by the claimant which should have been covered by reinsurance, ie $11m. This was a loss which it was part of the defendant's duty to prevent and it had been caused by his breach of that duty. The claimant also sought recovery of the further loss of $24m which would not have been covered by reinsurance even if it had been successfully obtained. It succeeded in doing so. The majority purported to apply the principles laid down by Lord Hoffmann in *SAAMCO*, but found that this was not a case in which the broker had only supplied information upon which the claimant would decide upon a course of action. It was established, as a matter of fact, that if the risk under the Bullen Treaty had been properly presented, no reinsurer would have been willing to provide the required reinsurance cover. The reinsurance which the claimant required was not available in the market. If the defendant had performed his duty carefully, he would have reported that this was the position and the market assessment of the reinsurance risks involved in the Bullen Treaty would have been apparent to the claimant. This was a case where, in reality, the defendant was advising

---

[23] Lords Lloyd of Berwick and Steyn, with whom Lords Slynn of Hadley and Browne-Wilkinson agreed.

[24] In strict terminology the case involved retrocession, but it was described as reinsurance throughout the proceedings and this was adhered to by the House of Lords.

[25] Under a quota share treaty, the (re)assured must cede a set proportion of every risk which falls within the criteria laid down in the contract. By contrast, a fac/oblig treaty gives greater discretion to the (re)assured and allows him to put onto his reinsurer the least attractive pieces of qualifying business in his book, while keeping what he considers to be the best business for himself.

on the commercial wisdom of the transaction contemplated by the claimant and should be held liable for all the losses incurred as a result of entering into it.

It is respectfully submitted that the conclusion reached by the majority in *Aneco* is wrong. There is little of real interest in this if it amounts to no more than a disagreement, on the facts, about the scope of the duty owed by the defendant.[26] It is further submitted, however, that the wrong conclusion was reached because of a continued blurring of the distinction between questions of duty and questions of causation. In simple terms, it is submitted that the conclusion of the majority is wrong because it does not produce a result consistent with the realistic allocation of risk between the parties. Adopting the same approach as was taken with *SAAMCO*, it is not difficult to imagine the following instruction from the claimant: 'I am considering reinsuring a share of the Bullen Treaty. I will take the decision whether or not to do so, but first I require confirmation that reinsurance of $11m is available.' In fact, this might be put in even simpler terms: 'If you obtain cover of $11m, I will reinsure a share of the Bullen Treaty.' The defendant's duty is fulfilled either by obtaining the cover of $11m, or paying damages in the same sum. Any loss above and beyond this did not fall within the scope of the defendant's duty.

The conclusion of the majority appears to have been reached because it asked the wrong question, or perhaps took the relevant questions in the wrong order. As Lord Millett pointed out in his dissenting speech, the court does not ask what would have happened if the defendant had performed his duty *and stated the true facts*. Yet this is precisely what the majority appear to do: if the defendant had performed his duty, no reinsurance could have been obtained; this would have informed the claimant (a) that no reinsurance was available, and (b) that the only credible reason for this was the market's assessment of the risks involved in the Bullen Treaty; *ipso facto* the defendant was under a duty to advise on the risks inherent in the transaction. In the end, the majority fall into the same trap as the Court of Appeal in *SAAMCO*: but for the negligence of the defendant, the claimant would not have reinsured a share of the Bullen Treaty and none of the losses *occasioned* by that decision would have been incurred. That much is true, but it does not follow that all of those losses fell within the scope of the defendant's duty and were therefore *caused* by a breach of it. When the defendant first approached the claimant, he was acting for the syndicates in the Bullen Treaty and did not assume any responsibility for advising on the risks inherent in reinsuring a share of it. When later he did act for the claimant, it was merely to provide informa-

---

[26] That is certainly how it was seen by Lord Steyn who thought that the defendant was fortunate in obtaining leave to appeal on what were no more than issues of fact.

tion, viz. the availability of reinsurance, upon which *the claimant made the decision* whether to write the Bullen Treaty.[27]

4. PLATFORM HOME LOANS LTD V OYSTON SHIPWAYS LTD[28]

In *Lamb v Camden LBC*, Lord Denning might easily have included contributory negligence among the 'devices by which the courts limit the range of liability for negligence.' If the concern in *SAAMCO* was to determine the proper relationship between duty and causation and its effect on the level of damages to be awarded, what is the further relationship with, and the effect of, any contributory negligence by the claimant? This was the issue before the House of Lords in the *Platform Homes* case. The lender had incurred a loss of around £612k.[29] The negligent over-valuation amounted to £500k. In addition, it was found by the trial judge that the lender was guilty of contributory negligence and he assessed this at 20 per cent. The principal issue[30] before the House was whether this should be applied to the loss actually incurred, so as to produce a figure of around £489k, or to the amount of the overvaluation so as to produce a figure of £400k. The majority applied it to the loss actually incurred.[31] It is submitted that they were right to do so.

In the *SAAMCO* appeal itself there had been a finding of contributory negligence. The lender's loss amounted to £9.75m, but there was a finding of 25 per cent contributory negligence on his part. The negligent over-valuation amounted to £10m. All of the loss therefore fell within the scope of the valuer's duty. The reduction for contributory negligence was applied to the loss incurred and not the overvaluation. The lender was awarded £7.3m. Unlike in the *Platform Homes* case, however, the point was not argued and, more importantly, the loss incurred was less than the overvaluation. Nonetheless, the unexplained application of the finding of contributory negligence to the loss incurred is instructive and is entirely

---

[27] For Lord Millett (at para [86]) this was confirmed by the evidence of Mr Crawley on behalf of Aneco which gave the impression that while he made the availability of reinsurance a condition of writing the Bullen Treaty, and would have felt disappointment at not being able to if it was not available, he would not have regarded such unavailability as indicating the undesirability of the venture.

[28] [2000] 2 AC 190.

[29] This had already been reduced on account of the claimant's failure to mitigate.

[30] The lenders argued that there should be no reduction at all from the maximum sum recoverable from the valuers, ie £500k, since this was not damage suffered 'as the result partly of his own fault and partly of the fault of any other person' within the meaning of the Law Reform (Contributory Negligence) Act 1945, s 1(1). This was rejected by the majority on the basis that the 'damage' referred to in the Act was the damage suffered by entering into the loan, viz. £612k. cf J Stapleton, 'Risk-taking by Commercial Lenders' (1999) 115 LQR 527.

[31] Lord Cooke of Thorndon dissenting.

consistent with the underlying basis of the principle formulated by Lord Hoffmann in *SAAMCO*. Any loss over and above the overvaluation supplied by the valuer was at the lender's risk. It is not too artificial to describe the additional non-recoverable loss as the consequence of the 'contributory negligence' of the lender.[32] Of course, it follows that where the lender is, in fact, guilty of contributory negligence, the additional non-recoverable loss may be increased so that the lender is worse off in terms of the damages to be awarded. In the *SAAMCO* appeal, he was, but in other cases this may not be the outcome. Consider the following examples:

(1) The lender incurs a loss of £1m. The negligent overvaluation amounts to £500k. In accordance with the *SAAMCO* principle, the lender recovers £500k.

(2) The facts are the same as in (1), but there is a finding that the lender was guilty of contributory negligence and this is assessed at 25 per cent. Adopting the approach taken in both the *SAAMCO* appeal and the *Platform Homes* case, the starting point is that the loss incurred is reduced to £750k, but the lender will still recover £500k as in the first example. He is no worse off than the lender in (1) who was not guilty of contributory negligence. This is because the aim in both cases is to leave with the lender losses which are attributable to the risks which were taken by him and were not caused by the valuer's breach of duty. In the case of the lender guilty of contributory negligence, some of the losses will be attributed to him regardless of the scope of the duty of the valuer, for example £250k in the example just considered. The remaining loss is, however, recoverable from the valuer up to the limit imposed by the scope of his duty.

(3) The facts in the *Platform Homes* case. A finding of 20per cent contributory negligence reduced the loss incurred to £489k. The scope of the valuer's duty was limited to protecting the lender from losses up to £500k, but only £489k was recoverable. The effect of the contributory negligence of the lender on the loss attributed to him is the same as in (2), but in this case it also accounts for part of the loss that would otherwise have been attributable to the breach of the valuer's duty.

(4) The facts in the *SAAMCO* appeal. The total loss incurred fell within the scope of the valuer's duty, but 25 per cent of it was attributable to the additional risks taken as a consequence of the lender's contributory negligence. The damages which would otherwise have been recovered from the valuer were therefore reduced by the 'full' 25 per cent.

---

[32] The artificiality may, in fact, lie in isolating some of the risks taken by the lender as instances of contributory negligence, but not others.

It is submitted that the very different results in each of these examples are consistent with the underlying basis of the principle in *SAAMCO*. The alternative of applying a finding of contributory negligence to the negligent overvaluation is flawed in at least two respects. First, there is no 'loss' involved in the overvaluation itself; it only determines how much of the loss which has been incurred may be recovered from the valuer. If the finding of contributory negligence in the *SAAMCO* appeal had been applied to the negligent overvaluation, the effect would have been to *increase* the damages recoverable by the lender. It is hoped that this is so counter-intuitive a result to contemplate that it requires no further comment. Secondly, there appears to be a concern to compare the position of the lender who has been guilty of contributory negligence with the lender who has not and ensure that, in terms of result, the former is worse off in a way which reflects the extent of his contributory negligence. The 'just and equitable' reduction in damages allowed for by the Law Reform (Contributory Negligence) Act 1945, s 1(1) is not concerned with a comparison between real and hypothetical claimants, but rather with 'the claimant's share in the responsibility for the damage.' That is precisely the basis upon which the results were reached in both *SAAMCO* and the *Platform Homes* case. Of course, this analysis assumes that the negligence of the lender has not caused or contributed directly to the overvaluation.[33] As Lord Millett acknowledged,[34] it may then be appropriate to apply any reduction to the amount of the overvaluation as well as to the overall loss.[35]

5. WIDER IMPLICATIONS

The emphasis thus far on cases involving the liability of valuers might give the impression that the principles under discussion have a restricted application. Nothing could be further from the truth. The fundamental proposition that a defendant is only liable for losses he may have caused if it was also part of his duty to prevent or avoid them is one of universal application, even if in many cases it is unnecessary to distinguish between the two, or in some it forms the unarticulated basis of the decision reached.

---

[33] This point is elaborated by Richard Butler in Chapter 8 in which he quite rightly points out that one must also take into account the nature and effect of the contributory negligence involved.

[34] [2002] 2 AC 190 at 215.

[35] In the *Platform Homes* case itself, there were two findings of contributory negligence by the lender: (1) it failed to pick up on a failure by the borrower to complete the application form showing the original purchase price of the property concerned, and (2) it was imprudent to have loaned 70 per cent of valuation to a 'non-status' borrower.

As Lord Hoffmann pointed out in a lecture to the Chancery Bar Association,[36] the latter category consists largely of those cases in which the issue has been addressed solely in terms of causation and has been described as a 'matter of common sense'.[37] The confines of space prevent this paper from re-visiting these cases, and others.[38] Instead it will conclude by dwelling on a further development which may be explained, at least in part, by the clearer division between questions of duty and questions of causation heralded by *SAAMCO*.

Earlier, it was submitted that the courts should first ask whether, as a question of law, the losses incurred by the claimant fell within the scope of the duty owed by the defendant and then ask whether, as a question of fact, such losses were caused by the defendant's breach of duty. Some may have been surprised both at the submission that causation is purely a question of fact and that one should first ask about the scope of the duty owed. It is perfectly possible to talk in terms of a legal requirement for causation; in the now forbidden Latin, to ask not only whether the defendant's breach of duty was a *causa sine qua non* of the loss (a factual cause), but also a *causa causans* (a legal cause). However, this is probably one area where the abandonment of the Latin may prove beneficial since all it does, like recourse to the phrase 'it is a matter of common sense', is disguise the fact that the latter question is really concerned with the scope of the duty owed by the claimant. The submission that causation is, therefore, strictly a question of fact in which no question of 'policy' should be involved is reaffirmed.

The submission that one should first ask about the scope of the duty owed is one that can be relaxed. In practice, it is often the case that the courts will first ask whether the loss incurred by the claimant has been caused by the defendant and then consider whether, and to what extent, such loss may be considered a consequence of the defendant's breach of duty. In some cases, this may assist in the proper resolution of the issues

[36] 'Common Sense and Causing Loss', 15 June 1999.

[37] For a good example, see a number of cases dealing with the potential liability of auditors for the trading losses incurred by companies which would have ceased trading if the auditors had exercised reasonable care and disclosed their insolvency: *Galoo Ltd v Bright Grahame Murray* [1994] 1 WLR 1360, CA; *BCCI v Price Waterhouse (No 3)* The Times, 2 April 1998, Laddie J.

[38] Including those where an appropriate emphasis on the duty owed by the defendant has the effect of establishing a liability which may not have been obvious from a purely causal perspective. For example, see most recently the decision of the House of Lords that the police should be held liable (subject to contributory negligence) for the suicide of a prisoner in a police cell: *Reeves v Commissioner of Police of the Metropolis* [2000] 1 AC 360. Once it had been established, as a question of law (or a matter of 'policy') that the police owed a duty to prevent the harm 'caused' by the prisoner's own act 'it would be absurd to retain a causal requirement that the harm should not have been so caused': *Fairchild v Glenhaven Funeral Services Ltd* [2002] 3 WLR 89, para [57] (*per* Lord Hoffmann).

before the court, as in the effect of contributory negligence in the *Platform Homes* case. In others, it will not prevent such proper resolution as long at it is recalled that the question *of the first order*, if not that first asked, is whether the loss fell within the scope of the duty owed by the defendant.

One consequence of first asking whether the loss incurred by the claimant was caused by the defendant is that it may serve to limit the nature of the loss for which it is thought that the defendant *may* be held responsible. In many cases, nothing will turn on this. In each of the appeals in *SAAMCO* the loss caused by the overvaluations, as a matter of fact, was all of the financial loss incurred by the lenders as a result of entering into the loans. It was then a question of how much of this loss could be attributed to the valuers' breach of duty. But what if it cannot be established that the 'loss' has been caused by the defendant at all? Is it possible that by reformulating the duty owed, another type of loss might be identified; one which was 'caused' both as a matter of fact, and in law, by the defendant's breach of duty? It is submitted that this is possible, or becomes more likely, it one does *first* ask what is the duty, or scope of the duty, which was owed by the defendant. It is also submitted that this is the key to a proper understanding of the decision in the recent case of *Fairchild v Glenhaven Funeral Services Ltd*.[39]

Fairchild may be viewed as a case primarily concerned with causation. The facts certainly throw up a classic causation conundrum. Mesothelioma is a form of cancer which can be, and most commonly is, caused by exposure to asbestos dust. The state of scientific knowledge in this area is incomplete, but what is known is that it can be triggered by a single asbestos fibre 'contaminating' a mesothelial cell. Consequently, if a potential claimant is negligently exposed to asbestos fibres over a period of time, it is impossible to say which fibre, or period of exposure, caused the mesothelioma. It may take as long as thirty to forty years from the first exposure to asbestos dust before mesothelioma develops. During this time, a claimant may have been negligently exposed to asbestos dust by several employers, any one of whom may have caused the disease. These were the circumstances of the several appeals before the House of Lords in the *Fairchild* case.

The Court of Appeal had felt obliged, albeit very reluctantly, to hold that the claims by the employees must fail.[40] The impossibility of establishing when the fatal contamination had occurred meant that it could not be proved that, but for the negligence of a particular employer, the claimant employee would not have developed mesothelioma. The employees' appeal to the House of Lords was allowed. Their Lordships each gave a reasoned speech, but the essential basis upon which they were willing to allow recovery may be summarized as follows: it was sufficient

---

[39] [2002] 3 WLR 89.   [40] [2002] ICR 412.

to show that a particular employer's breach of duty had materially increased the *risk* of developing mesothelioma. This was variously described by their Lordships as a 'variation' of the ordinary approach to proof of causation,[41] or the application of a 'different and less stringent' form of the 'but for' test.[42] In fact, what it really amounts to is an alteration to our understanding of the scope of the duty normally owed by an employer to an employee. Perhaps not surprisingly, this is most evident from the speech of Lord Hoffmann. For him, the House was required to say 'what should be the relevant causal connection for breach of a duty to protect an employee against *the risk* of contracting . . . mesothelioma by exposure to asbestos.'[43] Once it is determined that an employer has a duty not only to protect an employee against a disease, but also to protect against the *risk* of that disease, the difficulty of establishing the necessary causal connection is removed. Indeed, there is no difficulty in applying the ordinary approach to proof of causation; 'but for' the breach of duty by the employer, the employee would not have been exposed to the risk of contracting mesothelioma.

An analysis of the *Fairchild* case in terms of duty, rather than causation, highlights two potential problems; one relatively easy to overcome in practice, one far less so. The first takes us back to the starting point for this paper: what is the level of damages recoverable from the defendant? If all that can be proved is that a particular employer owed a duty to protect an employee from *the risk* of a disease and that his breach of that duty caused *the risk* to occur, he should not be made liable *for the disease itself.* Yet that was the outcome in the *Fairchild* case. In cases where the disease occurs after working for successive employers, all of whom have breached the relevant duty, the solution is for the employers to sue each other for a contribution. That, however, will not work where the disease may, in fact, have occurred as a result of an entirely non-negligent cause. That was the position in the earlier case of *McGhee v National Coal Board*[44] where the claimant had been exposed to an unavoidable, and non-negligent, period of exposure to brick dust. The negligence of his employer in not providing showers materially increased the risk of the dermatitis which he subsequently contracted and for which the employer was held liable, in full. There was no other tortfeasor from whom to seek a contribution.[45] The solution in such a case may be found at the quantification stage, ie in the

---

[41] ibid at para [35] (*per* Lord Bingham of Cornhill).
[42] ibid at para [45] (*per* Lord Nicholls of Birkenhead).   [43] ibid at para [49].
[44] [1973] 1 WLR 1.
[45] This problem does not arise with 'progressive diseases', ie those where the longer the exposure, the worse the disease becomes. In such cases, the defendant is liable for any material contribution to the disease itself, but only in proportion with his contribution: *Holtby v Brigham & Cowan (Hull) Ltd* [2000] 3 All ER 421.

valuation of the claim. In *Smith v Leech Brain & Co Ltd*[46] the claimant contracted cancer as a result of a burn to his lip caused by the negligence of the defendant. The claimant had a pre-existing susceptibility to cancer, but the application of the thin-skull rule meant that it could not be disputed that the defendant's breach of duty had caused the cancer. Nevertheless, the risk that cancer might have occurred in any event was taken into account in assessing the damages payable by the defendant. The same might be done in cases like *McGhee*. The employer should only have been liable for a sum which reflected the fact that dermatitis might have occurred in any event. The sum payable would reflect the basis of his liability, ie breach of his duty not to increase the risk of dermatitis.

This brings us to the second problem. By altering our normal perception of the duty owed by a defendant, we can make him liable not for causing a particular identifiable and tangible loss, but rather the risk of that loss. If that is the position which has been reached, is there any reason why it should be confined to cases like *Fairchild* and *McGhee*? For example, when a patient presents himself at hospital he may already be at the risk of further injury or disease. If he receives negligent treatment and goes on to suffer the injury or disease in question, it may not be possible to prove that such treatment caused the injury or disease, but it may have materially contributed to the risk of it. Such claims have previously been considered and rejected by the courts where they have been formulated in terms of 'the loss of the chance' of avoiding the injury or disease in question.[47] The terminology may be different, but the issue it is submitted is precisely the same.

In the *Fairchild* case, an attempt was made by some of their Lordships to distinguish the 'loss of a chance' cases in terms of causation. Whereas in the *Fairchild* case and *McGhee* the disease in question was caused by a single agent (asbestos and brick dust respectively), there were two or more possible agents involved in the loss of a chance cases.[48] As Lord Hoffmann pointed out, this is a far from principled distinction.[49] What if the claimant in the *Fairchild* case had been exposed to two different forms of dust, both of which created a material risk of mesothelioma, and it was impossible to say which had caused the fatal cell mutation? If, as seems certain, each of the successive employers would still have been found liable, then a different

---

[46] [1962] 2 QB 405.

[47] *Hotson v East Berkshire Area Health Authority* [1987] AC 570; *Wilsher v Essex Area Health Authority* [1988] AC 1074. For further comment, see: J Stapleton, 'The Gist of Negligence' (1988) 104 LQR 213 (pt I), 389 (pt II).

[48] In the *Wilsher* case the claimant suffered a condition which resulted in blindness. Due to the defendant's negligence, the claimant was given excess oxygen which may have caused the condition, but there were at least four other possible causes each due to the claimant's premature birth.

[49] [2002] 3 WLR 89, at para [72].

basis must be found for distinguishing the 'loss of a chance' cases. That basis is provided not by the principles of causation, but by considering the scope of the duty owed by the respective defendants. This is, of course, a question of law and therefore of policy. In the *Fairchild* case, the policy of the law came down in favour of the claimants. In the exceptional circumstances of that case, an employer's duty was extended to preventing a material increase in the risk of avoiding a disease. The potential implications of such an extension in cases of medical negligence are perhaps all too evident. As Lord Hoffmann acknowledged in the *Fairchild* case,[50] there are political and economic arguments involved in what would be a massive increase in the liability of the National Health Service. This is not to say that such a development may not be appropriate. If it is to take place, however, the relevant policy considerations must be taken into account. This requires it to be analysed properly as a question of duty and not disguised as a question of causation.[51]

6. CONCLUSION

The principal aim of this paper has been to clarify and re-emphasize the distinction which was drawn in *SAAMCO* between questions of duty and causation, and to assess their impact on the level of damages recoverable. Where the final result achieved by the courts has been called into question,[52] this has been primarily for the purpose of illustrating that it may have been reached by a failure to clarify the real issue. It has also been suggested that such clarification may herald further development in the scope of the duty owed by potential defendants in other areas, but without offering any definite conclusions in this regard. However, it is hoped that enough has been said to establish an irrefutable proposition, namely that one is far more likely to get the right answer if one begins by asking the right question.

---

[50] ibid.

[51] Whatever the other reasons which may have been offered by the majority of the Court of Appeal in *Gregg v Scott*, 29 October 2002 [2002] EWCA Civ 1471, it is submitted that their rejection of the claim made therein for a 'loss of a chance' (based in part on the *Fairchild* decision) is best explained as a straightforward policy decision about the scope of the duty of care which is owed by the medical profession: see Mance LJ (at para [85]), and Simon Brown LJ (at para [102]).

[52] As with *Aneco Reinsurance Underwriting Ltd v Johnson & Higgins Ltd*: above, p 60 *et seq*.

8

SAAMCO in Practice

1. SUMMARY

The themes of my paper are:

- What might be described as the wide *SAAMCO* principle (that is, for the defendant to be liable, the losses claimed must fall within the scope of the duty undertaken by the defendant) is correct.
- That said, the outcomes in the *SAAMCO* cases[2] do not generally reflect commercial expectations of risk apportionment so far as those engaged in the commercial property lending business are concerned.
- *SAAMCO* and its progeny create a number of practical problems in their implementation and in at least one respect are unworkable.
- *Platform Home Loans Ltd v Oyston Shipways Ltd* was wrongly decided.
- *Aneco Reinsurance Underwriting Ltd v Johnson & Higgins Ltd* highlights differing judicial perceptions of professionals in different disciplines. I speculate that this may have its origin in fiduciary duties.

2. BEFORE *SAAMCO*

Despite the criticisms of *SAAMCO* which follow, I should make it clear at once that I do not suggest we should turn the clock back to pre-*SAAMCO* days. To explain why that is, I start with a brief reminder of the approach which we used to take to valuers' negligence liability before *SAAMCO* was decided. I then take an even briefer look at the prevailing attitudes to causation from which that approach developed.

Here is a brief description of a typical *SAAMCO* case. A bank intends to lend money to a company to buy commercial property. It requires a valuer's report before it does so. It wants to know that, if it has to sell as mortgagee, the property will fetch a sufficiently large sum that the borrower's default does not leave the bank out of pocket.[3] The valuer negligently overstates the value and the loan transaction proceeds. The borrower

---

[1] Head of Research and Training, Commercial Litigation, Norton Rose.

[2] See n 17 below.

[3] Of course, the valuer does not have a crystal ball and is not expected to predict what the property will be worth in the future. Adverse market conditions which are already on the horizon are different, however. They *will* need to be taken into account to the extent that the relevant market is presently affected by them.

defaults and even after selling the property in exercise of its rights under the mortgage, the bank is out of pocket. Between the date of the loan and the date on which the bank sells the property, the price of commercial property has fallen across the country. That general fall in prices accounts for all or much of the shortfall in the sum recovered by the bank. Is the valuer liable for the entire shortfall?

Before *SAAMCO*, our analysis of these cases went like this. First, we would decide whether the valuer owed the bank a duty of care. We would look at the contract between the bank and the valuer and also consider any tortious duties. Usually the contract would set out the tasks which the valuer was to perform and it would be an implied term of the contract that those tasks would be performed with reasonable care and skill. The tortious duties would normally be the same and so this parallel source of duty would only come into play if some limitation issue arose. To this point, the exercise had no regard to damages.[4] It concerned liability, not quantum, which we began to consider only at the next stage.

Secondly, we would consider whether the valuer's breach of the duties which we had identified *caused* the bank's loss. We developed our own jargon to describe the two causal relationships which could exist. We might be dealing with a *no transaction* case or a *successful transaction* case. The first expression described a case in which, had the valuer reported the correct figure, the bank would not have loaned any money at all. The second described a case in which the bank would still have gone ahead, but would have loaned a smaller amount.

Next, we would conduct a foreseeability analysis. Since the possibility of *a* fall in property prices is reasonably foreseeable (even if the depth of the collapse is not), this analysis would not exclude from the range of recoverable losses, those losses flowing from market falls. So, in most cases, the determining factor would be the second analysis. If one was dealing with a *no transaction* case, one had the required causal link between the negligent act and the market losses—but for the negligence, the bank would not have advanced the money and so it would not have lost the money. In a *successful transaction* case, the bank would have advanced some money anyway (albeit a lower sum) and so the negligence did not cause the bank to be exposed to some market falls.

Whatever the fate of *SAAMCO* in the future, I think it is clear that there can be no return to those days. I will give my main reason for saying this in a moment. A subsidiary reason relates to the labels *no transaction* and *successful transaction* which I have just described. If you want a long-lasting

---

[4] Save to the extent that reasonable foreseeability of harm was material to the existence of a duty of care. As is generally accepted, market falls are reasonably foreseeable both for the purposes of remoteness and duty.

product life, you pay a PR consultant to brand your product effectively. It is my belief that if less awkward and poorly descriptive labels had been devised for these ideas, causation might not so readily have been edged off the shelves by the new market leader—scope of duty.[5] But it was not just a matter of ineffective branding. My main reason for saying that there can be no turning back relates to the concept of causation itself. As I must try to focus on the practical rather than the theoretical, I must not spend too long on this, but a brief excursion is necessary to my argument that there is no turning back.

An event happens because a number of conditions. If any of these conditions is absent, the event will not occur. To use an example from Edwin Peel's paper (Chapter 7, above), two of the many conditions for the accident in the *Tennessee Trailways v Ervin* case[6] were (1) that the deceased's motorcycle arrived at the junction at the precise moment at which the collision took place, and (2) that the defendant's bus was travelling at 73mph rather than at a reasonable 65mph. I characterize (2) as a condition for the accident because if the bus had been travelling at 65mph, it would have been several blocks short of the junction when the deceased's motorcycle passed by. The Tennessee Supreme Court did not promote this second condition to the status of a *cause*, however.

It is undeniably the case that all attempts by judges to formulate intellectually satisfying tests for identifying one of several conditions as causative, for liability purposes, have been failures.[7] The 'but for' test does no more than give you the starting line up of conditions—it gives no indication as to which of them should win the race. Notions such as *causa causans*, proximate cause, most potent causes and the like are rosettes awarded to the winner of the race,[8] but they provide no test for determining which condition should win it.

You do not need to be an out and out member of a school of legal realism to see that, in these circumstances, judges must be making a selection among the conditions before them on some unexpressed (or at least, unreasoned) basis reflecting their intuitive view of the correct outcome. This is possible because questions of causation, being questions of fact (or jury questions), call for no reasoning and are susceptible to treatment in

---

[5] In point of fact, the labels are still with us, but they have a new and reduced significance following *Nykredit Mortgage Bank plc* v *Edward Erdman Group Ltd (No 2)* [1997] 1 WLR 1627, HL, as discussed below.

[6] (1969) 438 SW 2nd 733.

[7] Attempts by lawyers to formulate a test, against the background of the treatment of the notion of causation by philosophers, is described in detail in HLA Hart and T Honoré, *Causation in the Law* (2nd edn, 1985).

[8] The losers are awarded the label 'occasion'. You can have more than one winner in these races. The winner of the race in *Fairchild v Glenhaven Funeral Services Ltd* [2002] 3 WLR 89, HL, was not an eligible entrant on any conventional set of race rules.

this sort of way: 'I consider . . . that what or who has caused a certain event to occur is essentially a practical question of fact which can best be answered by ordinary common sense rather than by abstract metaphysical theory'.[9]

It was this feature of the old approach which Lord Hoffmann found so objectionable. His solution was to remove the central determining factor in these cases from the province of fact and to make it instead a matter of law. That is, it becomes a question of the scope of the defendant's duty of care. That way, issues of policy can be allowed to play a spoken rather than an unspoken part in the judges' reasoning and judges must articulate their reasons by reference to principles rather than common sense alone. I for one find this wholly compelling and I would certainly not want to see a return to the old days.

3. LORD HOFFMANN'S SPEECH IN *FAIRCHILD*

All five members of the House of Lords in *Fairchild v Glenhaven Funeral Services Ltd*[10] believed that they should find a way of deciding the case in favour of the claimants. Their twin concerns were (1) to identify a legally and logically defensible way of doing so, and (2) to draw a boundary around their decision so that its consequences could be developed in a controlled way in future cases. In his *Fairchild* speech,[11] Lord Bingham identified four ways of rationalizing a decision in the claimant's favour culled from a comparative survey of tort law:

- Treat an increase in risk as equivalent to making a material contribution to the harm suffered.
- Put the burden of proof on the defendant.
- Treat the risk creators as if they were acting in concert.
- Base the decision solely on policy.

The House in the *Fairchild* case was unanimous[12] in adopting the first of these as the means of explaining its decision in favour of the claimant. The one point I want to develop relates to Lord Hoffmann's speech, given that

---

[9] Lord Salmon in *Alphacell Ltd v Woodward* [1972] AC 824, 847 described by Lord Hoffmann as being 'in the best tradition of English anti-intellectualism' and 'a good example of our characteristic polemical judicial style' in his lecture to the Chancery Bar Association: *Common Sense and Causing Loss*, 15 June 1999. This lecture provides an insight into Lord Hoffmann's thinking painted on a broader canvas than is possible in judicial pronouncements in individual cases. It is a great shame that it has never been published.

[10] [2002] 3 WLR 89.   [11] ibid, at [32].

[12] Lord Bingham at [34], Lord Nicholls at [42], Lord Hoffmann at [49], Lord Hutton at [116] and Lord Rodger at [168].

it represents another example of his insistence that causation questions must proceed from a careful analysis of the legal question to be answered.

An instance of this approach given by Lord Hoffmann in the *Fairchild* case was this. If a court must decide whether a police officer is liable to the family of a fully competent man because he commited suicide in custody, the decision that a duty of care exists must necessarily result in one of the usual rules of causation being switched off, that is the requirement that the harm was not caused by the deliberate action of another adult of sound mind.[13] The problem is the jump which has to be made from that proposition to that in the *Fairchild* case. It is one thing to say that the law can require you to ignore one of several causal agents for liability purposes. It is quite another to assert that the law can prescribe something as a causal agent when there is no factual basis for that proposition. The law is no more competent to prescribe that X caused Y than it is to say that Newton's first law of mechanics has no application in England and Wales.[14]

The root of the problem is that creating risk is just not the same as causing harm. Of course, risk can in itself be harmful. A man who has been exposed to asbestos dust may be unable to obtain private health cover or life assurance irrespective of whether he ever develops a disease. There is a demonstrable causal link between the creation of the risk and the harm suffered. To go further and to say that the risk-creator caused a disease, when there is no factual basis for saying so, is simply a misuse of the word.

In the *Fairchild* case, Lord Hoffmann said that 'there is no *a priori* reason or rule of logic which prevents the law treating [the creation of the risk] as sufficient to satisfy the causal requirements of the law of negligence.'[15] If this is understood as meaning that the law can treat certain risk creators *as if* they had caused an injury, then it is plainly correct. But that is not an application of the requirement for causation. It is the abolition of the requirement in the specified circumstances.

If one accepts, as I do, that a pragmatic exercise in compassion and justice was called for (and achieved) in the *Fairchild* case, one is necessarily accepting that an unattractive rationale is inevitable. The common law of negligence, the only tool at the disposal of the House, is not the right tool for the job. In my view, the second option canvassed by Lord Bingham (a shift in the burden of proof) would have been a less unattractive approach.[16]

---

[13] *Reeves v Commissioner of Police for the Metropolis* [2000] 1 AC 360, considered by Lord Hoffmann in *Fairchild v Glenhaven Services Ltd* [2002] 3 WLR 89 at 125.

[14] The same criticism applies to the weaker formulation: X contributed to Y.

[15] [2002] 3 WLR 89 at 127.

[16] It was the approach taken by Lord Wilberforce in *McGhee v National Coal Board* [1973] 1 WLR 1, 6–7.

4. PRACTICAL CRITICISMS OF *SAAMCO*

Although many practitioners do not agree with the *SAAMCO* decision, there seem to be few willing to criticize the general proposition that in order to succeed in a claim for contractual or tortious negligence, the range of losses claimed must fall within the duty of care owed by the defendant to the claimant. Practical criticisms tend to focus on three less central aspects of the decision. First, the way in which its implications for contributory negligence, interest, and limitation have been worked out in the later cases. Secondly, the difficulties in applying a principle, which must plainly have a wider effect, outside valuers' negligence cases, and thirdly, the unreality (when viewed in the light of the expectations of those in the commercial property lending business) of the actual scope of duty analysis in the *SAAMCO* cases themselves.[17]

(a) Working out SAAMCO's implications: I—Interest and limitation

One of the cases decided by the House of Lords in the *SAAMCO* appeal was *Nykredit Mortgage Bank plc v Edward Erdman Group Ltd*.[18] In that case, the valuers negligently valued a property at £3.5m when it was worth only £2m—a difference of £1.5m.[19] The bank advanced £2.45m. Three years later, after the borrower had defaulted, the bank sold the property for £345,000, suffering a total loss of £3m. The effect of the decision in *SAAMCO*[20] was that, of the £3m loss, only £1.5m fell within the scope of the duty of care owed by the valuer to the bank.

Unfortunately for the parties, this decision did not resolve all of the issues between them and they eventually ended up before the House of Lords again.[21] The unresolved question was, from which date should statutory interest run under the Supreme Court Act 1981, s 35A(1)? That section says that interest starts to run not earlier than the date on which the

---

[17] By 'the *SAAMCO* cases' I refer to the three appeals which were heard together in early 1996 and which are reported as *South Australia Asset Management Corp v York Montague Ltd* [1997] AC 191. These cases were (1) the *South Australia* case, (2) *United Bank of Kuwait plc v Prudential Property Services Ltd* and (3) *Nykredit Mortgage Bank plc v Edward Erdman Group Ltd*.

[18] [1997] AC 191. The *Nykredit* case is considered by Lord Hoffmann at 222–3.

[19] All figures used in this paper are rounded.

[20] As in all the cases heard by the House of Lords in the *SAAMCO* appeal, the valuer's task was characterized as the provision of information rather than advice. Unfortunately, this attempt to identify two categories in such a way as to point clearly to opposite conclusions just does not work on Lord Hoffmann's formulation. As Lord Millett explained in para 62 of *Aneco Reinsurance Underwriting Ltd v Johnson & Higgins Ltd* [2002] 1 Lloyd's Rep 157, a straightforward contraposition of information and advice is a distinction without a difference. Edwin Peel considers Lord Millett's reformulation in Chapter 7 at n 10.

[21] *Nykredit Mortgage Bank plc v Edward Erdman Group Ltd (No 2)* [1997] 1 WLR 1627.

cause of action arises.[22] In *Nykredit (No 2)* Lord Nicholls explained that the key to unlocking the problem as to when the cause of action accrues lies in the method of calculating the lender's loss. The starting point for this exercise is to put the transaction into one of the old 'no transaction/successful transaction' categories. In a no transaction case (had the valuer reported the correct value the bank would not have lent anything) the basic measure of loss is the difference between (i) the money which the bank would still have if it had not made the loan plus the bank's cost of borrowing,[23] and (ii) the value of what the bank has actually got as a result of the transaction. The latter will include the true value of the property and the value to the bank of the borrower's contractual obligation to pay the debt (in the jargon, 'the borrower's covenant').

In *Nykredit*, not only was the borrower's covenant worthless right from the date of the loan, but the property was worth less than the advance. It followed that a 'relevant, measurable loss' occurred on that day, which was therefore the date on which the cause of action in tort accrued. This creates two very real practical difficulties for practitioners:

Valuing the borrower's covenant—in a case in which the borrower's covenant is not initially worthless, any valuation exercise of this kind is fraught with difficulty.[24] In the nature of things, the lender's lawyers will not have the full facts and it is most unlikely that they will have the borrower's co-operation either. The difficulty has now been turned into an impossibility by the Court of Appeal decision in *DnB Mortgages v Bullock & Lees*[25] in which Robert Walker LJ held that the valuation must be performed by reference to the facts as they emerge with hindsight rather than as they would have appeared to the lender at the time. It follows that lawyers advising a bank on the important question of the expiry of the limitation period in tort cannot know with any certainty when that date will be.

Commencement date for statutory interest—my discussion of the *Nykredit (No 2)* case above does not cover all of the steps you need to take in working out when statutory interest starts to run. Although the date on which the cause of action accrues is the *earliest* date, in many cases the commencement date has to be deferred, for this reason. Banks borrow money in order to lend it. In the case of a large corporate loan, the borrowing may be a single inter-bank loan which is identifiably linked to the lending in

---

[22] The decision is therefore an important authority on the start of the limitation period in tort, though that was not an issue in the *Nykredit* case itself.

[23] Which is normally claimed as special damages.

[24] Lord Nicholls was of the view that it should not be unduly troublesome. The practical difficulties are mostly to do with investigative problems, which Lord Nicholls seems to ignore. Other difficulties relating to the borrower's covenant include ascribing a present value to an uncertain future income stream.

[25] [2000] Lloyd's Rep PN 290.

question. Otherwise it may be part of a larger borrowing arrangement. Either way, the bank will have to pay for the money it has borrowed in the form of interest. As we have already seen, in a valuer's negligence case this cost of borrowing forms part of the basic measure of the bank's loss. Because of the cost of borrowing element of these claims, an interest commencement date complication arises in one of two categories of case. Unfortunately, most cases probably fall into that category. Here are the two categories. The problem arises in the second one:

Bank's losses exceed *SAAMCO* 'cap' from day one—this could come about, for instance, because the borrower's covenant has little value and the security cover is exceeded by the amount of the overvaluation. In such a case, statutory interest will run on the capped figure from the date of the loan. The full recoverable loss has crystallized on that day.

Bank's losses do not reach the level of the *SAAMCO* 'cap' until later— this might be because the borrower's covenant initially has value and so the overvaluation figure is not reached until the borrowing costs have built up sufficiently. Alternatively, the lender may have applied a more cautious loan-to-value ratio and the lender may have issued a less inaccurate valuation. The point here is this. If statutory interest started to run on the date the cause of action accrued, the bank would effectively make a double recovery. Because the losses would still be building up to the maximum claimable sum (the *SAAMCO* 'cap'), the lender would be claiming cost of borrowing in respect of the same period for which it was claiming statutory interest. Consequently, despite the general rule that statutory interest starts running when the cause of action accrued, in this case it has to be deferred until the *SAAMCO* 'cap' is reached. This was, in fact, the result in the case of *Nykredit (No 2)*.[26]

These calculations include the requirement that the borrower's covenant has to be revalued over time, with the complications already discussed, but introduce further complications. First, the cumulative cost of borrowing has to be tracked over time, and secondly, every point to be plotted on the graph represents an expensive revaluation of the property. Statutory interest starts to run on the day the bank's basic loss calculated by reference to these variables reaches the amount of the *SAAMCO* 'cap' because that is the day on which the claim reaches its full *SAAMCO* potential. Such an exercise is wholly impracticable in most cases, with the result that, in practice, the cost of borrowing is continued through to trial in lieu of statutory interest. Which party benefits from this is debatable. My point is that the rule is unworkable.

---

[26] See Lord Hoffmann's speech, [1997] 1 WLR 1627 at 1627.

(b) Working out SAAMCO's implications: II—Contributory negligence and contribution between defendants[27]

In Chapter 7 Edwin Peel has considered the way in which the contributory negligence issues arising from *SAAMCO* have been worked out in *Platform Home Loans Limited v Oyston Shipways Ltd.*[28] I take a different view of the merits of the decision. Take a hypothetical example based on physical damage rather than economic loss:

The claimant owns two adjacent warehouse units, *A* and *B*. He employs a contractor, the defendant, to carry out work to *A*. Negligently, the defendant's workmen build a bonfire too close to building *A* and it burns down. By a freak and entirely unpredictable accident, the fire spreads to unit *B* and that burns down too. The claimant's loss in respect of each warehouse is £1m, but the incompetence of the claimant's own employees in their attempts to deal with the fires at both warehouses renders the claimant 20 per cent contributorily negligent. On the basis that the defendant has no liability in respect of unit *B*, because there was no relevant breach of duty,[29] what is their liability in respect of unit *A*? The only possible choice is £800,000 (method: £1m minus 20 per cent).

Suppose now, however, that the two fire fighting parties sent in by the claimant were not uniformly incompetent. Those in warehouse *A* were 20 per cent contributorily negligent whereas those in warehouse *B* were 80 per cent contributorily negligent. We now have a choice of methods we could use to quantify the defendant's liability. Is it (1) £800,000 (method: ignore warehouse *B*. It is £1m minus 20 per cent) two, or (2) £500,000 (method: (£1m minus 20 per cent) plus (£1 million minus 80 per cent) divided by two because the defendant is only legally responsible for warehouse *A*)?

In truth, there is no real choice at all. No-one would opt for solution (2). The causal link between the contractors' negligence and the damage to warehouse *B* provides no rational basis for introducing warehouse *B* (also known as the Red Herring Building) into the case at all. Having decided that the defendants' duty of care does not extend to that area of the loss which they have caused, we leave it out of account for all purposes.

---

[27] My attention is all on contributory negligence on the part of the claimant. However, the same issues arise when considering questions of contribution between defendants: see *Ball v Banner* [2000] EGCS 36.

[28] [2000] 2 AC 190.

[29] This is itself an application of the wider *SAAMCO* principle. I have emphasized the unpredictable mechanism of the fire spread, perhaps suggesting that lack of reasonable foreseeability is the reason why the defendant has no liability in respect of the damage to warehouse *B*. But foreseeability of harm is an important factor in the question whether there exists a duty of care also. As cases such as *Caparo Industries v Dickman* [1990] 2 AC 605 demonstrate, it is not sufficient to establish a duty of care, but it is necessary.

How does this reasoning apply to the type of case which we are considering? I think the following propositions (rejected by the House of Lords in the *Platform Home Loans* case) represent the only rational approach to the application of *SAAMCO* in split responsibility cases:

- In a valuers' negligence case, categories of loss which do not fall within the scope of the defendant's duty of care ('Red Herring losses') are no more part of the case than was warehouse B in my example.[30]

- More specifically, negligence on the part of the claimant lender which is material only to the Red Herring losses, such as a failure properly to investigate the borrower's creditworthiness, falls outside the ambit of the enquiry. In principle, the owner of warehouse B was entitled to employ clowns to damage his own property without thereby incurring liability to or relinquishing rights against a third party with no relevant interest in that warehouse. Similarly, in principle, the lender is entitled to risk its money by making non-status loans without losing its rights against a valuer who has caused the lender's loss and who has legal responsibility for an unrelated range of losses pertaining to lack of security cover. Now that the valuer has no responsibility for losses falling outside the scope of the duty assumed as a result of information which he has provided, the valuer has no legitimate right to question the way in which the lender conducted credit checks.[31]

- On the other hand, negligence on the part of the lender which *is* material to the range of losses claimed against the valuer, such as a negligent failure to provide the valuer with information about a recent transaction which could shed light on the market value of the property, should plainly be brought into account. In this instance, if the lender is considered to be responsible to the extent of 20 per cent as a result of that failure, the 20 per cent should go (in full and exclusively) to reduce the damages to which it relates—namely that part of the lender's overall loss which arises from the breach of the valuer's duty to provide accurate information on the value of the property.

It follows that, in my view, the majority decision of the House of Lords in *Platform Home Loans* is wrong in principle, however understandable it may be on the wording of the Law Reform (Contributory Negligence) Act 1945.[32]

---

[30] In a *SAAMCO*-type case the total loss will need to be proved, of course, but once it is established that a figure in excess of the *SAAMCO* 'cap' was suffered (and when) the excess has no further part to play in the action. It represents that part of the claimant's loss which is at its own risk.

[31] At any rate, once causation is no longer a live issue.

[32] The statutory construction turned on the word 'damage' as it appears, several times, in the expression '. . . the damages recoverable in respect of [the damage suffered by reason of the fault of the person suffering the damage] shall be reduced to such extent as the court thinks just and equitable having regard to the claimant's share in responsibility for the

(c) Working out SAAMCO's implications: III—Cases not involving negligent surveyors

There can be no real doubt that the wide *SAAMCO* principle is of general application in our law of negligence.[33] Indeed, in Lord Hoffmann's view, the reasoning applies even beyond cases in which the defendant owed the claimant a duty, to include such cases as fraud,[34] though the outcome in a fraud case will often be different.[35] The difficulty confronting professionals seeking to reduce their liability by reference to *SAAMCO* will be to show that their role was to provide information enabling their client to make a decision as opposed to providing advice on the correct course of action. Sometimes solicitors' duties are confined to the provision of information only,[36] but very often solicitors are credited (debited?) with having a more central advisory role in transactions, leading to responsibility for a wider range of losses.[37] Similarly other professionals.[38] I do not take issue with the proposition that certain professionals commonly or even characteristically advise on the viability of the transaction. My criticism is that, in commercial property transactions, valuers typically have a wider role than was ascribed to them in the cases before the House of Lords in *SAAMCO*.

5. THE OUTCOMES OF THE *SAAMCO* CASES

Believing, as I do, that the broad *SAAMCO* principle (losses claimed must fall within the scope of the duty undertaken) is correct, I nevertheless believe that the outcome of the *SAAMCO* cases was probably wrong. This

damage' (s 1(1)). The majority of the House of Lords considered that the 'damage' for these purposes was the whole of the lender's loss—not just that part of it which fell within the valuer's duty of care. It is respectfully suggested that the word 'damage' in this section is capable of bearing the meaning 'damage material to the claim' and that, for the reasons given in the text, it should have been given that meaning.

[33] Not in Australia, however. The High Court of Australia refused to follow *SAAMCO* in *Kenny & Good Property Ltd v MGICA (1992) Ltd* (1999) 163 ALR 611.

[34] It is not conventional, or justified, in the light of the separate historical development of deceit and negligence, to use the concept of duty in a fraud case.

[35] In his Chancery Bar Association Lecture, above n 8, Lord Hoffmann proposed a variation to the mountaineer's knee story. Instead of making an honest but negligent diagnosis of the mountaineer's knee injury, the doctor deliberately provides the wrong information. His object is to send the man on the mountaineering expedition so that he can have an assignation with his wife. As in all fraud cases, the range of losses caused by the fraud for which damages are available is widened.

[36] As in the *Colin Bishop* case in *Bristol & West Building Society v Fancy & Jackson* [1997] 4 All ER 582.

[37] For instance, in the *Steggles & Palmer* case in *Bristol & West Building Society v Fancy & Jackson*, ibid. And more recently, the Court of Appeal decision in *Portman Building Society v Bevan Ashford* [2000] PNLR 344.

[38] For instance, architects—*Hancock v Tucker* [1999] Lloyd's Rep PN 814 and the insurance brokers in *Aneco Reinsurance Underwriting Ltd v Johnson & Higgins Ltd* [2002] 1 Lloyd's Rep 157, HL.

is because, in my view, the scope of the duty of care held to have been undertaken by the commercial property valuers in the *SAAMCO* cases is unlikely to have reflected the commercial expectation of players in the market or their insurers.

In Chapter 7 Edwin Peel has used a very illuminating technique for analysing these scope of duty cases—positing an express term of the retainer to reflect the scope of duty as found by the court. I have tried using the same technique, but I find that I take a different view as to what it tells us. In my view, the decision of the House of Lords on the scope of the valuers' duty of care in the cases before the House is more consistent with an express term along these lines: 'We [the lender] intend to make a loan to [the borrower] in any event, but because we only lend a maximum of [ ]% of the present value of the property offered as security, before we do so, we would like you to tell us how much the property is worth.' Not only does such an instruction not reflect the usual express agreement, but neither, in my view, does it reflect the mutual expectations of a bank and a valuer in the sorts of transaction which we are considering. No doubt it is wrong to generalize too much about these things (and certainly wrong to assume that I can speak for the actual expectations of the parties in the *SAAMCO* cases), but in my experience of cases flowing from the early 1990s property crash, a typical story would run along the following lines.

A property investor would require a certain sum in order to buy a commercial building. Unless he could borrow the specified sum, there would be no transaction as far as he was concerned, because the property would be sold to someone else who *could* raise the necessary sum. The intending buyer would already have a valuation (often a 'desk top' valuation) prepared on his instruction for the information of potential funders. Having found a suitable bank (there would be many banks courting him—falling over each other to lend money—so he would have a choice) the loan application would be processed up to and even beyond the decision-in-principle stage on the basis of the details, including the desk top valuation, provided by the buyer. A bank official, or perhaps a credit committee, would then produce a list of outstanding items, or conditions to be fulfilled, before the loan could be completed. By this stage, all of the items on this list would be formalities, such as the execution of a charge. One of the items would be a valuation by reputable valuers certifying an open market value of no less than £X. The bank would then commission the valuation at the borrower's expense.

A valuation in these circumstances can be seen by the bank and the valuer alike to be decisive. If the valuer does not certify the required sum, the transaction fails. If he does, the transaction completes. The thing which the bank is buying from the valuer is insurance in respect of the transaction—that is clear from the heavy cost of valuations of this kind when compared with the work which the valuer would have to put into its preparation.[39] In my view, these commercial realities are overlooked in the actual *SAAMCO* outcomes. Why is it that '. . . where a negligent solicitor fails to provide information which shows that the transaction is not viable . . .' the solicitor is liable for all of the resulting losses[40] but a valuer who does the same thing is not. After all, the bulk of the cases raising these issues are, in the old terminology, 'no transaction cases'—had the valuer provided accurate information the transaction would not have proceeded—so why is the valuer's duty of care treated as if it was never intended or expected that it would have this decisive effect?

Where the parties both know that the information/advice to be tendered will in fact be relied on for the purpose of committing to a risky transaction, the advisor/information provider ought, in my view, to be entitled to limit liability only by the use of clear and unambiguous wording. There was no such wording in the *SAAMCO* cases and in my opinion, assuming they conformed broadly to the template I have described, the outcomes should in each case have been that the valuers were liable for the whole of the lender's loss. In the words of Lord Bridge in *Caparo Industries v Dickman*:[41]

> the defendant giving advice or information was fully aware of the nature of the transaction which the plaintiff had in contemplation, knew that the advice or information would be communicated to him directly or indirectly and knew that it was very likely that the plaintiff would rely on that advice or information in deciding whether or not to engage in the transaction in contemplation. In these circumstances the defendant could clearly be expected, subject always to the effect of any disclaimer of responsibility, specifically to anticipate that the plaintiff would rely on the advice or information given by the defendant for the very purpose for which he did in the event rely on it. So also the plaintiff, subject again to the effect of any disclaimer, would in that situation reasonably suppose that he was entitled to rely on the advice or information communicated to him for the very purpose for which he required it.

The decision of the majority of the House of Lords on the scope of the brokers' duty of care in *Aneco Reinsurance Underwriting Ltd v Johnson & Higgins Ltd*[42] is consistent with this view. It is submitted that the following factual parallels between *Aneco* and *SAAMCO* type cases ought to mean that the latter cases should normally be resolved in favour of the lender and not the valuer:

---

[39] The typical transaction which I have described has the valuation at the eleventh hour, which was and no doubt continues to be very common. Such timing is not important to my reasoning, however. If an 11th hour valuation is, because of its decisive effect, advice on the viability of the transaction rather than the mere provision of information, then it should make no difference whether it arrives at the first, fifth or eleventh hour.

[40] *Portman Building Society v Bevan Ashford* [2000] PNLR 344, CA.

[41] [1990] 2 AC 605 at 620–1. Lord Bridge was referring to *Hedley Byrne v Heller* [1964] AC 465 and *Smith v Eric S Bush; Harris v Wyre Forest DC* [1990] 1 AC 831. On the assumed facts in the *Caparo* case, of course, the auditors had no liability to prospective investors.

[42] [2002] 1 Lloyd's Rep 157.

Aneco	*SAAMCO type cases*

No express obligation to advise generally

There was no obligation on J&H to advise Aneco on the wisdom of entering into the Bullen Treaty.	There is generally no obligation on the part of the valuers to advise the lenders on the wisdom of entering into the loan agreements.

The contractual task

The contractual task of J&H was carefully to place $11m of Aneco's excess of loss risk with reinsurers.	The usual contractual task of the valuers is carefully to value the properties on a 'market value' basis.[43]

Assumption of duty

'J&H assumed[44] a duty to report correctly the current market assessment of the reinsurance risks which Aneco was proposing to undertake.'[45]	In *Aneco*, Lord Steyn went on to say:[46] 'This is far removed from the lender/valuer relationship and even from the client/professional adviser relationship to which the [*SAAMCO*] case applies, and even more so from the doctor and mountaineer.' On the highly restricted view of the valuers' duty which Lord Hoffmann accepted in

---

[43] With effect from 1 August 2002 the RICS has recommended valuation to the international 'market value' basis in the place of the old 'open market value' basis which had been in use for many years in this country. Even for mortgage valuations, the discredited bases of Estimated Realisation Price and Estimated Restricted Realisation Price have been swept away (Amendment 15, RICS Appraisal and Valuation Manual—'The Red Book'—issued in May 2002 in discussion with the British Bankers' Association).

[44] It appears that this assumption of responsibility came about after the brokers had agreed to act for Aneco. Since post-contractual behaviour is not usually admissible as evidence of the agreed terms (*Schuler AG v Wickman Machine Tool Sales* [1974] AC 235) it may be that liability in Aneco was tortious only.

[45] Lord Steyn [2002] 1 Lloyd's Rep 157, at para [40]. Lord Millett was disposed to see this as part of Aneco's underwriting risk and no part of the broker's responsibility, ibid, at paras [108]–[111].

[46] *per* Evans LJ in the Court of Appeal, [2000] Lloyd's Rep IR 12, paras [82]–[84].

Assumption of duty (cont.)	the *SAAMCO* cases, that would be correct. As explained, I do not consider this to be the correct view of valuers' duties in most commercial cases, in which the duty should be expressed in terms such as: A duty not to cause the lender to enter into the proposed transaction if the true value of the property was below that which formed the basis of the lender's decision to advance the money.

Causation

If J&H had carefully reported on the availability of reinsurance in respect of the Bullen Treaty, Aneco would not have entered into that treaty.	If the valuers carefully report on the value of the property, the lender would not advance anything to the borrower.

Defendant's knowledge of reliance

J&H knew that Aneco would not enter into the Bullen Treaty unless $11m of the risk was reinsured.	The valuers would ordinarily know that if they report a significantly lower value than that proposed by the borrower, the lender will not enter into the loan agreement.

Conclusion

'On the evidence Lord Justice Evans was correct to conclude that the brokers' breach of duty was their negligent advice "with regard to the availability of reinsurance (retrocession) and therefore on the current market assessment of the risk". In my view the conclusion of Lord Justice Evans is supported by the commercial realities and inherent probabilities in the relationship between broker and reinsured revealed by the documentary and oral evidence.'[47]	I suggest that if the duty is expressed in terms similar to the above, then the damages extend to all of the foreseeable losses which the breach caused

[47] Lord Steyn, ibid at 187.

Result

| J&H liable for all of Aneco's losses arising from the Bulletin Treaty and not just the sums which the reinsurers would have to pay on valid reinsurance arrangements | Valuers who know that their valuation will be decisive will be responsible for all foreseeable consequences of the transaction |

6. VALUERS AS SECOND CLASS PROFESSIONALS

Although it plays no part in the reasoning of the House of Lords in any but one[48] of the leading cases, it seems possible that fiduciary obligations have a subliminal role in shaping the judges' evaluation of the scope of the duties assumed by professionals. Solicitors owe their clients fiduciary duties and these duties percolate through to solicitors' rules of professional conduct, to the terms of their retainers and indeed to the scope of their duty of care in tort. To take just one example, a solicitor must act in the best interests of his or her client and not take advantage of the client.[49] The Code of Conduct under the Insurance Brokers (Registration) Act 1977 used to say that 'Insurance Brokers shall do everything possible to satisfy the insurance requirements of their clients and shall . . . place the interest of those clients before all other considerations.'[50] In the face of weighty professional duties of this kind, whether they form part of the contract or not, it is understandable that judges are reluctant to find that such professionals' liabilities to their clients are confined to the result of information provided being wrong.

Such a link between the fiduciary duties owed by a given professional person and the extent of the duty of care owed has historical justification. As Lord Browne-Wilkinson explained in *Henderson v Merrett Syndicates*

---

[48] The exception is Lord Browne-Wilkinson's speech in *Henderson v Merrett Syndicates Ltd* as discussed below.

[49] Solicitors Practice Rule 1 and Law Society Guidance 12.09 (conduct rules); *Bristol & West Building Society v Mothew* [1998] Ch 1 Millett LJ (fiduciary duties) and *Nocton v Lord Ashburton* [1914] AC 932 (duty in tort).

[50] No precisely equivalent language appears in the 2002 successor to that code, though *The General Insurance Standards Council Commercial Code* includes in its Core Principles an obligation that 'in the course of their general insurance activities, members should take reasonable steps to give Commercial Customers sufficient information in a comprehensible and timely way to enable them to make balanced and informed decisions about their insurance.' In *Kelly v Cooper* [1993] AC 205, 215 the Privy Council approved *North and South Trust Co v Berkeley* [1971] 1 WLR 470 (Donaldson J) which held that an insurance broker had a duty not to act for clients with conflicting interests.

Limited[51] the general principle enunciated by the House of Lords in *Hedley Byrne & Co v Heller & Partners*[52] was taken up and developed from *Nocton v Lord Ashburton*.[53] In that case, Viscount Haldane expressed the fiduciary duty owed by the solicitor Nocton to his client as 'being but one example of a wider principle, viz., that a man who has voluntarily assumed to act on behalf of, or to advise, another in law assumes a duty to that other to act or to advise with care.'[54] If this is, in truth, part of the unexpressed reasoning in these cases, it would follow that judges perceive valuers differently. The close identification of valuers with estate agents may fuel that perception,[55] but in my view a perception of this kind would be wrong. Analytical valuers who are chartered surveyors would consider themselves as much bound by client orientated professional obligations as would solicitors and insurance brokers.

---

[51] [1995] 1 AC 145, 204–6.   [52] [1964] AC 465.   [53] [1914] AC 932, 948.

[54] In Lord Browne-Wilkinson's words in *Henderson v Merrett Syndicates Ltd* [1995] 1 AC 145, at 204.

[55] Analytical valuers often practise in partnership with estate agents. Estate agents do not seem to owe such rigorous fiduciary duties to their clients as those owed by solicitors and insurance brokers—see, for instance, *Kelly v Cooper* [1993] AC 205, PC in which the Privy Council held that an estate agent acting for two separate owners of adjacent beach properties in Bermuda owed no fiduciary obligation to his principals to disclose the fact that a prospective buyer, Ross Perot, was in the process of buying both (thereby denying the principals the opportunity to realize marriage value).

9
SAAMCO: Review of Discussion

Much of the initial discussion on the issues raised by *SAAMCO*[1] was concerned with the correctness of the decision in *Aneco*[2] on the facts, ie regardless of the appropriate legal analysis (scope of duty, causation, etc). Opinion appeared to be divided. Some thought was given to the idea put forward by Richard Butler that certain categories of professionals (whether one might describe them as occupying a 'fiduciary' position or not) were perhaps more likely to be found to have 'advised' (for example, brokers, lawyers) than to have merely provided 'information'. Edwin Peel reiterated his view that while one might well reach different conclusions *on the facts* in a case like *Aneco*, the conclusion reached by the majority in the House of Lords may have been reached, at least in part, by a failure to follow the approach advocated by Lord Hoffmann in *SAAMCO*.

As far as *SAAMCO* itself was concerned, the view was advanced that, in addition to saying nothing new about the 'scope of the duty', it was not a decision which was likely to add anything in the majority of cases. One aspect of this view was the suggestion that 'scope of duty' was simply another way of dealing with 'legal causation', ie that another explanation for *SAAMCO* and the mountaineering example given by Lord Hoffmann was that there had been a break in the chain of causation. While it was noted that there was a clear and obvious link between the scope of the duty owed and *novus actus interveniens* (and *Reeves v Commissioner of Police of the Metropolis*[3] was cited as a recent example), it was said in response that the question of the scope of the duty owed by a particular defendant was, or may be, more fundamental than questions of *novus actus interveniens*; in *SAAMCO* (and in the mountaineering example) the House of Lords dealt with the appeal on the basis that the losses in the market were reasonably foreseeable, yet still found that they did not fall within the scope of the valuer's duty.

There was some debate as to the correctness of the decision in the *Platform Homes* case,[4] but opinion appeared to settle in favour of the view advanced in Richard Butler's paper (Chapter 8) that neither the majority, nor the minority, had sufficiently taken into account the *nature* of the contributory negligence involved, ie whether the fault of the lenders served to increase the loss which fell within the scope of the valuer's duty, or the loss which fell outside that duty. In the *Platform Homes* case, the findings of

---

[1] [1997] AC 191.   [2] [2002] 1 Lioyd's Rep 157.   [3] [2000] 1 AC 390.
[4] [2000] 2 AC 190.

contributory negligence appeared to be divided between the two and this had, perhaps, not been taken into account by the decision.

The latter part of this session was taken up with discussion of the decision of the House of Lords in the *Fairchild* case.[5] Some doubt was expressed at the suggestion that it should be seen as a case concerned with duty and that it was really just another example of the '*Cook v Lewis*[6] problem'. While it was conceded that it was an 'exceptional' case which required an exceptional solution, the view was advanced that the proper analysis of the approach taken by the House of Lords was to alter the scope of the duty owed by each employer, ie that each was found to owe a duty not to increase the *risk* of the disease. If that was correct, it was questioned whether this approach would have any application beyond the facts of this case. There was some discussion of the basis, if any, upon which the *Fairchild* case might be distinguished from the 'loss of a chance' cases in medical negligence (eg *Hotson*,[7] *Wilsher*[8]). There seemed to be little support for the distinction offered up in the *Fairchild* decision between cases of 'single agency' and 'multiple agency'. Instead, it was noted that the key feature of the *Fairchild* case was that the disease was undoubtedly caused by *a* negligent tortfeasor, whereas in the medical negligence cases it was possible that the injuries involved were due to an entirely non-negligent cause. On that basis, it was *McGhee*[9] which might be seen as the 'problem' case, rather than *Fairchild*.

[5] [2002] 3 WLR 89.   [6] [1952] 1 DLR 1.   [7] [1987] AC 570.
[8] [1988] AC 1074.   [9] [1973] 1 WLR 1.

PART B

Restitution and Punishment

10

Breach of Contract, Restitution for Wrongs, and Punishment

EWAN McKENDRICK[1]

The decision of the House of Lords in *A-G v Blake (Jonathan Cape Ltd, Third Party)*[2] is one of some significance for the law of civil wrongs generally and the law of contract in particular. The extent of its significance is, at present, difficult to discern. Its importance lies in the fact that it recognizes that an account of profits is, in principle, available as a remedy in respect of a breach of contract. *Blake* thus evidences the fact that the range of remedies available in respect of a breach of contract has increased in recent years. The decision of the House of Lords in *Kuddus v Chief Constable of Leicestershire Constabulary*[3] may herald a further expansion in the range of remedies available in that the abolition of the 'cause of action' test[4] for determining whether or not a claimant is entitled to recover exemplary (or punitive) damages holds out the possibility that a court might, in an appropriate case, see fit to award such damages for a breach of contract.[5] The addition of an account of profits and the potential addition of exemplary damages to the judicial weaponry raise important questions of principle. Who should decide when these remedies are to be available? Is it to be the courts or is primary importance to be attached to the wishes of the parties? Should fixed principles govern their availability or should availability depend upon the discretion of the court? The last question is an important one and the claim that greater emphasis should be placed on the appropriateness of the remedy on the facts of the case has its supporters[6] and its critics.[7]

    The aim of this paper is not to consider, as a matter of principle, whether or not an account of profits or exemplary damages should be available for

[1] Professor of English Private Law in the University of Oxford; Fellow of Lady Margaret Hall. I am very grateful to Martin Graham for his assistance in the preparation of this paper and to James Edelman, Felicity Maher and Robert Stevens for their helpful comments which saved me from a number of errors.

[2] [2001] 1 AC 268.   [3] [2001] 1 WLR 1789.

[4] According to which, in order to bring a claim for exemplary damages, a claimant had to show that exemplary damages had been awarded in respect of such a cause of action prior to the decision of the House of Lords in *Rookes v Barnard* [1964] AC 1129.

[5] See J Edelman, 'Exemplary Damages for Breach of Contract' (2001) 117 LQR 539.

[6] See, for example, P Finn, 'Equitable Doctrine and Discretion in Remedies' in W Cornish, R Nolan, J O'Sullivan and G Virgo (eds) *Restitution: Past, Present and Future* (Hart, Oxford, 1998) 251.

[7] See, for example, P Birks 'Rights, Wrongs, and Remedies' (2000) 20 OJLS 1, 22–4.

a breach of contract. These issues have been explored at some length in the literature both in the case of an account of profits[8] and exemplary damages[9] and it is not proposed to go over this ground once again. Rather, my concern is to ascertain the range of possible circumstances in which a court might award an account of profits or exemplary damages in respect of a breach of contract. Given that the decision in *Blake* unequivocally recognizes that a court can, in an appropriate case, award damages assessed by reference to the gain made by the party in breach, I shall focus principally upon the *Blake* case before going on, albeit more briefly, to consider the possible impact of the decision in *Kuddus*. The general picture that emerges from this study is that the remedial regime for breach of contract (and possibly for other wrongs) has become more complex[10] and that the immediate consequence of this is an increase in the level of uncertainty in the law. Whether this uncertainty will persist is a matter that remains to be seen.

It is necessary to make two preliminary points. Both relate to the scope of the paper. The first is that its focus is on breach of contract. It does not purport to deal other than by way of analogy with torts and equitable wrongs.[11] The second is that compensatory damages for breach of contract are also beyond the scope of this paper. They are dealt with elsewhere in this volume[12] but they nevertheless have a bearing on the subject-matter of this chapter. In the first place, acceptance of the proposition that English law permits a contracting party in certain circumstances to recover dam-

---

[8] See, for example, G Jones, 'The Recovery of Benefits Gained from a Breach of Contract' (1983) 99 LQR 443; A Farnsworth, 'Your Loss or My Gain? The Dilemma of the Disgorgement Principle in Breach of Contract' (1985) 94 Yale LJ 1339; P Birks, 'Restitutionary Damages for Breach of Contract; *Snepp* and the Fusion of Law and Equity' [1987] LMCLQ 421; R O'Dair, 'Restitutionary Damages for Breach of Contract and the Efficient Breach Theory: Some Reflections' (1993) 46 CLP 113; S Smith, 'Of Remedies and Restrictive Covenants' (1994) 7 Journal of Contract Law 164; L Smith, 'Disgorgement of the Profits of Breach of Contract: Property, Contract and "Efficient Breach"' (1994) 24 Canadian Business Law Journal 121; C Mitchell, 'Remedial Inadequacy in Contract and the Role of Restitutionary Damages' (1999) 15 Journal of Contract Law 133; J O'Sullivan, 'Reflections on the Role of Restitutionary Damages to Protect Contractual Expectations' in D Johnston and R Zimmermann (eds) *Unjustified Enrichment: Key Issues in Comparative Perspective* (Cambridge, 2002) 325.

[9] See, for example, N McBride, 'A Case for Awarding Punitive Damages in Response to Deliberate Breaches of Contract' [1995] Anglo-American Law Review 369 and, more generally, Law Commission, *Aggravated, Exemplary and Restitutionary Damages* (Law Com No 247, 1997).

[10] It is likely that the regime will become even more complex in the context of consumer contracts for the sale of goods when the Council Directive (EC) 1999/44 on Certain Aspects of the Sale of Consumer Goods and Associated Guarantees [1999] OJ L171/12 which adds repair, replacement, and price reduction to the remedial menu comes into force. Ratification of the Vienna Convention on Contracts for the International Sale of Goods will also add to this remedial complexity.

[11] The reason for this is, essentially, that the range of remedies available in respect of a particular wrong must depend, to a large extent, on the nature of the wrong at issue. It is therefore essential to focus attention in the first place on the nature of the cause of action and then consider whether or not a particular remedy is available in respect of that cause of action.

[12] See Part A, Chapters 1–9.

ages assessed by reference to the gain that the defendant has made from her breach of contract or, more radically, to recover exemplary damages means that damages for breach of contract should no longer be seen exclusively in compensatory terms. While it is likely that compensatory damages will remain the principal remedy for breach of contract, they are no longer the sole monetary remedy. Secondly, the broader the conception of loss which the law of contract adopts, the less need there will be in practice for a claimant to seek damages that are assessed by reference to the gain made by the defendant.[13] However, there is no need for the law to choose between the adoption of a broad approach to the concept of loss and the recognition of the possibility that damages can be assessed by reference to the gain made by the defendant. As Lord Millett observed in *Alfred McAlpine Construction Ltd v Panatown Ltd.*[14] 'there is room for both approaches'.[15] No further attempt will be made in this paper to address the issue relating to the view of loss that English law currently embraces. It suffices for present purposes to note that the two issues are conceptually distinct.

1. BLAKE AND ITS AFTERMATH

The decision of the House of Lords in *A-G v Blake* has already attracted a considerable degree of academic comment.[16] But, ultimately, the task of ascertaining its limits rests with the judiciary and they are now beginning to assume this task as the case is cited to them in different contexts.[17] The first signs are that the courts have been willing to apply the decision and

---

[13] A fact illustrated by the dissent of Lord Hobhouse in the *Blake* case in which he held that compensatory damages provided an adequate remedy on the facts of the case.

[14] [2001] 1 AC 518.   [15] ibid at 588.

[16] See, for example, P Jaffey, 'Disgorgement for Breach of Contract' [2001] RLR 578; A Phang and P-W Lee, 'Rationalising Restitutionary Damages in Contract Law—An Elusive or Illusory Quest' (2001) 17 Journal of Contract Law 240; R Cunnington, 'Equitable Damages: A Model for Restitutionary Damages' (2001) 17 Journal of Contract Law 212; J Edelman, 'Profits and Gains from Breach of Contract' [2001] LMCLQ 9; D Fox, 'Restitutionary Damages to Deter Breach of Contract' [2001] CLJ 33; S Hedley, '"Very Much the Wrong People": The House of Lords and Publication of Spy Memoirs (*A-G v Blake*)' [2000] 4 Web Journal of Current Legal Issues.

[17] See, for example, *Amec Developments Ltd v Jury's Hotel Management (UK) Ltd* [2001] EGLR 81; *Kuddus v Chief Constable of Leicestershire Constabulary* [2001] 2 WLR 1789; *CMS Dolphin Ltd v Simonet* [2001] 2 BCLC 704; *WWF—World Wide Fund for Nature v World Wrestling Federation Entertainment Inc* [2002] FSR 32 and *Esso Petroleum Co Ltd v Niad Ltd*, unreported, Chancery Division, 22 November 2001. It was also cited in passing by Lord Nicholls in his speech in *Kuwait Airways Corp v Iraqi Airways Co (Nos 4 and 5)* [2002] UKHL 19; [2002] 2 WLR 1353 para [87]. Further it has been considered in an arbitral award which, unusually, has been reported in part: *AB Corp v CD Co (The 'Sine Nomine')* [2002] 1 Lloyd's Rep 805. Finally, it been considered by the courts in Australia: see *Hospitality Group Pty Ltd v Australian Rugby Union* [2001] FCA 1040, (2001) ATPR 43, 325. The decision of the Court of Appeal in *Blake* was considered by Elias J in *University of Nottingham v Fishel* [2000] ICR 1462.

that their perception of its scope is, perhaps, broader than that intended by their Lordships in *Blake.*

(a) Blake: The facts

On 4 May 1989 George Blake entered into a contract with the publishers Jonathan Cape Ltd under which he granted to Jonathan Cape Ltd an exclusive right to publish his autobiography. Mr Blake had been a member of the security and intelligence services for a number of years but during that period he had betrayed his country by acting as an agent for the Soviet Union. In his book, entitled 'No Other Choice', Blake recounted some of his activities as a secret intelligence officer. The information disclosed in the book was, by the time of publication, no longer confidential, nor was its disclosure damaging to the public interest. Nevertheless, its disclosure was in breach of contract. On entry to the security and intelligence services Blake signed an Official Secrets Act declaration which included the following:

> I undertake not to divulge any official information gained by me as a result of my employment, either in the press or in book form. I also understand that those provisions apply not only during the period of service but also after employment has ceased.

In failing to submit his manuscript for clearance prior to its publication Blake committed a breach of this undertaking.[18]

Two points merit immediate attention. The first relates to the cause of action. The Crown's case was not initially based on the fact that Blake had broken one of the terms of his contract. The claim at first instance was based solely on the fact that Blake was alleged to have broken the fiduciary duties which he owed to the Crown. Sir Richard Scott V-C rejected this submission.[19] The Crown appealed to the Court of Appeal and sought leave to amend its statement of claim by the addition of a new claim. But that claim was not one for breach of contract. Rather, it was a public law claim, namely that the Attorney-General, as guardian of the public interest, had a duty to oversee the enforcement of the criminal law.[20] The entry

---

[18] This point has been challenged by Hedley ('"Very Much the Wrong People": The House of Lords and Publication of Spy Memoirs (*A-G v Blake*)' [2000] 4 Web Journal of Legal Issues) but it is not necessary to discuss this issue further here. The concern of this paper is with the remedial consequences of a breach of contract and not with the existence of a breach.

[19] [1997] Ch 84.

[20] The Court of Appeal held that Attorney-General was indeed entitled to an injunction restraining the defendant from receiving or from authorizing any person to receive on his behalf any payment or other benefit resulting from or in connection with the exploitation of the book. On appeal the House of Lords held that the court had no power to make such an order. This point will not be further discussed.

of breach of contract into the proceedings was as a consequence of the insistence of the Court of Appeal, not the choice of the parties.[21] Indeed, the Attorney-General declined to advance a submission that 'the Crown might have a private law claim to restitutionary damages for breach of contract',[22] but the Court of Appeal nevertheless proceeded to consider the issue and, in an extended obiter dicta, stated that the general rule that damages for breach of contract are compensatory and not restitutionary was not an absolute rule but was in fact subject to exceptions.[23] Even in the House of Lords it would appear that the primacy of the Crown's private law claim was attributable to an 'invitation'[24] from their Lordships rather than the initiative of the Attorney-General. While *Blake* will undoubtedly be remembered as a case concerned with the remedies available for a breach of contract, it is worth recording that the appearance of the claim was by no means obvious to the parties and its emergence was attributable to judicial insistence[25] rather than the initiative of the parties. The second point to note is that Mr Blake was never present before the court. He was resident at all times in Moscow where he fled after his escape from prison in 1966. His absence from the jurisdiction complicated matters somewhat. Under the terms of his contract with Jonathan Cape Ltd, Blake was entitled to £50,000 on signing the contract, £50,000 on delivery of the manuscript and £50,000 on publication. Of that figure some £60,000 had apparently been paid to Blake. The money so paid was stated to be 'in practice . . . irrecoverable.'[26] It was the £90,000 that remained to be paid to Blake by Jonathan Cape that was the subject of the claim by the Attorney-General. Jonathan Cape were third parties to the litigation, although they did not take part at any stage. The absence of Blake from the jurisdiction did have a significant impact on the case, particularly in terms of the order that was made by the court. There is no doubt that the order would have been different had Blake been present before the court.

It was held by the House of Lords that the Attorney-General was 'entitled to be paid a sum equal to whatever amount is due and owing to Blake from Jonathan Cape under the publishing agreement of 4 May 1989.'[27] It was entitled to recover this sum as a remedy for Blake's breach of contract.

---

[21] See [1998] Ch 439.   [22] ibid, at 456.

[23] The Court of Appeal identified two exceptions to the general rule. The first was described (ibid, at 458) as the case of 'skimped performance', namely where the 'defendant fails to provide the full extent of the services which he has contracted to provide and for which he has charged the plaintiff.' The second was the case in which the defendant obtained his profit 'by doing the very thing which he contracted not to do' (ibid, at 458). This identification of the exceptions did not, however, purport to be exhaustive.

[24] [2001] 1 AC 268, 277.

[25] Which, in turn, was based on research by academics. The role of academics in shaping the direction of the law was generously recognized by the Court of Appeal (see 456).

[26] [2001] 1 AC 268, 275.   [27] ibid at 288.

The 'exceptional'[28] facts of the case were held to demand that Blake account for the profit that he made from his breach. An award of compensatory damages would not have been a 'just response'[29] to his breach of contract. The decision gives rise to a number of issues. Four of these issues merit further consideration, namely: (i) the name given to the remedy, (ii) the circumstances in which the remedy is likely to be available, (iii) the measure of recovery, and (iv) the issues of election and multi-party litigation.

(b) The choice of label

There has been some discussion in the academic literature as to the label that is to be attached to this particular remedy. Should it be called 'restitutionary damages',[30] 'disgorgement damages'[31] or 'gain-based damages'?[32] The issue is not simply one of terminology. Underneath it all lies a debate as to the nature of the cause of action upon which the claimant relies.[33] Is the claim one in unjust enrichment or is it based on the particular wrong alleged to have been committed by the defendant? Lord Nicholls did not expressly enter into this debate, other than to say that he preferred to avoid 'the unhappy expression "restitutionary damages."'[34] But it seems clear from his speech that the cause of action in *Blake* was the breach of contract and that the issue before the court related to the Attorney-General's entitlement to a particular remedy. The name given to that remedy by Lord Nicholls was an account of profits. It could be said that the choice of label does not matter. But, as Lord Steyn observed, 'in law classification is important.'[35] The nomenclature adopted by the court

---

[28] ibid at 286.   [29] ibid.

[30] A phrase used by Professor Birks , 'Rights, Wrongs and Remedies' (2000) 20 OJLS 1, 6.

[31] Professor Lionel Smith has used the word 'disgorgement' but has not combined it with the word 'damages' ('Disgorgement of the Profits of Breach of Contract: Property, Contract and "Efficient Breach"' (1994) 24 Canadian Business Law Journal 121). On the other hand, Dr Edelman in his book *Gain-Based Damages: Contract, Tort, Equity and Intellectual Property* (Hart, 2002) uses the phrase 'disgorgement damages' to describe one of his two categories of gain-based damages. See further n 32.

[32] A generic term used by Dr Edelman in his book *Gain-Based Damages: Contract, Tort, Equity and Intellectual Property* (Hart, 2002). It is, however, important to note that Dr Edelman identifies two measures of gain-based damages, namely restitutionary damages and disgorgement damages. Thus, the label 'gain-based damages' is used at a higher level of generality than the other two labels.

[33] The significance of the distinction is discussed by E McKendrick, 'Restitution and the Misuse of Chattels—The Need for a Principled Approach' in N Palmer and E McKendrick (eds) *Interests in Goods* (2nd edn, 1998) 897, see especially 908–16.

[34] [2001] 1 AC 268, 284. Contrast the view of the Court of Appeal in the case ([1998] Ch 439, 458, 'it would surely be preferable, as well as simpler and more open, to award restitutionary damages').

[35] [2001] 1 AC 268 at 290. See, more generally, E McKendrick, 'Taxonomy: Does it Matter?' in D Johnson and R Zimmermann (eds) *Unjust Enrichment: Key Issues in Comparative Perspective* (Cambridge, 2001) 627.

may not always be significant of itself but, in so far as it provides insight into the nature of the remedy granted, it merits further examination.

The particular point that is worthy of note is Lord Nicholls' dislike of the expression 'restitutionary damages'. In this he is not alone. Dr Harvey McGregor has stated:[36]

> In my lexicon there is 'restitution' and there is 'damages'. I do not say that never the twain shall meet for they meet, and overlap, all the time. But they are entirely different concepts: one deals with assuring compensation for loss to a plaintiff, the other with extracting a benefit from a defendant. Damages should be restricted to compensation for loss. That is what damages are about . . .

The central point here is the attempt to confine damages to compensation for loss. As Dr McGregor acknowledges, this terminological point has implications elsewhere, in particular for nominal damages and exemplary damages. Consistently with this Dr McGregor maintains that nominal damages are 'not really damages at all'[37] and that exemplary damages are an 'anomaly'.[38] But, in the light of *Kuddus*, it is difficult to defend the view that exemplary damages remain an anomaly. They are now a recognized part of the remedial weaponry of the court. And, if the link between damages and compensation for loss can be broken in the case of 'exemplary damages' or 'punitive damages', why can it not also be broken in the context of 'restitutionary damages' or 'gain-based damages'? There is much to be said for the view advocated by Dr Edelman, namely that the word '"damages" can only mean money awards which respond to wrongs.'[39] On this view the word 'damages' is not tied to any particular measure of recovery. There is a range of measures available to the court, all of which can be described as different types of damages. Thus, we have nominal damages, compensatory damages, restitutionary (or disgorgement) damages, and exemplary (or punitive) damages.

However the reasons for Lord Nicholls' unhappiness with the expression 'restitutionary damages' may not be the same as those given by Dr McGregor. There are other possible objections to the phrase. In the first place, it can be objected that the word 'restitution' is ambiguous. It could mean either that the defendant must give up to the claimant the gain which he has made by subtraction from the claimant, or it could mean that the defendant must give up the gain which he has made from his breach of contract, whether or not the gain was made by subtraction from the claimant. As we shall see,[40] there is a difficulty over the measure of

---

[36] 'Restitutionary Damages' in P Birks (ed) *Wrongs and Remedies in the Twenty-First Century* (Oxford, 1996) 203.

[37] ibid ('they are damages in name only and are so described').　　　[38] ibid.

[39] J Edelman, *Gain-Based Damages: Contract, Tort, Equity and Intellectual Property* (Hart, 2002) at 22.

[40] At pp 114–16.

recovery in these cases and the difficulty is caused in part by the fact that the word 'restitution' is used in these two different senses. Secondly, it may be that Lord Nicholls' objection was not confined to the word 'restitutionary' but that it also extended to the word 'damages'. Damages are available as of right, whereas the emphasis in the speeches in *A-G v Blake* is on discretion (albeit a structured discretion) rather than entitlement. The decision to use the label 'account of profits' in preference to 'damages' may serve to emphasize that distinction, namely that the remedy of account of profits is never available as of right, as would be the case with an award of damages, but is an exceptional remedy which is only available in the discretion of the court. Thus, the significance of the choice of phrase may lie, not in the measure of recovery, but in the entitlement, or lack of entitlement, to the remedy.

One further point ought to be made in connection with the use of the language of account of profits, and that relates to its association with equity. The advantage is that it enables an easy link to be made with analogous cases decided in equity, principally cases involving breach of fiduciary duty[41] and breach of confidence.[42] But it must not be allowed to sever the link with analogous common law claims. As Dr Edelman has pointed out, 'precisely the same profit-stripping remedy is available at common law.'[43] Thus, damages assessed by reference to the gain made by the defendant have been awarded in relation to the following torts: trespass to land,[44] trespass to goods,[45] conversion,[46] deceit[47] and, more doubtfully, nuisance,[48] and inducing breach of contract.[49] Lord Nicholls intended no such bifurcation. He stated that it would be 'nothing short of sophistry'[50] to say that an account of profits may be ordered in respect of

[41] See, for example, *Regal (Hastings) Ltd v Gulliver* [1942] 1 All ER 378 and *Boardman v Phipps* [1967] 2 AC 46.

[42] See, for example, *A-G v Guardian Newspapers Ltd (No 2)* [1990] 1 AC 109 and *Peter Pan Manufacturing Corp v Corsets Silhouette Ltd* [1964] 1 WLR 96.

[43] See J Edelman, *Gain-Based Damages: Contract, Tort, Equity and Intellectual Property* (Hart, 2002) at 72. It should, however, be noted that not all of the cases cited at nn 40–5 below are examples of disgorgement damages (at least, in the sense that he uses that phrase).

[44] *Penarth Dock Engineering Co Ltd v Pounds* [1963] 1 Lloyd's Rep 359; *Ministry of Defence v Ashman* [1993] 2 EGLR 102; *Ministry of Defence v Thompson* [1993] 2 EGLR 107.

[45] *Oughton v Seppings* (1830) 1 B & Ad 241; *Strand Electric and Engineering Co Ltd v Brisford Entertainments Ltd* [1952] 2 QB 246.

[46] *Lamine v Dorrell* (1701) 2 Ld Raym 1216; *United Australia Ltd v Barclays Bank Ltd* [1941] AC 1; *Chesworth v Farrar* [1967] 1 QB 407.

[47] *Hill v Perrott* (1810) 3 Taunt 274, but contrast *Halifax Building Society v Thomas* [1996] Ch 217.

[48] *Carr-Saunders v Dick McNeill Associates Ltd* [1986] 1 WLR 922 (although no award was made on the facts of the case).

[49] There is no English case in point but such a claim has succeeded in America in *Federal Sugar Refining Co v The United States Equalisation Board* 268 F 575 (1920), which is frequently cited in English textbooks.

[50] [2001] 1 AC 268, 285.

the equitable wrong of breach of confidence but not in respect of the breach of the contract that governed the relationship between the parties. The jurisdictional divide was not allowed to stand in the way of the development of the law in *A-G v Blake* and it is to be hoped that courts in future cases will draw on the full range of authorities, both common law and equitable, when deciding whether or not it is appropriate to award damages assessed by reference to the gain made by the defendant from his wrong. But there must be a doubt about the ability of the language of account of profits to straddle the jurisdictional divide. It has too strong a bias towards equity and there may be a reluctance to use it to describe a gain-based remedy awarded in respect of a tort.[51] In the past differences in terminology have been allowed to obscure commonalities between remedies[52] and the use of account of profits for equitable wrongs and breach of contract, and restitutionary damages for torts, risks a repetition of this oversight. The law does have an interest in the development of secure and consistent terminology. In the long run it may be necessary to abandon the language of account of profits in favour of some more neutral term, such as 'restitutionary damages' or 'gain-based damages'.[53]

(c) When is an account of profits available?

The second issue that arises out of *A-G v Blake* relates to the circumstances in which the remedy of account of profits is likely to be available in respect of a breach of contract. In deciding that the Attorney-General was entitled to an account of the profit made by Blake as a result of his breach of contract, the House of Lords refused to lay down fixed rules to determine whether or not a claimant is entitled to an account of profits. Thus, Lord Nicholls stated:

> An account of profits will be appropriate in exceptional circumstances. Normally the remedies of [compensatory] damages, specific performance and injunction, coupled with the characterisation of some contractual obligations as fiduciary, will provide an adequate response to a breach of contract. It will be only in exceptional cases, where those remedies are inadequate, that any question of accounting for profits will arise. No fixed rules can be prescribed. The court will have regard to all the circumstances, including the subject matter of the contract, the purpose of the contractual provision which has been breached, the circumstances in which the breach occurred, the consequences of the breach

---

[51] In particular, to the extent that the language of equity might import a discretion where none had previously been thought to exist.

[52] See J Edelman *Gain-Based Damages: Contract, Tort, Equity and Intellectual Property* (Hart, 2002) at 114–18.

[53] It is also the case that account of profits seems to be an inappropriate term in the case where the defendant does not make a profit but simply does not incur an expenditure which it would otherwise have incurred.

and the circumstances in which relief is being sought. A useful general guide, although not exhaustive, is whether the plaintiff had a legitimate interest in preventing the defendant's profit-making activity and, hence, in depriving him of his profit.

The essence of the guidance given by Lord Nicholls can be summarized in three statements. First, the remedy of an account of profits will be available only where other contractual remedies are inadequate. Secondly, the claimant must generally have a 'legitimate interest' in preventing the defendant making or retaining his profit. Thirdly, the court must have regard to 'all the circumstances of the case'. It may fairly be said that these general guidelines largely beg the question: they necessitate definition of words such as 'adequacy' and 'legitimacy'. At this point the quest for legal certainty threatens to degenerate into a somewhat tedious semantic exercise. However, further light can be shed on these guidelines by analysing them within the context of Lord Nicholls' speech. At the same time, this tendency to extrapolate from Lord Nicholls' words must be tempered by the realization, first, that his speech, for all its authority, does not have the force of legislation and so should not be read or interpreted as such and, secondly, that these criteria are broad guidelines, so that it is dangerous to infer from them any principle too hard and fast in application. Indeed, such an extrapolation would be contrary to the central thrust of the speech of Lord Nicholls which is to confer on the court a structured discretion. Nevertheless, bearing these caveats in mind, it is possible to bring some more precision to the nature of the 'exceptional cases'[55] in which an account of profits may be awarded by exploring the three general guidelines that have been identified.

(i) The inadequacy of other remedies

The criterion of 'remedial inadequacy' would appear to be a condition precedent to the award of an account of profits. Plainly it is not a sufficient condition, but it seems to be a necessary one: in the words of Lord Nicholls, it is only where other remedies are inadequate 'that any question of accounting for profits will arise.'[56] Four points can be made in connection with the issue of 'remedial inadequacy'.

The first relates to the range of remedies to which the court must have regard when deciding whether or not they are inadequate. It is clear that Lord Nicholls envisaged remedial inadequacy in terms of all the contractual remedies. He expressly listed '[compensatory] damages, specific performance and injunction, coupled with the characterisation of some

---

[54] [2001] 1 AC 268, 285.   [55] ibid.   [56] ibid.

contractual obligations as fiduciary.'[57] This is an important point. The inquiry is not confined to a comparison with compensatory damages.[58]

This leads on to the second point which is the relationship between the remedy of account of profits and the remedies of specific performance and an injunction. Lord Nicholls expressly drew upon the language of these specific remedies in assessing the availability of an account of profits. Like an account of profits, these remedies are discretionary in nature, and they are available only in circumstances where damages[59] are inadequate. Thus, Lord Nicholls stated:[60]

> In the same way as a plaintiff's interest in performance of a contract may render it just and equitable for the court to make an order for specific performance or grant an injunction, so the plaintiff's interest in performance may make it just and equitable that the defendant should retain no benefit from his breach of contract.

What is the precise nature of the relationship between the specific remedies and an account of profits? The law could adopt one of a number of different positions. The first, which was considered and rejected by the Court of Appeal in *Surrey CC v Bredero Homes Ltd*[61] is that an account of profits should be available 'where the remedies of specific performance and injunction would have been available.'[62] The second is that account of profits should only be available when specific performance is unavailable. 'Unavailable' could here mean either unavailable as a matter of law (for example, one of the bars to specific performance is applicable) or unavailable as a matter of fact (it is not possible for the court to order specific performance because, for example, the breach cannot be undone). The third, and the position actually adopted by Lord Nicholls in the *Blake* case, is that an account of profits should be available only where specific performance

---

[57] ibid.

[58] Contrast *Esso Petroleum Co Ltd v Niad Ltd*, (ChD, 22 November 2001), discussed in more detail at pp 109–12 below.

[59] Although in the case of specific performance the issue is whether or not compensatory damages are inadequate, whereas in the present case the issue is whether or not all other remedies are inadequate. This being the case, a defendant who is faced by a claim for specific performance should not be entitled to claim that specific performance is not available as a remedy because damages (in the form of an account of profits) will be an adequate remedy. Rather, the court should first consider whether or not to grant specific performance and it is only when it has decided not to grant specific performance, or that it is not possible for it to grant specific performance, that it should give consideration to the issue of whether or not the claimant is entitled to recover the profits which the defendant has made from his breach.

[60] [2001] 1 AC 268, 285.   [61] [1993] 1 WLR 1361.

[62] ibid at 1370 *per* Steyn LJ. He dismissed the analogy as a 'bromide formula without any rationale in logic or commonsense.' To similar effect see the judgment of Dillon LJ (at 1368). More generally see R Nolan, 'Remedies for Breach of Contract: Specific Enforcement and Restitution' in F Rose (ed) *Failure of Contracts: Contractual, Restitutionary and Proprietary Consequences* (Hart, 1997) 35.

would be 'inadequate'. What does it mean to say that specific performance would be 'inadequate'? It may be 'inadequate' in the sense that, even if the court made the order, it would not be an adequate response to the breach. But 'inadequacy' may extend beyond that narrow category of case. In particular, it may suffice for a claimant to demonstrate that specific performance is inadequate when account is taken of the fact that it is no longer possible for the court to make a specific performance order. One such case is *Reid-Newfoundland Co v Anglo-American Telegraph Co Ltd*.[63] The defendant railway company agreed not to transmit any telegraph messages along a particular wire except those of the plaintiff telegraph company. It breached that undertaking and was held liable to account as trustee for the profits earned through breach of this undertaking. Had the action been brought prospectively, it seems clear that an injunction would have been available to prevent the breach taking place.[64] But the breach was, by the time of the hearing, a matter of past historical fact and could not be undone. Thus, one situation in which a court may be willing to order an account of profits is the case where it is no longer possible for the court to make a specific performance order or grant an injunction but, had the matter come before the court at an earlier point in time, a specific remedy would have been made available to the claimant. This does not mean 'inadequacy' will be demonstrated in every case where specific performance is no longer available at the time of the hearing before the court. 'Unavailability' cannot be equated with that 'inadequacy' and there may be cases where the factor that prevents the court from making a specific performance order will also persuade it not to order an account of profits.[65] But it would appear to follow from the fact that the specific remedies must be 'inadequate' that the task of the court is first to consider whether or not to make a specific performance order or to grant an injunction and it is only in the case where it concludes that such a remedy would be inadequate that it should give consideration to whether or not to order an account of profits.

The third point relates to the relationship between an account of profits as a remedy for breach of contract and an account of profits as a remedy

---

[63] [1912] AC 555.

[64] As to the limits of the analogy with specific performance, see discussion below (p 107) on the case of *WWF—World Wide Fund for Nature v World Wrestling Federation Entertainment Inc* [2002] FSR 32.

[65] This is a not unimportant point. Take the case of a contract for personal services. Traditionally, a court will not make a specific performance order in the case of a contract for personal services. The courts should be similarly reluctant to award an account of profits in such cases because the effect of making such an award may be indirectly to compel the defendant to remain a party to this personal relationship notwithstanding the defendant's wish to terminate the relationship and conclude a contract with another party: see *University of Nottingham v Fishel* [2000] ICR 1462, 1488.

for some other wrong, such as breach of fiduciary duty.[66] Lord Nicholls' statement that account must be taken of the 'characterisation of some contractual obligations as fiduciary' appears to suggest that in such a case the claimant should pursue its remedy for breach of fiduciary duty and, if that claim is successful, there is no remedial inadequacy and there is therefore no need to consider whether the claimant is entitled to an account of profits for the breach of contract.[67] This tells us that the remedy of account of profits for breach of contract is seen very much as a residual remedy. It is a remedy of last resort and not, as some commentators appear to think,[68] a remedy of primary resort. It is only when all other remedies fail to do justice on the facts of the case that a court should consider awarding an account of profits in respect of a breach of contract.

The final point relates to the meaning of the word 'inadequacy'. What does it mean, to say that other remedies are 'inadequate'? Does it suffice for the claimant to show that compensatory damages would be difficult to assess or are hard to prove? What of the case where the claimant could have, but did not, seek specific performance or an injunction? Can a defendant in such a case maintain that there is no remedial inadequacy because of the claimant's failure to avail himself of the range of remedies available to him? We shall return to some of these questions below.

(ii) Legitimate interest

The suggestion that the claimant must have a legitimate interest in depriving the defendant of his profit does not have the character of a necessary condition. It is a 'useful general guide' but 'non-exhaustive'.[69] The difficulty relates to the meaning of the phrase 'legitimate interest'. In *White & Carter (Councils) Ltd v McGregor*[70] Lord Reid flirted with a test based on whether or not the claimant had a 'legitimate interest, financial or otherwise, in performing the contract rather than claiming damages'[71] but

---

[66] Lord Nicholls stated that Blake's undertaking was 'closely akin to a fiduciary obligation' ([2001] 1 AC 268 at 287). Had it been a fiduciary obligation there would, presumably, have been no need to consider whether account of profits was available in respect of the breach of contract because it would have been available in respect of the breach of fiduciary duty. It was the fact that the breach was not a breach of fiduciary duty that compelled the court to consider whether or not account of profits could be available in respect of a breach of contract and the fact that the breach bordered on a breach of fiduciary duty may have been a factor which helped to persuade the court to order an account of profits.

[67] There may possibly be circumstances where there is no effective remedy in relation to the allegation of breach of fiduciary duty and it is necessary for the court to order an account of profits in respect of the breach of contract, but it is difficult to think of an example of this: cf Lawrence Collins J in *CMS Dolphin Ltd v Simonet* [2001] 2 BCLC 704, 747.

[68] See, for example, D Campbell and D Harris, 'In defence of breach: a critique of restitution and the performance interest' (2002) 22 LS 208.

[69] [2001] 1 AC 268, 285.   [70] [1962] AC 413.   [71] ibid, at 431.

subsequent judicial response to it has been distinctly frosty.[72] Thus, the guidance obtainable from other parts of the law of contract in terms of identifying the meaning of 'legitimate interest' is likely to be limited.

Must the claimant's legitimate interest relate to his interest in performance of the contract, his interest in preventing the defendant from making a profit, or both? While mention was made of the claimant's interest in performance,[73] the focus of this part of Lord Nicholls' speech was on the Crown's interest in preventing Blake from making a profit from his wrong. On this point he concluded that that 'the Crown had and has a legitimate interest in preventing Blake profiting from the disclosure of official information, whether classified or not, while a member of the service and thereafter.'[74] The need to maintain confidence, trust and morale among members of the secret services was held to be sufficient to give the Crown a legitimate interest in depriving Blake of his profit. The answer to the question of whether or not a particular claimant has a 'legitimate interest' in depriving the defendant of his profit will depend, to a substantial extent, on the facts of the individual case. But it is suggested that it will be difficult for a claimant to demonstrate the existence of such an interest in the case of a breach of an ordinary commercial contract. The mere fact that a contract has been concluded between the parties does not appear to be enough, of itself, to give rise to a legitimate interest. 'Something more' is required but the ingredients of that 'something more' largely remain to be established.

(iii) *The circumstances of the case*

Finally, Lord Nicholls stated that regard must be had to 'all the circumstances of the case'. His non-exhaustive list of these circumstances included:[75]

> the subject matter of the contract, the purpose of the contractual provision which has been breached, the circumstances in which the breach occurred, the consequences of the breach and the circumstances in which relief is being sought.

As far as the 'subject matter of the contract' is concerned it would appear that the courts may be more willing to award an account of profits where the subject matter of the contract concerns confidential information or property. But this will not always be the case. A claim for an account of profits in respect of a breach of contract was refused in *WWF—World Wide*

---

[72] See, for example, *Attica Sea Carriers Corp v Ferrostaal Poseidon Bulk Reederei GmbH (The Puerto Buitrago)* [1976] 1 Lloyd's Rep 250, 254–6 and *Clea Shipping Corporation v Bulk Oil International Ltd (The Alaskan Trader)* [1984] 1 All ER 129, 133–8.
[73] [2001] 1 AC 268, 285A.   [74] ibid, at 287.   [75] [2001] 1 AC 268 at 285.

Fund for Nature v World Wrestling Federation Entertainment Inc.[76] even though the relevant contract concerned the use of intellectual property rights. The claimant and the defendant each had registered trade marks which were in many respects similar to one another. In 1994 they entered into a contract which aimed to prevent either party infringing upon the merchandizing of the other. The claimant alleged that the defendant had breached the terms of this contract and sought to recover, *inter alia*, an account of profits and reliance was placed upon the decision in *Blake*. Jacob J. refused to order an account. He stated:[77]

> I can see nothing which makes this case of the exceptional character called for by the decision in *Blake*. All one really has here is a negative covenant. The fact that it relates to use of initials and so is a bit 'trademark-ish' or 'IP-ish' does not mean the common law should provide what Parliament provides by statute for an infringement of a registered mark or intellectual property right. It would indeed be odd if breach of an ordinary full restraint of trade clause (e.g. not to work in a defined area at a defined job for a defined period of time) did not attract an account [of profits], whereas breach of a lesser restraint (not to use a mark in a trade otherwise permitted) did.

It is clear, therefore, that subject-matter alone cannot be decisive. Contracts concerning proprietary interests and confidentiality have always received special protection in the courts, but only where those rights are such that compensatory damages would be inadequate to protect them effectively. In the *WWF* case, the court found that other remedies were in fact adequate to protect the claimant's interests, so no account of profits was necessary. This decision is interesting because it also illustrates the limits of the analogy with the specific remedies. Had the claimant sought an injunction at the time the breach commenced, the court would doubtless have awarded one. However, in the subsequent action for breach of contract, this fact was insufficient to convince Jacob J that an account of profits should be available in response to the breach. 'Remedial inadequacy' must therefore be assessed with close reference to the facts of each case.

The list of 'circumstances' provided by Lord Nicholls is also notable for its omissions. In particular, he omits from the list subjective considerations such as the defendant's motive or degree of intent.[78] Later in his speech he noted that the fact that the breach was 'cynical and deliberate' did not, of

---

[76] [2002] FSR 32. The Court of Appeal subsequently dismissed an appeal from the decision of Jacob J ([2002] EWCA Civ 196; [2002] FSR 33) but it was not necessary for them to consider the scope of the decision in *Blake*. The House of Lords on 10 June 2002 refused an application for leave to appeal from the decision of the Court of Appeal.

[77] [2002] FSR 32, at para [62] of the judgment.

[78] Unless this is encompassed within 'the circumstances in which the breach occurred.'

itself, amount to a good reason for ordering an account of profits. Counsel for Blake submitted that:[79]

> To concentrate on the motive of the party who committed the breach is contrary to the general approach to the assessment of damages in contract. It will lead to uncertainty in the assessment of damages in commercial and consumer disputes where predictability is important.

The response of their Lordships to the submission was to play down the relevance of the motive of the party in breach. The exception was the dissenting speech of Lord Hobhouse. He stated that the reasoning of Lord Nicholls did not reflect 'the essentially punitive nature of the claim.'[80] A cynical view of the *Blake* case would say that the majority underplayed the significance of the motive of the party in breach because they wished to cloak the quasi-criminal overtones of the order they were making. This is to over-state the case. It is clear that the judges had no sympathy for the position of Blake. But, at the same time, they were aware that their decision had implications beyond its immediate facts. In particular, they had to consider its impact on ordinary commercial contracts. A conclusion that the motive of the breaching party was the decisive factor would have had major (and undesirable) implications for ordinary commercial litigation. In order to avoid this, it was necessary to adopt a more balanced approach and their Lordships sought to do this by giving more emphasis to the interest of the claimant in performance, and in restraining the defendant from making a profit, than to the standard of conduct and the motivation of the defendant. In doing so they no doubt hoped to provide a secure framework for the future development of the law. Their hopes have not, as yet, been realized. The immediate impact of the decision in *Blake* has been to generate uncertainty and that uncertainty can be demonstrated by contrasting the reasoning in the following two cases.

(iv) Initial uncertainty

The first case is the decision of Morritt V-C in *Esso Petroleum Co Ltd v Niad Ltd*.[81] and the second is the award of an arbitral tribunal, partly reported under the name of *AB Corp v CD Co (The 'Sine Nomine')*.[82] These cases have not been chosen for their precedent value (the arbitral award does not

---

[79] [2001] 1 AC 268, 272.

[80] ibid, at 295. See to similar effect his conclusion (at 299) that the policy that was being enforced by the majority was one which required 'Blake to be punished by depriving him of any benefit from anything connected with his past deplorable conduct.'

[81] Unreported (ChD, 22 November 2001). While an appeal was made to the Court of Appeal, Civil Division, docket A3/2001/2785, filed 14 December 2001, the case has since been settled.

[82] [2002] 1 Lloyd's Rep 805, noted by J Beatson (2002) 118 LQR 377.

have any). Rather they have been chosen because they reveal very different perceptions of the scope of the decision in *Blake* and so illustrate the uncertainty that currently exists in commercial practice.

In *Esso v. Niad* the defendant ('Niad') sold petrol as a franchisee of the claimant ('Esso'). The parties had concluded an agreement whereby, as part of a national marketing campaign ('Pricewatch'), Niad undertook not to sell petrol above the maximum price recommended by Esso. In return, Esso paid Niad certain price-support payments. In breach of this contract, Niad repeatedly sold petrol at prices above the instructed maxima. Esso brought a claim for compensatory damages but the difficulty with this claim lay in establishing the value of the sales lost as a result of the defendant's failure to charge at or below the recommended price. So it advanced an alternative claim. Relying upon the decision of the House of Lords in *A-G v Blake*, it sought an account of the profits earned by the defendant as a result of selling petrol at the inflated price. Morritt V-C held that Esso was entitled to an account of profits. He relied upon four factors in reaching this conclusion, namely: (i) damages was an inadequate remedy; (ii) the obligation to implement and maintain the recommended pump prices was fundamental to Pricewatch; (iii) complaint was made of the defendant on four occasions and the defendant gave the appearance of complying with Esso's complaint when notified of it; and (iv) Esso had a legitimate interest in preventing the defendant from profiting from its breach of obligation.

On the other side of the line is *AB Corp v CD Co (The 'Sine Nomine')*, an arbitral award which, unusually, has been published in part in an English law report. The case concerned the wrongful withdrawal of a vessel from a charterparty by its owners ('the respondents'). The charterers sought to recover any profits made by the respondents from the alternative use made of the vessel and relied upon *A-G v Blake* to bolster their submission. The arbitrators rejected the claim for wrongful profits and did so in forthright language. They stated:[83]

> It is by no means uncommon for commercial contracts to be broken deliberately because a more profitable opportunity has arisen. Or the contract-breaker takes an over-generous view of his rights, knowing that the law may ultimately be against him. In such a case he may have little or nothing to lose by taking a chance; the downside at worst is that he will have to pay the costs of both sides. International commerce on a large scale is red in tooth and claw. We do not say that the Respondents' action was either deliberate or cynical wrongdoing in this case; they had a respectable argument on liability, although a commercial judge refused their application for leave to appeal.

---

[83] [2002] 1 Lloyd's Rep 805, 806.

Our solution to the present problem is that there should not be an award of wrongful profits where both parties are dealing with a marketable commodity— the services of a ship in this case—for which a substitute can be found in the market place. In the ordinary way the damages which the claimant suffers by having to buy in at the market price will be equal to the profit which the wrongdoer makes by having his goods or his ships' services to sell at a higher price. It is in the nature of things unlikely that the wrongdoer will make a greater profit than that. And if he does, it is an adventitious benefit which he can keep. The commercial law of this country should not make moral judgments, or seek to punish contract-breakers; we do not, for example, award triple damages, as in the USA.

The contrast between these two decisions is sharp. The arbitral award attempts, as far as possible, to confine the scope of *A-G v Blake*, whereas *Esso v Niad* demonstrates that an account of profits may be recovered in the case of a breach of an ordinary commercial contract.[84] Of the two decisions it is submitted that it is the decision in *Esso v Niad* that is the troublesome one.

Most of the elements relied upon by Morritt V-C to support his finding that Esso was entitled to an account of profits are a source of some concern. The first relates to his finding that damages were inadequate. The reason given for the inadequacy was that it was 'almost impossible to attribute lost sales to a breach by one out of several hundred dealers who operated Pricewatch.'[85] A number of difficulties arise here. The first is that it is not clear that problems of proof should lead to the conclusion that damages are not an adequate remedy. Should a claimant in such a case be entitled to abandon the normal forensic inquiry into proof of loss in favour of a claim based on a completely different method of assessment, namely the profit made by the defendant? Secondly, Esso's loss could have been quantified by means other than lost sales, for example, damage to reputation or loss of goodwill. This is especially relevant in a franchise situation, where the franchisee effectively rents the franchisor's brand, reputation, and goodwill to generate sales. Placing a figure on such a loss would undoubtedly involve an element of arbitrariness, but no more so than when the courts award sums for loss of life or limb (indeed less so, since business goodwill is a tradeable commodity upon which the market, and hence the court, is ready to place an objective value).[86] It is hard to see why such an award would not have been adequate to compensate Esso. Thirdly, it appears that Morritt V-C confined his consideration to the adequacy of compensatory damages. He did not consider the specific remedies. But he did consider another alternative claim, namely whether or not Esso had a claim to a 'restitutionary remedy.' He stated:[87]

---

[84] *Pace* Lord Hobhouse; [2001] 1 AC 268, 299.
[86] *Trego v Hunt* [1896] AC 7.
[85] ChD, 22 November 2001, para [63].
[87] ChD, 22 November 2001, para [64].

It is undoubted that Niad obtained a benefit, in the form of the price support, to which it was only entitled it if complied with its obligation to implement and maintain the recommended pump prices to be supported. In these circumstances it can hardly be denied that Niad was enriched to the extent that it charged pump prices in excess of the recommended prices. The enrichment was unjust because it was obtained in breach of contract. It was obtained at the expense of Esso because Esso was providing price support for a lower price than that charged by Niad. I can see no reason why this remedy should be unavailable to Esso if it wishes to pursue it. Indeed it appears to me to be the most appropriate remedy in that it matches most closely the reality of the case, namely that Niad took an extra benefit to which it was not entitled.

This statement is also problematic. In the first place the Vice-Chancellor does not identify the cause of action which entitles Esso to this 'restitutionary remedy' nor does he provide grounds for distinguishing it from the remedy of account of profits available in respect of the breach of contract. Secondly, to the extent that Esso was entitled to a restitutionary remedy one would have thought, on the basis of Lord Nicholls' speech in *Blake*, that it would have operated to deny to Esso its claim for an account of profits in respect of the breach of contract on the ground that the remedies available to Esso were no longer inadequate. This is particularly so if, as the Vice-Chancellor stated, the 'restitutionary remedy' was the 'most appropriate remedy' on the facts of the case. If the account of profits is truly an exceptional remedy for breach of contract then the availability of other adequate remedies should act to preclude it.

The second element relied upon by Morritt V-C, the importance of the term broken, is more straightforward. One would expect the court to have regard to this factor, although the weight to be attached to it is a more difficult matter. The third element, the conduct of the defendant, is more troublesome in so far as it gives prominence to a factor which the House of Lords was anxious to down play in *Blake*. It seems that the intentional nature of the breach, coupled with the defendant's deceitful conduct, influenced the Vice-Chancellor's decision to grant an account of profits. This highlights what may turn out to be a natural judicial tendency, namely to impose this extraordinary measure of liability in cases where a greater degree of fault or dishonesty can be proved. The courts will eventually have to decide whether the defendant's state of mind is relevant or irrelevant in assessing whether or not to order an account of profits.[88] Finally, in relation to the 'legitimate interest' factor, Morritt V-C offered no analysis. He simply concluded that Esso 'undoubtedly' had one. The

---

[88] Would Morritt V-C have granted Esso the account of profits if Niad had breached its contract inadvertently?

factor seems to have been used as a label to justify a decision that had already been reached and not as an element to be considered when deciding whether or not to grant the remedy.

In many ways the decision in *Esso v Niad* gives support to those who argue that the effect of *A-G v Blake* will be to introduce an unacceptable degree of uncertainty into commercial transactions. At this point it is necessary to recall the warning given by Lord Hobhouse in his dissenting speech in *Blake* :[89]

> I must also sound a further note of warning that if some more extensive principle of awarding non-compensatory damages for breach of contract is to be introduced into our commercial law, the consequences will be very far-reaching and disruptive. I do not believe that such is the intention of your Lordships but if others are tempted to try to extend the decision of the present exceptional case to commercial situations so as to introduce restitutionary rights beyond those presently recognised by the law of restitution, such a step will require very careful consideration before it is acceded to.

But it is submitted that it is *Esso v Niad* that is wrong and not *A-G v Blake*. The decision in *Esso* is wrong because it adopts too liberal an approach to the concept of remedial inadequacy and it fails to recognize the exceptional, subsidiary nature of the claim for an account of profits.

(d) The measure of recovery

A number of problems are likely to arise in terms of measuring the recovery to which the claimant is entitled. Here it suffices to point out three issues. The first relates to the definition of 'profit', the second relates to the share of the defendant's profit which the claimant is entitled to recover, and the third concerns the causation and remoteness rules that will be used to place a limit on the extent to which a defendant can be deprived of a profit he has made.

(i) What is a profit?

What is a profit for the purposes of the remedy of an account of profits? Does it mean net profit or gross profit? Will defendants be entitled to an allowance to the extent that their skill and enterprise contributed to the profit made? In the present state of the authorities, it is extremely difficult to answer these questions.[90] It seems clear that, on the facts of *A-G v Blake*,

---

[89] [2001] 1 AC 268, 299.

[90] Useful guidance as to possible answers can be gleaned from D Friedmann, 'Restitution for Wrongs: The Measure of Recovery' (2001) 79 Texas Law Review 1879.

profit meant gross profit and that Blake would not have been given any allowance for the time, skill, and effort which he put into writing the book. But, in terms of the measure of recovery, there may well emerge a difference between the position of the deliberate wrongdoer and the position of an innocent wrongdoer. The latter is much more likely than the former to be given an allowance for his skill and effort in making the profit.[91]

However, in *Blake* itself there are two apparent inconsistencies between the order as granted and the stated goal of requiring Blake to disgorge the profits which he earned through his breach of contract. The first was that, although the aggregate profits earned by Blake through his breach amounted to £150,000, the order only related to £90,000. But this was a reflection of the fact that, as has been noted, £60,000 had already been paid by Jonathan Cape, the publishers of the book, to Blake in Moscow and that sum was conceded to be practically irrecoverable. It might be argued that, in principle, the order for the account of profits should have extended to the full amount of the profits earned from the breach, notwithstanding any practical problems that might arise in the enforcement of that order. However, this sentiment contradicts the pragmatic tone of Lord Nicholls' speech. He would not have exercised the court's discretion to grant an exceptional remedy unless the order so granted was likely to be enforced.

The second inconsistency between the stated purpose of the *Blake* remedy and the order actually granted lay in the deductions that the third-party was allowed to make. Blake's publishers, Jonathan Cape, remained in possession of the £90,000. They were third-party litigants, as Blake brought third party proceedings against them for payment of the £90,000. The order granted by the House of Lords allowed Jonathan Cape to deduct from the sum payable to the Crown legal expenses incurred in resisting these actions. This deduction did not arise out of any pre-existing legal entitlement; set-off does not permit A to set off his liabilities to B against debts owed him by C.[92] The effect of the deduction was to reduce Blake's liability to an amount less than the 'profit' earned through the breach of contract. But the approach is doubtless justifiable on the facts of the case; it would offend commonsense to force the third party to bear its own costs while the claimant received what was ultimately a 'windfall' award. The Crown had a legitimate interest in 'depriving the defendant of his profit', but this does not necessarily translate into a legitimate interest in acquiring it itself. Therefore it may be that the 'profits' recoverable under the remedy in *Blake* are to be assessed on a pragmatic basis with deductions allowed in appropriate cases. That being so, it might be appropriate to say

---

[91] Perhaps on the basis of *Boardman v Phipps* [1967] 2 AC 46. cf *Guinness plc v Saunders* [1990] 2 AC 663.

[92] See, for example, *BCCI v Prince Fahd Bin Salaman Abdul Aziz Al-Saud* [1997] BCC 63.

that following *A-G v Blake* an account of profits is available in response to a breach of contract if *and in so far as* it is necessary to do justice on the facts of the case.

(ii) The amount of the profit recoverable

On the facts of *Blake* the House of Lords held that the Crown was entitled to recover the balance held by the third party, Jonathan Cape. This suggests that, had he been subject to the jurisdiction of the court, Blake would have been accountable to the Crown for the entirety of his profit. But in other cases it would appear that the claimant is only entitled to recover a portion of the profit made by the defendant from his breach of contract. *Wrotham Park Estate Co Ltd v Parkside Homes Ltd*[93] demonstrates this. The defendant built houses on its own land in breach of a restrictive covenant. Brightman J. awarded the plaintiff damages of £2,500, which represented some 5 per cent of the defendant's anticipated profits from the breach. In *A-G v Blake* Lord Nicholls noted[94] that the Crown sought to go further than Brightman J. had been prepared to go in *Wrotham Park Estate* in that the claim was for 'all the profits of Blake's book' and not simply for a 'reasonable payment in respect of the benefit' Blake obtained from his breach.

This difference in the measure of recovery between the cases of *Blake* and *Wrotham Park Estate* raises the question of whether or not the two cases are governed by the same principle. One view, adopted by Lord Hobhouse in his dissenting speech in *A-G v Blake,* is that *Wrotham Park Estate* is 'an example of compensatory damages'[95] on the basis that the plaintiff had lost 'the sum which he could have exacted from the defendant as the price of his consent to the development'.[96] On this view *Wrotham Park Estate* belongs in a different doctrinal category in that it is concerned with the recovery of losses not gains. While this view has its supporters,[97] it was not the view of Lord Nicholls.[98] He stated that *Wrotham Park Estate* was a case in which damages were measured by reference to the 'benefit gained by the wrongdoer from the breach.'[99] If this is so, on what basis should subsequent courts decide whether to award the claimant a per-

---

[93] [1974] 1 WLR 798.   [94] [2001] 1 AC 268, 284.   [95] [2001] 1 AC 268, 298.

[96] ibid.

[97] See, for example, R Sharpe and S Waddams, 'Damages for Lost Opportunity to Bargain' (1982) 2 OJLS 290.

[98] Although Lord Nicholls does accept that this 'analysis is correct' with respect to the cases in which damages were awarded under Lord Cairns's Act ([2001] 1 AC 268, at 281).

[99] [2001] 1 AC 268, 283–4.

centage of the defendant's profit or the entirety of that profit? One answer is that there is no principle capable of yielding an answer to this question. We must simply leave it to the (structured) discretion of the court and that, over time, guidance will emerge from reported cases that will assist the judges in the exercise of their discretion. An alternative view, powerfully advocated by Dr Edelman[100] is that there are two distinct measures of gain-based damages and that they are driven by different underlying principles. The first he terms 'restitutionary damages' which he defines as 'damages which reverse wrongful transfers of wealth from a claimant by subtracting the objective benefit received by the defendant.'[101] The second he labels 'disgorgement damages' and this is measured not by reference to what has been transferred by the claimant but by 'the actual profit accruing to the defendant from the wrong.'[102] *Wrotham Park Estate Co Ltd v Parkside Homes Ltd* is an example of the award of restitutionary damages, while *A-G v Blake* is an example of disgorgement damages. The rationales which underpin the two measures of recovery are different. In the case of restitutionary damages these 'should in theory always be available for wrongs'[103] and their rationale is that 'because the transfer was procured by the defendant's wrong the law should not recognise the validity of the transfer of the money or benefit transferred and should reverse the transfer from the claimant to the defendant.'[104] Disgorgement damages have a different rationale and their availability is, in consequence, more restricted. Their rationale is 'deterrence of wrongdoing'[105] and they should be available where compensatory damages are insufficient to deter wrongdoing.[106] The proposition that restitutionary damages should always in principle be available in respect of a wrongful transfer of wealth is one that requires careful consideration and it is beyond the scope of this paper to provide that consideration. Here it suffices to note that Dr Edelman does purport to provide a principled basis for distinguishing between the respective measures of recovery in the *Wrotham Park Estate* and *Blake* cases. In this respect it appears to offer a better alternative

---

[100] *Gain-Based Damages: Contract, Tort, Equity and Intellectual Property* (Hart, 2002). See in particular Chapter 3 where the division between the two measures is discussed in some detail. It is then applied to breach of contract in Chapter 5.

[101] ibid, at 68.   [102] ibid, at 72.

[103] ibid, at 81. This is subject to the caveat, important in the present context, that in the case of restitutionary damages for breach of contract the courts must consider whether or not the claimant has a 'legitimate interest' in depriving the defendant of his benefit: see ibid, 172–4.

[104] ibid, at 80.   [105] ibid, at 83.

[106] Dr Edelman identifies two circumstances in which compensatory damages are insufficient to deter wrongdoing. The first is where the wrong has been committed 'deliberately and cynically' (ibid, at 84), and the second is 'where there are institutions which require such a degree of protection that the prospect of gain for even inadvertent wrongdoing should be removed and potential defendants should be put on their guard' (ibid, at 85). Fiduciary relationships are 'institutions' that fall within the latter category.

than leaving the matter to the discretion of the court, although in favour of the latter approach it can be said that a discretionary approach, which has regard to the 'justice of the case' and to all the circumstances of the case, is more in keeping with the general tenor of Lord Nicholls' speech.

(iii) Causation, remoteness and mitigation

The third issue that merits discussion in terms of the measure of recovery relates to the development of rules that will place limits upon the liability of the defendant. What are the rules that will determine whether or not profit is attributable to the defendant's breach of contract? When will the profit be too remote a consequence of the breach of contract? Can a defendant deduct from the profit which he must disgorge to the claimant the profit he would have made in an alternative business or occupation in which he would have become involved had he not been involved in his wrongful conduct (the so-called 'mitigation' of profits)? In the present state of the authorities no clear answers can be given to these questions.

The Court of Appeal in *Blake* distinguished between profits that 'are occasioned directly by the breach' and cases where the breach 'merely provides the defendant with the opportunity' to make the profit.[107] This distinction may prove to be a difficult one to draw. An illustrative case is provided by the facts of *Teacher v Calder*.[108] The pursuer agreed to invest £25,000 in the defender's timber business. In return, the defender promised that he would keep at least £15,000 of his own money in the business. In breach of contract, the defender withdrew much of his capital from the business and invested the money in a distillery, where he earned large profits. The pursuer sought to recover, by way of damages, the profits which the defender had made as a result of his investment in the distillery. His claim failed. It was held that damages should be assessed by reference to the loss which the timber business had suffered as a result of the failure of the defender to keep the promised sum of money invested in the business. It is unlikely that the result in *Teacher v Calder* would be affected by *A-G v Blake*.[109] The pursuer's expectation was that a certain sum of money would be invested and retained in his business and the effect of the damages remedy was to put the pursuer into that position. There was no justification for going further and requiring the defender to disgorge the profit that he had made from his investment in the distillery. Two reasons can be given in support of this conclusion. The first is that compensatory damages were an adequate remedy for the breach so that

---

[107] [1998] Ch 439, 458.   [108] (1899) 1 F (HL) 39; [1899] AC 451.

[109] For a contrary view see D Campbell, 'The Treatment of *Teacher v Calder* in *AG v Blake*' (2002) 65 MLR 256.

the court never had a jurisdiction to award an account of profits. Secondly, it can be argued that there was no sufficient causal nexus between the breach and the profit.

What constitutes a sufficient causal nexus for this purpose? But for his breach of contract the defender, Mr Calder, would not have made his investment, and so would not have reaped his profit. However, anyone can make an investment; not everyone can turn it to profit. Mr Calder might have put the money in an ordinary bank account, or he might have kept the cash under his bed; he might have given it away to his friends, or he might have invested it poorly and lost the lot. His skill in choosing wisely among all the possible uses to which the money could have been put was not attributable to the breach of contract. It could be said that the defender's business acumen was a *novus actus interveniens* which operated to break the chain of causation between the breach of contract and the profit earned.[110] The defender's breach of contract occurred when he withdrew the £15,000 from the timber business. From that point forward he was liable to compensate the pursuer for his losses. The defender's liability to the pursuer should not then vary depending upon his fortunes on the stock market. The sufficiency of the causal nexus is unlikely to present significant difficulties in the case where the defendant makes his profit by doing the very thing that he contracted not to do. In such a case it is likely to be clear that the profit was occasioned directly by the breach. But in the case where the breach simply gives to the defendant a choice as to what is to be done with the resource that had been contractually committed to the claimant, causation problems are likely to be much more difficult to resolve. Either the courts will have to develop rules to distinguish between cases where the profits were occasioned directly by the breach and cases where the breach merely presented the defendant with an opportunity to make a profit, or they can develop more liberal rules of causation but then grant to defendants a (generous) allowance for their skill[111] in reaping the particular profit.

(e) Election and multi-party litigation

Two final issues fall to be considered in relation to the remedy of account of profits. The first is concerned with the application of the doctrine of election

---

[110] A different result is reached if a 'property'-based analysis is used based on cases such as *FC Jones (Trustee in Bankruptcy) v Jones* [1997] Ch 159. In such cases where the defendant invests the claimant's asset the earning potential inherent in the asset is attributed in law to the claimant and the defendant's business acumen is not a *novus actus interveniens*. For a critical analysis of the effect of property concepts and the law of tracing in this area see D Friedmann, 'Restitution for Wrongs: The Measure of Recovery' (2001) 79 Texas Law Review 1879, 1904–17.

[111] Or luck?

and the second with the problems that may arise where there are either multiple claimants or multiple defendants involved in the litigation.

(i) Election

In connection with the doctrine of election it is necessary to distinguish between two distinct issues. The first is whether or not the claimant has a free choice as between the different measures of recovery and the second is whether or not it is possible for a claimant to combine two different measures of recovery, (for example compensatory damages and an account of profits) within the same claim. The latter is properly the subject-matter of the doctrine of election. But it is also necessary to say something about the former issue. It is not the case that the claimant has a free choice as to whether or not to recover the profits that the defendant has made from the breach. As *Blake* makes clear it is for the court to decide whether or not an account of profits is an available remedy on the facts of the case and the claimant cannot insist that the court grant this particular remedy.[112] It is a discretionary remedy and the parties cannot exercise that discretion for the court. But, once the court decides that an account of profits is available as a remedy on the facts of the case, the claimant is then given a choice as to the remedy which she wishes to pursue. Thus, in *Esso v Niad* Morritt V-C had first to decide whether or not Esso was entitled to seek an account of profits and it was only once he had answered that question in the affirmative that he stated that 'Esso will have to elect which of these alternative remedies to pursue.'[113]

The statement that Esso must choose between 'alternative remedies' also answers our second question. A claimant cannot combine a claim for account of profits with a claim for compensatory damages.[114] He must choose between them.[115] This requirement has been criticized on the basis that there is no necessary inconsistency between a claim in respect of a loss suffered by the claimant and a claim to recover the profit made by the defendant provided that there is no element of double recovery.[116] The difficulty with the argument that it should be possible to combine claims in this way is that it might give rise to difficulty in practice in terms of deciding whether or not there has been any element of double recovery.

---

[112] Of course, the claimant can decide not to seek the remedy.

[113] ChD, 22 November 2001, para [65].

[114] In *Kuwait Airways Corp v Iraqi Airways Co (Nos 4 and 5)* [2002] UKHL 19 para [87] Lord Nicholls of Birkenhead stated that, in an appropriate case, damages may be awarded on the 'user principle' in addition to compensation for loss suffered. In the terminology of Dr Edelman this can be understood to mean that it is possible to claim both 'restitutionary damages' and compensatory damages so that the need to elect only applies as between 'disgorgement damages' and compensatory damages.

[115] *Tang Man Sit v Capacious Investments Ltd* [1996] AC 514.

[116] See Birks (1996) 112 LQR 375.

The rule that requires the claimant to make his election has the great merit that it is much easier to operate in practice and it should not give rise to injustice provided that the claimant is aware of the need to make a choice and chooses the remedy that is most appropriate on the facts of the case.

(ii) Multiple claimants and multiple defendants

What is to be done in the case where a number of defendants make a profit by committing the same breach of contract? Suppose that in *Esso v Niad* a number of garages had got together and had all broken their contracts with Esso? It is suggested that the addition of further defendants should not change the legal principle applicable. Each defendant would be accountable to Esso for the profit that it made from its breach of contract. But suppose that the problem was not one of multiple defendants but multiple claimants. Take the case where, in breach of contract, a supplier systematically over-charges its customers and makes an enormous profit in doing so. Assuming that the customers are entitled to an account of profits how should a court deal with litigation of this nature? No clear answer can be given to this question. It is, however, important to point out the nature of the problem in this case. It is not one that relates to the liability of the defendant because his liability cannot exceed the amount of the profit he has made from the breach. Rather, the problem is one which relates to the division of that profit among the various claimants.

2. PUNITIVE DAMAGES

The orthodox position is that punitive damages cannot be recovered for a breach of contract,[117] but that orthodoxy may come under some pressure as a result of the decision of the House of Lords in *Kuddus v Chief Constable of Leicestershire Constabulary*.[118] The narrow question before the House of Lords in that case was whether or not exemplary damages can be awarded for the tort of misfeasance in public office. However, the significance of the case transcends this relatively narrow point because, in order to reach their decision on the narrow point of law, their Lordships took the much bigger step of ridding the law of the 'cause of action' test which has for so long kept punitive damages in chains. Thus, in order to recover exemplary damages it is no longer necessary for a claimant to establish that exemplary damages had been awarded in respect of that particular cause of action prior to the decision of the House of Lords in *Rookes v Barnard*.[119]

---

[117] *Addis v Gramophone Co Ltd* [1909] AC 488.   [118] [2001] 2 WLR 1789.
[119] [1964] AC 1129.

The availability of exemplary damages in future cases will turn on whether or not they fall within the two categories of case recognized by Lord Devlin in *Rookes v Barnard*, namely oppressive, arbitrary or unconstitutional action by servants of the government and cases in which the defendant's conduct has been calculated by him to make a profit for himself which may well exceed the compensation payable to the claimant. The scope of these categories may change slightly over time[120] but they are likely to form the foundation for the modern law.

The extent to which this emancipation will result in the greater availability of exemplary damages is presently the matter of some doubt. It is possible to confine the abolition of the 'cause of action' test to tort claims. Such a restriction has little to commend it. Either the cause of action test has gone or it has not—and, if it has gone for torts, it must go for all causes of action unless the courts have already decided (or possibly subsequently decide)[121] that exemplary damages are not available in respect of that particular cause of action. This was, in essence, the conclusion of Palmer J in the New South Wales Supreme Court in *Digital Pulse Pty Ltd v Christopher Harris*[122] in deciding that exemplary damages could be recovered in respect of a breach of fiduciary duty. There was no Australian authority directly in point and academic authority was divided. Taking his lead from the decision in *Kuddus* Palmer J stated:[123]

> If, as Lord Nicholls suggests [in *Kuddus*], the availability of exemplary damages should be coextensive with its rationale, it is difficult to see why the remedy should be confined to causes of action in tort. Can it seriously be suggested that if my solicitor grossly deceives me in the course of his professional dealing with me and decamps with my life's savings, the law regards my sense of outrage as demonstrably greater if I sue him in a common law court for deceit than if I sue him in an equity court for breach of fiduciary duty? Is there any rational basis for believing that the policy of the law in such a case will permit the common law court to vindicate my outrage by an award of exemplary damages but will prevent the equity court from doing so? My answer to both these questions would be in the negative.

---

[120] In *Kuddus v Cheif Constable of Leicestershire Constabulary* ([2001] 2 WLR 1789) Lord Nicholls (at 1807) doubted the soundness of the distinction between government officials and others. He pointed out that national and international companies can exercise enormous power, as do some individuals. So there may not in future be a hard-and-fast line that will always exclude such companies and persons from the reach of exemplary damages. In relation to the second category Lord Nicholls pointed out that note must be taken of the decision of the House of Lords in *A-G v Blake* where their Lordships used the remedy of an account of profits to strip the defendant of the gains made from his wrong. It may be that an account of profits will prove to be a more suitable remedy in future cases in this category of case than the award of exemplary damages.

[121] It is possible that the courts may yet conclude that exemplary damages are not available in respect of a particular cause of action.

[122] [2002] NSWSC 33 (8 February 2002).   [123] ibid, para [156].

If this is the case in relation to a claim for breach of fiduciary duty should the same not follow for breach of contract cases? The answer to this question, at least in England and Australia, is that it does not. The reason for this is that in both jurisdictions there is binding authority for the proposition that exemplary damages cannot be recovered in respect of a breach of contract.[124] The question is whether or not these cases will survive further judicial scrutiny.

There is reason to believe that they will not. The Supreme Court of Canada has now recognized that punitive damages may be awarded in respect of a breach of contract upon proof of an independent actionable wrong arising out of the same facts as the breach.[125] In *Whiten v Pilot Insurance Co*[126] the defendant insurers repeatedly delayed making payment on a claim made by an insured whose house was destroyed in a fire. The defendant investigated the possibility that the plaintiff had started the fire deliberately but later conceded that there was no 'air of reality' to its allegation of arson. At trial the plaintiff led evidence to the effect that the defendant had prolonged its investigations into the cause of the fire with the aim of forcing the plaintiff to accept a reduced settlement. The trial judge instructed the jury to award punitive damages if they found that the defendant dealt with the plaintiff in a malicious, high-handed, arbitrary or capricious manner. The jury awarded the plaintiff compensatory damages of $345,000 and punitive damages of $1m. The Supreme Court of Canada upheld this award of punitive damages. It did so on the basis that the defendant had not only broken its contract with the plaintiff but had also broken the duty of good faith which it owed to the plaintiff. The breach of this contractual duty of good faith was held to be 'independent of and in addition to the breach of contractual duty to pay the loss.'[127] Thus, the 'independent actionable wrong' need not constitute a tort or even a breach of an equitable duty, such as a fiduciary duty. It can consist of a further breach of the contract provided that that breach constitutes an 'additional wrong'. It is difficult to discern the logic behind a rule which provides that two 'independent' breaches of contract can trigger an entitlement to punitive damages, when one breach cannot. *Whiten v Pilot Insurance Co* is unlikely to be the last word on the subject; it is more likely to be the penultimate stop on the journey to the conclusion that a breach of contract can, in an appropriate case, entitle a plaintiff to recover punitive damages.

---

[124] *Addis v Gramophone Co Ltd* [1909] AC 488 (England and Wales) and *Gray v Motor Accident Commission* (1998) 196 CLR 1 (Australia).

[125] *Royal Bank of Canada v W Got & Associates Electric Ltd* (2000) 178 DLR (4th) 385; *Whiten v Pilot Insurance Co* [2002] SCC 18 and *Performance Industries Ltd v Sylvan Lake Golf & Tennis Club Ltd* [2002] SCC 19. See more generally J Edelman, 'Exemplary Damages for Breach of Contract' (2001) 117 LQR 539.

[126] [2002] SCC 18, on which see M Graham [2002] LMCLQ 453 and G Fridman (2003) 119 LQR 20 .   [127] ibid, para [79].

Will the English courts eventually reach this conclusion? It is suggested that in time they will. If torts and equitable wrongs can generate a claim for punitive damages, why should a breach of contract never give rise to such a claim? As Lord Nicholls stated in *A v. Bottrill*[128] '"Never say never" is a sound judicial admonition.'[129] A refusal to recognize that a breach of contract can give rise to punitive damages will simply encourage claimants to characterize the breach as some other cause of action for the purpose of seeking punitive damages. This subterfuge will bring little credit to the law. The logic behind the abolition of the 'cause of action' test will eventually bring down the rule that a breach of contract can never give rise to a claim for punitive damages. But it does not follow from this that punitive damages will be widely available in contractual claims. On the contrary, cases in which punitive damages will be awarded are likely to be few and far between. There are essentially two reasons for this. The first is that, as both Lord Nicholls and Lord Scott pointed out in *Kuddus v Cheif Constable of Leicestershire Constabulary*,[130] the effect of *A-G v Blake* may well be to undermine Lord Devlin's second category in *Rookes v Barnard* on the basis that 'the profit made by a wrongdoer can be extracted from him without the need to rely on . . . exemplary damages.'[131] This being the case, punitive damages are only likely to be available where the breach of contract by the defendant is 'so outrageous, his disregard of the plaintiff's rights so contumelious, that something more is needed to show that the law will not tolerate such behaviour.'[132] Such cases are likely to be few and far between. In particular, the mere fact that the defendant has broken his contract with the claimant in order to pursue a more profitable relationship with another party will not suffice to entitle the claimant to punitive damages. Much more will be required before a finding is made that a defendant has behaved in an 'outrageous' fashion.

3. CONCLUSION

In the short run the decisions in *A-G v Blake* and *Kuddus v Chief Constable of Leicestershire Constabulary* will generate a degree of uncertainty in commercial transactions. This is particularly so in relation to *Blake* given that it recognized the existence of a claim for an account of profits in respect of a breach of contract but defined the limits of the claim in rather broad,

---

[128] [2002] UKPC 44, [2002] 3 WLR 1406.   [129] ibid, at para [26].

[130] At paras [67] and [109] respectively.

[131] ibid, para [109]. Lord Scott in fact referred to exemplary damages as an 'anomaly' but on this point he was in the minority. The point he makes holds good whether or not exemplary damages are seen as an anomaly.

[132] ibid, para [63].

discretionary terms. The impact of *Kuddus* is presently less marked but in the long run it may prove to be the more significant of the two decisions. However, the uncertainty generated by these cases should not be exaggerated. Two factors should reduce the uncertainty. The first is recognition of the fact that an account of profits should only be available as a remedy for breach of contract in an exceptional case (and punitive damages in an even rarer category of case). Account of profits is a subsidiary remedy for breach of contract, only to be invoked by the courts where all other remedies for the breach are inadequate and the claimant has a legitimate interest in depriving the defendant of the gain that he has made directly from his breach of contract. Secondly, as Lord Steyn noted in *A-G v Blake*, more detailed guidance as to the availability of these remedies is 'best hammered out on the anvil of concrete cases.'[133] Provided that judges hand down judgments that give clear and practical guidance as to the nature and scope of the remedy awarded, both *Blake* and *Kuddus* are likely to be seen in future years as cases that made a positive contribution to the development of English law in that they gave the judges the power that they needed to resort to exceptional remedies in cases where the justice of the case demand that they do so.

[133] [2001] 1 AC 268, 291.

11

Breach of Contract, Restitution for Wrongs, and Punishment: Comment

SAM EASTWOOD[1]

This comment is written from the perspective of a banking and commercial litigator.

In Chapter 10 Ewan McKendrick highlights the uncertainty about the significance and scope of the ruling of the House of Lords in *A-G v Blake (Jonathan Cape Ltd, Third Party)*.[2] Practitioners were never under any illusion that the remedial regime for breach of contract was straightforward but when distinguished academics pronounce that this area has become 'more complex' it is a cause for some concern.

The introduction of a new legal concept on the back of what everyone accepts is a truly exceptional case was always going to import a level of uncertainty: what are the exact principles involved and how would they be applied in any given instance? Practitioners, whilst interested in the theory, are more interested at a given moment about the application of that theory to the case at hand. This is even more true of our clients who, understandably, are far less interested in hypotheses, would prefer not to be in the contentious situation in the first place, and, with very few exceptions, have no interest in making legal precedent!

Ewan McKendrick asks whether fixed principles should govern the availability of this remedy or whether it should depend on the court's discretion. Fixed principles would give rise to greater certainty for practitioners to advise on when this remedy arises. However, there is always a balance between on the one hand a firm but inflexible description of when a remedy or doctrine may be used and on the other hand more general adaptable guidelines which may cover a wider range of factual scenarios. In *A-G v Blake* , Lord Nicholls clearly favoured the latter approach, and declined to set out any fixed rules to determine whether or not a claimant is entitled to an account of profits. Instead, he set out a few principles as guidance: inadequacy of other remedies; a 'legitimate interest' in preventing the defendant making or retaining the profit; and 'all the circumstances of the case'.

'Inadequate' should not be equated with 'unavailable' or even 'difficult to assess'. However, whilst in *Esso v Niad*[3] it may have been difficult to

---

[1] Partner, Norton Rose   [2] [2001] 1 AC 268.
[3] Unreported, 22 November 2001.

prove what Esso's loss of profits were, the court does not put it stronger than that. Difficult maybe, but not impossible. It probably could have been achieved with expert evidence. McKendrick puts forward the possibility of quantifying the claim in terms of loss of reputation or loss of goodwill. There seems some merit in this approach. The courts have in the past been willing to take a creative and common-sense view when it comes to assessing damages for, say, unprovable expectations. One would have thought that this possibility existed in *Esso v Niad*. Additionally, it is not clear what the position might be in the event that a claimant has mitigated his losses. Can he still look to the remedy of account of profits if otherwise no losses can be established on a compensatory basis and no other remedies are available or adequate?

What of the situation where there is an ongoing breach, where the defendant is making a profit, and the claimant wishes to stop future breaches? Here, would it be possible to seek an account of profits at the same time as seeking an injunction or specific performance? The remedy of specific performance/injunction may well be adequate in respect of future conduct but what if the defendant has already profited from his breach and the claimant cannot otherwise establish any loss or damage on ordinary compensatory principles?

The principle of 'legitimate interest' in preventing the defendant making or retaining the profit is nebulous. How legitimate does the interest have to be? What is the threshold? Try telling a client who has paid lawyers hundreds of thousands of pounds to negotiate a contract that his interest in seeing it performed is not sufficiently 'legitimate'. What person enters into a contract not caring if the other side performs his side of the bargain? In the case of *Esso v Niad* Morritt V-C determined that 'Esso undoubtedly has a legitimate interest in preventing Niad from profiting from its breach of obligation' without any further elaboration.

Finally, Lord Nicholls' non-exhaustive list of circumstances which also have to be taken into account add little certainty to our future advice.

Both the Court of Appeal and the House of Lords in the *Blake* case were at pains to play down the cynical and deliberate conduct of the defendant. There is, however, a sense that the courts, even if not expressly, will be prepared to take account of the conduct of the defendant when taking stock of the possible remedy of account of profits. The 'cynical view of Blake' has some attraction. As *Private Eye* said at the time: 'Four of the five law lords happily found in favour of the Crown, on the grounds that Blake was a "notorious traitor" who must be punished somehow, even if this meant bending the law.' Although the courts wish to be seen to be avoiding this approach, surely this factor is somewhere in their thinking. It is difficult to believe that the behaviour of the defendant does not influence the court in some way, even if it is not the decisive factor.

A-G v Blake is therefore not a useful precedent, particularly for commercial cases. The principles outlined by Lord Nicholls are sufficiently vague as to be uncertain for the purposes of advising a client accurately. What is clear, is that this new remedy can only be successfully invoked in 'exceptional circumstances.' But how exceptional is exceptional and how does one account for *Esso v Niad*? Having set out some guidelines, it is now up to other courts to build a body of precedent which over time will lend greater certainty to this area of law. It is early days certainly but, as stated above, commercial clients are not attracted by this uncertainty so of the few 'exceptional cases' that come to dispute, it is to be expected that even fewer will make it to trial. The body of precedent will be slow in coming. The fact that the *Niad* case has been settled prior to being heard by the Court of Appeal highlights this aspect.

Ewan McKendrick also raises the prospect of exemplary or punitive damages being awarded in cases of certain breaches of contract. Certainly this would be consistent with the erosion of the compensatory principle discussed above in connection with *A-G v Blake* , the decision in the *Kuddus* case,[4] the narrowing of the distinctions between remedies in tort and contract, authorities in other jurisdictions, and the continued expansion of remedies for breach of contract.

Practitioners take note. We have many times advised clients that, unlike say in the United States, punitive damages are not awarded in the case of a breach of contract. A note of caution should feature in any advice—and certainly where the proposed conduct of the contract-breaker appears to be calculated to make a profit which may well exceed the compensation payable. Whether you characterize the potential exposure as being liability for an account of profits/restitutionary damages or for punitive or exemplary damages will be of little consequence to the client. There is clearly an overlap.

---

[4] [2001] 2 WLR 1789.

12

Breach of Contract, Restitution for Wrongs, and Punishment: Review of Discussion

Lord Nicholls explained that the reason why he had preferred to avoid the term 'restitutionary damages' in *A-G v Blake*[1] was because, for many, damages are virtually synonymous with compensation. If one could therefore use terminology that avoided alienating or confusing such people that was preferable. In other words, the terminology of 'restitutionary damages' was an unnecessary additional complication to the acceptance of the new development in *A-G v Blake*. In his Lordship's view, an 'account of profits' was less problematic. Pressed with the point that an account of profits has its own historical baggage that means that it too cannot simply be equated with 'gain-based monetary remedy' (eg that an account of profits cannot be awarded where the defendant has made a loss, albeit less of a loss than if the wrong had not been committed; or that an account of profits cannot cover 'expense saved') his Lordship expressed the view that these were unprincipled (and, on the face of it, unnecessary) restrictions on that remedy. Once one had crossed the threshold for being able to recover an account of profits for breach of contract, rather than compensatory damages or specific relief, Lord Nicholls thought that the measure of recovery could extend from expense saved through to stripping a proportion of the profits made through to stripping all of the profits made from the breach. The *Wrotham Park Estate*[2] case (where 5 per cent of the profits had been stripped) was therefore based on the same principle as *A-G v Blake* (where all the profits had been stripped). Lord Nicholls also expressed the view that, while the fact that a breach of contract had been committed cynically was not a reason in itself for an account of profits, it might be a factor that, along with others, would exceptionally make that remedy appropriate. He emphasized that, in his view, an account of profits was a residual and exceptional remedy for breach of contract.

While some expressed the view that the principle in *A-G v Blake* was unacceptably uncertain, others saw it as an inevitable and natural progression: once one realized that an account of profits (or restitutionary damages) is available for intellectual property wrongs, proprietary torts (such as trespass to land and nuisance), and equitable wrongs (such as breach of confidence and breach of fiduciary duty), it was hard to defend a position that an account of profits is never available for breach of contract. In any event, the facts of a case like *Surrey CC v Bredero Homes Ltd*[3]

---

[1] [2001] 1 AC 268.   [2] [1974] 1 WLR 798.   [3] [1993] 1 WLR 1361.

showed that, unless one accepted this remedy, there would be an unacceptable lacuna in the law on contractual remedies which, in that case, allowed a cynical contract-breaker to operate without sanction and frustrated the operation of justifiable restrictive covenants.

Views differed as to the merits of the decision in *Esso v Niad*.[4] On one view, this was not such an exceptional case as to merit an account of profits. In particular, the assessment of compensatory damages, while difficult, would not be impossible. On another view, the case was close to *A-G v Blake*. There had been a continuing and flagrant breach of contract and it was hard to see how compensatory damages could be accurately assessed. More puzzling was Sir Andrew Morritt V-C's reference to a restitutionary remedy for unjust enrichment being the more appropriate remedy than an account of profits (and note that the contract had not been terminated, which would normally mean that one could not rest one's cause of action on unjust enrichment). It was unclear what precisely this referred to and, on the face of it, applying the step-by-step approach laid down in *A-G v Blake* an adequate remedy based on the cause of action of unjust enrichment should have precluded an account of profits for the cause of action of breach of contract. From the perspective of development of the law, it was disappointing to hear that *Esso v Niad* had settled and would not now be going to the Court of Appeal.

The possibility that the *Kuddus* case[5] has opened the door to punitive damages being awarded for breach of contract means that a useful way of viewing the law is that there is a hierarchy of remedies for breach of contract. Compensatory damages are always available and are the normal remedy. But if inadequate, specific performance or an injunction can be awarded. If both of those are inadequate, an account of profits may exceptionally be awarded. If even that is inadequate (in the sense that a court remains outraged by the breach), punitive damages may be granted.

[4] ChD, 22 November 2001.   [5] [2001] 2 WLR 1789.

13

Restitution of Unjust Enrichment

PETER BIRKS[1]

There are two principal commercial contexts in which the law of unjust enrichment operates. The first is transactions which one way or another come to grief after value has passed between the parties. A decade of litigation over void interest swaps provides the most dramatic illustration in recent memory. The second comprises all those situations in which funds have been misdirected. That is a large and diverse category. It includes innocently mistaken payments and massive frauds. A theme running through both is the search for a solvent defendant and, failing that, for priority over other claimants.

This book is about remedies in commercial contexts. The term 'remedies' is used in at least four senses. Unjust enrichment is a cause of action or more accurately, like tort, a generic description of a whole family of causes of action. Nonetheless it is often contemplated as a remedy because the very existence of the cause of action offers a cure for a grievance. Secondly, the rights which arise from unjust enrichment attract a narrower application of the metaphor. An unjust enrichment is not a wrong, but just as rights arising from wrongs are referred to as remedies so rights arising from unjust enrichment are easily perceived as relieving pain or warding it off. Thirdly, and more narrowly still, the metaphor can be used of the orders which courts make to realize the rights which arise from the event. Fourthly, since even those orders only generate another tier of rights, we might say that, just as a prescription is only a bird in the bush until the pharmacist puts the pills in your hand, your remedy for unjust enrichment is not the judge's order but the execution of that judgment. The relativity of 'remedy' is vividly evident in the fact that from the standpoint of the fourth the third usage is incorrect, and so on.

This paper has three parts. After a short introduction which fills in the background, the second part takes remedy in the first and largest of these four senses. It uses six cases to show how this cause of action should be analysed. The third part then switches to the second understanding of remedy and asks what kinds of right arise from unjust enrichments.

---

[1] Regius Professor of Civil Law in the University of Oxford; Fellow of All Souls.

1. INTRODUCTION

Most of the rights which we seek to realize in court arise either from manifestations of consent, such as contracts, conveyances, declarations of trust, and wills, or from wrongs, such as torts, breaches of equitable duty, breaches of statutory duty, and breaches of contract. Some rights arise from events which are neither manifestations of consent nor wrongs. This residual miscellany of causative events yields up one more generic category, namely unjust enrichment at the expense of another. That still leaves a reduced residual miscellany. There are therefore four categories of causative event: rights arise from consent, from wrongs, from unjust enrichments, and from miscellaneous other events.

History shows that manifestations of consent and wrongs are so much easier to identify and understand than unjust enrichment and the residual miscellany that lawyers have been constantly tempted to over-extend their explanatory effect. That 'ghost from the past', the implied contract theory of unjust enrichment, is only the most famous case.[2] Presumed and constructive intentions to create a trust do similar work. We have never had implied wrongs, but we do have cases where the language of wrongdoing is used without any care taken to ensure that the conduct in question necessarily takes effect as a breach of duty.[3]

It has taken a long time for common lawyers to draw unjust enrichment out of these shadows. Understanding is still held back by unfamiliarity. Lawyers who recognize its utility are still cautious, for fear that others, especially judges, will turn out to be sceptics. Critical commentary is absolutely necessary, but out and out scepticism is perverse. Yet in Cambridge Mr Hedley leads the English sceptics[4] and in Australia last year Gummow J said from the bench that Australian law knew no such category, preferring an undifferentiated category of unconscionable behaviour, with no tie to enrichment.[5]

The law of restitution is all the law of gain-based recovery. Compensation is loss-based recovery. Both are multi-causal. Like other

---

[2] G Jones (ed) Lord Goff of Chieveley and GH Jones, *The Law of Restitution* (5th ed Sweet & Maxwell London 1998) 5–11.

[3] Undue influence, for example, is constantly referred to as a wrong: *Barclays Bank Plc v O'Brien* [1994] 1 AC 180 (HL); *Royal Bank of Scotland v Etridge (No 2)* [2001] UKHL 44; [2001] 3 WLR 1021 (HL).

[4] S Hedley *A Critical Introduction to Restitution* (Butterworths London 2001); S Hedley *Restitution: Its Division and Ordering* (Modern Legal Studies Sweet & Maxwell London 2001). These offer no alternative to the bubble which they seek to burst.

[5] *Roxborough v Rothmans of Pall Mall (Australia) Ltd* [2001] HCA 68 [70], (2001) 185 ALR 355 (HCA) [70] noted J Beatson and G Virgo (2002) 118 LQR 352–8, P Birks (2002) Oxford U Commonwealth LJ 1.

rights a right to restitution may arise from a contract, from a wrong—a tort, breach of contract or breach of equitable or statutory duty—or from unjust enrichment or from an event in the residual miscellany. Within this series created in answer to the question from what events rights can arise unjust enrichment, is *sui generis*. The key to its independence is that, by comparison with claimants who seek to make their defendants worse off, usually by shifting to them a loss which they themselves would otherwise suffer but sometimes by stripping them of wrongful gains or inflicting penal award, those who want to do no more than recover a gain made at their expense need to point only to very slight facts.

As you are leaving a shop an assistant tells you that he accidentally gave you change for a £50, instead of a £20. It is no good your saying that you never even noticed or that he for his part was very careless. Such protestations do not touch the strength of his claim to the extra £30. You are only being asked to return to the position in which you ought to have been all along. In every unjust enrichment there is enrichment at the expense of the claimant and there is a reason, not being a contract or a wrong, why that enrichment should be given up to the claimant. And liability is in principle strict. There is strict liability to give up a gain to the person at whose expense it was acquired notwithstanding the absence of a wrong or a contract or other manifestation of consent. Even if there were only one case in which it was instantiated it would be impossible to deny the distinctive character of this causative event. The boundary of the class, whatever its size, is drawn by the limits of the logic which explains this example of overpaid change.

A-G v Blake[6] falls outside that boundary.[7] At issue was only gain-based recovery for breach of contract—restitution for a wrong. Unjust enrichment comprises only those enrichments at the expense of another which have to be given up independently of consent and wrongs. Dual analysis is sometimes possible but not in the *Blake* case. A payment obtained by fraud can be presented as a wrongful enrichment or, dispensing with the allegation of fraud, as an unjust enrichment of the species payment by mistake. The traitor Blake had promised not to write unauthorized books about his experiences as a secret agent. Had he profited from his breach, his gain could not be presented other than as a wrongful enrichment. For without relying on the facts in their character as a wrong the Crown could not have created any connection at all between it and the gain in question.

Every problem in unjust enrichment can be unlocked by a five-question analysis derived, with two necessary additions, from the full name of the event, unjust enrichment at the expense of another: (i) Was the defendant enriched? (ii) Was it at the expense of this claimant? (iii) Was it unjust?

---

[6] [2001] AC 268 (HL).　　[7] Compare McKendrick Chapter 10 in this volume.

(iv) What kind of right did the claimant acquire? (v) Does the defendant have a defence?

The first question is almost never problematic when the defendant has received money. This paper, by sticking to money cases, avoids the complications which arise in relation benefits in kind. The second question uses 'at the expense of' as a convenient way of asking what amounts to a sufficient connection between claimant and enrichment. The phrase should not be construed as though it were taken from a statute. In the third question 'unjust' indicates a reason for restitution which is not a wrong or a contract or other manifestation of consent. The fourth question principally asks whether the claimant has a personal or a proprietary right and, if the latter, whether it is immediately vested or a power to vest. Five is self-explanatory, except to say that defences now carry a good deal of the law of unjust enrichment.

2. APPLYING THE FIVE-QUESTION ANALYSIS : SIX CASES

(a) Scottish Equitable Plc v Derby[8]

Mr Derby ran into financial trouble as he neared retirement. He finally made up his mind to take part of his pension early. Later, as he came to 65, he inquired about the value of his remaining rights. Though he tried to make clear his situation, the quotation he received assumed that he had never touched his fund. This was due to a series of internal errors on the part of Scottish Equitable. He was ultimately paid £172,451 too much. He honestly believed his policy had done surprisingly well. It was not until sixteen months later that the demand for restitution came. He had to repay almost all the overpayment.

(i) Question three: careless claimants and innocent defendants

This partly re-runs *Kelly v Solari*.[9] Was the enrichment unjust? Derby argued that the payees had been careless in making the mistake and he had been completely honest. Some jurisdictions have held that the mistake must be excusable. Scots law has recently withdrawn from that position.[10] South African law still adheres to it.[11] In England *Kelly v Solari* already laid

---

[8] [2001] 3 All ER 818 (CA).

[9] (1841) 9 M&W 54; [1835–1842] All ER Rep 320; 152 ER 24.

[10] *Morgan Guaranty Trust Co of New York v Lothian Regional Council* 1995 SLT 299, 316 (Court of Session).

[11] *Willis Faber Enthoven Pty Ltd v Receiver of Revenue* (1992) (4) SA 202 (AC) (Supreme Court of South Africa, Appellate Division).

down that, unless the payer had deliberately waived all inquiry and intended the recipient to have the money without regard to the truth of the belief later falsified, it did not matter how carelessly the mistake was made. Parke B observed:

> but if it is paid under the impression of the truth of a fact which is untrue, it may, generally speaking, be recovered back, however careless the party paying may have been, in omitting to use due diligence to inquire into the fact. In such a case the receiver was not entitled to it, nor intended to have it.[12]

This was endorsed by Robert Goff J in his radical review of the cases in *Barclays Bank Ltd v WJ Simms Son & Cooke (Southern) Ltd.*[13] In *Scottish Equitable Plc v Derby* the Court of Appeal again confirmed it. The unjust factor is a mistake which causes the payment. Negligence on the part of the payer does not disqualify, nor does innocence on the part of the recipient excuse.

The liability is strict, subject to defences. As long as the entire fund of the defendant's wealth is in unjust surplus, so that his making restitution will not leave him any worse off than he would have been, neither his innocence nor the payer's fault weakens the case for restitution. The word 'unconscionable' has nothing to add. If it says anything it says that money which ought to be given back ought to be given back. That circularity shows it is only by applying the law of unjust enrichment that you reach the conclusion that retention would be unconscionable.

(ii) Question five: change of position

It had taken sixteen months for Scottish Equitable to discover its mistake and demand repayment. During that time Mr Derby had used the money to discharge part of his mortgage, to buy a pension from Norwich Union, and in small ways to raise the standard of living of his family. He was now in his late sixties. The effect of the order to repay would leave him with the prospect of a bleak old age, with his total income reduced by a half. His position was aggravated by other financial problems, by the collapse of his marriage, and by ill health.

These hardships invited sympathy, but the Court of Appeal refused to dissolve the claim in a saucer of good will. The defence of change of position was not a matter of discretionary allowances. Following the line advocated by Professor Andrew Burrows,[14] the Court agreed that the law must take as broad a view of the defence as could be taken within the requirement that a relevant change of position must consist in a detriment caused

---

[12] (1841) 9 M&W 54, 59; [1835–42] All ER Rep 320, 322; 152 ER 24, 27.

[13] [1980] QB 677, 686.

[14] A S Burrows *The Law of Restitution* (Butterworths London 1993) 425–8. See now 2nd edition (2002) 512.

by the enrichment. The £9,662 which had marginally raised the family's standard of living was an expenditure so caused. The Court would not put the defendant to rigorous proof of specific items of expenditure, nor charge him with too heavy an onus. But the onset of old age, the dearth of job opportunities, and his other personal problems had not been caused by the payment. The discharge of the mortgage and the purchase of the pension had been, but, given that the mortgage would have had to be paid off anyhow and the Norwich Union was willing to unwind the contract for the annuity, neither were detriments.[15]

There was therefore no relevant change of position beyond the outlay of the £9,662. Two troubling points remain. One is that special consideration will have to be given to the case of defendants who run out of money altogether. A lowest intermediate balance rule must apply. In a rare case, the entire aggregate of the defendant's wealth will fall below the amount received. If this happens while the defendant is still entitled to the defence, it cannot thereafter be said that he has not been disenriched at least to the extent of that deficiency. At the moment when the credit side of his balance sheet falls below the amount received and to the extent that it does, he must have used up his unjust enrichment. His wealth cannot be swollen by more than that intermediate lowest balance. This is perfectly compatible with the causal approach, but its compatibility needs to be spelled out.

Secondly, a court must soon ask whether the name of this defence does not wildly overstate its scope. We should immediately separate disenrichment from other changes of position, if any there be. It seems doubtful that the latter category will turn out to have content. Meanwhile, the defence of disenrichment can be developed without the distraction of overblown terminology.

The disenrichment sector of the defence, which reduces the liability of the recipient to the extent that the swelling of the assets has been eliminated, protects the interest in the security of receipts, for it means that the recipient can safely do what he likes with whatever appears to be at his disposition, but it also draws a line around the strict liability in such a way as to preserve its rationale, namely that very slight facts, independent of consent and wrongs, suffice for the relocation of gains at the claimant's expense. To deny the existence of a law of unjust enrichment is to deny that proposition.

(iii) Question five: estoppel

Mr Derby had another string to his question five bow, namely estoppel. He had sought confirmation and been told all was in order. Estoppel and

---

[15] [2001] 3 All ER 818 [30]–[36] (Robert Walker LJ), [53]–[54] (Simon Brown LJ).

change of position are historically related but functionally very different defences.[16] Change of position is about, or chiefly about, confining claims in unjust enrichment to the amount by which the recipient's assets are still swollen at the moment at which an honest recipient would have ceased to regard the addition as at his disposition. Estoppel in this context is a cousin of a contract for finality. The defences have quite different work to do. Their separation removes the old temptation to discover binding representations. In the *Derby* case and again shortly afterwards in *National Westmister Bank Plc v Somer International (UK) Ltd*[17] differently constituted Courts of Appeal had to confront the new relationship between the two defences.

In the latter the defendants were suppliers of computers who had been waiting for a substantial payment from a fragile customer. When the bank notified them that their account had been credited they released more goods to the customer. The bank then discovered that the credit was for another account-holder with a similar name. Meanwhile, Somer's fragile customer went under. Somer was certainly entitled to reduce its restitutionary liability by the value of the goods it had released, but it maintained that the bank was estopped from bringing any claim at all. Estoppel was similarly Mr Derby's last hope. On this all-or-nothing argument his detrimental reliance of less than £10,000 would have allowed him to hold on to more than ten times that much.

There is earlier Court of Appeal authority for the all-or-nothing view of estoppel,[18] seemingly endorsed in the House of Lords by Lord Goff: *Lipkin Gorman v Karpnale Ltd*.[19] In both the recent cases the Court of Appeal refused the defence. At first instance in the *Derby* case Harrison J had formulated an exception to the effect that one way or another steps would be taken to prevent a grossly disproportionate outcome. That provided the way out.

Robert Walker LJ was attracted by an ingenious and crisper argument.[20] Since change of position would now automatically charge reliance expenditure to the other side it could not amount to detrimental reliance for the purpose of perfecting an estoppel. This encounters obstacles. First, it is unusual to prevent a party from using facts in different characters. Secondly, it entails awkward distinctions between acts of reliance which are technically chargeable to the claimant as changes of position and others which are not. Thirdly, it overlooks the functional contrast between the two defences, excluding one of them on grounds which are unrelated to its function.

---

[16] From the first edition *Goff & Jones* led the campaign to separate them: R Goff and G Jones *The Law of Restitution* (Sweet & Maxwell London 1966) 486.

[17] [2001] EWCA Civ 970; [2002] 3 WLR 64 (CA).

[18] *Avon County Council v Howlett* [1983] 1 WLR 605 (CA).

[19] [1991] 2 AC 548 (HL) 579.   [20] [2001] 3 All ER 818 (CA), paras [45]–[47].

The better approach will be to leave the *Avon* logic intact while construing most representations as revocable. Exceptional circumstances apart, it accords with ordinary expectations to construe a representation as reliable unless and until corrected. It does not make sense to give relief in respect of mistaken payments while denying all possibility of correcting mistaken representations. Representations construed so as to allow the representor to retract so long and to the extent that he can obtain restitution without leaving the defendant to bear the ill consequences of any detrimental reliance would yield the same results as change of position. Room will then be left for the rare case in which on unequivocally strong facts estoppel can still be as absolute a defence as a contract not to sue.

(b) Dextra Bank & Trust Co Ltd v Bank of Jamaica[21]

Here fraud on the part of third parties induced Dextra to draw a cheque for US$2,999,000 in favour of the Bank of Jamaica. Dextra was made to believe that this was to be a loan. At the same time the rogues led the Bank of Jamaica to believe that the cheque represented foreign currency which its agents had bought. The bank of Jamaica was so comprehensively deceived that, by the time the cheque came into its hands, its agents had already paid the supposed vendors and had in their turn been reimbursed. Dextra's restitutionary claim failed.

(i) Question five: anticipatory disenrichment

Scottish Equitable v Derby shows that the defence of disenrichment, while it cannot dissolve into a discretionary expression of sympathy, must, within its proper sphere, be interpreted liberally. *Dextra* was Lord Goff's last judgment, given jointly with Lord Bingham. When he first introduced the defence he said that one consequence would be to allow a less restrictive attitude to the unjust factors themselves.[22] This trade-off will not work unless the defence is indeed construed generously. There is a price to be paid in that worthy claimants sometimes have to be defeated. Broadening the defence, Lord Goff here insisted, first, that only the dishonest would be disqualified, and, secondly, that anticipatory disenrichment would suffice.

The Bank of Jamaica had paid the supposed price of the dollars before actually receiving them. The American *Restatement of Restitution* expressly says that the detriment required for change of position must come after the payment.[23] In *South Tyneside MBC v Svenska International* that caused

---

[21] [2002] 1 All ER Com 193 (PC) noted M McInnes (2002) 119 LQR 208.

[22] *Lipkin Gorman v Karpnale Ltd* [1991] 2 AC 548 (HL) 581.

[23] American Law Institute (Reporters: A Scott and W Seavey) *Restatement of the Law of Restitution* (ALI Publishers St Paul 1937) s 142(1).

Clarke J some anxiety.[24] The *Dextra* facts demonstrate that 'after' cannot be rationally defended. If the question is whether the enrichment has been wholly or partly eliminated, the timing of the outlay caused by the enrichment, so long as it is so caused, was manifestly irrelevant. Effects do not of course usually precede causes, but where the modality of causation is reliance they can do so, since reliance can look forwards to events about to happen.[25]

(ii) Question three: mistakes and mispredictions

Dextra would, it seems, have lost anyway. The Privy Council restated two essential elements of a claim based on mistake. First, the mistake must be shown to have caused the payment. This, as will be seen below, must never be left unqualified, for if there is a contract between the parties it can give the wrong result.[26] Secondly, it must be a mistake of present fact or law and not a misprediction of the future. The latter implies no impairment of the decision to make the payment and therefore merits no relief. A misprediction is merely an incorrect assessment of uncertainty. The following paragraphs show that their Lordships thought that Dextra had either made no more than a misprediction, or, so far as it could be said to have made a mistake, it had not in any way been influenced by that mistake. That is, its mistake, if it made one, had not been causative.

> [29] Here, unfortunately, Dextra failed to communicate directly with the BOJ to make sure that the BOJ understood that the money was being offered as a loan. Instead, it left the communication of this vital matter to its agent, Phillips. Dextra's misplaced reliance on Phillips led it to assume that a loan would result; and this prediction proved to be mistaken. But a misprediction does not, in their Lordships' opinion, provide the basis for a claim to recover money as having been paid under a mistake of fact.
>
> [30] Dextra did, however, argue that it suffered under a mistake of fact when it was deceived by Wildish into believing that the BOJ had previously agreed to take a loan from Dextra. In fact, the BOJ had not so agreed. But, although this can be regarded as a mistake of fact on the part of Dextra, it cannot be said to have caused Dextra's payment to the BOJ. This is because it was overtaken by the specific instructions given by Dextra to Phillips that the cheque was not to be handed over to the BOJ except against the delivery to him of a promissory note evidencing the loan and its terms. It was upon the compliance by Phillips with this instruction that Dextra relied to ensure that a loan was made upon the terms acceptable to it. The significance of the earlier deception by Wildish was only

---

[24] [1995] 1 All ER 545.

[25] Comparative support: M Jewell 'Change of Position' in P Birks and F Rose (eds) *Lessons of the Swaps Litigation* (LLP London 2000) 273, 284–90.

[26] Text between n 47 and n 55 below.

that it contributed to Dextra instructing Phillips to ensure that the cheque was handed over as a loan. Dextra's payment was not, however, caused by any such mistake of fact as that now alleged by Dextra; it was caused by a misprediction by Dextra that Phillips would carry out his instructions and that a loan would eventuate.

The principle is certainly right, but its application to the facts is problematic. There are real difficulties in distinguishing *Jones v Waring & Gillow*,[27] where the claimants drew cheques to Waring & Gillow having been deceived into believing that they would acquire rights in respect of an Italian car which was coming on to the market. They recovered their payment. It is hard to avoid the conclusion that Dextra would never have paid if they had not, however carelessly, formed the view that all the preparations were being made because of an in principle commitment on the part of the Bank of Jamaica to the dollar loan.

(c) Lloyds Bank Plc v Independent Insurance Co Ltd[28]

Here the bank had made a large payment to one of its customer's creditors. The payment was made by mistake. Had the mistake not been made, Lloyds would never have paid. Nevertheless, the bank failed in its attempt to recover. The bank's customer was an insurance agency, WF, which had fallen behind in its duty to pay over premiums to Independent. It had virtually nothing in the bank. Its manager was desperately making arrangements to cover the debt to Independent. Some cheques payable to WF came in. The manager took them to the bank and asked that £162,387.90 be paid to Independent as soon as possible. The cheques amounted to £172,131.97, the bulk of this sum being contributed by one for £168,000, the Kaffco cheque. Lloyds told the manager that the transfer to Independent could not be made until the cheques had been cleared. Three days later a CHAPS transfer was made to Independent in the belief that they had been cleared. Shortly afterwards the Kaffco cheque was dishonoured. The consequence was that the WF account went into massive overdraft. Some £55,000 later came in from Kaffco. This was an unsuccessful attempt to recover £107,387.90 from Independent, as money paid by mistake.

At first instance the judge construed the facts as amounting to a payment without the customer's authority. He took the view, highly favourable to the bank's present claim, that the customer had given only a conditional authority to transfer: 'If you receive the funds represented by these cheques, transfer £162,387.90 to Independent.' The condition never having been fulfilled, the judge was able to hold that the bank had made a mistake as to the existence of the customer's authority to pay and he there-

---

[27] [1926] AC 670 (HL).   [28] [1999] 2 WLR 986 (CA).

fore held that the bank was entitled to recover. The judge's major premise was right. That a payment without authority is recoverable was laid down by Robert Goff J in *Barclays Bank Ltd v WJ Simms & Son (Southern) Ltd*.[29] The Court of Appeal rejected the minor premise: the facts would not bear the construction that this was a payment without authority. It was obvious that WF wanted the transfer made just as soon as it could be made. The bank's mistake was, not that it wrongly thought it had the customer's authority, which it did have, but that it had formed an incorrect view of the funds available to the customer. In short it thought the Kaffco cheque had been cleared when it had not been cleared. In the result it had extended overdraft facilities to the customer in circumstances in which it would not have wished to do so.

(i) Question three or question five?

The outcome of *Lloyds Bank Plc v Independent Insurance Co Ltd* is identical to that of *Aiken v Short*.[30] A third party, Carter, had borrowed from bank S and then from bank A. Both bankers thought they had good real security. Bank A was willing to increase its exposure to Carter and paid off the S debt. The assumptions as to security were then destroyed by the discovery of a new will made by the testator from whom Carter thought he had received the interest which he had twice mortgaged. A could not recover from S.

Until Robert Goff J's judgment in *Barclays Bank Ltd v WJ Simms & Son (Southern) Ltd* there was a perfectly good question three explanation. There was no unjust factor because the restrictive approach used in a world without the defence of change of position required the mistake to be one which gave the payer the impression of being under a liability. Robert Goff J's radical review widened liability mistake to causative mistake but protected *Aiken v Short* by creating a 'good consideration' exception. In his judgment he listed some exceptions, amongst which this appeared as (2)(b):

(2) [The Plaintiff's] claim may however fail if . . . (b) the payment is made for good consideration, in particular if the money is paid to discharge, and does discharge, a debt owed to the payee (or to a principal on whose behalf he is authorized to receive the payment) by the payer or by a third party by whom he is authorized to discharge the debt.

A few lines later the exception was then itself qualified:

However, even if the payee has given consideration for the payment, for example by accepting the payment in discharge of a debt owed to him by a third party

---

[29] [1980] QB 677 (QBD).   [30] (1856) 1 H&N 210; 25 LJ Ex 321; 156 ER 1180.

on whose behalf the payer is authorised to discharge it, that transaction may itself be set aside if the payer's mistake was induced by the payee, or possibly where the payee, being aware of the payer's mistake, did not receive in good faith.[31]

This drew a sharp distinction between mistakes which went to the authority to pay and mistakes which left that authority intact. In the latter case the debt would be discharged and the payment could not be recovered from the creditor. It also appears to move the explanation from question three to question five: there is a good unjust factor but 'I gave consideration' is a defence to the action based on it. American law also solves the problem under question five. The American position is, however, more extreme. The bank there has no direct action for repayment from the creditor-payee even where the bank has no authority to pay. The *Restatement of Restitution* says, at section 14(1):[32]

> A creditor of another or one having a lien on another's property who has received from a third person any benefit in discharge of the debt or lien is under no duty to make restitution therefor, although the discharge was given by mistake of the transferor as to his interests or duties, if the transferee made no misrepresentation and did not have notice of the transferor's mistake.

The *Restatement* expressly says that the defence is a specific application of the underlying principle of bona fide purchase, presumably meaning bona fide purchase from the debtor.[33] An attempt to narrow this defence was firmly scotched by the New York Court of Appeals.[34] The ultimate outcome is not that the payer has no claim at all but that he is subrogated to the payee's claim against the customer.[35]

It is not altogether easy to explain that defence, whether in its American or its English version. Suppose bank's immediate payee is not a creditor but a donee. A father asks his bank to send £5,000 to his son. The bank does so, overlooking a sudden deterioration in the father's finances. The 'good consideration' defence would leave the son exposed. It seems unlikely that that was intended. A question two analysis may be more successful.

(ii) Question two: not at the expense of the bank?

A question two analysis will explain *Aiken v Short* and *Lloyds Bank Plc v Independent Insurance Co Ltd* and protect the son in the father-son hypo-

---

[31] [1980] 1 QB 677, 695. [32] *Restatement* (n 23) s 14(1).

[33] 'The rule stated in this Section is a specific application of the underlying principle of bona fide purchase' *Restatement* (n 23) s 55.

[34] *Bank Worms v Bankamerica International* 77 NY 2d 362, 570 NE 2d 189 (1991). Cf *Shield Benefit Administrators v University of Michigan* 225 Mich App 467, 571 NW 2d 556 (1997).

[35] Uniform Commercial Code #4-407 discussed in A Kull 'Rationalizing Restitution' 82 California L Rev 1191, 1230–2 (1995).

thetical. The bank has no cause of action because the defendant receives at the immediate expense of the customer, not the bank. The bank's immediate enrichee is the customer. The bank is trying to leapfrog its immediate enrichee, which it may not do. However badly a bank may be mistaken in paying the defendant a sum due from a third party, yet if it paid out on the credit of the third party (the customer) and has a right under this contract with the third party (the customer) to charge the sum to that customer, the defendant will be able to remit the bank or other payer to an action against the customer. In other words, the payer has to take the risk of his contractual partner's insolvency.

The nearest congeners of this kind of case look superficially quite different. Suppose a garage does work on a car which has been damaged in a crash. The car's owner is the ultimate beneficiary of the work. However, in almost all cases the garage will be doing the work under a contract with an insurance company. It has been held that if, after the work is done and the customer has taken the car back into his possession, the insurance company becomes insolvent, the unpaid garage has no claim against the owner. The work is done for the insurance company. The garage has to take the risk of the insolvency of the insurance company with which it validly contracted. It cannot say to the customer that the customer was enriched at its expense.[36]

The question two solution only explains the case in which the bank does have authority to pay. It does not explain the American extension of the defence to cases where the mistake goes to that authority. It also does not explain the qualifications which both Robert Goff J and, much less tentatively, the *Restatement* put on the creditor-payee's privileged position. They say that the immunity is forfeited if the creditor himself misrepresents or has notice of the payer's mistake. These qualifications are easier to explain when the creditor-payee is contemplated as having a defence of bona fide purchase. They then operate because, and so far as, they undermine the defence. If, however, the plaintiff payer is contemplated as having no cause of action against the creditor, the facts mentioned must supply one.

(d) Roxborough v Rothmans of Pall Mall Australia Ltd[37]

This is the case in which Gummow J rejected the very existence of the category of unjust enrichment. He rewrote the history in such a way as to justify a future attempt to empty the law of unjust enrichment into equitable

---

[36] *Brown and Davis v Galbraith* [1972] 1 WLR 997 (CA); *Gray's Truck Centre Ltd v Olaf L Johnson Ltd* (CA 25 January 1990).
[37] [2001] HCA 68, (2001) 185 ALR 355 (HCA).

unconscionability. The other judges did not support these preparations but also put up no resistance to them. For Gummow J the five-question analysis is irrelevant, but at this point we are concerned with a level of detail which is not touched by his attempt to repaint the larger picture.

Roxborough, the appellant claimants, were retailers of cigarettes. The respondents were wholesalers. Roxborough bought a month's supply of cigarettes from the respondents for a price which included, separately quantified, a tax disguised as a recurrent licence fee. Both parties understood that the wholesalers would pay over the tax element to the New South Wales government, while the retailers would pass it on in the price charged to the smoking public. At a time when the retailers had already sold on but the wholesalers had not yet paid over to the government, the High Court of Australia decided that the tax was void.[38] The retailers' claim to get it back failed in the Federal Court but succeeded in the High Court.

There was no issue under the first or second question. The enrichment was a large sum of money received from the claimants. There was also no issue under question four. The right which the claimants sought to realize was the common or garden personal right *in personam* correlating with an obligation incumbent on the defendants to repay. The problems arose under question three, unjust, and under question five, defences.

(i) Question three: failure of basis within a valid contract

The court held, Kirby J dissenting, that the wholesalers had received the tax element of the price upon a consideration which had subsequently failed. The judgments, not least that of Gummow J, make an important contribution to the understanding of failure of consideration in this context. At the beginning of the nineteenth century Sir William Evans showed that Lord Mansfield had employed the phrase in this context as the English translation of 'causa data causa non secuta' which the Romans used to denote one ground of non-contractual indebtedness.[39] In his essay on the action for money had and received Evans expounded failure of consideration with an eye constantly on its Roman original.[40] Gummow J now says, 'Here "failure of consideration" identifies the failure to sustain itself of the state of affairs contemplated as a basis for the payments the appellants seek to recover.'[41] Evans would certainly agree that that captures

---

[38] *Ha v New South Wales* (1999) 187 CLR 465 (HCA).

[39] WD Evans (tr) Robert Joseph Pothier *A Treatise on the Law of Obligations or Contracts* vol 2 (Strahan London 1806) 380.

[40] WD Evans *Essays: On the Action for Money Had and Received, on the Law of Insurances, and on the Law of Bills of Exchange and Promissory Notes* (Liverpool 1802) 25–34. The essay on money had and received is reprinted in [1998] Restitution L Rev 1–33.

[41] [2001] HCA 68 [104], (2001) 185 ALR 355 (HCA) [104].

well the sense of the almost untranslatable Latin 'Things given on a basis, that basis not following.'

It would avert a recurrent misunderstanding if 'failure of basis' could once and for all displace 'failure of consideration'. The resonance between consideration in this context and the doctrine of consideration in contract has repeatedly led judges to think that the only possible failure of basis was failure of contractual consideration.[42] In fact failure of contractual reciprocation is but one example of the failure of the basis of a transfer. The confusion would never have arisen if we had followed Sir William Evans in keeping our eyes on 'causa data causa non secuta'. Whether or not the terminology shifts to 'failure of basis', the *Roxborough* case should ward off further error. The majority judgments are absolutely clear that failure of contractual reciprocation is only one manifestation of failure of basis.[43] Here the tax element was paid, as both sides knew, on the basis that the tax was valid and the sum would have to be handed over to the government. There was no promise on the part of the wholesalers to hand it on, merely a shared assumption as to the basis on which the money was paid and received.[44]

Alongside failure of basis the other central unjust factor is mistake. The two often overlap. A claimant can recover for mistake without showing that the mistake was shared by the defendant, whereas there can be no failure of basis unless the basis is manifest. And a claimant can recover for failure of basis even though the shared basis consisted in future acts and facts, whereas a mistake must be as to the present or past. But if I mistakenly pay you money to discharge a supposed liability and it is manifest that that is the basis of my payment, there is no reason why if there was no such liability I should not rest my case for restitution on either or both unjust factors. Since both English and Australian law now allow recovery for mistakes of law,[45] it would seem that if Roxborough could have restitution for failure of basis it could equally have it for mistake of law, at least

---

[42] *Fibrosa Spolka Akcyjna v Fairbairn Lawson Combe Barbour* [1943] AC 32 (HL) corrected the view that, once the defendant had given consideration sufficient to make the claimant promise binding, only rescission *ab initio* could bring about a failure of consideration. Yet in *Westdeutsche Landesbank Girozentrale v Islington LBC* [1996] AC 669 (HL) it still remained doubtful whether there could be a failure of consideration other than within the context of an initially valid contract. Lord Goff's opinion, obiter as he thought (but see text between n 103 and n 106), was that there could [1996] AC 669 (HL) 682–3; cf W Swadling 'Restitution for No Consideration' [1994] RLR 73, 78–9; E McKendrick 'The Reason for Restitution' in P Birks and F Rose (eds) *Lessons of the Swaps Litigation* (LLP Mansfield London 2000) 84, 100–6.

[43] [2001] HCA 68, (2001) 185 ALR 355 (HCA) [16] (Gleeson, Gaudron, Hayne JJ), [102]–[104] (Gummow J).

[44] [2001] HCA 68, (2001) 185 ALR 355 (HCA) [16], (2001) 185 ALR 355 (HCA) [16]. (Gleeson, Gaudron, Hayne JJ).

[45] *David Securities Pty Ltd v Commonwealth Bank of Australia* (1992) 175 CLR 353 (HCA); *Kleinwort Benson v Lincoln CC* [1999] 2 AC 349 (HL).

according to the broad understanding of mistakes of law adopted by the House of Lords.[46] They paid because they mistakenly believed the tax on cigarettes was valid.

Kirby J's dissent was founded largely on the fact that Roxborough had paid under a valid contract which had never been discharged except by full performance.[47] This seems at first sight to be an insuperable objection. The orthodox doctrine is that an enrichment transferred under a valid contract cannot be recovered unless the contract is rescinded or terminated.[48]

The majority judgments barely address this obstacle. They appear to assume that it is covered by the weakening of the old rule that there could be no recovery for failure of consideration.[49] By accepting apportionment they hope to escape the bar to restitution of benefits transferred under a valid contract.[50] That will not quite do. A mistake which would otherwise indisputably require restitution will be ineffectual if the value in question passed under a contract. The claimant will then succeed only if he can show that the mistake destroyed the contract itself.[51] By parity of reasoning, in the very rare case that a failure of consideration can be made out despite the validity and indeed the performance of the contract, the contract remains an obstacle to the claim to restitution.[52] The rationale behind the bar can be expressed in the proposition that contracts must not be subverted or that irreconcilable contradictions between the law of contract and the law of restitution cannot be tolerated.

Orthodoxies are sometimes stated too widely. This one has been much discussed.[53] Professor Beatson has argued, rightly, that a more sophisticated analysis would conclude that this bar is not absolute. In particular he says that a distinction should be drawn between cases in which restitution

---

[46] Too broad according to P Birks 'Mistakes of Law' [2000] CLP 205; to the contrary J M Finnis 'The Fairy Tale's Moral' (1999) 115 LQR 170, D Sheehan 'What is a Mistake?' (2000) 20 LS 538.

[47] [2001] HCA 68 [165–66], (2001) 185 ALR 355 (HCA) [165–66].

[48] Goff & Jones (n 2) 47–48; AS Burrows *The Law of Restitution* (Butterworths London 1993) 271–2; K Mason and J Carter *Restitution Law in Australia* (Butterworths Sydney 1995) [909].

[49] E McKendrick 'Total Failure of Consideration and Counter-Restitution: Two Doctrines or One' in P Birks (ed) *Laundering and Tracing* (OUP Oxford 1995) 217; P Birks 'Failure of Consideration' in F Rose (ed) *Consensus* ad idem (Sweet & Maxwell London 1996) 179.

[50] [2001] HCA 68, (2001) 185 ALR 355 (HCA) [18]–[19] (Gleeson, Gaudron, Hayne JJ), [105]–[109] (Gummow J), [198]–[199] (Callinan J).

[51] *Bell v Lever Bros* [1932] AC 161 (HL).

[52] SA Smith 'Concurrent Liability in Contract and Unjust Enrichment: The Fundamental Breach Requirement' (1999) 115 LQR 245, 247–8, rightly distinguishing the requirement of total failure from that of discharge of the contract.

[53] G Mead 'Restitution within Contract' (1991) 11 Legal Studies 172; D Friedmann 'Valid, Voidable, Qualified and Non-Existing Obligations: An Alternative Perspective on the Law of Restitution' in AS Burrows *Essays on the Law of Restitution* (OUP Oxford 1991) 247; Swadling (n 52 above); J Beatson 'The Temptation of Elegance: Concurrence of Restitutionary and Contractual Cliams' in W Sadling and G Jones *The Search for Principle: Essays in Honour of Lord Goff of Chieveley* (OUP Oxford 1999) 142.

would disturb legitimate hopes and fears inherent in the bargain and others where it would not. In the latter the orthodox rule should give way.[54] That seems to be exactly the right way to approach this case. The crucial fact is that neither the payment of the tax nor the amount of that payment were viewed as negotiable. There were no hopes and fears in that regard. No tax, no payment. As between the parties there is no doubt whatever that restitution of the tax returned them to exactly the position they would have been in if, to their knowledge, the tax had been annulled or repealed before the payment.[55]

If in this way the orthodox rule proves more flexible than has been thought, serious attention will have to be paid to the outcome of *Orphanos v Queen Mary College*.[56] In that case a student who should have been charged fees on the home scale was charged on the higher overseas scale. When the mistake was discovered he sought to recover the difference. The House of Lords rejected his claim. The contract between him and the college was not invalidated by the mistake. Yet there was again no element of bargaining. There were simply two scales, and he had mistakenly been charged according to the wrong one.

We have allowed ourselves to speak of a 'bar' to restitution within a valid contract, language which suggests a defence under question five. But this is probably better viewed as question three matter, going to the definition of the unjust factors. There is no operative mistake where relief would redistribute risks distributed by the contract, and there is no failure of basis where the basis upon which the transfer was made included the running of such risks.

(ii) *Question five: disimpoverishment*

There was some question five matter. The wholesalers argued that the retailers could not recover because they had recouped their loss from consumers who had paid the prices fixed so as to include the tax. This defence has been upheld in some jurisdictions, notably Canada.[57] However, it has come under very severe criticism,[58] and, although it has been imposed by

---

[54] J Beatson (previous note) 142, esp 151–4.

[55] One important paragraph brings these factors together: [2001] HCA 68, (2001) 185 ALR 355 (HCA) [21] (Gleeson, Gaudron, Hayne JJ) and could be taken as in effect endorsing the approach of Beatson (n 53 above).

[56] [1985] AC 761 (HL). Cf *David Securities Pty Ltd v Commonwealth Bank of Australia* (1992) 175 CLR 353 (HCA) where there was also no need to protect the bargain, not because the mistaken payment had not been bargained for but because the matter was not as a matter of law open to private bargaining.

[57] *Air Canada v British Columbia* [1989] 1 SCR 1161, 59 DLR (4th) 161 (SCC).

[58] P Michel 'Restitution, Passing On, and the Recovery of Unlawfully Demanded Tax: Why *Air Canada* Doesn't Fly' (1995) (1) U Toronto Faculty L Rev 130; FD Rose 'Passing On' in

statute in relation to a number of indirect taxes, in Australia and England it has not been accepted in the absence of such a statute.[59] On this occasion the dissenting judgment would have allowed the defence on the ground that the cases only ruled it out against public authorities.[60] The majority ruled it out altogether, regarding it as profoundly flawed.[61]

There is a relation at this point between question five and question two, which identifies the claimant. In a system which recognizes unjust enrichment as an independent cause of action, the rejection of the defence of passing on is consonant with the view that, as in Germany, there is no absolute requirement that the claimant must have suffered a loss corresponding to the gain which he seeks to take from the defendant. The focus is on the enrichment of the defendant, not the impoverishment of the claimant. This is not to say that the enrichment must not in some way come from the claimant, but it does mean that in exploring that 'from' one must not start with a preconceived notion that there must be a simple plus and minus. This is very important. The range of the law of unjust enrichment is much reduced by the simple plus and minus understanding of 'at the expense of'.

(e) Lipkin Gorman v Karpnale Ltd[62]

This great case, in which the House of Lords accepted for the first time that English law did recognize a law of restitution of unjust enrichment, has been found difficult. Mr Virgo has gone so far as to expel it. He thinks it was a vindication of property rights and had nothing to do with unjust enrichment.[63] It certainly was not a vindication in the usual sense of that word, in which it denotes a direct assertion of a property right. It was, in the old language, an *indebitatus assumpsit*, a debt collected through *assumpsit*, a personal claim to a sum of money. The *causa debendi*—the causative event creating the debt—was unjust enrichment. There was a proprietary question, but it arose only in the attempt to build a sufficient connection between the claimant's and the defendant. It is not clear that that attempt succeeded.

P Birks (ed) *Laundering and Tracing* (OUP Oxford 1995) P Birks 'Private Law' in P Birks (ed) *Lessons of the Swaps Litigation* (LLP Mansfield 2000) 1, 36–9.

[59] *Mason v New South Wales* (1959) 102 CLR108 (HCA) 146 (Windeyer J); *Commissioner of State Revenue v Royal Insurance Australia Ltd* (1994) 182 CLR 51 (HCA) (Mason ACJ); *Kleinwort Benson Ltd v South Tyneside MBC* [1994] 2 All ER 972, 987; *Kleinwort Benson Ltd v Birmingham City Council* [1997] QB 380 (CA) 400.

[60] [2001] HCA 68 [127]–[143]; (2001) 185 ALR 355, [127]–[143] (Kirby J). His conclusion in favour of the availability of the defence to a non-governmental party is somewhat tentative and confined to the case in which the factual problems can be overcome [143].

[61] [2001] HCA 68 [25]–[29]; (2001) 185 ALR 355, [25]–[29] (Gleeson, Gaudron, Hayne JJ), [8]–[9] (Gummow J).

[62] [1991] 2 AC 548 (HL), Birks [1991] LMCLQ 473–97, McKendrick (1992) 55 MLR 377.

[63] G Virgo *Principles of the Law of Restitution* (OUP Oxford 1999) 592–4.

The facts were that over a long period a partner in a firm of solicitors had fed his addiction to gambling from the firm's client account. By the time he was found out the gambling partner was penniless. He was sent to prison. The question was whether the firm could recover from the casino in which he had gambled away hundreds of thousands of pounds. In the House of Lords the firm laid aside equitable arguments and confined itself to its common law rights. On that narrow basis it nevertheless won.

(i) Question two: at the expense of the claimant

The casino had received money. There was no contest under question one. Most of the difficulties are concentrated on question two. The casino did not receive from the firm but from the gambler. Had the money used by him belonged to the firm, there would have been no difficulty. One who receives my property receives from me. The House of Lords squeezed the facts into that model. There was an obstacle. The gambler was an authorized signatory. Their Lordships refused to reverse authority to the effect that property in money paid by a bank to an authorized signatory passes to that signatory even if he has an unauthorized purpose in mind.[64] So the money was not the firm's money but belonged to the gambler.

Lord Goff, giving the leading speech, circumvented this obstacle by recourse to the law of tracing. The money, though it belonged to the gambler, was the traceable product of the bank account which belonged to the firm. From this he inferred that the firm had a power to assert a right in it and that that power, though never actually exercised while the money remained traceable in the casino's hands, was sufficient to entitle the firm to make this claim.

This argument does not work unless supplemented by a proposition which was never secured. A key element in Professor Lionel Smith's work on tracing has been the proposition that tracing is neutral as to rights.[65] The rules of tracing tell whether one asset is the substitute for another. But substitution is itself neutral as to rights. If I show that the picture on your wall is the traceable substitute for the money I gave you for your birthday, I do not thereby establish any right in it. Nor does it make any difference that I can show that on the morning of your birthday that money was mine, just before I gave it to you. Similarly, in the *Lipkin* case, on the face of things the firm achieved nothing at all by showing that the account which Cass rifled belonged to them before he rifled it. They had to establish a proprietary base, not the moment before he received the money, but

---

[64] *Union Bank of Australia Ltd v McClintock* [1922] 1 AC 240 (PC); *Commercial Banking Co of Sydney Ltd v Mann* [1961] AC 1 (PC), approved [1991] 2 AC 548 (HL) 573.
[65] LD Smith *The Law of Tracing* (OUP Oxford 1997) 10–14, 299.

the moment after. Given the rule that the property passed to the authorized signatory, the firm could not show that at that moment the money
was theirs.

Given that the property in the money passed to the gambler, the proprietary base could only be compatibly established in one of three ways.
First, their Lordships might have held that the gambler had a voidable title
at law. Secondly, if equitable arguments had not been cut out, it could
have been said that he had only the bare legal title. Thirdly, more complex,
it could have been affirmed that as a signatory the gambler was, in relation
to the bank account, in the same position as a bailee of the firm's money,
in that the account was already in his hands before he misapplied it, so
that the tracing exercise could start from that asset rather than the
money.[66]

These are the only ways of salvaging the proprietary link between
Lipkin Gorman and the casino. None of them deals with the problem that
the power to vest was never exercised in relation to any specific thing and
therefore has to be seen as sufficing in itself to create the link. We have to
say that the power itself, unexercised, was sufficient.

The more radical alternative is to abandon the proprietary connection
and say instead that it suffices to establish a causal connection between a
claimant in unjust enrichment and the enrichment which he wants to
claim: if Cass had not enriched himself from the firm, the casino would
never have received. Tracing is not strictly necessary for a causal argument, but it could be understood as part of a very restrictive view of a
sufficient causal link for these purposes. Not only would the casino not
have received from Cass if Cass had not taken from the claimants but,
additionally, the money he passed to them was the very money he took or
its traceable substitute. All the same, without the proprietary link we
would have to see a more elaborate explanation of the firm's having been
able to leapfrog the gambler. Causation can establish a link but it does not
explain why the leapfrog is allowed. One crucial fact is that the casino
could not plead the defence of bona fide purchase from third party. It was
technically a donee, on account of the statutory nullity of its contracts. But
we have just observed in connection with *Lloyds Bank v Independent
Insurance* that it is not permissible to leapfrog a contractual relationship.
There was a contractual relationship between the firm and Cass, a contract
of partnership. In the absence of a proprietary link that would seem to be
an insuperable obstacle.

---

[66] This may be Professor Smith's meaning in a difficult passage: LD Smith (n 65) 363.

(ii) Question three: unjust

If the casino could be said to have established a sufficient proprietary link between it and the enrichment of the casino, the third question required it to identify an unjust factor. Why was the enrichment at their expense unjust? The judgments do not explicitly address this question. However, it is not really problematic. If mistake works as an unjust factor because it shows that the claimant's consent to the transfer was defective, complete absence of consent must necessarily work in the same way.

On the present hypothesis the gambler was secretly using money which, for the purposes of a claim in unjust enrichment, though not for a claim in tort, sufficiently belonged to the firm. The firm gave no consent at all to that user by either party. It knew nothing of it. 'No consent' has different manifestations. Ignorance (not knowing that wealth was passing) and powerlessness (knowing but not being able to prevent wealth passing) are the obvious cases. So long as we suppose that the proprietary connection was established, then the same unjust factor works for every recipient, for it is equally true of all who receive or deal with my property that they do so without my consent.

If the connection was merely causal and the objection to leapfrogging could be overcome, the third question would have to be answered differently. The absence of my consent ceases to be relevant, for the recipients are now dealing with what has become their own. Where the causal argument works under question two, it is not necessary to establish an independent unjust factor against the remote recipient. The relevant proposition is that the unjust factor good against the immediate recipient is good against his donee, simply because the donee cannot be in a better position as a holder in due course. Suppose a mistaken payee is led into making a donation to a charity. The mistaken payer probably has a claim against the charity, even without establishing any proprietary link. The mistake is the only unjust factor. The charity is liable because a donee cannot be in a stronger position than the donor.

(iii) Question four and question two: interaction

A claimant who wants to establish a proprietary connection between himself and an enrichment received by the defendant may or may not rely on the law of unjust enrichment to do it. In the simplest model *C* draws £50 from a cash machine and drops it on the way home, so that *D* finds it. Here there is no recourse to the law of unjust enrichment to establish *C*'s proprietary right. Lipkin Gorman could not establish the connection in that simple way, for the reasons just discussed. The firm thus argued that the casino had received, not their asset, but the traceable substitute for their asset over which they had a power to vest it in themselves. The discussion of the next case will show that it is a matter of dispute whether substitution is a species of unjust enrichment at the expense the owner of the original. If it is, the case illustrates the fact that one reason why a claimant will try to establish that the enrichment gave rise to a proprietary right is precisely in order to provide the foundation for a proprietary answer to question two. In other words question four, which asks what kind of right arises from the unjust enrichment which has occurred, sometimes becomes relevant only because of the need to answer question two.

(iv) Question five: defences

The *Lipkin Gorman* case also secured the place of change of position in the law of unjust enrichment, laying down at the same time that bona fide purchase from a third party cannot be relied upon by a recipient whose exchange with the third party was void, as the casino's was with the gambler. Had his taste been for champagne at the Ritz, the Ritz would have had an absolute defence as bona fide purchaser.

Under the heading of change of position the casino was allowed to deduct the payments which it had made because of the money received by Cass, namely his occasional winnings. There are many difficulties lurking here, but they lie outside the central purpose of this paper, which is to show that the five-question analysis identifies and tests a liability which is *sui generis*.

(v) Summary

The casino was enriched at the firm's expense either because it received money which in a limited but sufficient sense was the property of the firm or else, possibly, because it would not have received anything from the gambler if he, Cass, had not enriched himself at the firm's expense, that causal link being underpinned by the fact that the money was traceably the very money taken from the firm. As for the unjust factor, it was 'no consent' in the form of 'ignorance'—the firm did not know its money was being used. In the alternative it might be said that the absence of consent consisted in a prohibition disobeyed. On the second hypothesis as to the answer to question two, the causal answer, there was no independent unjust factor applying to the casino, which was only caught by a proposition to the effect that donee cannot be in a stronger position that the donor. As for question four, the firm only asserted a right *in personam* although it may be correct to say that they answered question four in order to obtain a favourable answer to question two. Under the fifth question, the case was the first to reduce the liability of a defendant explicitly for change of position: its receipts had caused some payments out, in the form of the gambler's winnings.

(f) Foskett v McKeown[67]

The latest manifestation of insecurity in relation to unjust enrichment is to be found in this important case. The House of Lords held that it had nothing to do with unjust enrichment. Unless that is correct, it is an important fourth question case, an example of an unjust enrichment which gives rise not only to a personal right but a proprietary right. To decide whether it is correct, we have to answer the first three questions of the five-question analysis. The is also a hidden fifth question point.

Money was stolen by a trustee and used to pay premiums on an expensive insurance policy. The dishonest trustee killed himself. His family received £1m in death benefit. For present purposes we need not bother with some complications lurking in these facts. The terms of the insurance policy were unusual and led to some disagreement as to whether and to what extent the £1m was indeed the traceable substitute for the stolen money. There is no need to get bogged down in the intricacies of tracing, for tracing is only the process of identification which tells whether and to what extent a given asset is the substitute for another. Our concern is their Lordships' analysis of the law applicable to an undoubted substitute.

Suppose a simpler scenario in which a trustee takes £100,000 of trust money and, with £50,000 of his own, buys himself a Rolls Royce. The House of Lords approached the more complex real facts on the basis that in this simpler case the beneficiaries under the trust have an option. They can elect to have a beneficial interest in the car proportionate to their contribution or a lien on the car for the sum of money taken. The choice will depend on the current value of the car. If the proportionate interest would be worth less than the contribution, the lien for the whole sum will be preferable.

(i) Fictitious persistence

Their Lordships' explanation of the claimants' rights in the substitute, here the Rolls Royce, was that their proprietary rights in the original asset simply persisted. Thus Lord Millett, who gave the leading speech, said 'The plaintiffs claim a continuing beneficial interest. . . . The transmission of a claimant's property rights from one asset to its traceable proceeds is part of our law of property, not of the law of unjust enrichment.'[68] This

---

[67] [2000] 2 WLR 1299 (HL).   [68] [2000] 2 WLR 1299, 1322H–1323A; cf 1327CD.

represents an adoption, almost verbatim, of the position taken in Mr Virgo's book.[69]

Property and unjust enrichment cannot be opposed in this way. A right belongs in the law of property by virtue of its nature as a proprietary right, a right *in rem*, just as a right *in personam* belongs in the law of obligations by virtue of its nature as such. Since the nature of a right as *in rem* or *in personam* is not determined by its causative event, every right necessarily belongs not only in the law of property or the law of obligations but also in the law of its own causative event. A property right which arises from a wrong, belongs in the law of property and the law of wrongs. A right *in personam* which arises from an unjust enrichment belongs in the law of obligations and in the law of unjust enrichment. When their Lordships said the case arose in property not in unjust enrichment, they no doubt meant to contrast causative events. They meant that the right in the substitute was not generated by unjust enrichment but by the same event—express declaration of trust—as the right in the original and, having been generated, simply persisted.

Professor Burrows has shown that this persistence is a fiction.[70] In our example it cannot be said, except fictitiously, that the beneficiaries' right in the Rolls Royce arose from the declaration of trust which earlier gave them their right in the money which was stolen. Not only was there no Rolls Royce in sight at the beginning of the story but by the end of the story the right in the Rolls Royce has mutated. It has become an undivided two-thirds share. At the election of the claimant it might have become a lien. The fiction of the persistence of the original right is a familiar kind of lawyerly evasion. It hides an event which is difficult to analyse. That event we may call substitution without the consent of the owner or, somewhat shorter, non-consensual substitution.

(ii) *Questions one, two, and three*

Professor Burrows says, correctly in my view, that the event is an unjust enrichment.[71] The first three questions of the five-question analysis confirm this, though not without one hiccup. Was the trustee enriched? Yes, by using the beneficiaries' money and his own in the proportion 66.6:33.3 the trustee was able to buy himself a Rolls Royce. Was it at the

---

[69] Virgo (n 63 above) 12–13, 17, 592–3.

[70] A Burrows 'Proprietary Restitution: Unmasking Unjust Enrichment' (2001) 117 LQR 412.

[71] Burrows (n 70 above) esp 418–19. Compare LD Smith *Tracing* (n 65 above) 300, 305–10. Rotherham also accepts the unjust enrichment explanation, but he appears to think of the effects given to substitutions as a blunt instrument for deciding what enrichment survives in the assets of the defendant, a role which is primarily discharged by the defence of change of position: C Rotherham *Proprietary Remedies in Context* (Hart Oxford 2002) 108–14.

expense of the beneficiaries? Yes, as to 66% the Rolls Royce came from the claimant beneficiaries because it was obtained with their money. Was the enrichment unjust? Yes, the unjust factor was the absence of their consent, in the form of 'ignorance'—not knowing their money was being used. Ignorance is *a fortiori* from mistake. One who transfers money by mistake gets it back because his consent to the transfer was impaired. One from whom wealth moves absolutely without his knowledge must have a parallel case for restitution. And here the law does give it back. It does so by raising a new proprietary right in the substitute.

The hiccup, and hence the weakest link in the argument, is the answer to question two. Was the car acquired at the expense of the beneficiaries? The money was subtracted from them but the car was not. Nevertheless there was an interceptive subtraction, in that in using their money the trustee intercepted the opportunities inherent in their ownership of the money. A system committed to the proposition that the claimant in unjust enrichment must show a loss corresponding to the defendant's gain could not accept the notion of an interceptive subtraction of this kind, but not all systems do so insist, and ours seems not to.[72]

(iii) Question four: a property right arising from unjust enrichment

The House of Lords avoids the analysis of substitution by hiding it behind a fiction. Professor Burrows treats it as an unjust enrichment. Mr Swadling does not avoid the issue but comes to a different conclusion, for he places non-consensual substitution in the miscellaneous fourth category, where it joins accessions, mixtures, specifications, and so on.[73] However, if we followed him in taking it out of unjust enrichment, we would come up against a serious difficulty. What other reason can be given why the law should give substitution any proprietary effect? No other rationale seems plausible.

If it is correct to say that the first three questions yield affirmative answers, the new right in the substitute does arise from unjust enrichment, and non-consensual substitution is a species of unjust enrichment which

---

[72] On this basis even the claim which was made in the famous Kentucky Cave case, *Edwards v Lee's Administrators* 96 SW 2d 1028 (1936), can be understood as based on an interceptively subtractive enrichment: E Weinrib 'Restitutionary Damages as Corrective Justice' (2000) 1 Theoretical Inquiries into Law 1, cf E Weinrib 'The Juridical Classification of Obligations' in P Birks (ed) *The Classification of Obligations* (OUP 1997) 37, 47; P Birks and C Mitchell in P Birks (ed). *English Private Law* (OUP 2000) vol 2 [15.000]. This is not to say that the Kentucky case cannot be explained as restitution for the wrong as such, only that it can by alternative analysis also be explained as an interceptive unjust enrichment. The same is true of *Trustee of FC Jones & Sons v Jones* [1997] Ch 159 (CA), although there no attempt at all is made to build the conclusion on a wrong (conversion of the cheques).

[73] WJ Swadling 'Property' in P Birks (ed) *English Private Law* (OUP 2000) vol 2 para 4.777; contrast para 15.191 (Birks).

gives rise to a proprietary right. The next section returns to that. If the right
in the substitute, more accurately the power to impose that right on the substitute,[74] does after all arise from unjust enrichment, it must so arise regardless of the nature of the event from which the right in the original asset
arose. The claimant's right in the original may have arisen from some manifestation of consent on the part of a predecessor in title. More rarely it may
have arisen non-consensually. If *X*, a fiduciary, takes a secret commission,
which he then holds on trust for his beneficiary, *Y*, *Y*'s equitable interest in
that money arises from the wrong of breach of fiduciary duty. If *X* then
invests and reinvests until *Y* claims a farm as the traceable substitute, the
power and the beneficial interest which comes with its exercise arise from
non-consensual substitution and, on this view, from unjust enrichment.
Attorney-General for Hong Kong v Reid thus begins with a property right arising from a wrong but ends with one which arises from unjust enrichment.[75]

(iv) Question five: change of position

One pressingly practical issue is whether the right in the substitute is
immune to the defence of change of position. That defence, in its disenrichment form, is tied into the central rationale of unjust enrichment. It marks
the point at which the relocation of gains turns into the allocation of losses.
It has no similarly necessary application to claims arising from any other
causative event. *Foskett v McKeown* answered this question by affirming
that the right in the substitute did not arise from unjust enrichment. But,
because of the fiction of persistence, the causative event was never
identified. All rights which arise from unjust enrichment are subject to the
defence of change of position. A particular defendant may be disqualified.
The defence only applies to those who change their position in good faith.

3. THE FOURTH QUESTION

So far this paper has not attempted a general answer to any of the five
questions. This section seeks to give such an answer to the fourth. It gets
special treatment, not because of its special difficulty, but because, as was
explained at the beginning, the metaphor of remedy raises expectations
here which are not provoked by the other four. The right arising from a
troublesome event is often called a remedy, although there would be less
danger of confusion if 'remedy' were saved for the court's order or,
slightly wider, for all means of realizing the right. What follows is too
short and done with too broad a brush. One large excision is the incidence
of subrogation.

[74] Text to n 110, below.   [75] [1994] 1 AC 324 (PC).

(a) The meaning of the fourth question

The central purpose of the question is to find out whether the right which arises from any particular unjust enrichment falls in the law of obligations or the law of property. In other words, is it a right *in personam* correlating with an obligation incumbent on the defendant to make restitution, or is it a property right, a right *in rem*? If it is a property right, the principal question requires two sub-inquiries, first whether the right is a power *in rem*, by the exercise of which the claimant can alter the status of the thing, or an immediately vested right—this terminology is not entirely satisfactory, because a power *in rem* is strictly speaking itself a vested right, albeit one limited by its nature as a power—secondly whether, when vested, it is a security right or a beneficial right. This latter sub-question will not be pursued here.[76]

We may assume that the law's common or garden response to an unjust enrichment is a right *in personam* or, synonymously but looking from the other end, an obligation to make restitution. The difficult questions are whether or not, in addition to the personal right, or instead of it, the law raises a property right of one of the kinds mentioned in the previous paragraph, and, if it does, of which of those kinds.

This amplification of the question will be disputed by some scholars. In particular it will not be accepted by those who think that property and obligations ought not to be contrasted at all, nor by those who think that the contrast cannot be expressed as that between rights whose exigibility is confined to the person or persons against whom they originally arose (rights *in personam*, anglicized to personal rights) and rights whose exigibility is defined by the location of a thing (rights *in rem*).

(b) The moment of receipt

Until we expressly return to traceable substitutes, the paragraphs which follow must be understood to speak only of the law as it applies at the moment at which an enriching asset first comes into the defendant's hands. In practice many proprietary claims are made in respect of traceable substitutes. The importance of the original asset and the moment of receipt is then that, unless the claimant establishes a proprietary base in that asset at that moment, successful tracing to a substitute will yield no proprietary rights in the substitute.[77]

---

[76] The option in relation to traceable substitutes was mentioned above, text to n 67. Sometimes only a lien arises: *Lord Napier and Ettrick v Hunter* [1993] AC 713 (HL).

[77] Burrows (n 70) 429; LD Smith *The Law of Tracing* (OUP Oxford 1997) 301, cf 11–14.

We want to know whether and when an unjust enrichment gives rise to a proprietary right. At the moment of receipt the situation will be that the transferor either has a proprietary right in the asset received or has not. If he has not, the question drops away. If he has, it will either be the same right as he had before the transfer—in other words the property in the asset will not have passed—or it will be a brand new right. If it is the same proprietary right, it is highly unlikely to have arisen from unjust enrichment, certainly not from the unjust enrichment of the recipient. In ninety-nine cases out of a hundred it will have arisen consensually. Thus, if I lose my wedding ring or part with it under a mistake so fundamental as to prevent the property passing, my property right surviving in the ring now in the hands of the defendant is same the right I acquired by delivery from my wife, she having purchased it from the goldsmith who made it.

The other case is that in which the claimant acquires—obtains, not retains—a brand new proprietary right in the thing. That right may also have arisen consensually. I transfer my ring to X and Y on express trust for myself. My equitable beneficial interest is brand new. It arises from the fact that the transfer was, as I declared and they accepted, made upon trust. Alternatively, the new interest may have arisen by operation of law independently of the consent of parties. In that case the event which has had the effect of raising the new property right must be a wrong, an unjust enrichment, or a causative event of some other kind.

We know from *Attorney-General for Hong Kong v Reid*, if we did not know it before, that there is at least one acquisitive wrong, namely breach of fiduciary duty, which generates a proprietary right in its victim.[78] The Hong Kong government's equitable right in the bribes taken by the corrupt prosecutor arose from that acquisitive wrong. We also know that there are some non-consensual property rights which arise neither from wrongs nor from unjust enrichments. When your paint accedes to my car it becomes mine. That accession does not operate in the character of a wrong and, far from reversing an enrichment at my expense, it enriches me at your expense. We need not explore non-consensual property rights arising from wrongs or from miscellaneous other events. We need only to be aware that those categories exist.

Our concern is with the remaining non-consensual category, namely unjust enrichment. Do property rights arise from unjust enrichments? Mr Swadling thinks that the answer ought to be that they never do, though he admits that that happily simple conclusion is not yet represented in the cases.[79] Mr Virgo thinks that proprietary rights are definitively outside the

---

[78] [1994] 1 AC 324 (PC).
[79] WJ Swadling 'Property and Unjust Enrichment' in JW Harris (ed) *Property Problems from Genes to Pension Funds* (Kluwer London 1997) 130.

law of unjust enrichment,[80] but in so doing he is forced to take a position which has no rationale, namely that the list of events which generate property rights must be shorter than the list of the events which create personal rights. It is not to be overlooked that the House of Lords appears to have been moving towards the Swadling-Virgo position, both wanting and finding less proprietary responses to unjust enrichment.[81]

The question can only be answered by working through the cases on every known species of unjust enrichment. The exercise is made no easier by the fact that people do not instantly agree on what counts as a species of that genus or how best to review them all. In every case there must be an enrichment at the expense of the claimant and an unjust factor which, not operating as a manifestation of consent or a wrong, provides the reason for restitution. Dividing according to the nature of the unjust factor, there are four groups:

(a) the claimant gave no consent at all,
(b) the claimant's intent to transfer was defective, as by reason of mistake, pressure, or want of autonomy arising from a relationship or other disadvantage,
(c) the claimant's intent was qualified and the qualification cannot now be purified, or
(d) some other good reason why the enrichment should be given up.

The last of these must now drop out. It requires disproportionate space.

Category (a) is not in play at the moment of receipt, because there property does not pass at all. The transferor has a property right but it is the right he had all along. It certainly has not arisen from the unjust enrichment of the transferee. Category (a) includes cases in which the claimant had no knowledge that his wealth was passing to the recipient or where he was helpless to prevent it doing so. Very similar but probably best left in (b) are extreme cases of mistake and pressure which have the same effect of preventing the property passing.

Category (b) contains all the cases of defective intent. Many we instantly recognize as factors which render the transfer as voidable, so that the claimant obtains a power *in rem* either at law or in equity to vest in himself the *res* which is voidably transferred. This is true of induced mistake, of illegitimate pressure, and certainly of the relational want of autonomy usually called undue influence. Other cases of want of autonomy require more prolonged and individual consideration and must be put on one side.

---

[80] Virgo (n 63) 15–17, 591–5.
[81] As witness *Westdeutsche Landesbank Girozentrale v Islington LBC* [1996] AC 669 (HL); *Foskett v McKeown* [2000] 2 WLR 1299 (HL).

Nowadays it seems to be agreed that when a transfer is voidable in equity the claimant does not have an immediate vested equitable interest. The American *Restatement of Restitution* assumes a different model, namely that voidability in equity produces an immediate constructive trust, the beneficiary of which is then able on ordinary principles to recall the legal title.[82] Voidabilty in equity is thus focused only on the behaviour of the legal estate.The legal estate is voidable because of the immediate trust imposed by equity. But this view has apparently been abandoned in recent cases. What the transferor now has is, as at law,[83] a power to give himself an equitable interest, the power itself being something less, 'a mere equity'.[84]

Spontaneous mistake is more difficult. If sufficiently fundamental, it will prevent the property passing. These are the examples with affinity to category (a). It is still controversial whether or not in equity a lesser spontaneous mistake can render a transfer voidable.[85] The right answer is probably that in bargaining situations it cannot but in non-bargaining situations it can. *Chase Manhattan Bank NA Ltd v Israel-British Bank (London) Ltd*, nowadays the subject of criticism, would be inexplicable if that were not minimally the case.[86] There a bank mistakenly paid a large sum twice. There was no element of bargaining. The view was taken that a mistaken payment turned the recipient into a trustee for the transferor. The transferor had, not a power, but an immediate vested beneficial interest in the money received. This is compatible with the older view of what voidability meant in equity. The result of the case would not be inexplicable if on second thoughts the right was re-analysed as initially a mere power *in rem*. In a non-bargaining situation it would be odd if there were much difference between a spontaneous mistake and one which was innocently

---

[82] *Restatement* (n 22) sections 163, 166, with comments thereto. It is fair to say that in the meantime the American view of a constructive trust has departed from that of English law. It now more resembles a personal right to the conveyance of an asset enforceable specifically but giving the claimant a property right only from judgment: *Re Omegas Group* 16 F 3d 1443 (6th Cir 1994) followed with some reluctance in *Re Dow Corning Corp* 192 BR 428 (Bankr E D Mich 1996) resisted in A Kull 'Restitution in Bankruptcy' 72 American Bankruptcy J 265 (1998).

[83] *Car & Universal Finance Co Ltd v Caldwell* [1965] 1 QB 525 (CA).

[84] *Lonrho Plc v Fayed* [1992] 1 WLR 1, 11–12 (Millett J); *Bristol and West BS v Motthew* [1998] Ch 1, 22–3 followed in *Twinsectra Ltd v Yardley* [1999] Lloyd's Rep Banking 348, 461–2 (CA) aff'd on other grounds [2002] UKHL 12, [2002] 2 WLR 802 (HL). This was resisted in favour of an earlier preference for an immediate trust in R Chambers *Resulting Trusts* (OUP Oxford 1997) 170–84. Compare R Chambers 'Constructive Trusts in Canada' (part II) (2002) 16 Trust Law Intl 2, 15.

[85] *Great Peace Shipping Ltd v Tsavliris Salvage (International) Ltd* (2001) 151 NLJ 1696 (QBD Comm Ct) aff'd [2002] EWCA Civ 1407.

[86] [1981] Ch 105, criticized and explained in terms of fault in *Westdeutsche Landesbank Girozentrale v Islington LBC* [1996] AC 669 (HL) 714 (Lord Browne-Wilkinson). Compare Lord Millett: The Rt Hon Sir Peter Millett 'Restitution and Constructive Trust' (1998) 114 LQR 399, 412–13.

induced. It would be very odd if Chase Manhattan had been accorded no proprietary interest at all because its mistake was spontaneous when it would have had such an interest if its mistake had been induced by an innocent misrepresentation. Where there is no bargain there is no difference between the two.

It is possible that the resulting trust which arises by presumption from transfers which have the externalities of gift ought to be placed here in category (b). It depends what fact the presumption presumes. If it presumes an intent to create a trust, the resulting trust is an express trust found with the help of a presumption. If it presumes no more than the absence of an intent to benefit the transferee, it may be best placed here. This argument cannot be pursued here, though it will crop up once more in this paper.[87]

To sum up at this point, where the transferor gives no consent at all, and in extreme cases of mistake and pressure, no property passes. The transferor literally retains his original right. In cases of defective consent, the transferor generally obtains a power *in rem*, a power to vest the asset in himself. In spontaneously mistaken transfers of the kind in which the legal property does pass it may be that the transferor obtains an immediate equitable interest, though this might easily be brought into line with the power which is the response to induced mistakes. Into this picture we still have to throw the disruptive swaps cases. We will come back to them.

Category (c) includes two kinds of qualified intent, failure of consideration, better called failure of basis, and absolutely qualified intent, where the transferor intends to transfer but only on condition that the transferee never takes any benefit. An important difference between category (c) and category (b) is that in (c) the unjust factor may not operate at the moment of the receipt.[88] That is, there may be a lapse of time between receipt and activation of an obligation to make restitution. For the purposes of our fourth question it makes a great deal of difference whether in that lapse of time the value in question is or is not ring-fenced. It is ring-fenced if the recipient is obliged not to apply it to his own benefit in the manner in which he may apply his own property. Usually this means he must apply it to particular purposes, but on occasion it means only that he must not use it for himself.[89]

Here it is certain that if the qualified transfer puts the value transferred freely at the disposition of the recipient at the moment of the transfer, the transferor will never have a proprietary interest even if a restitutionary obligation is triggered later. I pay you £5,000 in advance on the basis that you are going to build me a garage. We have a contract to that effect. If you

---

[87] Text to n 97.   [88] Chambers *Resulting Trusts* (n 84) 145–6, 148.

[89] As where a trust fails to dispose of the beneficial interest and, most obviously, where it fails for want of any objects: *Vandervell v IRC* [1967] 2 AC 291 (HL).

do not build the garage and the contract is brought to an end, you will incur a personal liability to make restitution. However, for the moment you are not under any restitutionary liability. Furthermore, in the interval between receipt and restitutionary liability there is no ring-fencing. In that sense the money is at your disposition, even though you have a potential restitutionary liability in the event of the basis of the transfer failing.

So far as *Re Goldcorp Exchange*[90] was decided on the ground of failure of basis, it vividly illustrates this negative certainty. Many New Zealanders had invested heavily in in a scheme run by Goldcorp under which gold which they bought from the company was to be safely kept for them and insured. No gold was ever appropriated to any contract and no attempt was made to maintain a store of customer gold. The investors, having paid for gold and further services, had received nothing. They undoubtedly had a personal claim for the amount of their payments, but in the insolvency of the sellers the crucial question was whether they had any proprietary right in the money which they had paid over. The answer was an emphatic negative. There was no point in beginning a tracing exercise because the property in the money had passed to Goldcorp and had been at that moment freely at the company's disposition. Hence one certainty is that, in the absence of ring-fencing, when the basis of a payment fails after it has been received there is no proprietary right.

Subject once again to the law as applied in the swaps saga, in all cases in this category in which there was no moment at which the defendant recipient was free to treat the money as being at his own disposition, a proprietary interest has arisen. There are cases in which the value in question is first ring-fenced and then the basis fails, and there are other cases in which the unjust factor bites *ab initio*. These represent two different but sometimes concurrent ways in which the value in question is prevented from ever being freely at the disposition of the recipient.

Four cases can be identified. Thus, there may be: (i) a Quistclose tie,[91] (ii) an express trust which fails to dispose of the entirety of the beneficial interest,[92] (iii) a transfer which is absolutely qualified by intent that the transferee should not benefit,[93] (iv) a simple failure of basis where the basis has already failed at or before the moment of receipt.[94] Example (i) is

---

[90] [1995] 1 AC 74 (PC).

[91] *Barclays Bank Ltd v Quistclose Investments Ltd* [1970] AC 567 (HL), reanalysed in *Twinsectra Ltd v Yardley* [2002] UKHL 12, [2002] 2 WLR 802 (HL).

[92] *Air Jamaica Ltd. v Charlton* [1999] 1 WLR 1399 (PC).

[93] *Hodgson v Marks* [1971] Ch 892 (CA), on which Chambers *Resulting Trusts* (n 84) 139 and R Chambers 'Resulting Trusts in Canada' (Part 1) (2002) 16 Trust Law Intl 104, 116–17. To the contrary W Swadling 'A Hard Look at *Hodgson v Marks*' in P Birks and F Rose (eds) *Restitution and Equity* (LLP Mansfield London 2000) 61. Of the same kind but presumptive: *Tinsley v Milligan* [1994] 1 AC 340 (HL).

[94] *Neste Oy v Lloyds Bank* [1983] 2 Lloyd's Rep 658.

a case of initial ring-fencing and, usually, later failure of basis. Example (ii) is a case of ring-fencing in which the failure of basis is usually immediate and initial, though the failure is not necessarily and invariably initial. Example (iii) is not a case of failure of basis but of absolute qualification, which takes effect immediately, and example (iv) is completely independent of ring-fencing .

There is no doubt whatever that a proprietary interest arises in the transferor in the ring-fenced cases (i), (ii), and (iii). The only debate is as to whether it arises from unjust enrichment. The one serious counter-argument is that it arises consensually, by way of express trust, albeit sometimes with the help of a presumption. As a matter of authority the consensual explanation is currently dominant in (i),[95] but that explanation may be flawed. In (ii) the consensual argument will certainly not work, since it is nearly always clear on the evidence that the transferor had no intention at all as to the destination of the undisposed interest.[96] It has been objected instead that (ii) is a case in which the transferor necessarily, or 'automatically', retains a pre-existing interest, but that view has also been rejected.[97] In (iii) the express trust explanation works in cases in which there is no requirement of writing, but where writing would be required the resulting trust is better explained as arising to reverse the enrichment of a recipient towards whom the transferor had no beneficial intent.

We have seen that there is a question whether (c) (iii) is the proper home for the cases in which the requisite intent is established by the presumption arising from gratuitous transfers outside the relationships of 'advancement'. It is probably better returned to category (b).[98] Mr Swadling's argument that these are genuine express trusts established with the aid of an evidential presumption has been commended in the House of Lords.[99] But the evidential presumption cannot realistically establish more than an absence of beneficial intent. To press it further is to engage in the same kind of fiction as the old implied contract theory of unjust enrichment. If the fact presumed were that the transferor positively intended to create a trust or to retain the benefit, the presumption would

---

[95] *Twinsectra Ltd v Yardley* [2002] UKHL 12, [2002] 2 WLR 802 (HL) esp Lord Milllett. Professor Chambers's objections to the analysis preferred in that case weigh heavily and remain to be answered more fully, Chambers *Resulting Trusts* (n 84) 73–7.

[96] *Re Gillingham Bus Disaster Fund* [1958] Ch 300, 310 (Harman J), aff'd [1959] Ch 62 (CA).

[97] *Westdeutsche Landesbank Girozentrale v. Islington LBC* [1996] AC 669 (HL) 706 (Lord Browne-Wilkinson). There are compelling arguments in Chambers 'Resulting Trusts in Canada' (n 93 above) 114–15.

[98] Text to n 87 above.

[99] WJ Swadling 'A New Role for Resulting Trusts?' (1996) 16 Legal Studies 110, cited with approval in *Westdeutsche Landesbank Girozentrale v Islington LBC* [1996] AC 669 (HL) 708 (Lord Browne-Wilkinson).

be recurrently rebutted by affirmative evidence that he never thought of such a thing.[100]

There are loose ends in this account, which for want of space cannot be tucked in. One crucial fact is that nothing at any point turns on fault of any kind.[101] The proprietary interest turns on timing.[102] Was there any moment at which the value transferred was freely at the disposition of the recipient? If not, the transferor has a proprietary interest. Fault creeps in from an alien context. Sometimes proprietary effects can be simulated by fault, as for instance when a contractual licence is made binding on a third party, not because the licence is a right *in rem*, but because the third party interfering with the licence came on the scene with notice of it. Nothing like that is happening here. The immediate recipient's notice of the claimant's right to restitution is totally irrelevant to the question whether the claimant has a proprietary interest which will bind other parties.

(c) The swaps cases

The swaps cases now have to be taken into account. They have made the picture much more difficult. In the *Westdeutsche* case the issue which brought the fourth question into play, and ultimately the only issue to reach the House of Lords, was compound interest. Did restitution under a void swap carry simple or compound interest? The only orthodox basis on which the claimant could claim compound interest was to show that the defendant had used money in which the claimant had an equitable proprietary interest. If the case was regarded as one in which money had been paid on a basis which failed after and not at the time of the receipt, there was a clear answer. On that view the money had been at the disposition of Islington, not ring-fenced, until the swap was interrupted. There could be no proprietary interest. But there was no analysis of the unjust factor and hence no firm conclusion that the case was of that kind.

Hobhouse J, who concluded that the claimants did obtain an equitable proprietary interest in the money transferred, had decided that the case was not of that kind and, in the concurrent *Sandwell* case,[103] a closed swap, had demonstrated it made no difference whether void swap was open or closed. The relevant unjust factor operated *ab initio*. Hobhouse J's finding

---

[100] Chambers 'Resulting Trusts in Canada'(n 93 above) 117–19.

[101] To the contrary the *Westdeutsche* case [1996] AC 669 (HL) in which Lord Browne-Wilkinson's speech espouses a general theory that guilty knowledge on the recipient's part is the key (705–6, 714). In similar vein: *Triffit Nurseries v Salads Etcetera Ltd* [2000] 1 All ER (Comm) 737 (CA), distinguishing *Neste Oy v Lloyds Bank* [1983] 2 Lloyd's Rep 658 as requiring an extreme degree of wickedness.

[102] Similarly: Chambers *Resulting Trusts* (n 84 above) 148–61, 23–6.

[103] *Kleinwort Benson Ltd v Sandwell BC* (decided and reported with the *Westdeutsche* case) [1994] 4 All ER 890.

that the claimants did have a proprietary interest was therefore absolutely in accord with the picture outlined above.

There was no appeal in the *Sandwell* case. The Court of Appeal upheld all aspects of Hobhouse J's *Westdeutsche* judgment but somewhat blurred the picture of the unjust factor in that it held that it could have been decided on the ground of failure of consderation, which he had expressly rejected.[104] The House of Lords then reversed his decision as to the proprietary interest and compound interest, saying very little about the unjust factor. Subsequent cases on closed swaps then confirmed that he had been correct in saying that the unjust factor operated *ab initio*.[105] Either on the ground of mistake of law or on the more shadowy ground of 'absence of consideration' the obligation to make restitution had been in place from the moment of the first payment. In other words there was no instant during which the enrichment was freely at the disposition of the parties. The restitutionary obligation was in place all along. Yet the claimant was still assumed to have no proprietary right in the value transferred.

The crucial flaw in the *Westdeutsche* case was the assumption that it was possible to consider question four without closely analysing the nature and operation of the causative event. The only issue in the appeal was compound interest, which, in the majority's view, turned solely on the answer to question four: if the claimants had had no proprietary right at the moment of the receipt they were not entitled to compound interest. But question four turned on question three: what was the unjust factor and when did it operate? This flaw infects the overruling of *Sinclair v Brougham*.[106] If that case is viewed as turning on the fact that the ultra vires depositors had suffered a failure of consideration in that they had not received the counter-performance on the basis of which they had paid money into their accounts, then it is squarely within *Re Goldcorp Exchange Ltd*[107] and cannot support any proprietary interest. On the other hand if it is contemplated as turning on an unjust factor which bit *ab initio*, whether mistake of law or some other, the case for overruling it looks very different.

These cases do not put in issue any case discussed above in which the enrichment was ring-fenced. There was no ring-fencing in any swaps case. On the other hand they appear to destroy the proposition that in any case in which the liability in unjust enrichment bites from the instant of the receipt the claimant has not only a personal claim but also a proprietary interest in the money or other value transferred. Yet since Hobhouse J in *Sandwell* no judge who has had to apply the unjust factor *ab initio* has actually considered that proposition. The proprietary question was never

---

[104] [1994] 4 All ER 957 (CA).
[105] *Guinness Mahon & Co Ltd v Kensington and Chelsea Royal London BC* [1999] QB 215 (CA); *Kleinwort Benson v Lincoln CC* [1999] 2 AC 349 (HL).
[106] [1914] AC 348 (HL).   [107] [1995] 1 AC 74 (PC), discussed in text to n 90 above.

reviewed after the *Westdeutsche* case even though a different ground for restitution later moved to the centre of the stage, and the *Westdeutsche* case itself could have been decided on the same ground and with the same conclusion as the *Goldcorp* case, which is the paradigm of the unjust enrichment which does not give rise to any proprietary interest.[108] We will attempt a resolution of these intricacies in the final section of this discussion.

(d) Traceable substitutes

At this point we have briefly to turn again from the original asset and its condition at the moment of the receipt to the traceable substitute for the asset originally received. Let it be supposed that the rules of tracing allow us to conclude that a Rolls Royce in the recipient's garage is wholly or partly the traceable product of £200,000 earlier received. In discussing *Foskett v McKeown* we have seen that the law is that, from whatever facts his interest arose, a claimant who had a proprietary interest in the £200,000 at the moment of the receipt, will have a proprietary interest in the traceable substitute. Substitution without consent has that effect. It is apparent from the same case that the right in the substitute asset may ultimately be either a beneficial interest or a lien for the amount traceable to its acquisition. The general rule is that the claimant may choose.[109]

The immediate effect of a non-consensual substitution is not a vested right but a power to claim the currently traceable substitute, which may of course not be the first but the tenth or twentieth link in a chain of substitutions. The analysis of the right as initially a power is not uncontroversial, but it was clearly adopted in *Lipkin Gorman v Karpnale Ltd.*[110] The other view, that there is a vested interest in every link of the chain, leads to grave practical difficulties, although it still has strong support.[111] Since in many cases the right in the original asset is itself a power and in many others the only reason for establishing a proprietary right in the original asset is to found a proprietary claim to subsequently traceable substitutes, in practice the analysis of the right in the substitute as a power goes a long way towards unifying our picture. That is to say, it will very commonly be the case that if a claimant seeks to realize a proprietary right arising from unjust enrichment, it will turn out that he has a vested interest only if he has exercised what was initially a power *in rem*. There is nothing outlandish about this. The model is the perfectly familiar power to avoid a voidable title.

---

[108] Chambers *Resulting Trusts* (n 84 above) 158–62.   [109] Text from n 67 above.
[110] [1991] 2 AC 548 (HL) 573.
[111] LD Smith *Tracing* (64) 358–61, preferring *Cave v Cave* (1880) 15 ChD 639, a decision of first impression of Fry J, criticized in *Re ffrench's Estate* (1887) 21 LR Ir 283 (Ir CA).

(e) Elusive coherence

Professor Burrows has recently aligned himself with those who think that the way to achieve coherence is to ask who deserves priority against an insolvent defendant and who should join the queue of unsecured creditors waiting to share the residual dividend, if any.[112] Quite apart from the fact that property determines many other issues too, that question is for those charged from time to time with reforming the insolvency laws, not for a court presiding over a particular disaster which nobody deserved. The complex rationality of 'women and children first' is not to be re-examined as each ship goes down.

Priority attaches to property rights. The incidence of property rights arising from unjust enrichment has been unclear because of the obscured overview of the law of unjust enrichment itself. The clouds might with better luck have blown away before the great swaps cases. That did not happen. In the result those cases have disrupted the picture that was emerging. The principal propositions are now hard to reconcile with each other. Eight follow. The first two are secure. This is not a programme for improvement. It is an attempt to describe the way the law now stands.

(1) Where the defendant received value which was at his disposition free from any immediate claim in unjust enrichment and was not consensually ring-fenced, the claimant will never have a proprietary interest in it, even if the recipient later comes under an obligation to make restitution as where the basis of the receipt subsequently fails.

(2) Where the defendant holds a traceable substitute for the asset received, then, if the claimant had a proprietary right in the asset originally received, he will have a power to impose either a lien or beneficial interest on the substitute.

(3) Where the value received was never freely at the defendant's disposition, either (a) because the liability in unjust enrichment bit at once, or (b) because, although it bit later, the value in question was in the meantime consensually ring-fenced, the claimant has normally been held to obtain a proprietary interest in the asset at the moment of its receipt.

(4) So far as concerns the original asset received the proprietary interest in cases under (3)(a) has generally been a power *in rem* while under (3)(b) it has been an immediately vested right. In some cases within (3)(a) it has also been treated as immediately vested. In traceable substitutes the right is a power *in rem.*

---

[112] Burrows (n 70 above) 424–8.

(5) The closed swaps litigation, so far as it assumed on the strength of the *Westdeutsche* case that claimants had no proprietary interest in the payments received by their counter-parties, cannot be reconciled with (3a). The *Westdeutsche* case, itself an interrupted swap, could have been decided under (1), which gives no hope of any proprietary interest. However, the unjust factors relied upon in the closed swap cases— mistake and absence of consideration—were such as to bite *ab initio*, whether the swap was open or closed

(6) Proposition (3) is expressed as the normal rule, but the swaps cases cannot easily be explained as exceptions. The closed swaps cases, which can only be explained by unjust factors operating *ab initio* and which did not reconsider the *Westdeutsche* denial of a proprietary interest, would be more easily explained by a general proposition that no proprietary claims should arise from unjust enrichment within (3)(a). However, that would involve a radical review of all the law relating to voidable title in cases of mistakes induced by misrepresentation and so on. The preferred *Westdeutsche* doctrine would explain those proprietary interests in terms of fault, but that criterion is inherently unsound.

(7) The law's best hope of coherence is now (a) to treat the power *in rem* as the standard proprietary response in cases in which there is no ring-fencing but the unjust factor operates immediately upon receipt, and (b) to recognize the immediate proprietary interest as the universal response in cases in which, whenever the unjust factor operates, the assets in question are ring-fenced. The first limb of this proposition will require the *Westdeutsche* denial of any proprietary interest to be confined to cases where the unjust factor is a supervening failure of consideration and there is no ring-fencing.

(8) It does not automatically follow that compound interest should have been awarded in the swaps cases. If it were held that the swaps cases did after all fall within the normal rule for (3)(a) above, where the proprietary interest is initially a power *in rem* and not an immediately vested interest, it would remain true that in none of the swaps cases was the power exercised in relation to identifiable assets. It follows that it was only in the weakest possible sense that it could be asserted that the defendants had used money which belonged to the claimants. It belonged to them only in the sense that they had an unexercised power over it. The orthodox view of the availability of compound interest would have had to be expanded to reach that case.

4. CONCLUSION

The principal aim of this paper has been to show that the five-question analysis has real work to do in identifying, analysing, and implementing the independent cause of action in unjust enrichment. The constantly underlying truth is that where the relocation of a gain is at stake the facts which suffice to ground a strict liability to disgorge do not have to amount to a contract or a wrong. The law of unjust enrichment collects together all those not-wrongs/not-contracts which have this purpose and effect. It has nothing to say where the reason for the relocation is one of those well-known heavyweights. If it is, the case belongs to them. There is contractual restitution and there is restitution for wrongs. The law of unjust enrichment is the law of enrichments which are unjust despite the absence of any contract or wrong. Out-and-out scepticism as to the existence of this category of causative event is rationally indefensible. Its effect is to push unjust enrichments back into the world of pretended contracts, imaginary declarations of trust, and supposed wrongs which usurp that name. The business has always been done. Scepticism is a preference for doing it covertly.

The last section of the paper turned to the difficult fourth question which asks what kind of right is generated by an unjust enrichment, whether *in rem* (in the law of property) or *in personam* (in the law of obligations). The difficulties encountered in that section are also ultimately due to the long failure to identify the law of unjust enrichment and to see it as a whole. The problems are similar to those found in the law of limitation and capacity, in neither of which can one yet see rules for unjust enrichment as such.

Those days are nearly behind us. Thanks to all the work done on the law of restitution, above all by Lord Goff and Professor Gareth Jones, we are on the brink of being able to assert with confidence that we do have a law of unjust enrichment, the principal but not the only cause of restitution. With confident recognition of the unity and independence of this causative event will come the ability to review it as a whole and to maintain consistency across the full range of unjust enrichments.

14

Proprietary Remedies for Unjust Enrichment

RICHARD CALNAN[1]

1. BIRKS' FIVE-QUESTION ANALYSIS

This book is about commercial remedies. In his paper, 'Restitution of Unjust Enrichment' (Chapter 13 above), Professor Peter Birks has given the expression 'remedy' a broad meaning and I will adopt the same approach.

Much of Professor Birks' wide-ranging paper is a defence of the law of unjust enrichment and a plea for the use of a 'five-question analysis which is capable of unlocking every problem in this field'. One of the problems with the way in which the law of restitution has developed over the last twenty-five years has been that there have not only been rapid developments in the law, but also wholesale changes to the vocabulary by which the underlying concepts are described. Indeed, a practitioner could be forgiven for thinking that the academic developments in this area have spawned the creation of a new language produced by academics for academics, which many practitioners have not had the time to assimilate.

For a practitioner who is not an initiate into the mysteries of the law of unjust enrichment, the importance of the five-question analysis lies in the first two questions. They require us to consider whether the defendant has been enriched at the expense of the claimant. And it is this which distinguishes unjust enrichment from contract and tort. As Professor Birks has made clear, an analysis in terms of unjust enrichment does not encompass all cases in which a remedy is available outside contract or tort. But a recognition that enrichment at the claimant's expense is a category of recovery which the law recognizes does give cohesion to an area of law which has often been seen as an agglomeration of isolated incidents.

The other three questions raise more difficulties. To ask the third question—whether the enrichment was 'unjust'—does not carry the analysis forward. It simply recognizes that it is only in some circumstances that the law permits the recovery of enrichment. It does not give any clue as to what those circumstances are. An analysis of whether the enrichment is unjust therefore requires an examination of those types of case in which

[1] Partner, Norton Rose.

the common law (and, sometimes, equity) has required restitution. However much this may seem inconvenient to the twenty-first century restitution lawyer, the starting point in such an analysis remains the old common counts in *indebitatus assumpsit*.

The fifth question—does the defendant have a defence to the claim?—is similarly incapable of revealing any answers. It states the obvious, that claims frequently have defences, but gives no clue as to the circumstances in which a defence is available. That again requires an analysis of the cases, although this is an area which has seen substantial developments in recent years, particularly in relation to the defence of change of position.

To an outsider, it sometimes seems that the law of unjust enrichment is developing entirely by reference to the fifth question (whether there is a defence) rather than the third (whether the enrichment is unjust). And, if cases focus on the defences, they obscure the real issue, which is whether the enrichment was of a type for which the law ought to give a remedy.

Take payments by mistake as an example. Is it the case that every payment made by mistake is recoverable in the absence of a defence? Until 1980, it was only mistakes as to liability which enabled recovery to be made. In *Barclays Bank v Simms*,[2] Robert Goff J swept that restriction away, but did not replace it with an alternative. The problem has been exacerbated now that recovery is permitted for mistakes of law, as well as mistakes of fact.[3] In the law of contract, operative mistakes are limited by concepts such as reasonableness and materiality.[4] Similar concepts are required in the law of restitution.

2. THE FOURTH QUESTION: PROPRIETARY CLAIMS

(a) Preliminary points

But it is the fourth question on which this paper will focus. In what circumstances is an unjust enrichment claim proprietary? In practice, the main reason why a claimant will want to establish that his claim is proprietary is because the defendant is insolvent. As Professor Birks points out in his paper, a proprietary claim can assist in two ways.

In the most common type of case, the claimant will attempt to take priority over the other creditors of an insolvent defendant by establishing a proprietary claim over an asset in the defendant's hands. If he can do so,

---

[2] *Barclays Bank Ltd v WJ Simms & Son (Southern) Ltd* [1980] QB 677.

[3] As a result of the decision of the House of Lords in *Kleinwort Benson v Lincoln City Council* [1999] 2 AC 349.

[4] See, for instance, the approach of Steyn J in *Associated Japanese Bank v Credit du Nord* [1989] 1 WLR 255.

the asset concerned will be taken out of the insolvency and returned to the claimant.[5] An example of such an attempt is the *Chase Manhattan* case.[6]

An alternative use of a proprietary claim is to extend the category of defendants beyond the scope of those who are insolvent. This can be done if the claimant can establish that his asset was delivered by the insolvent person to a third party and that the third party has a duty to return it, or its proceeds. An example of such a case is *Lipkin Gorman v Karpnale*.[7]

There is little consensus, either in the cases or amongst the commentators, as to the circumstances in which a proprietary claim is available in respect of unjust enrichment. The cases are difficult to reconcile, and all that can be attempted in the brief compass of this paper is to suggest a method of approaching the issue. Space does not permit a detailed analysis of the cases, and the discussion will therefore concentrate on the main principles.

Three preliminary points need to be made. The first is that the fact of the defendant's insolvency is irrelevant to the question of whether or not the claim is proprietary. The policy of insolvency law is, with very few exceptions, to treat all creditors equally unless, at the time of the insolvency, they had a proprietary claim against the debtor.[8] An understandable wish to protect a claimant against his defendant's insolvency should not be achieved at the expense of preferring that creditor to other unsecured claimants. The proprietary claim must exist at the inception of the insolvency; it cannot be created as a result of the insolvency. A remedial constructive trust is, therefore, not available to the claimant, at least in an insolvency.[9]

The second point is to draw the obvious distinction between:

- an asset in which the claimant has retained a proprietary interest (an 'original asset'); and
- an asset in which the claimant did not have a proprietary interest when the defendant acquired it (a 'new asset').

In other words, there is a distinction between retaining a proprietary interest to an original asset and obtaining one in a new asset.

In the first type of case, the issue is whether the claimant has retained a legal or beneficial interest in the asset or has a right to have legal or beneficial title re-vested in him. But it is the second type of case on which

---

[5] *Godfrey v Furzo* (1733) 3P Wms 185; *Burdett v Willett* (1708) 2 Vern. 638; *Whitecomb v Jacob* (1710) 1 Salk 161.

[6] *Chase Manhattan Bank NA v Israel-British Bank (London) Ltd* [1981] Ch 105.

[7] [1991] 2 AC 548, HL.

[8] Insolvency Act 1986, ss 107, 328 and 329; Insolvency Rules 1986, r 4.181(1); and see the cases cited in n 5 above.

[9] *Re Goldcorp Exchange Ltd* [1995] 1 AC 74; *Re Polly Peck International plc* [1998] 3 All ER 812, CA.

this paper will concentrate. Should the claimant be given a proprietary interest in a new asset?

New assets fall into two categories. A new asset might be the product of an original asset of the claimant (a 'substitute asset') or it might be wholly unconnected with an asset owned by the claimant (an 'unconnected asset'). An example of a substitute asset is the proceeds of bonds owned by the claimant which are wrongfully disposed of by the defendant (as in *Re Hallett's Estate*).[10] An example of an unconnected asset is a bribe or secret profit received by a fiduciary (as in *A-G for Hong-Kong v Reid*).[11]

The third point is that a proprietary remedy in such a case cannot solely depend on the law of unjust enrichment, but requires a consideration of the law of property.

In his discussion of *Foskett v McKeown*,[12] Professor Birks criticizes Lord Millett's statement in that case[13] that '[t]he transmission of a claimant's property rights from one asset to its traceable proceeds is part of our law of property, not of the law of unjust enrichment.' He does so on the basis that 'unjust enrichment is an event from which rights, including property rights, arise' and therefore that 'property and unjust enrichment cannot be opposed in this way.'

That is true but, I would suggest, misleading. It is true in the sense that property rights often arise from the law of obligations. In the same way, contract and property cannot be opposed in this way, since most property rights arise from contract.

The reason why I suggest it is misleading is that, in the case of a contract, it is not just the contract itself which creates property rights. The principles of the law of contract will establish if there is a binding contract and its terms. Where assets are involved, it will decide whether the parties intend to create a proprietary interest in them. But the law of contract cannot answer the question whether a proprietary interest has, in fact, been created. That is the province of the law of property.

Similarly, the law of unjust enrichment can establish that the defendant ought to reverse the effect of unjust enrichment, but it cannot, of itself, establish whether the claimant's rights are proprietary. In a case where the parties intend to create a proprietary interest, they cannot do so without satisfying the requirements of the law of property. Why should a claimant not have to do so where there is no such intention?

To adopt any other approach would not only create uncertainty, but would result in rules for the creation of proprietary rights being based on different principles, depending on whether they were created consensu-

---

[10] (1880) 13 ChD 696, CA.   [11] [1994] 1 AC 324, PC.   [12] [2001] 1 AC 102, HL.
[13] ibid, at 127.

ally or non-consensually. It could also enable the introduction of alien concepts, such as a change of position defence, into proprietary claims.

In his article, 'Proprietary Restitution: "Unmasking Unjust Enrichment"',[14] Professor Andrew Burrows makes the important point that it is a fiction to say that a claimant owns a substitute asset because ownership of the original asset continues through to the substitute asset. It does not necessarily follow that ownership of one asset automatically confers ownership of a substitute asset. He goes on to argue that:[15]

- the reason why a claimant is entitled to a proprietary claim over a substitute asset is because the defendant has been unjustly enriched at the claimant's expense; but that
- a proprietary claim should only be available if 'the claimant is, or is analogous to, a secured creditor who has not taken the risk of the defendant's insolvency.'

The problem with the first proposition is that the defendant will not be unjustly enriched if the claimant is not given a proprietary interest in the substitute asset. The claimant will always have a personal remedy. Something more must be needed to found a proprietary remedy.

The second proposition also creates difficulties. It is clearly necessary to restrict the first proposition unless all unjust enrichment claims are to be proprietary. But basing the existence of a proprietary claim on whether or not the claimant has taken the risk of the defendant's insolvency is not an answer. It is not the basis on which proprietary claims have historically been established, and it would apply equally to tortious, as to restitutionary, claimants. Even more importantly, it is, itself, a fiction. Because the claimant's rights arise by operation of law, he would never have considered the question of the defendant's insolvency. To accept the proposition would be to require the imputation to the claimant of a risk-assessment which he never performed. In the case of a mistaken payment, for instance, if the payer had known the truth, he would not have asked for security, he would simply not have made the payment.

It is therefore suggested that the law of unjust enrichment, by itself, cannot provide the answer to the question whether the claimant has a proprietary claim. It is beyond the scope of this paper to consider in any detail the cases in which the issue has been discussed. Suffice it to say that it is impossible to find a common thread running through the cases. They can be used to justify almost any proposition concerning the availability or otherwise of proprietary claims in cases of unjust enrichment. When searching for a principle which can explain the circumstances in which an unjust enrichment claim will be proprietary, a better starting point is to

---

[14] (2001) 117 LQR 412.   [15] ibid, at 427.

consider, by analogy, the circumstances in which proprietary rights arise in other cases. Since most proprietary rights arise by contract, that is an appropriate starting point. Non-consensual security interests may also provide a useful analogy.

(b) Consensual proprietary rights

In essence, a person who wishes to establish a consensual proprietary right has to show three things:

- first, that there is an identifiable asset of a type which the law recognizes as property over which the claim can be made;
- secondly, that there was an express or implied intention to create or transfer a proprietary interest over that asset in his favour; and
- thirdly, that there has been a sufficient objective manifestation of the transaction (ie the formalities of property law have been complied with).

These requirements apply to varying degrees at common law and in equity, and are relevant both to outright transfers (such as sales) and to transfers by way of security (such as mortgages or charges).

The first requirement is that the asset concerned is identifiable. As Lord Mustill said in *Re Goldcorp Exchange*[16] 'it is the very nature of things ... that it is impossible to have a title to goods, when nobody knows to which goods the title relates'.

The asset must also be of a type recognized as constituting property. At common law, there is a clear distinction between ownership and obligation, and there are still certain types of asset (particularly intangibles) which the common law does not recognize as constituting property. Property which it does recognize, such as land and goods, is only capable of being transferred if, at the time the transfer is to take place, the asset concerned existed and was owned by the transferor. In relation to outright transfers, this principle is manifested in the Sale of Goods Act 1979 in the principle that legal title to goods can only pass in relation to unascertained goods once they have been ascertained. Where the transaction is by way of security, *Lunn v Thornton*[17] establishes that a person cannot create a legal mortgage over assets which he does not own at the time. The transfer of legal title requires a new act to be performed by the putative transferor at the time he becomes the owner of the asset.

In equity, any type of asset is capable of being transferred; and, in many cases, an agreement to transfer future property will be effective to transfer the beneficial interest in the property as soon as it becomes owned by the

---

[16] [1995] 1 AC 74 at 92, PC.   [17] (1845) 1 CB 379.

transferor, without the necessity for any further action on his part. Where the interest is created by way of security and the loan has been made, this is the case in relation to all types of asset.[18] In relation to agreements to transfer property outright, it is only the case in relation to land.[19]

As Lord Macnaghten made clear in *Tailby v Official Receiver*,[20] the transfer is effective because, where there is an agreement for value to transfer assets, the contract is binding on the conscience of the transferor and, as soon as the assets which are the subject matter of the contract come into existence and become owned by the transferor, equity treats as done that which ought to be done. But, even in equity, it is necessary to be able to identify the assets concerned at the time the equitable right is enforced.[21]

The second requirement of a consensual proprietary claim is that the parties intend to create or transfer a proprietary interest in the asset concerned. This is the same both at common law and in equity. The intention may be express, or it may be implied from surrounding facts.[22]

The third requirement is that there has been a sufficient objective manifestation of the transaction, in other words that the parties have complied with the formalities required by the law of property. These are treated very differently at common law than in equity. At common law, formalities are frequently required in order to effect the transfer of legal title (for instance registration at the Land Registry in relation to land or registration in the register of members in relation to shares). As would be expected, the position in equity is much more flexible. There are fewer formalities and, in many cases, an effective trust, assignment, or charge can be created simply by evidence of intention. As Browne-Wilkinson J explained in *Swiss Bank Corp v Lloyds Bank*,[23] this is because equity acts on the conscience of the putative transferor and treats as done that which ought to be done.

It is important to stress that all equitable proprietary interests which arise consensually are ultimately dependent on the maxim that equity treats as done that which ought to be done. This is most apparent in relation to future assets, but the maxim also underlies the creation of equitable rights over existing assets. They are enforced because, although the common law formalities have not been complied with, equity will treat them as having been done. It is only because of the maxim that the beneficiary of a trust, an equitable assignee, and a chargee is entitled to enforce his rights not only against the putative transferor, but also against his liquidator, administrator, or trustee in bankruptcy (and, indeed, against third parties other than a bona fide purchaser of the legal title to the assets

---

[18] *Holroyd v Marshall* (1862) 10 HLC 191, HL.
[19] Compare *Lysaght v Edwards* (1876) 2 ChD 499 with *Re Wait* [1927] 1 Ch 606.
[20] (1888) 13 App Cas 523, at 547–8, HL.
[21] *Berrington v Evans* (1839) 3 Y & C Ex 384; *Mornington v Keane* (1858) 2 De G & J 292.
[22] As in *Re Kent & Sussex Sawmills Ltd* [1947] Ch 177.   [23] [1979] 1 Ch 548, 565.

concerned for value without notice). The clear line which exists at common law between ownership and obligation is less rigid in equity.

In practice, therefore, consensual proprietary interests are treated very differently at common law than in equity. At common law, there are very material restrictions on the types of asset which are capable of being transferred, and there are frequently significant formalities required. In equity, on the other hand, there are no restrictions on the type of asset over which a proprietary interest can be created, and there are few formalities to be complied with. Accordingly, the intention of the parties to create or transfer a proprietary interest over an identifiable asset is, in equity, the most important consideration. And, although a legal interest is often preferable to an equitable one in a priority dispute, the distinction is immaterial in an insolvency. Both are equally effective against the defendant's liquidator or trustee-in-bankruptcy.

(c) Non-consensual security interests

At common law, security interests created by operation of law are very limited. Common law liens only exist where the debtor's goods are in the possession of a person to whom he owes a liability;[24] and, even then, they only arise in limited cases. Particular liens are limited to those who improve goods and to those who have duties imposed on them under the general law in relation to goods;[25] and general liens, which derive from mercantile custom, only apply to a limited category of persons.[26]

Equitable liens are much more difficult to pin down than common law liens, but perhaps the most important equitable lien is that of the unpaid vendor of land. It only applies to sales of land and only gives the vendor rights over the land which he previously owned.[27] In essence, it is an implied restriction on the purchaser's rights over the asset he has acquired, and it can be seen as an example of the way that courts of equity have approached proprietary issues more liberally in relation to land than in respect of other assets.[28]

(d) Proprietary claims for unjust enrichment

How do these principles assist in establishing when a proprietary claim is available in respect of unjust enrichment? To what extent do the

[24] See, for instance, the judgment of Diplock LJ in *Tappenden v Artus* [1964] 2 QB 185, CA.
[25] See, for instance, the judgment of Stephen J in *Majeauw Carrying Co v Coastal Rutile* (1973) 129 CLR 48, HCA.
[26] See, for instance, the judgment of Lord Campbell LC in *Bock v Gorrissen* (1860) 2 De G F & J 434.
[27] *Mackreth v Symmons* (1808) 15 Ves 329.
[28] Compare, for example, the cases cited in n 19 above.

requirements of consensual proprietary claims apply to unjust enrichment claims?

Because the claim arises by operation of law, the requirement of intention will not apply. But the other two requirements will continue to apply.

There must still be an identifiable asset. It is in the nature of a proprietary interest that it can only be created over an identifiable asset. At common law, the restrictions on the types of asset over which proprietary rights can be created or transferred will continue, and even in equity many potential proprietary claims will fail because the claimant is unable to identify a particular asset over which the claim can be made. This is a particular problem in relation to monetary payments, and it significantly reduces the availability of a proprietary claim in such cases. It is instructive that the *Chase Manhattan* case[29] was decided on a preliminary point of law; the process of identification was not attempted before the preliminary point had been decided.

In principle, the same requirements for the objective manifestation of the transaction should apply whether it is consensual or non-consensual. In practice, this means that a common law proprietary claim will be much less likely to succeed than an equitable one, in view of the greater requirement for formalities at common law in relation to the transfer of most assets other than goods.

At common law, therefore, little hope for a proprietary remedy can be given to the claimant in unjust enrichment. If he can show that he did not intend to transfer the original asset to the defendant, and it remains in the defendant's hands, he will retain title to it.[30] But he will have great difficulty in calling on the common law to aid him in a proprietary claim in respect of new assets, even if they are substitute assets. Although there is some authority for the ability of a claimant to trace at law into substitute assets, its historical and conceptual basis is open to challenge and, even more importantly in practice, its scope is very limited.[31]

Pursuit of an equitable remedy is more tempting and, in principle, more likely to succeed. It is available in relation to any type of asset, and it requires very few formalities. In establishing proprietary rights over new assets, the common law generally looks to the intention of the transferor. But equity will look at the transferee and ask whether he ought, in conscience, to hold the assets concerned for the benefit of someone else. If so, although he remains the legal owner, the beneficial interest will vest in that other person, by way of trust, assignment, or charge.

---

[29] See n 6 above.

[30] *Re Reed, ex p Barnett* (1876) 3 ChD 123. Alternatively, he may have a right of rescission.

[31] It is beyond the scope of this paper to consider the so-called 'exchange-product' theory of common law tracing. For a recent, if puzzling, example of its use, see *Lipkin Gorman v Karpnale* [1991] 2 AC 548, HL.

Unlike the common law, equity does have a conceptual basis to enable the claimant to obtain a proprietary remedy over a new asset. If the claimant can show that the defendant ought to hold an identifiable asset for his benefit, the maxim that equity treats as done that which ought to be done will have the effect of conferring an equitable proprietary interest on the claimant, even though the defendant will retain the legal title. It has been seen that this is the basis for the creation of consensual equitable propriety interests, and it would be curious if it did not also underlie equitable interests which are not created by agreement.

Where consensual claims are concerned, it is the agreement between the parties which makes the principle apply. Without such an agreement, it is obviously more difficult to establish when the defendant has a duty to hold the asset concerned on behalf of the claimant. If the defendant has not agreed to do so, in what circumstances should he be required to do so?

There is a natural concern that the use of such a mercurial maxim will provide very little certainty as to the circumstances in which it will be applied. But, in fact, the application of the maxim is more limited than might appear at first blush. Space does not permit a detailed analysis of the types of case which can arise, but a few general observations can indicate that the maxim is very limited in its application.

First, in the absence of an agreement to do so, the courts should be slow to create an obligation on a defendant to hold an asset on behalf of a claimant. The circumstances in which the law imposes non-consensual security interests are extremely limited; and they are overridden by an express or implied agreement to the contrary. They suggest, by analogy, that proprietary claims for unjust enrichment should only arise in very limited circumstances. Intention is the key to most equitable proprietary interests, and only in exceptional circumstances should it not be required.

Secondly, in order to create a proprietary claim, it is necessary to establish that the duty of the defendant is to hold an asset on behalf of the claimant. This requires an analysis not only of the nature of the asset concerned, and whether it is sufficiently identifiable, but also of the nature of the defendant's obligation in relation to that asset.

Cases on implied trusts and charges[32] show that it is not sufficient to establish that the defendant has an obligation to the claimant which can be expressed by reference to the asset. It must be clear that the duty of the defendant is to hold that particular asset solely for the claimant's benefit, and on terms that the claimant has no rights to it whatsoever (except, in relation to a security interest, as a result of an equity of redemption). The analysis which the courts apply in deciding whether or not there is an

---

[32] Such as *Palmer v Carey* [1926] AC 703, PC, *Swiss Bank Corp v Lloyds Bank* [1982] AC 584, CA & HL, and *Re Kayford* [1975] 1 WLR 279.

implied trust or charge is equally applicable to constructive trusts. They can only arise if the duty imposed on the defendant is to hold the entirety of his interest in the asset solely for the benefit of the claimant, and so that the defendant has no rights to the asset.

Thirdly, since the doctrine only applies if the defendant ought, in conscience, to hold the asset on behalf of the claimant, the defendant can only be bound to do so if he is aware that he has received the unjust enrichment. In the *Westdeutsche* case,[33] Lord Browne-Wilkinson suggested that, if the defendant had innocently received the claimant's original asset, a constructive trust might be imposed over that asset if the defendant subsequently discovered the truth whilst he still held it. That would have the effect that a proprietary interest could arise in an asset subsequently to its receipt, and it could create substantial uncertainty. Even though this principle could only apply if the defendant remained in possession of the original asset at the time he became aware of the true position, it might be preferable if a proprietary remedy were only available if the defendant had the requisite knowledge at the time he received the asset. Either way, even if the claimant does have a proprietary interest in the original asset, he will only be able to claim a proprietary interest in a substitute asset if the defendant was aware of the true position at he time he made the substitution.

There are some cases which do not fit this analysis, but the same could be said for any principle which tried to impose order on the unruly body of conflicting cases which make up the law in this area. In particular, there is authority for the proposition that a volunteer may be treated differently from a purchaser: if a volunteer innocently receives an asset belonging to the claimant, the claimant may have a proprietary interest in a substitute asset even if the volunteer was not aware of the true facts at the time he made the substitution.[34] Although equity often treats volunteers more harshly than purchasers, it is suggested that such an approach is wrong in principle. It is one thing to enable the claimant to follow his equitable interest in an original asset into the hands of an innocent volunteer. It is something very different to impose a proprietary interest over a substitute asset in circumstances where the volunteer was not aware of the facts.[35]

In his paper, Professor Birks emphatically takes a different view: on his analysis nothing at any point turns on fault of any kind. It is 'substitution without consent' which gives the claimant the right to the substitute asset.[36] The essence of a proprietary right is that it does not just affect the

---

[33] *Westdeutsche Landesbank Girozentrale v Islington LBC* [1996] AC 669, HL.

[34] *Re Diplock* [1948] Ch 465, CA.

[35] The approach of the Court of Appeal in *Re Diplock* must be open to re-examination. Their decision was based on *Sinclair v Brougham* [1914] AC 398, HL, which is no longer good law following the *Westdeutsche* case.

[36] See above Chapter 13, esp pp 154, 166. See also *English Private Law* P Birks (ed) at 15.186.

immediate parties, but others; and there is therefore much to be said for the view that the state of mind of the defendant should be irrelevant to those others. But this is to ignore the conceptual basis for the creation of proprietary interests in new assets. It is extremely difficult to justify the creation of such a proprietary interest at common law. It is possible in equity, but only if the conscience of the defendant is affected. Any other approach would undermine the unity of the way in which equitable proprietary rights are created, whether consensually or by operation of law.

Fourthly, it should be much easier to impose a duty on a defendant to hold a new asset on behalf of the claimant when the asset is a substitute asset than if it is an unconnected asset. Where the defendant has received the original asset from the claimant, whether or not such a duty is imposed in relation to a substitute asset will depend on how the substitution occurred.

If it is done with the express or implied agreement of the claimant, there can be no room for the imposition by law of such a duty. Whether or not the defendant has a duty to hold the substitute asset on behalf of the claimant will depend on the express or implied intention of the parties.[37] It will arise consensually, or not at all.

If, on the other hand, the defendant knows that he has no express or implied authority to dispose of the claimant's asset, he will hold its proceeds on behalf of the claimant, provided that they can be identified in accordance with the rules of equitable tracing.[38] The reason he will do so is because he has wrongfully dealt with an asset owned by the claimant. He ought to have held the original asset on behalf of the claimant and, having disposed of it wrongfully, he ought to do the same with the proceeds. In such a case, it is easy for the court to decide that the defendant ought, in conscience, to hold the substitute asset on behalf of the claimant.

Fifthly, although it is not logically necessary to restrict the availability of a proprietary remedy to substitute assets, it ought not to be available in relation to unconnected assets. In other words, a proprietary remedy should not be available in respect of a new asset where the asset concerned is not the traceable proceeds of the claimant's original asset.

There is no conceptual reason why the courts cannot use the maxim that equity treats as done that which ought to be done to require the defendant to hold an unconnected asset on behalf of the claimant. An example where this has been done in the past is *A-G for Hong Kong v Reid*,[39] in which a bribe received by an agent was held on constructive trust for his principal.

---

[37] As in *Aluminium Industrie Vaasen v Romalpa Aluminium* [1976] 1 WLR 676, CA, and the cases which followed it.

[38] As in *Re Hallett's Estate* (1880) 13 ChD 696, CA, and in *Foskett v McKeown* [2001] 1 AC 102, HL.

[39] [1994] 1 AC 324, PC.

But there are policy issues involved, not the least of which is whether the claimant ought to have priority over the defendant's other creditors in his insolvency. Although it is open to the courts to impose a proprietary remedy in such a case, it is not a necessary conclusion from the receipt of a bribe by an agent that it is held on trust for his principal. The outcome depends on the way in which the court describes the duty of the defendant. Is it to hold the particular asset which he received on behalf of the principal, or is it simply to account to his principal for the profit he has made as a result of his wrongful act? The choice does not depend on logic, but on policy—and I would suggest there is no policy reason to impose a trust in such a case.

The use of the expression 'constructive trust' in such cases can be misleading. Constructive trusts are imposed for two different purposes. They can be used to create a proprietary interest which would not otherwise exist; or they can make a person who is not otherwise a trustee personally liable as if he were. There is no logical reason why the imposition of a proprietary right by means of a constructive trust should necessarily impose upon the defendant the personal obligations of a constructive trustee. Even more importantly in this context, the converse is equally true. The requirement for a defendant to account, as a constructive trustee, for a benefit received by him, does not necessarily mean that benefit is held on trust for the claimant.

Sixthly, in practice the main type of asset which will be the subject of an unjust enrichment claim is money, and there are particular problems involved in establishing proprietary claims over money. To some extent, they are practical problems of identification, which are exacerbated when bank accounts are in overdraft.[40] But there are two more fundamental problems.

The first is that, in most cases, the defendant will have received the payment concerned by bank transfer. The payment will have been made by the debiting and crediting of various bank accounts, and the claimant will not have received an asset belonging to the claimant. If the defendant's bank account is in overdraft, he will not own an asset over which a proprietary claim can be established. If it is in credit, he will own an asset (ie a proportion of the debt due from his bank) which represents the payment received, but he will not have received it from the claimant.[41] If he has been unjustly enriched at the claimant's expense, he may have a duty to return an equivalent amount, but it is difficult to see why the claimant should have a proprietary remedy. Bank balances can be traced in equity,

---

[40] As in *Bishopsgate Investment Management v Homan* [1995] Ch 211, CA.

[41] See R Calnan Proprietary Claims for Mistaken Payments, F Rose (ed), in '*Restitution and Insolvency*' (2000).

but only if the defendant has initially received an asset belonging to the claimant.

The second problem is that money (whether in the form of bank payments or cash) is fungible. It is a means of payment for a commodity; it is not itself a commodity. A proprietary remedy requires the law to impose an obligation on the defendant to hold a particular asset on the claimant's behalf, and not to claim any interest in it himself. The nature of money means that it is extremely unlikely that the defendant will owe such a duty in relation to money he has received. He will have a duty to pay an equivalent amount to the claimant, but not to hold the particular money received on behalf of the claimant.[42]

3. CONCLUSION

This paper can do no more than to propose a method of approaching the problem of when a claimant will have a proprietary remedy for the recovery of unjust enrichment.

It is not possible to look solely to the law of unjust enrichment in order to establish when a claim for unjust enrichment is proprietary. The principles of the law of property must be complied with.

The best approach to the problem is by analogy with consensual proprietary rights and non-consensual security interests.

A common law proprietary remedy is likely to be extremely limited in its scope.

An equitable proprietary remedy should, however, succeed if the claimant can identify a specific asset in the hands of the defendant which, in conscience, the defendant ought to hold solely for the benefit of the claimant.

This is easy enough to establish if the defendant has wrongfully dealt with the claimant's asset. But it should not be the case where the obligation of the defendant is simply to account to the claimant for benefits received from a third party. Nor is it generally appropriate where the defendant has received money, the receipt of which, by its very nature, normally gives rise to purely personal rights.

---

[42] ibid.

15

Restitution of Unjust Enrichment: Review of Discussion

Much of the discussion focused on what Peter Birks had labelled 'the fourth question'. That is, when may proprietary, rather than merely personal, restitution be given to reverse an unjust enrichment? The Birksian view was that it was incorrect to say that all this was a matter for the law of property and not the law of unjust enrichment because that is to misunderstand one's categories. The question at issue is whether unjust enrichment generates proprietary rights. It is no more helpful to say that this is a matter for property law and not unjust enrichment than it would be to say, in the realm of personal rights, that it is all a matter for the law of obligations and not unjust enrichment. Unjust enrichment is a source of proprietary rights just as it is a source of personal rights. Moreover, it is of little or no assistance to turn to the law on the *consensual* creation of proprietary rights in deciding whether unjust enrichment *should* trigger proprietary rights because one is here concerned with the non-consensual creation of such rights. To do so runs into the danger of committing the same error in the realm of proprietary rights as was historically committed in the context of personal rights by those adhering to the now discredited 'implied contract' theory.

The contrary view put forward by Richard Calnan was that the question of whether or not there is a proprietary remedy cannot be left to the law of unjust enrichment but is a part of the law of property; that there are certain features common to all proprietary interests; and that, in the light of the confused state of the cases, it is useful to try to find analogies with other types of property interests, particularly consensual proprietary interests (because they are so much more numerous) and non-consensual security interests (because they, like claims arising from unjust enrichment, arise by operation of law).

Some doubted whether there is any case in English law where the courts have clearly applied unjust enrichment reasoning to trigger proprietary rights. The counter-argument put to this was that the history of the English law of restitution shows that unjust enrichment reasoning has often been hidden and that what one is seeking to do is to bring into the open reasoning that has often been obscure and based on fiction. This was said to be rationalization not empire-building. It was additionally counter-argued that the cases on rescission (of contracts transferring property) for misrepresentation and undue influence, non-contractual subrogation to secured rights, equitable liens and trusts imposed following tracing, let alone the admittedly controversial case of *Chase Manhattan Bank NA Ltd v Israel-British Bank (London) Ltd*,[1] all illustrate unjust enrichment triggering proprietary rights.

One suggestion made was that, while it was indeed fictional to say that a lien or trust imposed after tracing was the continuation of pre-existing proprietary rights into a new product, what was triggering the newly-created proprietary right was not the defendant's unjust enrichment but a *wrongful* substitution. This, it was suggested, is consistent with the way in which equity approaches the question of the creation of proprietary interests in other cases. A possible difficulty with this analysis is that in some cases proprietary remedies after tracing are imposed against a defendant who has innocently made the substitution (see, eg, *Re Diplock*).[2] In such cases, at least, unjust enrichment subject to defences, such as change of position and bona fide purchase, seems a better explanation of the newly created proprietary right in the substitute asset than does the commission of a wrong.

It was pointed out that a good practical test for whether unjust enrichment is, or is not, triggering proprietary restitution is whether change of position is a defence or not. Those adhering to the 'this is all a matter of property law' approach would deny any scope here for change of position. Those taking the 'unjust enrichment' view would argue that change of position should be a defence to proprietary, as well as personal, restitution.

The argument was also made by some that one cannot simply answer these questions by looking at past cases. Rather there are real policy questions to be answered, in particular in determining whether the claimant *should* have priority on the defendant's insolvency.

One view put forward is that many practitioners are hostile to, and sceptical of, the law of restitution because the language used by academics is unfamiliar, and there is a fear that unjust enrichment is taking over, and uprooting, well-settled areas of law. A plea was made for writing on the law of restitution to be made more accessible and readily comprehensible to practitioners.

On the issue of whether change of position has killed off estoppel, as raised by cases like *Scottish Equitable plc v Derby*,[3] different views were expressed. One approach was to say that estoppel was analogous to a contract of settlement and therefore had a different role to play from change of position and must survive. The alternative approach was to argue that in very few (if any) cases was the estoppel analogous to a contract of settlement and, where not so analogous, it merely performed crudely the role which change of position now achieved in a finely-tuned way. The

---

[1] [1981] Ch 105.   [2] [1948] Ch 465.   [3] [2001] 3 All ER 818.

'novel and ingenious argument'[4] of junior counsel in *Scottish Equitable plc v Derby*, which the Court of Appeal had found attractive, was regarded as convincing by some (because change of position removes the ability to prove the 'detrimental reliance' needed for estoppel) but problematic by others.

---

[4] ibid at para [45].

PART C

Agreed Remedies, Human Rights,
and Conflict of Laws

16

Agreed Remedies

LOUISE GULLIFER[1]

It is a widespread practice for contracting parties to include in their contract terms specifying remedies in the event of breach. These clauses can take a variety of forms: a clause may specify a sum payable on an event or on breach, or give the innocent party the right to terminate the contract or to retain a sum of money already paid.

Parties may include agreed remedies in a contract for a number of reasons,[2] including

(1) avoiding expensive assessment of damages in the event of a breach;[3]
(2) enabling each party to plan for the financial consequences of breach;[4]
(3) enabling the 'innocent' party to recover for losses that might otherwise be irrecoverable under the ordinary rules of assessment of damages;[5]

---

[1] Fellow and Tutor in Law, Harris Manchester College, Oxford.

[2] Other reasons might be:

(1) protecting the innocent party in the event of breach without having to sue for damages, eg by the forfeiture of a deposit or by the termination of the contract (*Scandinavian Trading Tanker Co AB v Flota Petrolera Ecuatoriana (The Scaptrade)* [1983] 2 AC 694),

(2) enabling a party to terminate a contract or otherwise protect itself if the other party becomes a bad credit risk (*Goker v NWS Bank plc* (CA, 1st August 1990) *per* Lloyd LJ, *Lordsvale Finance plc v Bank of Zambia* [1996] 3 WLR 688),

(3) enabling a party to terminate a contract to protect its artistic integrity or reputation (*Crittall Windows Ltd v Stormseal (UPVC) Window Systems Ltd* [1991] RPC 265 (unauthorized use of trade marks); *Python (Monty) Pictures Ltd v Paragon Entertainment Corp* [1998] EMLR 697 (not including certain anti-cutting provisions in licenses of film)),

(4) ensuring that to take the benefit of a contract a party also has to bear the burden (*Nutting v Baldwin* [1995] 1 WLR 201),

(5) enabling a party to know the precise proprietary and possessory consequences of breach, eg, whether it has the right to sell land that was the subject matter of the contract (*Union Eagle Ltd v Golden Achievement Ltd* [1997] AC 514).

[3] *Robophone Facilities v Blank* [1966] 1 WLR 1428, 1447. Settlements are also promoted: PR Kaplan, 'A critique of the penalty limitation on liquidated damages' [1977] 50 Southern Californian Law Review 1055, 1058.

[4] ibid.

[5] For example, as suggested by Lord Diplock in *Robophone Facilities v Blank* [1966] 1 WLR 1428, 1448, losses falling under the second limb of *Hadley v Baxendale* (1854) 9 Exch 341; idiosyncratic or non-pecuniary losses (see M Chen-Wishart, 'Controlling the power to agree damages' in P Birks (ed), *Wrongs and Remedies of the Twenty-first Century* (1996), 271, 276, and CJ Goetz and RE Scott, 'Liquidated damages, penalties and the just compensation principle' (1977) 77 Columbia Law Review 554, 572; covering the cost of cure where compensatory damages might be limited to difference in value (see D Harris, D Campbell and R Halson, *Remedies in Contract and Tort* (2nd edn, 2002), 138, 146.

(4) enabling the innocent party to recover where damages would be difficult to assess;[6]
(5) enabling the parties to allocate the risk of particular losses occuring;[7]
(6) acting as an incentive to performance, where performance is more valuable to the paying party than damages.[8]

The law generally enforces such clauses, but only within certain limits. Restrictions on enforcement have developed in a piecemeal fashion from the common law, equity, and statute. It is hard to define a unifying principle behind these restrictions, which appear to cut across the fundamental principle of freedom of contract.[9]

1. RESTRICTIONS ON AGREED REMEDIES: THE OVERALL MAP

A contractual provision may either stipulate an amount of money payable by a party in breach, or give the innocent party the right to terminate the contract on breach.[10] The former is subject to the rule against penalties, namely that the provision will only be enforced if it is a genuine pre-estimate of loss: if it is not, then the courts will not enforce it, but will allow recovery by the innocent party under the normal damages rules.[11] There are three possible effects of the exercise of a right to terminate:

(1) damages for the innocent party's loss of bargain become payable,[12]
(2) any sums of money already paid by the guilty party may be irrecoverable,
(3) the guilty party loses the benefit of the bargain.

[6] *Widnes Foundry (1925) Ltd v Cellulose Acetate Silk Co* [1931] 2 KB 393, 406 *per* Scrutton LJ.

[7] D Harris, D Campbell, and R Halson, *Remedies in Contract and Tort* (2nd edn, 2002), 141. Here the agreed remedies clause performs a similar function to a limitation clause, or an express notification of likely loss under the second limb of *Hadley v Baxendale*, above n 5. The cost of this risk allocation may be reflected in an increase or decrease in the contract price.

[8] Such a clause might in theory be unenforceable if it operated *in terrorem* (though this part of the test seems to be less important than the compensatory principle: see below). However, it is clear from recent developments in the law of contractual remedies that there is a growing recognition that there is more to the innocent party's performance interest than pecuniary loss. See: *Farley v Skinner* [2001] 3 WLR 899; the speeches of Lord Millett and Lord Goff of Chievely in *Alfred McAlpine Construction Ltd v Panatown Ltd* [2001] 1 AC 518; *A-G v Blake* [2001] 1 AC 268; E McKendrick and M Graham, 'The Sky's the Limit: Contractual Damages for Non-pecuniary Loss' [2002] LMCLQ 161.

[9] PR Kaplan, 'A critique of the penalty limitation on liquidated damages' [1977] 50 Southern Californian Law Review 1055.

[10] Either expressly or by providing that the term breached is a condition.

[11] In *Jobson v Johnson* [1989] 1 All ER 621, Nicholls LJ suggested that the courts do enforce penalty clauses, but only up to the extent of the actual loss. This (as opposed to recovery under the normal damages rules) would need to be the position if the penalty jurisdiction was extended to payments not consequent on breach: see below.

[12] As in *Lombard North Central v Butterworth* [1987] 2 WLR 6. Unless the contract stipulates the amount of damages payable, no control is exerted over this.

The second and third effects present two distinct solutions, between which a guilty party may have a choice. The contract may be treated as at an end, and the guilty party may seek to be put back in the position that he would have been in if the contract had not been made, the innocent party being protected by his right to sue for damages.[13] To achieve this result the court has to consider whether the guilty party should recover back money already paid under the contract which would otherwise be irrecoverable[14] ('relief against forfeiture: recovery of payments'). However, in order to retain the benefit of the bargain, the guilty party may wish to argue that he should be entitled to continue the contract, subject to remedying the breach and indemnifying the innocent party against any loss arising from the breach.[15] This may be permitted by the court under an equitable doctrine ('relief against forfeiture: allowing the contract to continue').

Other restrictions on agreed remedies are in more general terms. In *Interfoto Picture Library Ltd v Stiletto Visual Programmes Ltd*[16] the Court of Appeal held that a potentially penal clause had not been incorporated into the contract, using the same technique that had in the past been used to control exclusion clauses.[17] There is also control under the Unfair Terms in Consumer Contracts Regulations 1999, though only in relation to contracts with consumers.[18]

The three specific areas of control of agreed remedies[19] have largely been treated separately by the courts, and will be dealt with separately in this paper. However, many attempts have been made to argue that the whole jurisdiction should be come under one unifying principle[20] or that it should form part of a general jurisdiction to relieve against unconscionable bargains.[21] While such arguments will be referred to below, the main focus is on the current law and possible developments within its existing structure. Within the general overview, there will be particular focus on the following issues:

---

[13] This is called 'the restitution solution' by L Smith in 'Relief against forfeiture: a restatement' (2001) 60 CLJ 178, 182.

[14] See below for a detailed consideration of this area.

[15] Smith calls this 'the perfection solution': above n 13.   [16] [1989] QB 433.

[17] eg, *Spurling v Bradshaw* [1956] 1 WLR 461.

[18] Who are defined as natural persons, acting outside their trade, business, or profession (reg 3(1)). The 'grey' list in Sch 2 of terms which may be regarded as unfair contains both agreed damages clauses (para 1(f)) and clauses providing for the forfeiture of payments (para 1(d)). The Law Commission is considering extending similar protection to standard terms in business-to-business contracts, although such terms would not be regarded as presumptively unfair: *Unfair Terms in Contracts* (Law Com Consultation Paper No 166, August 2002) Pt V.

[19] The rule against penalties and the two types of relief against forfeiture.

[20] For example, in the Scottish Law Commission, *Report on Penalty Clauses* (Scot Law Com No 171, 1999).

[21] T Downes, 'Rethinking penalty clauses' and M Chen-Wishart, 'Controlling the power to agree damages' in P Birks (ed), *Wrongs and Remedies of the Twenty-first Century* (1996).

(1) In relation to the rule against penalties, the approach of the courts to large scale commercial transactions and the scope of the penalty jurisdiction.
(2) In relation to relieving against forfeiture by allowing recovery of money paid, the nature of the test for relief.
(3) In relation to relieving against forfeiture by allowing the contract to continue, the use of such relief in the context of financing transactions.

2. THE RULE AGAINST PENALTIES

The rule against penalties originated in the courts of equity to relieve against penal bonds,[22] but the modern doctrine dates from Lord Dunedin's judgment in *Dunlop Pneumatic Tyre Co v New Garage & Motor Co*.[23] The basic test asks whether the amount payable is a genuine pre-estimate of loss or whether it is 'stipulated *in terrorem* of the offending party'.[24] The cases considering the application of the test have generally focused on the first part: how to determine whether the amount is a pre-estimate of loss. The principles deployed in making this determination originate from the *Dunlop* case and are as follows:

(1) The label used by the parties is not conclusive: whether a clause is penal is a matter for the courts to decide.[25]
(2) Whether the clause is penal is to be judged at the time of contracting rather than at the time of breach.[26]

---

[22] Giving a right to an action in debt payable if a condition was not fulfilled: the condition could be the payment of a lesser sum of money or performance of another obligation. Where the obligation was to pay money, equity would only require the payment of the lesser sum, but where it was performance, there was only limited relief until section VIII of the statute of 8 & 9 Will 3, Ch 11 suspended the verdict on a penal bond but allowed the innocent party to sue for damages. See G Muir, 'Stipulations for the payment of agreed sums' (1985) Sydney Law Review 503, 503–8.

[23] [1915] AC 79.

[24] *Dunlop Pneumatic Tyre Co v New Garage & Motor Co*, above n 23. The '*in terrorem*' part is rarely examined, and is, to some extent, a fiction since many parties are not in the least terrorised by them (see Lord Radcliffe in *Bridge v Campbell Discount Co Ltd* [1962] AC 600, 622).

[25] *Clydebank Engineering and Shipbuilding Co Ltd v Don Jose Ramos Yzquierdo y Casteneda* [1905] AC 6, 17; *Commissioner of Public Works v Hills* [1906] AC 368, 375; *Dunlop Pneumatic Tyre Co v New Garage & Motor Co* [1915] AC 79, 86. This is consistent with the approach of the courts in a variety of categorization issues, eg: whether an agreement creates a lease or a tenancy; whether an agreement is a sale or for security; whether an agreement creates a fixed or floating charge.

[26] *Comr of Public Works v Hills* [1906] AC 368, 375; *Dunlop Pneumatic Tyre Co v New Garage & Motor Co* [1915] AC 79, 86. The position in the USA is different in that the clause is compared to what actually happened on breach, thus prompting criticism that the penalty rule fails to take account of the parties' allocation of risk at the time of the contract (see PR Kaplan, 'A critique of the penalty limitation on liquidated damages' [1977] 50 Southern Californian Law Review 1055, 1072).

(3) The basic principle involves comparing the stipulated sum with what the innocent party is likely to recover in damages were the breach to occur.[27] Certain specific situations will give rise to certain presumptions:

   (i) It will be a penalty if the sum is extravagant and unconscionable compared to the greatest loss[28] that could be proved to follow from breach.[29]

  (ii) It will be a penalty if the breach is failure to pay a sum of money and the sum stipulated is greater than the unpaid sum.[30]

 (iii) There is a presumption that it is penal when a single lump sum is made payable on the occurrence of one or more of several events, some of which may occasion serious damage and some only trivial damage.[31]

 (iv) It is not an obstacle to a sum being liquidated damages if pre-estimation is very difficult: here an agreed damages clause is likely to represent a genuine allocation of risk between the parties.[32]

(4) The rule is limited in scope to provisions stipulating sums payable on breach.[33]

(5) The doctrine does not just apply to terms providing for the payment of money: provisions stipulating for the transfer of property on breach are also included.[34]

[27] 'The compensatory principle': see M Chen-Wishart, 'Controlling the power to agree damages' in P Birks (ed) *Wrongs and Remedies of the Twenty-first Century* (1996).

[28] It appears that this loss is not limited by the first rule in *Hadley v Baxendale,* since the inclusion of the agreed damages clause gives the other party notice of likely loss (*Robophone Facilties v Blank* [1966] 1 WLR 1428, 1448 *per* Lord Diplock). It is not clear how far this principle could be extended to include other types of irrecoverable loss, eg, the cost of cure when this would be considered unreasonable under the principle set out in *Ruxley Electronics & Construction Ltd v Forsyth* [1996] 1 AC 344.

[29] *Clydebank Engineering and Shipbuilding Co Ltd v Don Jose Ramos Yzquierdo y Casteneda* [1905] 6, 16 (Lord Davey); *Dunlop Pneumatic Tyre Co v New Garage & Motor Co* [1915] AC 79, 87, relying on Lord Halsbury in the *Clydebank* case, whose judgment supports the 'extravagant and unconscionable' part of the proposition but not the comparison to the greatest loss.

[30] *Kemble v Farren* (1829) 6 Bing 141, 130 ER 1234. This is likely to be interpreted liberally today, since foreseeable loss flowing from non-payment is now recoverable (*Wadsworth v Lydall* [1981] 1 WLR 598). A clause increasing the rate of interest payable once the borrower was in default has recently been upheld: *Lordsvale Finance plc v Bank of Zambia* [1996] 3 WLR 688.

[31] *Lord Elphinstone v Monkland Iron and Coal Co Ltd* (1886) 11 App Cas 332.

[32] *Dunlop Pneumatic Tyre Co v New Garage & Motor Co* [1915] AC 79, 88. *Lordsvale Finance plc v Bank of Zambia* [1996] 3 WLR 688 is indicative that the courts are prepared to let parties agree risk allocation where it makes commercial sense.

[33] See below for further discussion.   [34] *Jobson v Johnson* [1989] 1 All ER 621.

(a) The approach of the courts to large scale commercial transactions

In relation to the control of penalty clauses there is a tension between the wish to uphold the bargain of the parties, and the wish to protect parties against oppression. The problem with the *Dunlop* test is that it is a blunt instrument with which to distinguish between true oppression and fairly negotiated clauses. Applied literally, it takes no account of the nature of the parties, their respective bargaining power or the circumstances in which the contract was made.[35] This led the Scottish Law Commission[36] to propose that the test be changed to whether the penalty is 'manifestly excessive'.[37] It has been argued that to enforce agreed damages clauses in freely negotiated commercial contracts actually increases efficiency, and that the only control should be that of unconscionability, applied chiefly in consumer contracts.[38] Now that the Unfair Terms in Consumer Contract Regulations 1999 control agreed remedies clauses in consumer contracts by subjecting them to a test of good faith,[39] there is much to be said for abolishing the common law jurisdiction altogether.[40]

The courts, too, are now interpreting the test differently in relation to freely negotiated commercial contracts. The decision of the Privy Council in *Phillips Hong Kong Ltd v The A-G of Hong Kong*[41] is illustrative of this approach.[42] The Government of Hong Kong contracted directly with seven contractors in relation to the building of a highway project. Each contractor was to carry out a different aspect of the work, and each knew each other's timetable so that the work could be dovetailed. Each contractor was obliged to meet certain 'Key Dates' to enable the other contractors to operate. The contract contained clauses providing for liquidated damages at a daily rate for failure to meet each Key Date and also for failure to complete on time. Phillips caused delay and, pending arbitration, applied

[35] See M Chen-Wishart, 'Controlling the power to agree damages' in P Birks (ed), *Wrongs and Remedies of the Twenty-first Century* (1996).

[36] *Report on Penalty Clauses* (Scot Law Com No 171, 1999).

[37] Wording that follows Article 9.509 of the Principles of European Contract Law and Article 7.4.13 of the Unidroit Principles for International Commercial Contracts.

[38] PR Kaplan, 'A critique of the penalty limitation on liquidated damages' [1977] 50 Southern Californian Law Review 1055, 1089.

[39] Regulation 5(1).

[40] An alternative argument is that it should be brought in line with the jurisdiction over limitation clauses (which are another means of risk allocation), so that all such clauses in consumer contracts are controlled and a flexible test of reasonableness applies to standard term commercial contracts (as under the Unfair Contract Terms Act 1977). See now the Law Commission's proposals in *Unfair Terms in Contracts* (Law Com Consultation Paper No 166, 2002) Pt V.

[41] (1993) 61 Building Law Reports 49.

[42] Although this is a decision of the Privy Council, there is evidence that this approach is being adopted in English decisions: see below.

to the court for a preliminary ruling on whether the liquidated damages clause was capable of operating as a penalty.

The commercial nature of the arrangement clearly coloured the Privy Council's reasoning and approach to the evidence in every respect:

(1) They accepted the government's justification for the formula stipulated in the contract for calculating the loss, and for the absence of any double compensation when sums were payable both for missing a Key Date and for missing the final completion date.[43]

(2) They rejected the argument that the clause must be penal because there might be hypothetical situations when the amount payable was more than the loss actually suffered, saying that 'the use in argument of unlikely illustrations should . . . not assist a party to defeat a provision as to liquidated damages.'[44] Where there was no inequality of bargaining power, the advantages of agreeing and knowing in advance what damages were payable outweighed the disadvantages of the sums being possibly too great in some situations.[45]

(3) They said that the use of the words 'liquidated damages' in the contract is not to be disregarded, but raises a strong inference which the party in breach has to rebut.[46]

(4) Further, although whether the clause is penal is to be judged at the time the contract is made, what happens after the contract is made can provide valuable evidence as to what the parties could reasonably expect to be the loss.[47]

(5) Furthermore, they said that 'the fact that two parties who should be well capable of protecting their respective commercial interests agreed the allegedly penal provision suggests that the formula for calculating liquidated damages is unlikely to be oppressive.'[48]

The decision is based on two strands of reasoning which are likely to govern the courts' approach to penalty clauses in the future. One is that the true purpose of the jurisdiction is to relieve against oppression,[49] the other

---

[43] (1993) 61 Building Law Reports 49, 60–3.

[44] ibid, 59. Compare the approach set out in the text to n 31, above. See also Article 9.509 of the Principles of European Contract law and Article 7.4.13. of the Unidroit Principles for International Commercial Contracts, where the 'grossly excessive' test is applied in relation to the loss relating from the non-performance and other circumstances (as opposed to all possible breaches). However, there is a fine line to be drawn between this approach and the US system of *ex post facto* assessment of agreed damages clauses.

[45] (1993) 61 Building Law Reports 49, 54.

[46] ibid, 59. Compare the approach set out in the text to n 25, above.

[47] ibid. Compare the approach set out in the text to n 26, above.   [48] ibid, 59.

[49] As shown by the citation with approval by the Privy Council of the view of Dickson J in the Supreme Court of Canada in *Elsey v JG Collins Insurance Agencies Ltd* (1978) 83 DLR 1, at 15: 'It is now evident that the power to strike down a penalty clause is a blatant interference with freedom of contract and is designed for the sole purpose of providing relief against oppression for the party having to pay the stipulated sum. It has no place where there is no oppression.'

is that there is a clear distinction between consumer-type cases of unequal bargaining power and commercial cases, where 'what the parties have agreed should normally be upheld.'[50]

Two more recent English decisions reflect this approach. In *Lordsvale Finance plc v Bank of Zambia*,[51] the court considered whether a default interest rate uplift in a syndicated loan agreement was penal. Colman J held that so long as the increased rate only applied prospectively from the date of default, then unless the increase was exceptionally large, it was not penal. He took account of commercial realities in two ways: by accepting the argument that the increase was commercially justifiable, on the grounds of the increased credit risk once the borrower was in default;[52] and by regarding it as important that English courts should not be inconsistent with courts in New York, the other major centre of international syndicated loans as well as London.[53] In *Cenargo Ltd v Izar Construcciones Navales SA*[54] a ferrybuilding contract provided for liquidated damages of $150,000 for each trailer space by which the ship was deficient. The breach that in fact occurred was extremely minor. Rather than argue that the clause was penal and should be struck down the builder argued successfully that the clause did not apply to the breach in question. In the court's view, this kind of reasoning prevented the penalty jurisdiction striking down commercially useful clauses[55] and fair bargains.[56] In commercial transactions the courts should, and do, acknowledge the advantages of agreed remedies clauses and are prepared to uphold them if there is a commercially justifiable reason for them.

(b) The scope of the penalty jurisdiction

The court's power to control the enforcement of penalties only extends to where the penal consequences occur on breach.[57] There are a number of reasons for this, which have been the subject of considerable criticism:[58]

---

[50] (1993) 61 Building Law Reports 49, 59.   [51] [1996] 3 All ER 156.
[52] ibid, 167.   [53] ibid, 169.   [54] [2002] EWCA Civ 524.
[55] ibid, para [27] *per* Longmore LJ.
[56] ibid, para [30], approving a passage from G Treitel, *The Law of Contract* (10th edn, 1999) 932.
[57] *Associated Distributors Ltd v Hall* [1938] 2 KB 83; *Bridge v Campbell Finance Ltd* [1962] AC 600; *Alder v Moore* [1961] 2 QB 57; *Exports Credit Guarantee Dept v Universal Oil Products Co* [1983] 1 WLR 399; *Lombard North Central plc v Butterworth* [1987] QB 527; *Transag Haulage Ltd v Leyland DAF Finance Co* [1994] 2 BCLC 88; *Nutting v Baldwin* [1995] 1 WLR 201; *Jervis v Harris* [1996] Ch 195.
[58] T Downes, 'Rethinking penalty clauses' in P Birks (ed), *Wrongs and Remedies of the Twenty-first Century* (1996) 259; M Chen-Wishart, 'Controlling the power to agree damages', ibid, 286–7; G Treitel, *The Law of Contract* (10th edn, 1999) 934–6; Law Commission, *Penalty Clauses and Forfeiture of Monies Paid* (Law Com Working Paper No 61) (1975) paras 17–26; *Report on Penalty Clauses* (Scot Law Com No 171, 1999) Pt 4.

(1) The jurisdiction to control agreed remedies has grown up in a piece-meal fashion. This was considered preferable to a general jurisdiction to control the fairness of bargains, and to some extent the piecemeal approach is replicated in other areas of contract law.[59]

(2) Control of penalties is based on the principle that the party claiming the agreed sumn should not recover more than a genuine pre-estimate of loss.[60] This has been interpreted to constitute loss recoverable at law, ie damages for breach of contract.[61]

(3) It is not considered desirable for the courts to control the substance of the parties' primary obligations, and in particular the adequacy of the price charged for them.[62] Since the courts generally control the substance of secondary obligations, they are happier to control the parties' agreement as to these.[63]

(4) By stipulating for payments on certain events, the parties are allocating the risks connected with the contract, and the courts should not interfere with this.[64]

---

[59] For example, undue influence, duress, misrepresentation, and the statutory control of unfair terms. However, although there is no overriding principle of good faith (*Interfoto Library Ltd v Stiletto Ltd* [1989] QB 433, 439), or any general principle governing inequality of bargaining power (*National Westminster Bank v Morgan* [1985] AC 686, 708), arguably these other areas reflect more conceptual coherence than the control of agreed remedies.

[60] Arguably, the advent of the restrictive scope of the penalty jurisdiction is co-extensive with the development of the compensatory principle, as strictly construed. The original equitable jurisdiction against penalties involved a comparison between the sum payable under the contract and the actual loss suffered (rather than the damage that a court would award) and so the question of whether the sum was payable on breach was of lesser importance. See the analysis in *AMEV-UDC Finance Ltd v Austin* (1986) 162 CLR 170, paras 4–5 (Deane J), paras [27]–[35] (Mason and Wilson JJ).

[61] Although even the compensatory principle allows pre-estimate of loss outside the rigid rules of contractual damage: see nn 4 and 27 above.

[62] eg, there is no requirement that consideration be adequate (G Treitel, *The Law of Contract*, (10th edn, 1999) 70); parties will not be relieved from bad bargains (*Bridge v Campbell Discount Co Ltd* [1962] AC 600, 626 *per* Lord Radcliffe); terms concerning the price cannot be challenged under the Unfair Terms in Consumer Contracts Regulations 1999 (reg 6(2)). The Law Commission (*Penalty Clauses and Forfeiture of Monies Paid* (Law Com Working Paper No 61, 1975) para 22) has said: '. . . it is not our intention that every price payable under a contract should be subject to judicial control.'

[63] The distinction between secondary and primary obligations is heavily criticized by M Chen-Wishart, 'Controlling the power to agree damages' in P Birks (ed), *Wrongs and Remedies of the Twenty-first Century* (1996), 273–7.

[64] See, eg, *Nutting v Baldwin* [1995] 1 WLR 201, where the contract was for membership of an association of Lloyds names for the purpose of recovering losses in litigation. The offending clause provided that any member who failed to contribute to the costs of the litigation could not share the benefits. See also *Moss' Empires Ltd v Olympia (Liverpool) Ltd* [1939] AC 544, where a clause requiring the lessees to spend £500 a year on repairs or, if less was expended, to pay the difference to the lessors, was said by the House of Lords not to create an obligation to do repairs up to the sum of £500 but to 'constitute a provision for the mutual advantage of lessors and lessees under which one or the other stand to gain according as more or less repairs are found to be required, and, so far as the lessees are concerned, they put a limit upon their obligations' (559 *per* Lord Porter). This argument could, of course, also

Against this, the following criticisms have been made:

(1) There are many provisions in contracts which are equally penal but do not occur on breach. It is unfair that these are not controlled.[65]

(2) Where a clause has penal consequences some of which arise on breach and some not, a party is better off in breach (as he can then challenge the clause), than not.[66]

(3) Parties wishing to impose penalties can do so by clever drafting which takes them outside the jurisdiction.[67]

(4) The distinction between primary and secondary obligations is not clear-cut enough to warrant different treatment.[68]

(c) The current law: illustration of problems

Hire-purchase agreements usually contain a clause requiring payment of all or a proportion of unpaid instalments on termination of the agreement ('minimum payment clauses').[69] Whether the penalty jurisdiction applies depends on how such payments are triggered:

(1) If the trigger is a repudiatory breach by the hirer, the sum is clearly payable on breach and the jurisdiction applies,[70] though if the clause only provides for loss of bargain[71] it will not be penal since the innocent party is entitled to compensation for this.[72]

(2) If the trigger is the exercise by the owner of a right to terminate which arises on a non-repudiatory breach by the hirer, then the jurisdiction applies, even though the right to terminate and the payment may be triggered by other non-breach events as well.[73] Strictly speaking, here the trigger is the termination by the owner rather than the breach.[74]

---

apply to clauses stipulating sums payable on breach: see PR Kaplan, 'A critique of the penalty limitation on liquidated damages' [1977] 50 Southern Californian Law Review 1055.

[65] Scottish Law Commission, *Report on Penalty Clauses* (Scot Law Com No 171, 1999) Pt 4.

[66] *Bridge v Campbell Discount* [1962] AC 600, 629 *per* Lord Denning.

[67] E McKendrick, *Contract Law* (4th edn, 2000) 433.

[68] M Chen-Wishart, 'Controlling the power to agree damages' in P Birks (ed) *Wrongs and Remedies of the Twenty-first Century* (1996), 274–5.

[69] This discussion relates solely to contracts which are not regulated agreements under the Consumer Credit Act 1974. Under that Act the hirer is entitled to terminate upon payment of one half of the price, and the court can order the payment of a smaller sum if it decides that this represents the owner's loss.

[70] *Lombard North Central v Butterworths* [1987] QB 527, 535 *per* Mustill LJ.

[71] Payment of future rentals (adjusted for acceleration) less the value of the repossessed goods, ie loss of profit.

[72] H Beale (ed), *Chitty on Contracts* (28th edn, 1999), para 38-314. *Robophone Facilities Ltd v Blank* [1966] 1 WLR 1428.

[73] *Bridge v Campbell Discount Co Ltd* [1962] AC 600; *Cooden Engineering Co Ltd v Stanford* [1953] 1 QB 86.

[74] See the dissenting judgment by Jenkins LJ in *Cooden Engineering Co Ltd v Stanford*, ibid.

However, because the payment is originally triggered by breach, the jurisdiction is said to apply. The position is unsatisfactory[75] in that it is not always clear whether the test for whether the clause is penal is comparison with potential loss flowing from the termination or from the breach. Some cases appear to favour the former,[76] but most cases compare the payment with the loss flowing from the breach, ie the amount of the unpaid instalments.[77]

(3) If the trigger is the hirer's option to terminate, the penalty rule does not apply and the receiving party is able to protect itself against loss flowing from termination.[78]

(4) If the trigger is another event, eg the hirer's insolvency or the appointment of a receiver, which gives the owner the right to terminate, again the penalty rule does not apply.[79]

Lords Denning and Devlin in *Bridge v Campbell Discount*[80] considered that there should be no difference between (2) and (3), to avoid the paradox that the hirer was better off breaching the agreement by non-payment than exercising his option to terminate.[81] However, if the jurisdiction were to apply to (3), a comparison would need to be made with the loss flowing from termination (ie loss of bargain) and if the clause were struck down as a penalty, it could only be to the extent that the payment exceeded the former. In that case, the exercise of the jurisdiction under (2) would also have

---

[75] G Treitel, *The Law of Contract* (10th edn, 1999) 935; *AMEV-UDC Finance Ltd v Austin* (1986) 162 CLR 170 para [10] *per* Dawson J.

[76] In *Bridge v Campbell Discount* and *Cooden Engineering v Stanford* the judges appeared to apply loss of bargain reasoning by comparing the position of the owner in receipt of the minimum payment (and the goods) with its position had the contract been performed. The alternative possible calculation of loss flowing from the termination would be the cost of restoring the owner to the position before the contract was made, ie compensation for depreciation of the goods, but not for loss of profit. As Lord Radcliffe points out in *Bridge v Campbell Discount* (at 622), this is unrealistic as on any view there is no obligation on the hirer to prevent wear and tear or to compensate for adverse movements of the market. It could well be argued that the breach in that case was repudiatory, since the hirer returned the vehicle and evinced an intention not to carry on with the contract: [1962] AC 600, 632 *per* Lord Denning and his views in *Financing Ltd v Baldock* [1963] 2 QB 104, 112. It is less easy to see the breach in *Cooden Engineering v Stanford* as repudiatory. See also *O'Dea v Allstates Leasing System (WA) Pty Ltd* (1983) 152 CLR 359.

[77] *United Dominions Trust (Commercial) Ltd v Ennis* [1968] 1 QB 54; *Financings Ltd v Baldock* [1963] 2 QB 104; *AMEV-UDC Finance Ltd v Austin* (1986) 162 CLR 170 (Deane J dissenting).

[78] *Associated Distributors Ltd v Hall* [1938] 2 KB 83; *Bridge v Campbell Discount Co Ltd* [1962] AC 600 (but this case only supported *Associated Distributors Ltd v Hall* by a majority).

[79] *Re Apex Supply Co Ltd* [1942] Ch 108; *Transag Haulage Ltd v Leyland DAF Finance Co* [1994] 2 BCLC 88.

[80] [1962] AC 600.

[81] In both *Bridge v Campbell Discount* and in the later case of *United Dominions Trust (Commercial) Ltd v Ennis* [1968] 1 QB 54 the court took a very strict view of what amounted to exercise of the option to terminate, saying that the hirer needed to be aware that he was subjecting himself to the minimum payment clause: this is clearly a device to enable the penalty jurisdiction to apply.

to be reformed so that loss of bargain became the point of comparison and the amount recoverable: it would be inconsistent if loss of bargain were recoverable if the minimum payment were triggered by the hirer's termination, but not by the owner's termination.[82] A similar problem arises with situation (4) above: should the point of comparison be loss of bargain, or would any pre-estimate of loss suffice providing that it is genuine? Further, if a payment clause triggered by a non-breach event were declared penal, should it be totally unenforceable, which would give the owner no protection against loss flowing from the termination?[83] Or should such a clause be enforceable only to the extent that it is reasonable (or reflects a genuine pre-estimate of loss)?[84]

The situation in (4) also raises the question of whether the court's jurisdiction should extend to the right to terminate, which itself could be said to be oppressive (as could the right under (2)). This question has been addressed in *Transag Haulage Ltd v Leyland DAF Finance plc*[85] and *On Demand Information plc v Michael Gerson*,[86] from which it appears that equity will, in a proper case, relieve against forfeiture of the possessory rights to the goods under a finance lease.[87] If the law will intervene to keep the contract going, why should it not control the terms upon which it ends? The absence of control over the payment clause could lead to courts granting relief against forfeiture of possessory rights where termination would be more appropriate, merely because there is no relief from an oppressive payment clause.

In situation (2) above, an attempt to protect loss of bargain by a minimum payment clause is likely to be unsuccessful.[88] However, if the breach is characterized as repudiatory, the innocent party can accept the repudiation and sue for loss of bargain under the general law. The Court of Appeal in *Lombard North Central v Butterworth*[89] reluctantly held that there is no form of control over the characterization in the contract of the term as a condition, though they commented that this result enabled the penalty jurisdiction to be sidestepped by drafting.[90] Of course, if the penalty jurisdiction were to be extended so that losses on termination

---

[82] A point made by Deane J in *AMEV-UDC Finance Ltd v Austin* (1986) 162 CLR 170 paras [15]–[22].

[83] Since there is no possibility of the owner suing for damage for breach.

[84] This is a technique used in the Code Civil (Article 1152), the BGB (the German Civil Code) (§343), and in Article 9:509 of the Principles of European Contract Law. In its *Report on Penalty Clauses* (Scot Law Com No 171, 1999) the Scottish Law Commission, who proposed extending the penalty jurisdiction beyond agreed payments on breach, proposed that a court should have the power to modify an excessive penalty for this very reason (paras 6.16, 6.20 and 6.22).

[85] [1994] 2 BCLC 88.

[86] [2002] 2 WLR 919, HL.

[87] The 'perfection solution' (discussed below).

[88] Above n 76.

[89] [1987] QB 527.

[90] See criticism in G Treitel, *The Law of Contract* (10th edn, 1999) 794.

were recoverable under any penalty clause operating on termination, then the *Lombard* case loses its sting in relation to minimum payment clauses. However, it may have a wider application, as the device could be used in any context to enable damages for termination to be recovered, rather than just damages for breach.[91] A clause deeming a contractual term a condition would fall within the ambit of the Unfair Terms in Consumer Contracts Regulations 1999 if the contract was made with a consumer.[92]

In many cases there is a very fine distinction between payment triggered by breach and payment which is conditional on an event other than breach.[93] In *Alder v Moore*,[94] a sum paid by an insurance company to a footballer on injury was recoverable by the company if he ever played football professionally again. One analysis would have been that there was an obligation under the contract not to play football professionally, in which case the repayment would have been triggered by breach and the penalty jurisdiction would have applied. In fact the Court of Appeal (by a majority) held that it was a payment to be made on a contingency: the insurance company had no interest in whether the player played professionally again, but this was an indication that he had not been permanently disabled (the original criterion for liability) and they were entitled to protect themselves with such a clause. Similarly, in *Coneco Ltd v Foxboro Great Britain Ltd*,[95] a contract for engineering services between A and B provided that, if the value of the invoices provided by B to A were less than £150,000 in any year, A was to pay B the balance. The Court of Appeal held that this did not create an obligation on A to place orders worth £150,000 with B (in which case the payment would have been damages for breach), but an agreed sum payable on a contingency.

---

[91] See H Beale (ed), *Chitty on Contracts* (28th edn, 1999) paras 27-118, where this technique is seen as a way of avoiding the whole law of penalties. This is something of an overstatement, since the *Lombard* case has no application (a) where the innocent party does not want the contract terminated on breach, or (b) where the breach is repudiatory but the innocent party wants to obtain more than it would have done under the general law, eg (arguably) *Bridge v Campbell Discount Co Ltd* [1962] AC 600 and any case where the amount recoverable under the clause means that the innocent party is better off than if the contact had been performed (see, eg *Transag Haulage Ltd v Leyland DAF Finance Co* [1994] 2 BCLC 88).

[92] Such a clause does not obviously fall within any of the terms in the grey list in Sch 2 of the Regulations, although one could argue that it is included within the spirit of either para 1(e) or 1(f). It would seem to fall within the wider scope of the Regulations, and would, presumably, also fall within the extension to standard terms in business-to-business contracts proposed by the Law Commission in *Unfair Terms in Contracts* (Law Com Consultation Paper No 166) Pt V.

[93] Other examples of clauses which appear to fall outside the penalty jurisdiction are provisions in instalment contracts that on default of one payment the entire sum becomes due (H Beale (ed), *Chitty on Contracts* (28th edn, 1999) para 27–115) and provisions for higher payments for early completion of work, or discounts for early payment.

[94] [1961] 2 QB 57.   [95] Court of Appeal, 24 February 1992.

One can criticize such cases on the basis that the difference is one of form and not substance, and thus the rule against penalties can be avoided by clever drafting.[96] There are several answers to this. First, where the contract is between commercial parties or parties of equal bargaining power, different conclusions based on form are not necessarily objectionable, since both parties will know where they stand. Secondly, such clauses can be just as much a matter of risk-sharing between the parties as one party protecting itself against a specific loss, and the courts should not interfere with this.[97] As a result, it is very difficult to apply any variant of the compensatory principle to such clauses, since many factors other than compensation are taken into account when fixing the relevant amount.[98]

(d) The way forward

It is quite clear from the House of Lords decision in *ECGD v Universal Oil Products*[99] that the limits on the penalty jurisdiction are secure at the moment. It is hard to see that any change could be made to the jurisdiction of the courts while the compensatory principle remains in its present form.[100] If, however, the test became more general[101] it would be possible to apply it to payments not triggered by breach.[102] In this area, the compromise between the freedom of contract argument and the anti-oppression argument involves narrowing the criterion for interference to a test which will only result in striking down truly oppressive clauses, such as the Scottish Law Commission's test of 'manifestly excessive' and widen-

---

[96] See *Penalty Clauses and Forfeiture of Monies Paid* (Law Com Working Paper No 61, 1975) para 18 which gives two examples: (a) X hereby agrees to clean the windows on January 1 and in default of so doing to pay Y the sum of £100 as liquidated damages for the breach; (b) X hereby agrees to clean the windows on January 1 or, at his option, to pay Y the sum of £100 instead and X shall be taken to have exercised his option to pay the £100 if he does not clean the windows on January 1.

[97] See *ECGD v Universal Oil Products* [1983] 1 Lloyd's Rep 448 (CA), 456 *per* Waller LJ, supporting the view that the courts should not interfere with the allocation of risk where the clause provided for payment on another party's default under a closely related contract.

[98] See M Chen-Wishart, 'Controlling the power to agree damages' in P Birks (ed), *Wrongs and Remedies of the Twenty-first Century* (1996) 275.

[99] [1983] 1 WLR 399.

[100] Because of the difficulties analysed above of applying such a principle to losses triggered by events other than breach, and because of the 'risk sharing' element also referred to above.

[101] For example, 'manifestly excessive' as suggested in the Scottish Law Commission, *Report on Penalty Clauses* (Scot Law Com No 171, 1999), or based on a test of whether there is oppression, reflecting the approach of Dickson J in the Supreme Court of Canada in *Elsey v JG Collins Insurance Agencies Ltd* (1978) 83 DLR 1, 15, apparently endorsed by the Privy Council in *Phillips Hong Kong v A-G of Hong Kong* (1993) 61 Building Law Reports 49 (see n 49 above).

[102] Although there would still be the problem highlighted in the text to nn 83 and 84 above.

ing the scope but only to a limited extent, either based on the function of the payment clause[103] or the payment trigger.[104]

3. RELIEF AGAINST FORFEITURE (1): THE RECOVERY OF PAYMENTS ON TERMINATION

Frequently a contract may involve a party paying part of the money consideration before receiving complete performance from the other party.[105] If the contract is terminated[106] before performance is completed, does the paying party have a right to recover any of the money already paid?[107] Since the termination is only prospective, one can argue that all payments made under the contract before termination cannot be unwound.[108] There are two interrelated exceptions to this, which threaten to undermine the whole principle.[109] The first is where the paying party has a restitutionary right to recover the payment. The second is where the contract expressly or impliedly provides that the performing party should not be entitled to retain any payment. These two exceptions overlap but are not necessarily co-extensive.[110] Where payments are not otherwise recoverable, equity will sometimes give relief against the operation of the strict law.

---

[103] Such as contractual obligations which secure a particular result, as suggested in Law Commission, *Penalty Clauses and Forfeiture of Monies Paid* (Law Com Working Paper No 61, 1975) para 26.

[104] Such as a rule covering cases 'where the penalty is due if the promisor fails to perform, or to perform in a particular way, or where there is an early termination,' suggested in the Scottish Law Commission, *Report on Penalty Clauses* (Scot Law Com No 171, 1999) para 4.10.

[105] In this section the party who has paid is called 'the paying party' and the party who has received the money is called 'the performing party'.

[106] Prospective termination as opposed to being rescinded *ab initio*.

[107] Quite often this question arises in the context of whether a performing party can sue for instalments, the liability for which accrued before the contract was terminated. The principle should be the same whether payments have been made or not: (i) the paying party should not be able to put himself in a better position by not paying (*Dewar v Mintoft* [1912] 2 KB 373); (ii) if the paying party were ordered to pay the instalments they could counterclaim for them on the grounds of total failure of consideration. The principle that the same criteria apply to both cases seems to have been accepted by the House of Lords in *Stocznia Gdanska SA v Latvian Shipping Co* [1998] 1 WLR 574, following *Hyundai Heavy Industies Co Ltd v Papadopoulos* [1980] 1 WLR 1129. In both these cases the performing party was suing for accrued instalments.

[108] See J Beatson, 'Discharge for breach: the position of instalments, deposits and other payments due before completion' (1981) 97 LQR 389, 390.

[109] Some writers state the principle the other way round, ie that payments are recoverable unless there is a reason they should not be, eg D Harris, D Campbell, and R Halson, *Remedies in Contract and Tort* (2nd edn, 2002) 58 and G Treitel, *The Law of Contract* (10th edn, 1999) 937–42. See also *Dies v British and International Mining and Finance Corp* [1939] 1 KB 724, 743.

[110] See J Beatson, above n 108, 416.

(a) Whether payments are recoverable: the restitutionary position

If there is a total failure of consideration, then money paid pursuant to the contract will be recoverable.[111] It should not make any difference that the party seeking to recover payment is in breach of contract, in that the performing party is otherwise unjustly enriched: it gets the payment and has not had to provide the performance.[112] The requirement that failure of consideration must be total restricts this ground of recovery very considerably. If, for example, the contract is for services, then any part performance of those services before termination will prevent recovery.[113] If the contract is for hire or hire purchase of goods, then granting of possession to the hirer, even for a limited time, will constitute part performance.[114] Could this problem now be solved by enabling the paying party to recover part of the money paid on the grounds of partial failure of consideration?[115] While this has the benefit of overcoming technicalities associated with the total failure limit,[116] there would be, in many cases, considerable difficulties in assessing what proportion of the consideration had failed. Such assessment would be possible in a contract for the sale of goods by instalments.[117] However, there are at least two possible measures in contracts for goods and services, or for just services: (a) the value of the benefit to the paying party, and (b) the cost of the work done to the performing party. Depending on the stage of performance at which the contract is terminated, there can be a great disparity between these two measures.[118] Lord Goff made it clear in the *Stocznia* case that the test for whether consideration had failed was 'not whether the promisee has received a specific benefit but rather whether the promisor has performed any part of the contractual duties in respect of which the payment is due,'[119] but that was in the context of whether the sellers could sue for the whole payment rather than in the context of apportionment. In relation to a contract of hire purchase, or a finance lease, it has been argued that part of the considera-

---

[111] For example, if no goods are delivered under a contract for the sale of goods, the buyer can recover the price (Sale of Goods Act 1979, s 54)

[112] See *Clough Mill v Martin* [1985] 1 WLR 111, 117–8 *per* Robert Goff LJ who envisages a restitutionary claim in such a situation. The right to recover in these circumstances is also assumed by the House of Lords in *Stocznia Gdansak SA v Latvian Shipping Co* [1998] 1 WLR 574.

[113] *Hyundai Heavy Industies Co Ltd v Papadopoulos* [1980] 1 WLR 1129.

[114] *Brooks v Beirnstein* [1909] 1 KB 98; *Chatterton v Maclean* [1951] 1 All ER 761 and see L Smith, 'Relief against forfeiture: a restatement' [2001] CLJ 178, 183.

[115] On the basis of *Goss v Chilcott* [1996] AC 788.

[116] eg, the difficulties caused by the decision in *Rowland v Divall* [1923] 2 KB 500.

[117] *Rugg v Minett* (1809) 11 East 211, 103 ER 985.

[118] A problem that is particularly evident on frustration and which is tackled to some extent in the complex provisions of the Law Reform (Frustrated Contracts) Act 1943.

[119] [1998] 1 WLR 574, 588.

tion is the use of the goods, and that part is the right to purchase, or to sell the goods, at the end of the contractual period.[120] This again raises the problem of from whose perspective is the benefit/cost to be assessed, with the added complication that in neither case is the result of the assessment obvious.

The partial failure of consideration solution thus has a number of drawbacks. First, it involves complex and unrealistic assessment exercises. Secondly, if such assessment exercises are to be undertaken, they would be better done as part of a discretionary jurisdiction of relief, taking into account all the circumstances of the case, rather than as an exercise in precise restitution. There is very little authority for this solution, and in the most recent House of Lords case, *Stocznia Gdanska SA v Latvian Shipping Co*,[121] Lord Goff, though he acknowledged criticism of the total failure rule, expressly declined to depart from it.

(b) Whether payments are recoverable: the contractual position

The alternative rationale is to say that when a contract terminates, the nature of the rights that accrue depend on their nature under the contract. It is possible for the right to claim or retain a payment to depend upon full performance (conditional) or to be unconditional,[122] conditional payments being recoverable by a paying party on termination. Whether a payment is conditional or unconditional is a matter of construction of the contract.

One type of unconditional payment is a payment given as security or 'earnest' for the performance of the contract by the paying party, often called a deposit. Many contracts will provide expressly for the forfeiture of a deposit if the paying party does not perform, but even without this express provision the nature of a deposit is that it can be retained in the event of default.[123] Another type of unconditional payment is a payment which is not conditional upon full performance by the performing party: 'part performance payments'. Thus, any payment which is referable to performance which has taken place before the termination comes into this category. There is very considerable overlap with the restitutionary reasoning here, which is apparent from the reasoning of Viscount Dilhorne and Lord Fraser in *Hyundai Heavy Industries Co Ltd v Papadopoulos*.[124] In that case, there was a contract for the building of a ship, the payment obligations of the buyers being guaranteed by the defendant. When considering the buyer's liability for instalments accrued before termination for default in payment (with which the defendant guarantor's liability was

---

[120] L Smith, 'Relief against forfeiture: a restatement' [2001] CLJ 178.
[121] [1998] 1 WLR 574, 588.   [122] *McDonald v Dennys Lascalles* (1933) 48 CLR 457.
[123] *Howe v Smith* (1881) 27 ChD 89.   [124] [1980] 1 WLR 1129.

co-extensive), Lord Fraser relied on two express contractual provisions,[125] whereas Viscount Dilhorne based his decision on the absence of total failure of consideration.

Except in these two cases, payments made under a contract are generally seen as conditional upon full performance and are recoverable in the absence of such performance. In *Dies v British and International Mining and Finance Corp*,[126] the contract was for the sale of ammunition and arms, with payment by instalments. The buyer paid £100,000 then defaulted, both by non-payment and by failure to take delivery. Stable J clearly based the buyer's right to recover the money paid on his interpretation of the contract, which did not give the seller any right to retain the money, expressly rejecting the ground of total failure of consideration (which he said was unavailable because the buyer was in default).[127]

The position from the cases appears to be that while the restitutionary position is useful in considering the overall picture, when it comes to deciding specific cases it is necessary to look closely at the contract between the parties to see the nature of the right to payment. Since the contract will itself determine what amounts to performance, construction of the contract is in any event crucial in deciding whether consideration has totally failed. Conversely, where any performance has taken place by the time of termination, it is very likely that the true construction of the contract will be that the payment is to be retained.[128]

(c) Relief against forfeiture of payments made

Even where the contract gives the performing party the right to retain the payment, this is subject to the control of the courts. The situation falls between the two jurisdictions: the penalty jurisdiction and the doctrine of relief against forfeiture of proprietary or possessory interests, and the courts have borrowed elements of each in their reasoning. It could be argued that the compensatory principle, as exemplified in the penalty rule, can justify control[129] on the basis that the pre-payment fulfils the

---

[125] One 'that the contract price "shall include payment for services in the inspection, tests, survey and classification of the vessel" and also "all costs and expenses for designing and supplying all necessary drawings for the vessel in accordance with the specifications"', the other that 'in the event of such cancellation by the builder of this contract due to default in payment of the ... second ... instalment as provided for in paragraph (a) above, the builder shall be entitled to retain the instalments already paid by the buyer to the builder.'

[126] [1939] 1 KB 724. See also, in the context of sale of land, *Mayson v Clouet* [1924] AC 980.

[127] [1939] 1 KB 724, at 744. See text to n 112 above.

[128] See G Treitel, *The Law of Contract* (10th edn, 1999) 942.

[129] Alternative justifications could be procedural unfairness (see T Downes, 'Rethinking penalty clauses' in P Birks (ed), *Wrongs and Remedies of the Twenty-first century* (1996)), substantive unfairness (see M Chen-Wishart, 'Controlling the power to agree damages' ibid.), or that events that have happened make it unfair for the innocent party to insist on his rights

same function as an agreed damages clause, the only difference being that the performing party already has the money. This is supported by the terms of some of the clauses themselves, which specify the purpose of retention as being agreed compensation for breach.[130] However, the fact that the money has already been transferred to the performing party changes the courts' attitude,[131] so that the strict penalty jurisdiction is said not to apply,[132] and the control is an equitable one based on more general considerations than the penalty rule.[133]

The exact nature of the equitable control is still rather unclear. The majority[134] in *Stockloser v Johnson*[135] specified two criteria: (a) that the forfeiture was penal, and (b) that it would be unconscionable for the performing party to retain the money. A case can be made for a distinction between deposits and other payments, so that deposits are always enforceable unless unreasonable,[136] while a more general equitable jurisdiction to relieve applies to other payments. It is, however, hard to see why the

under the contract (see C Harpum, 'Relief against Forfeiture and the Purchaser of Land' [1984] CLJ 134, and *Stern v. McArthur* (1988) 165 CLR 489).

[130] eg, the clause in *Commissioner of Public Works v. Hills* [1906] AC 368 read: 'The 10% retention money under this agreement, together with the 10% retention money . . . shall be forfeited to the Colonial Government as and for liquidated damages sustained by the said Government for the non-completion of the said line.' The Privy Council in that case found the clause penal and ordered repayment, subject to a reduction for the performing party's actual loss.

[131] The Law Commission could see the only justification for the distinction as the fact that the paying party is more likely to be aware that he will lose the deposit if he defaults. They concluded that the distinction between penalties and pre-payments was not justified and that they should be treated similarly: *Penalty Clauses and Forfeiture of Monies Paid* (Law Com Working Paper No 61, 1975) para 59. The Scottish Law Commission made a similar recommendation in its *Report on Penalty Clauses* (Scot Law Com No 171, 1999) para 5.9.

[132] This stems from an obiter dictum of Jessel MR in *Wallis v Smith* (1879) 21 C D 243, which was confirmed by Bigham J in *Pye v British Automobile Commercial Syndicate Ltd* [1906] 1 KB 425, although he said that the cases cited by Jessel MR did not support the proposition. The anomalous nature of deposits was noted by Lord Browne-Wilkinson in *Workers Trust & Merchant Bank Ltd v Dojap Investments Ltd* [1993] AC 532.

[133] *Stockloser v Johnson* [1954] 1 QB 476, 489, *per* Denning LJ, and *Else (1982) Ltd v Parkland Holdings Ltd* [1994] 1 BCLC 130, 135, *per* Evans LJ. The view that there is no such jurisdiction was upheld by Romer LJ in the *Stockloser* case, who said that in the absence of fraud, sharp practice, or other unconscionable conduct there is no equitable jurisdiction to recover payments, on the grounds of freedom of contract. This view has been followed at first instance in *Galbraith v Mitchenall Estates Ltd* [1965] 2 QB 473 and *Windsor Securities Ltd v Loreldal Ltd*, The Times, 10 September 1975. The point, in relation to part performance payments, was left open by the Privy Council in *Workers Trust & Merchant Bank Ltd v Dojap Investments Ltd* [1993] AC 532.

[134] Denning and Somervell LJJ.   [135] [1954] 1 QB 476.

[136] See the judgment of the Privy Council delivered by Lord Hailsham in *Linggi Plantations Ltd v Jagatheesan* [1972] 1 Malaysian Law Journal 89. The idea of an unreasonable (that is, grossly excessive) deposit being unenforceable was also supported by an example given by Denning LJ in *Stockloser v Johnson* [1954] 1 QB 476, 491 of a 50 per cent deposit. Recovery of deposits paid under contracts for the sale of land is governed in England and Wales by s 49(2) of the Law of Property Act 1925, which gives the court a discretion to relieve against forfeiture: see *Universal Corp v Five Ways Properties Ltd* [1979] 1 All ER 552.

difference should be anything but a matter of emphasis,[137] although the fact that deposits are 'arbitrary sums, seen not as potential compensation but as . . . inducements to perform'[138] means that any test based on the compensatory principle would be inappropriate, and the fact that the breaching party agreed to a deposit makes it less likely to be unconscionable for it to be forfeit.[139]

(d) The test for relief: deposits

The Privy Council in *Worker's Trust & Merchant Bank Ltd v Dojap Investment Ltd*[140] formulated the test for enforceability of deposits as one of reasonableness.[141] The contract in this case, for the sale of land at auction, provided for a 25 per cent deposit, which the vendor forfeited as the purchaser did not complete in time, time being of the essence. Lord Browne-Wilkinson said that the starting point when considering reasonableness was whether the deposit was larger that the customary sum;[142] if so the vendor must justify the deviation. It appears that the following may justify such a deviation: (a) a reasonable amount to act as 'earnest';[143] or (b) an amount to cover expenses the vendor would incur on completion.[144]

The emphasis is clearly on reasonableness rather than applying the compensatory principle. First, Lord Browne-Wilkinson did not consider the question of compensating the vendor for loss suffered by the loss of the bargain, which would depend on whether the vendor was able to resell

[137] C Harpum, 'Relief against Forfeiture and the Purchaser of Land' [1984] CLJ 134, 164.

[138] Law Commission, *Penalty Clauses and Forfeiture of Monies Paid* (Law Com Working Paper No 61, 1975) para 45.

[139] Another way forward would be to apply a test of reasonableness to all agreed remedies clauses: see n 40 above.

[140] [1993] AC 532.

[141] The actual reasoning was rather circuitous, in that the amount, being unreasonable, was not a deposit; therefore it was a sum paid 'by way of security for performance,' therefore the case was similar to *Commissioner for Public Works v Hills* [1906] AC 368 and repayment could be ordered after accounting for any actual loss. However, the *Hills* case can be distinguished (a) on the grounds that the sum was there said to be forfeit 'as and for liquidated damages', and (b) some of the money was never actually transferred to the performing party but held by the Agent-General as security money (see Denning LJ in *Stockloser v Johnson* [1954] 1 QB 476, 488 and Hoffmann LJ in *Else (1982) Ltd v Parkland Holdings Ltd* [1994] 1 BCLC 130, 146).

[142] Which had by long usage been 10 per cent in the United Kingdom and formerly in Jamaica, where the case originated.

[143] The vendor said that the customary amount in Jamaica had risen to cover tax which had to be paid within 30 days of the contract, and which was usually paid by the vendor out of the deposit. These considerations were dismissed as irrelevant to encouragement to perform the contract.

[144] The vendor also sought to justify the amount by referring to such expenses: Lord Browne-Wilkinson did not dismiss this as irrelevant but said that the amount was far in excess of such expenses. He also intimated that the tax argument did not work as the expenses were never incurred, first because in this case the tax was not payable as completion was 14 days after contract, and secondly because there was no liability to pay tax if the contract was not completed.

the property and mitigate his loss, and would therefore vary according to the state of the market. The fact that the vendor suffers no actual loss does not prevent the recovery of a reasonable deposit.[145] Secondly, the Privy Council's view of a 'customary sum' itself contains elements of reasonableness. It was argued that the customary sum in Jamaica was now higher than 10 per cent as it was common practice for banks selling at auction to demand deposits of between 15 per cent and 50 per cent. Lord Browne-Wilkinson rejected the test of 'common practice' as 'to allow the test of reasonableness to depend upon the practice of one class of vendor, which exercises considerable financial muscle, would be to allow them to evade the law against penalties by adopting practices of their own.' The test of reasonableness has considerable merit in this context and can take into account both substantive[146] and procedural[147] unfairness.

(e) The test for relief: part performance payments

There is less authority on how the penal requirement would be applied in the case of a part performance payment. It would seem that the point of the jurisdiction here is to avoid unjust enrichment,[148] but it must be remembered that the performing party can justifiably seek to protect his loss of bargain[149] by the forfeiture as well as his reliance interest. Any attempt to calculate precisely what amount is required to cover past performance plus future loss is fraught with difficulty, even taking into account the actual events that have taken place,[150] as exactly the same problems arise as with calculating partial failure of consideration.[151] Therefore the test is likely to be that the clause will not be penal unless its operation leaves the performing party manifestly better off than they would have been had the contract been performed.[152]

---

[145] *Linggi Plantations Ltd v Jagatheesan* [1972] 1 Malaysian Law Journal 89.

[146] Including factors such as the nature of the parties and the overall bargain as well as the actual loss likely to be sustained from breach, see M Chen-Wishart, 'Controlling the power to agree damages' in P Birks (ed), *Wrongs and Remedies of the Twenty-first Century* (1996) 296–8.

[147] Including factors such as notice of the forfeiture term, equality of bargaining power and freedom of choice: see H Beale, 'Unreasonable Deposits' (1983) 109 LQR 524.

[148] See Denning LJ in *Stockloser v Johnson* [1954] 1 QB 476, 492.

[149] See, eg, the following clause from the contract in *Stocznia Gdanska SA v Latvian Shipping Co* [1998] 1 WLR 574: 'In the event of rescission by the Seller of this Contract due to the Purchaser's default . . . the seller shall be entitled to retain and apply the instalments already paid by the Purchaser to the recovery of the Seller's loss and damage.' The House of Lords did not consider the issue of relief against forfeiture in that case.

[150] Denning LJ makes it clear that these are relevant in *Stockloser v Johnson* [1954] 1 QB 476, 492.

[151] See above.

[152] G Treitel, *The Law of Contract* (10th edn, 1999) 941 makes the point that relief is only possible in cases of provision of services where payment contains a heavy element of 'front loading.' Such considerations are also seen as relevant to the question of unconscionablity: see Somervell LJ in *Stockloser v Johnson* [1954] 1 QB 476, 484 and Hoffmann LJ in *Else (1982) Ltd v Parkland Holdings Ltd* [1994] 1 BCLC 130, 146.

The second requirement of unconscionability is wide and seems to cover a number of factors:

(1) the relative bargaining powers of the parties and whether it was a commercial transaction;[153]
(2) the fact that the paying party knew that he was likely to lose the payment if he was in breach;[154]
(3) delay in asking for relief;[155]
(4) how much had already been paid;[156]
(5) whether the paying party is willing and able to perform.[157] Somervell and Denning LJJ in the *Stockloser* case rejected the view that this was a condition precedent for relief,[158] although Romer LJ dissented from this. It is difficult to see that it has any relevance where the restitutionary solution is sought rather than the perfection solution.[159]

4. RELIEF AGAINST FORFEITURE (2): ALLOWING THE CONTRACT TO CONTINUE

There are two aspects to this area: first, in what situations a court has jurisdiction to relieve against forfeiture, and secondly, when the jurisdiction will be exercised.[160] There is jurisdiction where the forfeiture is of a proprietary or possessory interest,[161] but not of future contractual rights,[162] and where forfeiture is to secure the payment of money or the primary object of the bargain.[163] The effect of this jurisdiction in relation

---

[153] *Mussen v Van Diemen's Land Co* [1938] Ch 253, 262; *Else (1982) Ltd v Parkland Holdings Ltd* [1994] 1 BCLC 130, 146.   [154] [1938] Ch 253, 263.

[155] ibid. This factor was explained by Denning LJ in *Stockloser v Johnson* [1954] 1 QB 476, 492 as affecting the value of the land already conveyed to the paying party so that he had had his money's worth.

[156] Denning LJ in *Stockloser v Johnson* [1954] 1 QB 476, 492, apparently because there would not then be unjust enrichment.

[157] *Steedman v Drinkle* [1916] 1 AC 275. cf *Mussen v Van Diemen's Land Co* [1938] Ch 253, 263–5.

[158] [1954] 1 QB 476, 487, 489.

[159] See C Harpum, 'Relief against Forfeiture and the Purchaser of Land' [1984] CLJ 134, 156–61, and nn 175 and 176 below.

[160] The exercise of jurisdiction, which will not be examined in detail here, depends on a number of factors, such as the conduct of the parties, the nature and gravity of the breach and its relation to the value of the property forfeited (*Shiloh Spinners v Harding* [1973] AC 691, 723–4), and whether the defendant would otherwise obtain a windfall (*Transag Haulage Ltd v Leyland DAF Finance plc* [1994] 2 BCLC 88).

[161] *The Scaptrade* [1983] 2 AC 694; *BICC v Burndy* [1985] 1 Ch 232; *Transag Haulage Ltd v Leyland DAF Finance plc* [1994] 2 BCLC 88; *On Demand Information plc v Michael Gerson (Finance) plc* [2002] 2 WLR 919, HL.

[162] *Sport International Bussum BV v Inter-Footwear Ltd* [1984] 2 All ER 321; *Python (Monty) Pictures Ltd v Paragon Entertainment Corp* [1998] Entertainment and Media Law Reports 697.

[163] Per Lord Wilberforce in *Shiloh Spinners v Harding* [1973] AC 691, 723, cited with approval in *Transag Haulage Ltd v Leyland DAF Finance plc* [1994] 2 BCLC and *On Demand Information plc v Michael Gerson (Finance) plc* [2000] 4 All ER 734, CA: this aspect of the decision was not challenged in the House of Lords.

to transactions relating to personal property used as alternatives to secured lending[164] will be considered here. In such contracts A extends credit to B and protects itself either by retaining title and providing for forfeiture of B's possession in the event of default,[165] or by providing for forfeiture of B's proprietary rights[166] in the event of default.

Why might a party want to continue the contract if he is in default: (1) to carry on using the asset;[167] (2) to gain the benefit of the bargain;[168] or (3) where the hirer has already made considerable payments, which will not be recoverable on forfeiture?[169] The early cases, which are concerned with forfeiture of interests in land, are predicated on the defaulting party having motive (1).[170] The reasoning therefore was that so long as the innocent party could be protected financially, relief could be given. If the innocent party had a good non-financial reason for wanting forfeiture[171] relief would be refused. If, however, the defaulting party's motives are purely financial ((2) or (3)) the dynamics of the question change. It can be argued that the forfeiture of the proprietary/possessory interest is merely instrumental in achieving the parties' financial ends. Therefore what the court has to consider is how the losses and gains should be distributed between the parties, given the bargain made between them.

One analysis is that the transaction is merely one of security.[172] In relation to (2) above, it can be argued that the parties intend that the paying party should eventually have the asset or its value, and so is entitled to the benefit of any rise in value.[173] The performing party's interest is merely

---

[164] 'Quasi-security' transactions. These methods of financing are used to avoid registration of charges, and for tax and accounting reasons.

[165] As in a conditional sale, hire purchase, or finance lease, and also an operating lease when used for off balance sheet financing.

[166] Maybe a situation like *Jobson v Johnson* [1989] 1 All ER 621 (though for procedural reasons this was treated as a penalty case: the defendant's counterclaim for relief against forfeiture had been struck out for failure to comply with certain undertakings to the court). Another example would be *BICC v Burndy* [1985] 1 Ch 232 where proprietary rights in patents were forfeited.

[167] For example, a lessee of property may want to continue working from the premises, a hirer of goods may wish to continue using them in its business, eg, *Transag Haulage Ltd v Leyland DAF Finance plc* [1994] 2 BCLC 88, or a conditional purchaser of land may want to continue living there, eg, *Legione v Hateley* (1983) 152 Commonwealth Law Reports 406.

[168] eg, where the value of the asset has risen or will rise above the amount paid for it.

[169] Because the payments were unconditional (see above) and a restitutionary solution is not available.

[170] That is, a non-financial motive.

[171] For example, that he did not want to remain in a 'relation of neighbourhood with a person in deliberate breach of his obligations' (*per* Lord Wilberforce in *Shiloh Spinners v Harding* [1973] AC 691, 725) or where certainty was at a premium as he needed to know whether he could resell land (*Union Eagle Ltd v Golden Achievement Ltd* [1997] AC 514).

[172] L Smith, 'Relief against forfeiture: a restatement' (2001) 60 CLJ 178.

[173] And also takes the risk of any fall in value: in such a situation the paying party would seek the restitution solution. The question arises whether a defaulting party should be allowed this choice.

obtaining his money back plus interest and costs, and so long as this interest can be protected, relief should be given. The situation is said to be closely analogous to relief against forfeiture of a mortgage.[174] In situation (c), restitution[175] should be as satisfactory as perfection.[176] However, where the payments relate to hire[177] rather than, or as well as, the purchase price, there is no total failure of consideration,[178] and the difficulties of determining what amounts to partial failure of consideration[179] mean that restitution is not a viable option.[180]

(a) The limits of the jurisdiction

One explanation for the scope of the jurisdiction is that if the doctrine operates to protect the creditor's security interest, the debtor must have some kind of remaining beneficial interest, and this cannot be the case with contractual rights between the parties.[181] Further, in relation to forfeiture of contractual rights, the complaint is that the clause is unfair since the paying party loses the (financial) benefit of the contract because of a trivial breach or event. This is analogous to the situation where a term is characterized in the contract as a condition,[182] which, except for specific exceptions,[183] is not controlled at present. It is difficult to see why commercial parties should not be held to their bargain here.[184]

It is now clear that the jurisdiction applies to finance leases[185] and hire purchase agreements.[186] In relation to operating leases, the interest of the debtor is possessory, and so prima facie falls within the jurisdiction. If the forfeiture provisions are for the purpose of securing the primary object of

---

[174] See the reasoning of Deane and Dawson JJ in *Stern v McArthur* (1988) 165 CLR 489.

[175] Return of payments made.

[176] Continuation of the transaction on payment of money outstanding.

[177] As in a hire purchase agreement, a finance lease, or an operating lease.

[178] As there could be in a conditional sale, by analogy with the retention of title cases: see, eg, *Clough Mill v Martin* [1985] 1 WLR 111 and n 112 above.

[179] See above.

[180] See L Smith, 'Relief against forfeiture: a restatement' (2001) 60 CLJ 178 at 183–4.

[181] ibid, 194 explaining the decision in *The Scaptrade* [1983] 2 AC 694.

[182] As in *Lombard North Central plc v Butterworth* [1987] QB 527.

[183] Under the Unfair Terms in Consumer Contract Regulations 1999 and s 15A of the Sale of Goods Act 1979. Forfeiture clauses in consumer contracts would anyway be controlled under the 1999 Regulations.

[184] See the reasoning of Lord Diplock in *The Scaptrade* [1983] 2 AC 694, 703 and Lord Templeman in *Sport International Bussum BV v Inter-Footwear Ltd.* [1984] 2 All ER 321, 325, who both emphasized the need for certainty in these commercial transactions.

[185] *Transag Haulage Ltd v Leyland DAF Finance plc* [1994] 2 BCLC 88; *On Demand Information plc v Michael Gerson (Finance) plc* [2002] 2 WLR 919, HL.

[186] *Goker v NWS Bank plc*, 1st August 1990, CA.

the transaction,[187] which would usually be the payment of money, the jurisdiction would seem to apply whether the function of the transaction was financing or purely operative.[188] However, in the former case the ability to reconstitute might not be critical, while in the latter case it would be.[189]

(b) Where it is not possible to restore the proprietary or possessory interest in the asset to the paying party at the time of relief

In situations (2) and (3),[190] the asset is seen as a source of value. This is a different perspective from that of the courts in the earlier cases, where one criterion for relief was that the contract could be specifically performed,[191] since what the party asking for relief wanted was the equivalent of specific performance. But all that is sought in situations (2) and (3) is the financial equivalent of continuance of the contract. This issue was raised in *On Demand Information plc v Michael Gerson (Finance) plc*[192] where, by the time the court came to consider the application for relief, the goods had been sold by the administrative receiver pursuant to a court order, as part of the sale of the debtor's business. It was argued that because the transaction could not be reconstituted, relief could not be given. The House of Lords rejected this argument on the grounds that the order for sale was not intended to change the parties' rights, so that if relief would have been granted immediately before the order for sale, the court would make an order putting the parties in the same financial position as if the relief had been given. It is possible to see the decision as turning on the particular circumstances of the court order and sale.[193] However, if the security argument is accepted, the impossibility of reconstitution should never provide

---

[187] *Shiloh Spinners Ltd v Harding* [1973] AC 691, 722; *On Demand Information plc v Michael Gerson (Finance) plc* [2000] 4 All ER 734 CA.

[188] The point was considered arguable in relation to a simple operating lease in *Barton Thompson & Co v Stapling Machines Co* [1966] Ch 499.

[189] And the court would also take into account the severity of the breach in relation to the detriment to the debtor on forfeiture. Readiness and willingness to pay arrears would be a condition of relief (*Barton Thompson & Co v Stapling Machines Co* [1966] Ch 499, 510).

[190] As opposed to (1) see above p 213.

[191] Entitlement to specific performance was always seen as a precondition for imposing the perfection solution: this had the effect that if specific performance was not available because the party seeking relief was in breach of a term making time of the essence, relief against forfeiture of land was not available (*Steedman v Drinkle* [1916] 1 AC 275). That the perfection solution was seen as amounting to an order for specific performance appears from *The Scaptrade* [1983] 2 AC 694 where the fact that an order for specific performance could not be made in respect of a time charter (since it was a contract for services) was one of the reasons relief against forfeiture was said to be inappropriate.

[192] [2002] 2 WLR 919.

[193] In that the order was given on the basis that the sale was not to prejudice the parties' rights.

a bar to relief, so long as the parties can be put in the same financial position as though the contract had been performed.[194] This brings the doctrine of relief against forfeiture a long way from its roots, ie to enable a party to keep something which had a value to them other than money, by paying the money that was due. Although the security argument in one sense supports the exclusion of forfeiture of contractual rights from the jurisdiction of relief,[195] if reconstitution is not seen as important the analogy with loss of potentially profitable contractual rights becomes much closer. However, this also means that the argument that parties are to be held to their agreement[196] becomes stronger.

(c) The security argument as an interim measure pending reform

If the security argument prevails, quasi-security transactions[197] gain both the first and the second of the incidents of security set out by Romer LJ in *Re George Inglefield Ltd*.[198] The debtor, by being able to retain the goods even in the event of default, is given an enhanced right to redeem,[199] while the lender is only entitled to recover the amount of loan plus interest and costs, and is not entitled to any profit made from the sale of the goods. The third incident is already present: the contract will normally provide that if the recovered asset is not enough to repay the lender, he can recover the balance. It is, of course, possible to structure a quasi-security transaction which includes a right to redeem,[200] and which provides contractually that the lender accounts for surplus.[201] But such a transaction risks being characterized as a charge and being void for non-registration. The forfeiture route seems to avoid this danger: the transaction on its face is not a

---

[194] L Smith, 'Relief against forfeiture: a restatement' (2001) 60 CLJ 178, 196, where the analogy of redeeming a mortgage on default is used. It is, of course, important that the lender is fully compensated for the loss flowing from early redemption.

[195] Above.

[196] Above. This has some force where the parties have deliberately chosen a particular contractual structure to avoid registration, tax, or accounting requirements.

[197] Which do not amount to security transactions for the purposes of registration (Companies Act 1985, ss 395–6).

[198] [1933] Ch 1 at 27–8, namely, a right to redeem and an obligation on the lender to account for profit. This formulation is relied upon in numerous characterization cases, such as *Welsh Development Agency v Export Finance Co Ltd* [1992] BCLC 148, 161; *Re Curtain Dream plc* [1990] BCLC 921, 936; *Orion Finance Ltd v Crown Financial Management Ltd* [1996] 2 BCLC 78, 84.

[199] Which may not even depend on reconstitution.

[200] On payment of the debt, interest, and costs, although the penalty jurisdiction does not apply to the obligation to pay these as it does not arise on breach.

[201] See Law Commission, *Registration of Security Interests: Company Charges and Property other than Land* (Law Com Consultation Paper No 164, July 2002) para 6.5, n 6. There is, of course, the danger that if all the incidents of security are present then the transaction will be characterized as security.

charge, and the parties gain the benefits of this,[202] and yet on default, the court treats it as a security transaction by using the relief against forfeiture route. This seems wrong, though less so if one looks at the interests of the various parties. Those who are potentially injured by the non-registration of the transaction are the other creditors of the debtor. However, on default[203] these also suffer most from refusal of relief:[204] the benefit is for the lender. Thus, where the transaction is functionally a security agreement, it seems hard to insist on enforcing the agreement according to its form.

One can argue, as Smith does,[205] that the problem is that the law has a formal rather than functional approach to the classification of security, and until this is reformed it is best for debtors who enter into quasi-security transactions to be protected by relief against forfeiture. Certainly, the prospects for reform of the law are now looking brighter. The Law Commission Consultation Paper on Registration of Security Interests[206] proposes that quasi-security transactions be registrable[207] under a notice filing system, and that the incidents of security should necessarily apply to them.[208] If these proposals become law, the scope of relief against forfeiture should narrow again to situation (1), ie where the party asking for relief genuinely wants reconstitution of the precise transaction.

5. CONCLUSION

The law on agreed remedies fundamentally concerns the relief of parties from the effect of terms in the contract which operate oppressively or unfairly in the situation before the court. The courts have developed different criteria for relief in each of the three areas discussed above.[209] One

---

[202] For example, there is no obligation to register. Usually this benefits the debtor in particular, though the benefits may be shared between the two parties.

[203] Especially on the debtor's insolvency.

[204] Since they lose the benefit of the surplus.   [205] See n 13 above.

[206] Law Com Consultation Paper No 164, July 2002.

[207] Pt VII. This includes hire-purchase and conditional sale agreements (para 7.22), retention of title clauses (para 7.24), and leases, although they are undecided as to whether these should be leases over a minimum period or leases with a security function (para 7.30–4).

[208] Pt XI (although restraints of time might mean that the registration scheme would be introduced at an earlier date than the restatement of the law of security, including the provisions applying the incidents of security to quasi-security transactions). The incidents of security would include an accounting for surplus, a right to redeem and possibly a right to reinstate the security agreement (B.61–2). This last-mentioned right is based on s 133 of the New Zealand Personal Property Security Act 1999, and was introduced because the Act gives the parties the ability to agree that very minor events should constitute default, so s 133 allows the debtor to cure a minor breach and reinstate the agreement (see Widdup and Mayne, *Personal Property Securities Act, A Conceptual Approach* (2000) 322). The reasoning behind this seems very much in line with that of penalties and relief against forfeiture.

[209] The rule against penalties and the two types of relief against forfeiture.

possible rationalization would be for all contractual provisions concerning remedies to be unenforceable if they were unconscionable.[210] This would have the benefit of simplicity, and would also enable the court to hold parties to freely negotiated bargains while protecting vulnerable parties against oppression, by placing more emphasis on procedural fairness rather than the compensatory principle. However, a general test of unconscionability might be considered too uncertain and more specific rules for different situations would inevitably develop. A more limited rationalization might be to extend the existing control of unfair terms in non-consumer contracts to agreed remedies provisions.[211]

The shortcomings of the compensatory principle have already been recognized by the courts in relation to large-scale commercial transactions, where clauses are only likely to be struck down if they are oppressive. This approach could easily be reflected in any general doctrine. Further, with a general doctrine of unfairness fine distinctions between payments triggered by breach, and those triggered by non-breach, events, would no longer apply. It would, however, be necessary to limit the courts' ability to consider the fairness of the price agreed between the parties.[212] It would also be necessary to consider what, if any, sum were payable on the occurrence of the non-breach event, since none would be payable under the general law.[213]

The current law regarding relief from oppressive provisions regarding irrecoverable payments would fit reasonably well into a more general doctrine. Parties are held to their bargain as regards deposits, unless the deposit is unreasonable, and this test can include elements of both substantive and procedural unfairness. The criteria for relief in relation to part performance payments could also be built into a more general test, although it is clear that some consideration of circumstances after the

---

[210] Alternative tests could be 'grossly unfair' or 'oppressive'.

[211] See n 40 above. Arguably this would be the case in relation to business-to-business contracts if the proposals in *Unfair Terms in Contracts* (Law Com Consultation Paper No 166, August 2002), Pt V were implemented. It is proposed that this would only cover terms which were standard, or that have not been individually negotiated. It would be for the party challenging the clause to show that it was unreasonable, as agreed remedies clauses are not included in the proposed list of terms which are presumptively unfair (paras 5.84–8), although they are included on the equivalent consumer list in the Unfair Terms in Consumer Contracts Regulations 1999 (Sch 2, para (1)(d) and (e)). As regards consumers, the Law Commission proposes that Sch 2, paras (1)(d) and (e) should be reformulated to better reflect the general law, although it is not clear how it is envisaged that the statutory and common law controls would coexist.

[212] This is done in the Unfair Terms in Consumer Contracts Regulations 1999 by reg 6(2), although the interpretation of 'price' is not always clear: see *Unfair Terms in Contract* (Law Com Consultation Paper No 166, August 2002) paras 3.27–34 and 4.6–8. Other possible limits are those described in nn 103 and 104 above.

[213] Whereas on breach the ordinary rules of damages would apply. See text to nn 83 and 84 above.

conclusion of the contract would be necessary. It is submitted that the question of whether the paying party is willing and able to perform the contract should not be part of the criteria.

Relief against forfeiture of a proprietary or possessory interest can either enable the party in default to continue using an asset or can be used to give the transaction the same effect as a security agreement. In both cases the test is whether it is unconscionable for the performing party to insist on the agreed remedy given the position currently before the court.[214] If terms providing the right to terminate were subject to a general control of unconscionable terms, the application of the term to the parties' current situation would have to form part of the review.[215] The current jurisdiction can be used to impose upon parties the incidents of a security agreement even where that was not the form agreed: the issue here is not fairness between the two parties, but between the performing party and the other creditors of the paying party. Arguably a better way of dealing with the problem is the enactment of the Law Commission's proposals to turn quasi-security interests into security interests, thus removing these agreements from the equitable jurisdiction altogether.

[214] Including whether the paying party is willing and able to pay the arrears and subsequent payments, whether the performing party has a good reason to want to terminate the arrangement (though the latter is less important where the paying party's claim is purely financial as in *On Demand Information plc v Michael Gerson (Finance) plc* [2002] 2 WLR 919).

[215] This would also extend the jurisdiction beyond the current limits as there would be no reason not to include terms providing for forfeiture of contractual rights.

17
Agreed Remedies: Comment

JOHN SHELTON[1]

1. A GENERAL DOCTRINE OF UNCONSCIONABILITY

Whatever else the English law of contract may be, it is a product for which the world-wide business community are customers. The views and expectations of the customer should be influential, even if they are not conclusive, in any discussion about reform of the law of contract. What would a commercial party expect to be its position and liability if it failed to perform its side of the bargain, or if other foreseen events occurred through no failure on its part? A number of observations may be made in this regard.

First, this question should be asked as of the time the contract is made. In the context of relief against oppression, one has to look at when that oppression will have been applied. We would say that this is when the contract is being made.

Secondly, from a commercial person's perspective, provisions dealing with the premature end of the transaction are just one part, and possibly a not very important part, of a process of risk and reward allocation which includes the assessment of the quality of those risks and rewards, and the likelihood of them materializing. Against that background, the commercial party is unlikely to be able to see a meaningful distinction between aspects of its contract which are primary and those which are secondary. Nor, one suspects, will it see any obvious reason why a court should have the power to re-allocate transaction risks and rewards some years later where *a breach* is involved, but not in other circumstances.

Finally, even if the commercial party sees its bargain as being 'bad', or at least not ideal, we do not imagine that it will often, or reasonably, see itself as a victim of 'oppression', however disgruntled it may be about the terms it achieved. Commercial parties seldom have equal bargaining power when they (freely) negotiate a contract. Obviously both parties have an interest of some kind in doing the deal but equality of enthusiasm for reaching a deal on particular terms is not routine.

These assumed views of a hypothetical commercial party may suggest support for the view that there should be some general law on

---

[1] Partner, Norton Rose.

unconscionable bargains or unfair contract terms for commercial trans-actions. Certainly, whatever doctrine is formulated to enable the courts to rewrite contracts, it should apply logically and simply in a way which commercial parties can readily and, preferably, instinctively understand at the outset of their transaction, so that they can factor its application into their commercial analysis.

However, one must be extremely cautious about any doctrine which 'rewrites' the contract between commercial parties. Consumers of English contract law are of course exposed to a number of uncertainties as to the enforceability of contracts apart from common law and equit-able doctrines concerning agreed remedies. Legal opinions in financing or quasi-financing transactions will enumerate pages of factors which may prevent a financing contract from being enforced in accordance with its terms (despite what the parties may have agreed), for example: (a) the discretionary nature of specific relief; (b) the voidability of transactions at an undervalue; (c) the protection that the appointment of an administra-tor may give against the creditors of the other party; and, of course, (d) the rule against penalties (and perhaps now the risk of relief from forfeiture). Many of these qualifications to such an opinion are explicable to commercial parties, but if one were to add to that list, even in substi-tution for the last item, the ability of a court to rewrite a contract based on 'reasonableness', or 'fairness', the competitive edge of English law would suffer. Such concepts are too uncertain, too grey, for commercial comfort, and too unreal in the harsh commercial world of the global economy.

Parliament has clearly seen the consumer as a potential victim of oppression and taken action to provide certain protections for the consumer (and not just within the law of contract) but should we see com-mercial parties in the same light, however unequal their bargaining posi-tions? Even if a commercial party is weak in the context of its bargaining power in a particular transaction, is there a public policy imperative that they should be protected from the consequences of that weakness, or a stronger imperative that they are not? If inequality of bargaining power, or some other circumstance, results in some kind of abuse which Parliament (or the European Union) wishes to prevent (let us say abuse of a dominant market position), surely the way to tackle that abuse is by a regulatory framework which directs itself at wider issues than the termin-ation provisions in a particular contract. Should that really be the business of the law of contract in this highly regulated age? We have domestic and European competition law for that.

If the control of pricing of transactions is considered to be a public pol-icy objective, should that not be achieved by legislation controlling extor-tionate credit bargains and the like, even in a commercial, non-consumer, context? A minimum payment provision in a lease is just one aspect of defining the pricing of the transaction.

Protection of the guilty party's other creditors is advanced as a reason for having such a power, but if the protection of creditors is the objective, surely we have the Insolvency Act for that. Why formulate a doctrine of general application to contracts to protect creditors: enforcement of the contract in accordance with its terms does not necessarily involve the insolvency of the guilty party?

One could consider protection of the guilty party's shareholders as a justification but then shareholders have power, whatever one thinks of its effectiveness, to appoint and remove the directors of the company: should they not be bound by the decisions and actions of those they appoint? Should they not seek their remedies against their directors for breach of fiduciary duty if their directors fail to exercise their authority in the commercial interests of the company? If the other party is privy to such a breach of fiduciary duty the constructive trust mechanism is available to achieve justice to shareholders against the other party to an improper contract.

The English and Scottish Law Commission working papers on these topics give virtually no attention to these questions. The assumption seems to be that oppression, unconscionability, excess, or unreasonableness are bad in themselves.

If we are, however, to go down the path of a general power to relieve a party from oppression expressed in contractual terms triggering or concerning the termination of the contract, I think it has to be just that: a test of exploitation which is severe and obvious from the beginning. Expressions like 'extravagant and unconscionable' may perhaps suit the purpose but 'unconscionable' is too archaic an expression. Tell a commercial client that he must not act unconscionably in agreeing his contract and he won't know what you are talking about, especially if you explain the case law. It requires a very vituperative epithet.

2. THE SECURITY ARGUMENT

There is perhaps a case for applying to financing transactions which take the form of a lease or hire purchase agreement the kind of treatment given to certain aspects of a secured loan. For example, one might decide to characterize a quasi-security transaction as requiring filing in a public register as if the lessee owned the leased asset, although those doing business with a company learn little or nothing of value from the register of charges unless, perhaps, they plan to take security over that asset. I do not see the need for a contract law doctrine to act as an interim measure to reform any imperfections in the law relating to the registration of charges, or the protection of creditors generally. The lessee of a tangible asset will not, in any event, grant security over that asset to a creditor (except, in an economic sense, to the lessor). It may, however, give security over its contractual rights under the lease to receive the benefits of 'quasi-ownership' which the lease is intended to confer. The law on registration of charges ought to be directed to the registrability of charges over those rights.

Deciding which leasing transactions are quasi-security transactions, and which are not, is a topic in itself. The issue is essentially one of economic effect and substance, and is greatly exercising accounting bodies these days. The debate seems to be whether the decision to account for a lease as a loan is to be determined, US style, by a series of detailed rules or, British style, by the application of general principles.

If the law is to develop a meaningful approach to such transactions which is consistent with its approach to secured loans, it may perhaps have to defer to the accountants. Commercial parties see the logic of that: financing contracts which restrict borrowing or contracts of similar economic effect will usually rely on the accounting treatment of a lease to bring it within or exclude it from the scope of the provision.

If we are going to have a judicial power to amend termination provisions in contracts by reason of oppression, in determining whether oppression exists one needs to look at the economic purpose and effect of the contract. If the elements of a lease transaction feature the functional equivalent of the elements of a secured loan transaction, there may be logic in approaching them in a similar way. If one would not regard a lender's right to end the loan and require immediate repayment as oppressive, against the background that the borrower is entitled to receive any surplus proceeds of realization of the security, it ought to be the case that a finance lessor's right to require payment of a termination sum equivalent to principal and interest should be upheld where the lessor has agreed to credit the proceeds of resale of the asset to the lessee's account.

I think that brings us to looking at issues such as the fettering of the equity of redemption and whether a general power to control or modify termination provisions needs to deal cohesively with all types of contract, rather than by the present rather fragmented accumulation of doctrines.

18
Agreed Remedies: Review of Discussion

The discussion of agreed remedies was concentrated on the rule against penalties. In part, it sought to clarify the precise nature and scope of the current rule. First, that the 'loss' to which reference should be made is the actual loss suffered (or likely to be suffered) by the innocent party (see *Robophone Facilities v Blank*),[1] rather than the legally recoverable loss (eg after allowing for remoteness, mitigation, etc). Secondly, the rule is only invoked against clauses which do not represent a *genuine* pre-estimate of loss, as opposed to a reasonable loss. The latter is most evident in cases like *Dunlop v New Garage*[2] and *Phillips v A-G of Hong Kong*[3] where the potential losses were very difficult to assess, but the court was none the less willing to enforce what was viewed as the parties' *genuine* estimation.

There was some discussion as to whether the current scope of the rule can be attributed to its historical and somewhat piecemeal development and whether it has, as a result, failed to keep pace with other developments. For example, it was suggested that recent developments in the awarding of an account of profits or punitive damages (see Chapters 10 to 11) might mean that any prior agreement of the parties as to the availability of such remedies should be enforceable. Against this, it was argued that while there may be scope for the parties to agree on the level of compensatory damages to be paid, it may be another matter to leave in their control remedies which are still regarded as 'exceptional'. In a similar vein, it was queried whether the courts would, or should, enforce a clause in which the parties agreed to the specific performance of the contract: some expressed the view that, unlike damages, this was a remedy only available at the discretion of the court which could not be ousted by the parties' agreement; others saw no reason in principle why such a clause should not be enforceable, unless it purported to compel specific performance in circumstances where there was some fundamental objection to such a remedy.

Even with the benefit of clarification, there was widespread (and possibly uniform) agreement that the present scope of the rule against penalties was difficult to justify. Leaving aside consumer cases (where there may be additional protection in the form of control over unfair terms generally, eg under the Unfair Terms in Consumer Contracts Regulations 1999), numerous examples were given, such as incentive payments, price variation clauses, entire contracts, and 'non-breach' termination clauses (see *Bridge*

---

[1] [1966] 1 WLR 1428.   [2] [1915] AC 79.   [3] (1993) 61 Building Law Reports 49.

v Campbell Discount Co)[4] to illustrate the incoherence of confining the rule against penalties to sums payable *upon breach*.

There was less agreement about the best way to tackle this incoherence. Among the practitioners there appeared to be a greater adherence to an absolute view of freedom of contract. Even if the parties had not always turned their minds to the clause in question or, if they had and had been too optimistic about their prospects of avoiding it, it was preferable that the courts should enforce the parties' agreement. There might be some scope for interference by the courts in 'extreme' cases, but this was not elucidated further. The contrary view (voiced mainly by the academic audience) was precisely that parties are often too optimistic about the future. It was difficult to adhere to an absolute view of freedom of contract unless one was prepared to countenance the abandonment of certain fundamental rules such as the equity of redemption; even commercial parties did not always look after their own interests properly.

Some were concerned to take a step back from the rule against penalties and ask what precisely it was intended to achieve, eg if one of the aims of a 'penalty' clause was to deter breach, then this was all the more reason why it should be enforced since otherwise the deterrent value was undermined. It was also suggested that too often the real concern of the courts in refusing to enforce a penalty clause was the protection of the defendant's creditors and that, if this was the case, the appropriate controls should be found in, or developed as part of, the current insolvency regimes.

There was some brief discussion of relief against forfeiture. There was a considerable measure of support both among the practitioner and academic audience for the recent developments in the case of *On Demand Information v Michael Gerson*,[5] extending relief to the forfeiture of possessory rights.

---

[4] [1962] AC 600.   [5] [2002] 2 WLR 919.

19

Private Law Remedies and the Human Rights Act 1998: An Overview

NICHOLAS BAMFORTH[1]

It has been clear since the Human Rights Act 1998 ('the 1998 Act') came into force that private law remedies have been affected by the bringing into domestic law of most European Convention rights. However, there has been considerable debate about the mechanism or mechanisms by which the relevant Convention rights affect private law, together with questions concerning the degree (in a substantive sense) to which they do so. Both issues are addressed in this chapter. The analysis will proceed in three stages. First, the role of the Human Rights Act in litigation between private parties—and in consequence, the powers of the courts to apply Convention rights in the area of private law remedies—will be considered. It will be argued that Convention rights can be and have been used by courts when interpreting statutory rights and remedies (due to s 3 of the Human Rights Act 1998) and when interpreting and developing the common law, but that courts are not free to create new, free-standing causes of action between private parties in order to give effect to Convention rights. Secondly, the requirements of the relevant Convention rights—most notably, in this context, Article 6 (the right to a fair and public hearing in the determination of one's civil rights), Article 8 (the right to respect for private and family life), Article 10 (the right to freedom of expression), and Article 1 of the First Protocol to the Convention (the right to peaceful enjoyment of possessions)—will be discussed. Thirdly, some of the scenarios in which these rights have arisen—or might arise—in the context of private law remedies will briefly be explored.[2]

---

[1] Fellow and Tutor in Law, The Queen's College, Oxford.

[2] It should be noted that the distinction between rights and remedies has long been a cause of controversy at both practical and theoretical levels. It will be assumed in this chapter that a remedy can be categorized as the law's response to a litigant having established a cause of action. Although this assumption begs many questions—not least in the context of estoppel and constructive trusts—it will be used to confine the scope of the chapter to remedies, so defined. In consequence, the controversy concerning the impact of Article 6 on causes of action in tort law, characterized by cases such as *Osman v UK* (1999) 29 EHRR 245, *Barrett v Enfield LBC* [2001] 2 AC 550, and *Z v UK* (Case 29392/95), will not be discussed.

1. WHEN DO CONVENTION RIGHTS APPLY IN ENGLISH PRIVATE LAW?
SECTIONS 3, 6 AND 12 OF THE HUMAN RIGHTS ACT 1998

As a general matter, the Human Rights Act 1998 provides for at least three sets of circumstances in which Convention rights may come into play in litigation.[3] It is uncontroversial to assert that two of these, governed—respectively—by ss 3 and 12 of the Act, apply in the course of private law litigation; however, controversy surrounds the third situation, governed by s 6. In this part of the chapter, s 3 will first be considered, followed by s 6.[4] The analysis will proceed in this order because larger questions have so far arisen—both practically and in the academic literature—concerning these two sections of the Act. Section 12 will be considered afterwards.

(a) Section 3

Section 3(1) of the Human Rights Act 1998 provides that: '[s]o far as it is possible to do so, primary legislation and subordinate legislation must be read and given effect in a way which is compatible with Convention rights.'[5] Given that s 3 applies whoever the parties to a case may be, it brings Convention points into play in private law litigation whenever one party relies upon statutory provisions which fall within the ambit of a Convention right.[6] The central question to which s 3 gives rise is thus how strong an obligation it imposes to interpret legislation in the light of Convention rights. It is clear from the wording of s 3(1) that it cannot be an absolute obligation: for s 3(2)(b) provides that s 3(1) 'does not affect the validity, continuing operation or enforcement of any incompatible primary legislation', while section 4(2) stipulates that where a court decides that legislation is incompatible with a Convention right, 'it may make a declaration of that incompatibility'—albeit, as s 4(6) makes clear, a declaration which does not affect the 'validity, continuing operation or enforcement' of the offending legislation, and which is not binding on the parties to the case. Were s 3(1) to accord an absolute role to Convention rights in

---

[3] A fourth context is in devolution disputes concerning the powers of the Scottish Parliament, the Welsh Assembly, and the Northern Ireland Assembly, but this is not relevant for present purposes.

[4] It should be noted that in public law, there is a substantive overlap between these two sections: see further PP Craig, *Administrative Law* (4th edn, 1999) 556–7; however, this is not relevant here.

[5] According to s 3(2), this obligation applies to primary and subordinate legislation whenever it was enacted.

[6] See also I Leigh, 'Horizontal Rights, the Human Rights Act and Privacy: Lessons from the Commonwealth?' (1999) 48 ICLQ 57, 76; G Phillipson, 'The Human Rights Act, 'Horizontal Effect' and the Common Law: a Bang or a Whimper?' (1999) 62 MLR 824, 825.

the interpretation of all legislation—whatever its wording—neither s 3(2)(b) nor s 4 would make sense.[7] It is therefore clear that there must be limits to how *far* courts may interpret legislation using s 3.[8]

Significant judicial guidance concerning s 3 has been offered in four cases, two in the House of Lords and two in the Court of Appeal.[9] Taken together, these cases suggest that the limits of the s 3 interpretative obligation are still far from settled. The first case to be decided, chronologically speaking, was *Poplar Housing Association v Donoghue*,[10] where the Court of Appeal issued guidance, albeit obiter, concerning the effect of ss 3 and 4. Lord Woolf CJ suggested that 'subject to . . . not requiring the court to go beyond that which is possible, [section 3] is mandatory in its terms.'[11] It required the courts to interpret pre-Human Rights Act legislation which would otherwise conflict with the Convention in a manner which they would not have done had the 1998 Act not been in force. Lord Woolf suggested that the courts should no longer see themselves as primarily concerned to give effect to the intentions of Parliament *in general*: rather, they must now give effect to the *specific* direction of the legislature contained in s 3. In consequence, '[i]t is as though legislation which predates the Human Rights Act 1998 and conflicts with the Convention has to be treated as being subsequently amended to incorporate the language of section 3.'[12] Lord Woolf went on to make certain more specific suggestions. First, unless the legislation under scrutiny would otherwise be in breach of the Convention, s 3 could be ignored. In other words, courts should first seek to interpret legislation using ordinary techniques, before relying on s 3. If the ordinary techniques disclosed no breach of Convention rights, s 3 did not need to be considered. Secondly, if the court had to rely on s 3, it should limit the extent of its reinterpretation to that which was necessary to achieve compatibility with the Convention. Thirdly, s 3 entitled the court to interpret but not to legislate. Lord Woolf acknowledged that this

---

[7] See further C Gearty, 'Reconciling Parliamentary Democracy and Human Rights' (2002) 118 LQR 248, esp 250–8.

[8] For significant pre-Human Rights Act analysis, see R Clayton and H Tomlinson, *The Law of Human Rights* (2000), chs 3 and 4; S Grosz, J Beatson, and P Duffy, *Human Rights: the 1998 Act and the European Convention* (2000) ch 3; Lord Irvine LC, 'The Development of Human Rights in Britain' [1998] PL 221, 232–3; G Marshall, 'Interpreting interpretation in the Human Rights Bill' [1998] PL 167; G Marshall, 'Two kinds of compatibility: more about section 3 of the Human Rights Act 1998' [1999] PL 377; *McCartan Turkington Breen v Times Newspapers Ltd* [2000] 4 All ER 913, Lord Steyn and Lord Cooke. For a further example of the use of Convention rights when interpreting legislation, see *Graham v JA Pye (Oxford) Ltd* [2001] Ch 804 (but cf the House of Lords' view that the Convention was not relevant on the facts: *JA Pye (Oxford) Ltd v Graham* [2002] 3 WLR 221, paras [65] (Lord Browne-Wilkinson), [73] (Lord Hope)).

[9] Professor Gearty suggests—n 7 above, 263–6—that a significant flaw in the Privy Council's reasoning in *Brown v Stott* [2001] 2 WLR 817 lies in the fact that s 3 was not given independent consideration.

[10] [2002] QB 48. [11] ibid, para [75]. [12] ibid, para [75].

was a 'most difficult' distinction to draw, and suggested that courts would have to be guided by the 'practical experience of seeking to apply section 3', albeit subject to the point that if it was necessary to 'radically alter the effect of the legislation this will be an indication that more than interpretation is involved.'[13] Fourthly, Lord Woolf pointed out that a court was not *required* to issue a declaration of incompatibility where it proved impossible to interpret a statute compatibly with Convention rights. Rather, it should exercise its discretion and be guided by 'the usual considerations which apply to the grant of declarations.'[14]

In policy terms, Lord Woolf's assertions are perhaps unsurprising. However, they are couched in rather general terms, and—as Lord Woolf acknowledged in relation to the distinction between (permissible) interpretation and (impermissible) judicial legislation—beg difficult definitional questions. Such a lack of specificity is perhaps inevitable in the early stages of the life of a statute such as the Human Rights Act 1998, but the dicta in *Poplar Housing Association v Donoghue* nonetheless highlight the uncertainties with which the courts now have to deal. Thus far, only a small amount of practical guidance has been offered by the House of Lords. At House of Lords level, both cases in which s 3 has been discussed at length—namely *R v A*[15] and *R v Lambert* (which has since been qualified on the issue of the retrospective application of the 1998 Act)[16]—concerned the proper interpretation of provisions of criminal statutes in the light of Article 6 of the Convention. Most important, for present purposes, is the fact that the two cases involved a difference of opinion within the House of Lords—articulated in *R v A*—concerning the proper scope of s 3. In *A*, Lords Steyn and Hutton seemingly took a broader view than did Lord Hope. Lord Steyn suggested that the:[17]

> interpretative obligation under section 3 of the 1998 Act is a strong one. It applies even if there is no ambiguity in the language [of the relevant statute] in the sense of the language being capable of two different meanings. . . . Under ordinary methods of interpretation a court may depart from the language of the statute to avoid absurd consequences: s 3 goes much further. . . . It is a general principle of the interpretation of legal instruments that the text is the primary source of interpretation: other sources are subordinate to it. . . . Section 3 of the 1998 Act qualifies this general principle because it requires a court to find an interpretation compatible with convention rights if it is possible to do so.

Lord Steyn went on to suggest that it would therefore 'sometimes be necessary to adopt an interpretation [of legislation] which linguistically may

---

[13] ibid, para [76].   [14] ibid, para [75].

[15] [2002] 1 AC 45, concerning s 41 of the Youth Justice and Criminal Evidence Act 1999.

[16] [2001] 3 WLR 206, concerning ss 5 and 28 of the Misuse of Drugs Act 1971; on the retrospectivity point, cf *R v Kansal* [2002] 2 AC 69; *JA Pye (Oxford) Ltd v Graham*, n 8 above.

[17] [2002] 1 AC 45, para [44].

appear strained.'[18] As both Lord Steyn and Lord Hutton—who agreed with Lord Steyn's approach—suggested, this approach to interpretation appeared to prioritize s 3 over s 4 of the 1998 Act. Lord Steyn asserted that the declaration of incompatibility was 'a measure of last resort' which 'must be avoided unless it is plainly impossible to do so'.[19] In similar vein, Lord Hutton argued that the court should 'seek to avoid having to make a declaration of incompatibility' under s 4 unless 'the clear and express wording' of the provision under scrutiny made such avoidance 'impossible'.[20]

Lord Hope's approach to s 3 was, by contrast, narrower. As a general matter, Lord Hope suggested in *R v A*—relying, intriguingly, on the distinction drawn by Lord Woolf CJ in the *Poplar Housing Association* case— that while compatibility with Convention rights was the 'sole guiding principle' and 'paramount object' of s 3, the section was 'only a rule of interpretation' which did not 'entitle the judges to act as legislators'.[21] In relation to the statutory provision in issue in *A*, he thus asserted that in the absence of adequate factual detail concerning the impact of that provision on Convention rights, it was not appropriate to use s 3 to 'modify, alter or supplement the words used by Parliament'.[22] This could only have been done if 'the words used by Parliament were unable, when they were given their ordinary meaning, to stand up to the test of compatibility.'[23] Lord Hope went on, albeit obiter, to adopt a broader view of s 4 than Lords Steyn and Hutton. Having emphasised that compatibility under s 3 was 'to be achieved only so far as possible', he suggested that legislation could fall within section 4 if it contained provisions which were incompatible with Convention rights either expressly *or by necessary implication*:[24] a clearly wider remit for s 4 than that allowed for in Lord Steyn's and Lord Hutton's references to impossibility, or in Lord Hutton's stipulation concerning the clear *and express* wording of legislation. Lord Hope took care to repeat this analysis of section 4 in his judgment in *Lambert*,[25] where he also made two practical suggestions concerning the operation of s 3. First, great care had to be taken, in cases where a court felt obliged to give a different meaning to legislation from the ordinary meaning of the words used in the statute, to identify *precisely* the word or phrase which would be incompatible if given its ordinary meaning, and to say how that word or phrase was to be construed so as to make it compatible. Lord Hope even suggested that, so far as possible, 'judges should seek to achieve the same attention to detail in their use of language . . . as the parliamentary draftsman would have done if he had been amending the statute.'[26] Secondly, and subject to the proviso against judicial amendment of statutes, courts

---

[18] ibid.   [19] ibid.   [20] ibid, para [162].   [21] ibid, para [108].
[22] ibid, para [106].   [23] ibid.   [24] ibid, para [108].   [25] n 16 above, para [79].
[26] ibid, para [80]. This appears to build on Lord Hope's suggestion in *R v A*, n 15 above, para [110].

were not bound—when s 3(1) came into play—by previous authority concerning the meaning of a statute.

It is unclear what effect Lord Hope's two practical suggestions are likely to have on the lower courts (although, at this stage in the life of the 1998 Act, it might not be unfair to say that all practical suggestions are to be welcomed). At a deeper level, it is difficult to discern from *A* and *Lambert* how far the general approaches advocated by Lords Steyn and Hutton, on the one hand, and by Lord Hope on the other, are likely to differ in practice. It would appear from Lord Hope's observations in *A* that he feared that the approach advocated by Lords Steyn and Hutton might encourage courts to reconstruct legislation to an impermissible extent under the guise of interpretation, thereby trespassing into the territory of the legislature and upsetting the proper balance between ss 3 and 4 of the 1998 Act. Lord Hope made this concern explicit in *Lambert*, where he asserted that s 3(1) 'preserves the sovereignty of Parliament. It does not give power to the judges to overrule decisions which the language of the statute shows have been taken on the very point by the legislature.'[27] It would seem, therefore, that Lord Hope feared that the approach to s 3 advocated by Lords Steyn and Hutton would upset the distinction between interpretation and judicial legislation drawn by Lord Woolf CJ in the *Poplar Housing Association* case and approved in Lord Hope's judgment in *Lambert*.

However, it is difficult—with respect—to assess how realistic Lord Hope's fear may turn out to be. Two practical examples demonstrate why this is so. First, despite important differences in reasoning, Lord Hope arrived at the same conclusion as Lord Steyn concerning the interpretation of the legislation in question in both *A*,[28] and—save for the point (mentioned above) concerning the possible retrospective impact of the Human Rights Act—in *Lambert*.[29] Indeed, each went out of his way, in both cases, to express his agreement with the other on the substantive issue. Secondly, in *Wilson v First County Trust (No 2)*[30]—the second Court of Appeal case concerning s 3, in which judgment was given shortly prior to that in *A*— Morritt V-C appeared to adopt a similar, broad approach to s 3 to that adopted by Lords Steyn and Hutton in *A*, but nonetheless went on to issue a declaration of incompatibility concerning the legislation in question (s 127(3) of the Consumer Credit Act 1974). Morritt V-C suggested that the combined effect of ss 3 and 4 was that:

> where a court is faced with a provision in primary legislation which appears to require it to make an order which would be incompatible with a Convention

---

[27] n 16 above, para [79].   [28] n 15 above, paras [46] (Lord Steyn), [110] (Lord Hope).

[29] n 16 above paras [42] (Lord Steyn), [94] (Lord Hope).

[30] [2002] QB 74. For comment, see N Bamforth, 'Human Rights and Consumer Credit' (2002) 118 LQR 203.

right, the court must consider whether it is possible to read and give effect to that provision in a way which does not lead to that result. If it is possible to do so, then the court must take that course. The court will make an order which is not incompatible with the Convention right.

Where legislation appeared to be incompatible with Convention rights, s 3(1) thus required the court to consider whether such a conclusion could be avoided by another interpretation which was within the realm of what was legally possible. However, if the legislation could not be read so as to avoid incompatibility, the court could not use s 3 and might issue a declaration of incompatibility (like Lord Woolf CJ in *Poplar Housing Association v Donoghue*, Morritt V-C stressed the discretionary nature of the declaration). By talking of what a court *must* do, and about what was legally possible, Morritt V-C thus stressed the obligatory and wide nature of the s 3 obligation, *despite* going on to make a s 4 declaration on the facts. The adoption of a wide approach to s 3 did not, in other words, push the court into inappropriate territory properly reserved for Parliament.

In conclusion, it is clear that s 3 applies in litigation between private parties concerning private law matters—*Wilson v First County Trust (No 2)* provides an excellent example, given that it concerned the correct interpretation of the Consumer Credit Act 1974 in a dispute between private parties over a loan—and that, given the general nature of the interpretative obligation imposed by the section, statutory causes of action and remedies must be interpreted in the light of relevant Convention rights. However, the exact strength of the interpretative obligation imposed by s 3 currently remains uncertain. In *A*, Lords Steyn and Hutton appeared to favour a wider approach to s 3 than that advocated by Lord Hope, but thus far we lack any concrete indications about whether the two approaches are likely frequently to produce divergent outcomes, or that the wider approach will inevitably leave an unduly narrow role for s 4. Beneath these questions lies a deeper, effectively constitutional uncertainty concerning the proper location of the boundary between permissible interpretation and impermissible judicial legislation. It may be, as Lord Woolf CJ suggested in the *Poplar Housing Association* case, that clarity concerning such issues will only be provided as the case law develops. In the meantime, s 3 leaves us with considerable uncertainty concerning how far courts will go in practice—within the limits imposed by the drafting of the section—when interpreting legislation so as to give effect to Convention rights in disputes between private parties.

(b) Section 6

Whatever uncertainties surround s 3, it is at least clear that the section has a role to play in litigation between private parties. By contrast, the very role of s 6 has given rise to heated debate. This is due to the drafting of the section. Section 6(1) makes it unlawful for public authorities to act in contravention of Convention rights, but places no analogous duty on private parties. However, s 6(3)(a) makes clear that courts and tribunals are counted, for the purposes of the Act, as public authorities which are required to respect Convention rights in every case which comes before them: prompting speculation that they are thereby subjected to some sort of obligation to determine cases, or at least to interpret the law, in accordance with Convention rights, even where only private parties are involved.

It is important to clarify the nature of the question to which s 6 gives rise: for failure to do so will obscure the proper role of s 6 in the scheme of the Human Rights Act 1998. Before the 1998 Act came into force, the debate concerning s 6 was often presented as involving a choice between views whereby, either due to or despite the drafting of *s 6*, the *entire* Human Rights Act should be categorized as allowing Convention rights to have only 'vertical effect'—that is, effect against public authorities—or also some degree of 'horizontal' effect in litigation between private parties.[32] As the Court of Appeal's decision in *Wilson v First County Trust (No 2)*— discussed in the previous section—demonstrates, however, to present the debate in such a way ignores the role of s 3. In the *Wilson (No 2)* case, it was *s 3* of the Human Rights Act 1998 which provided the obvious basis for giving effect to Convention rights in a 'horizontal' dispute between private parties where statutory interpretation was involved. There was no need for the Court of Appeal to consider s 6: since the case turned on statutory interpretation, it could be resolved using s 3 (and, on the facts, s 4, given that the legislation in question turned out to be incompatible with Convention rights). This being so, the debate about the correct interpretation of s 6 seems, in practice, to be significant only in 'horizontal' cases which do *not* involve statutory interpretation, or which perhaps— given that interpretation of statutes is frequently influenced by common law precedent—do not turn *overwhelmingly* on statutory interpretation (the correct formulation has yet to be determined). This point seems to have been recognized by Mummery LJ in the Court of Appeal in *Graham v JA Pye (Oxford) Ltd*. Although the House of Lords ultimately rejected any role for Convention arguments in the case, Convention rights were held by the Court of Appeal to be relevant to the correct interpretation of the Limitation Act 1980. Mummery LJ stated, however, that it was unnecessary to express any view concerning the effect of s 6(1) 'on private law

---

[31] [2002] QB 74, para [10].

[32] See, eg, Sir William Wade, 'Human Rights and the Judiciary' [1998] EHRLR 520; 'Horizons of Horizontality' (2000) 116 LQR 217; Sir Richard Buxton, 'The Human Rights Act and Private Law' (2000) 116 LQR 48.

issues arising between one citizen and another': for the arguments deployed by both sides 'focused on one main point, namely the impact of section 3 of the 1998 Act on the interpretation of the relevant provisions of the 1980 Act.'[33] It is therefore unhelpful to present the debate concerning section 6 as a debate about whether Convention rights have 'horizontal effect' under the 1998 Act *per se*. For it is clear that, when s 3 is invoked in litigation between private parties, Convention rights can have such an effect via statutory interpretation. The debate concerning s 6 can more usefully be characterized as a debate about whether s 6(3)(a), when read together with s 6(1), opens up an important *additional* route whereby Convention rights can play a role in such litigation.

It should be reiterated, for the sake of clarity, that if a body counts as a *public authority* falling within the scope of s 6(1), a suitably qualified litigant may seek a remedy against it directly for the violation of a Convention right. This is illustrated by the proceedings in *Marcic v Thames Water Utilities Ltd*, where the claimant was held at first instance to be entitled to bring an action in damages against the defendant, as a public authority, in respect of its violation of his Convention rights and consequent breach of s 6.[34] Although the Court of Appeal ultimately resolved the case using the common law rather than s 6, it did not overturn the finding that the claimant's Convention rights had been violated: a conclusion which appears to leave in place the possibility that, where Convention rights are involved, a claimant might rely upon the Act—where a common law cause of action such as nuisance would be inadequate—in order to seek damages against a public authority.[35] This possible use of the Act to supplement private law remedies tells us nothing about the proper approach to 'horizontal effect', however: for the *Marcic* case is an example of the wholly uncontroversial point that s 6 allows for the development of remedies against *public authorities*; by contrast, the question of remedies for the actions of private parties—the central question in the debate concerning 'horizontal effect'—is simply not in issue.[36]

In outline, three broad responses can be identified to the question whether s 6 opens up an additional route allowing Convention rights to be invoked in litigation between private parties. The first response—that the Act has 'full horizontal effect'—has been championed by Sir William Wade. Wade argues that since courts are deemed by s 6(3)(a) of the Act to be public authorities, they are bound by s 6(1) to apply Convention rights

---

[33] n 8 above, para 51.   [34] [2002] QB 929, esp paras [54], [60], [65], [76].
[35] ibid, esp paras [103], [104], and [111]. On the question of remedies, see also *Marcic v Thames Water Utilities Ltd. (No 2)* [2002] QB 1003, paras [15]–[17].
[36] This being so, Andrew Henderson's apparent categorization (in Chapter 20) of *Marcic* as a case with significant implications for the debate concerning s 6 is, with respect, somewhat puzzling.

in every case which they hear, including cases which involve only private parties. On this view, Convention rights have full 'horizontal effect' due to s 6; they take effect against public authorities and private parties in equal measure, with the Act leading to the direct creation of new causes of action between private parties.[37] In direct contrast, Sir Richard Buxton has contended—under the second response—that no 'horizontal effect' should be possible since Convention rights are by definition applicable only against public authorities and the 1998 Act does nothing to alter their content.[38] In consequence, Convention rights have only 'vertical effect', regardless of the drafting of s 6. The third response, supported by the majority of commentators—including the present author—maintains that Convention rights may have partial 'horizontal effect' via judicial interpretation: for they are used in statutory interpretation in cases falling within s 3 which involve only private parties (subject to the constraints imposed by that section), whilst courts are enabled to interpret and develop the common law—in so far as the provisions of statute permit—in accordance with the Convention.[39] The courts thus develop statutory rules and the common law by interpretation, rather than by the direct creation of new causes of action—as Wade would seemingly demand—in accordance with the Convention jurisprudence. It will be suggested in this section of the chapter that the case law since the 1998 Act came into force is, by and large, consistent with the third, interpretation-based, response.

Different versions of the third response can, however, be identified. Commentators differ about the exact degree to which courts may develop the common law in actions between private parties.[40] Furthermore, some believe—even while discounting the Wade theory—that s 6(1) imposes a general and enforceable obligation on courts to interpret statutes and the common law in accordance with Convention rights; others (including the present author) doubt whether talk of a general obligation can be meaningful.[41] In favour of an obligation lies the actual drafting of section 6(1) coupled with s 6(3)(a).[42] Against lies the difficulty of talking of s 6 as imposing any type of *general* judicial obligation. Such an obligation would require remedies to be widely and generally available against courts, whereas the 1998 Act makes only limited and narrow provision for them. This being so, it is submitted that any 'unlawfulness' involved in a court's

---

[37] n 32 above (Wade).   [38] ibid (Buxton).

[39] M Hunt, 'The 'Horizontal' Effect of the Human Rights Act' [1998] PL 423, 435–42; A Lester and D Pannick, 'The Impact of the Human Rights Act on Private Law: the Knight's Move' (2000) 116 LQR 380; N Bamforth, 'The True "Horizontal Effect" of the Human Rights Act 1998' (2001) 117 LQR 34.

[40] Compare, eg, Phillipson, n 6 above; Leigh, n 6 above.

[41] Compare Hunt, n 39 above, 437–41; Lester and Pannick, n 39 above, 381, 383; Bamforth, n 39 above, 38–9.

[42] See further *Wilson v First County Trust Ltd (No 2)*, n 30 above, paras [10]–[11].

failure to act in accordance with Convention rights is best seen—subject to what is said below—as being of a symbolic nature.[43]

The qualification which must be entered at this point is that, in some cases since the 1998 Act came into force, dicta concerning s 6 have—as we shall see shortly—presented the judiciary as being placed under an obligation by the section, although no meaningful remedy to give effect to that obligation has been mentioned. The strongest supporter of the argument that courts *are* obliged to give judgment in accordance with Convention rights, while being free only to develop the common law by interpretation, is Murray Hunt.[44] Hunt believes that s 6 places courts under an obligation to apply rights between parties—whether public or private—whenever law is involved, given that the state 'lurks behind' all law.[45] While 'private relationships are left undisturbed' by human rights norms 'insofar as they are not regulated by law . . . once law becomes involved in regulating those relationships, they have lost their truly private character and the State, as the maker, the administrator, the interpreter and the applier of the law which governs those relationships, is bound to act in all those roles in a way which upholds and protects' the relevant human rights.[46] Hunt suggests that courts are included as public authorities in s 6(1) to ensure that all law, other than legislation which is deemed incompatible under s 4, will be subjected to Convention rights. Hunt thus suggests that the Convention applies to all law, and is therefore potentially relevant in proceedings between private parties, but falls short of being fully 'horizontally effective' on the Wade model since courts cannot develop entirely new causes of action. This means, in other words, that Convention rights will—in private law—take effect through judicial interpretation of existing causes of action between private parties, this being a result of the drafting of s 6.

Since the Act came into force, the impact of Convention rights in common law cases involving only private parties has received particular attention in *Douglas and Zeta-Jones v Hello! Ltd*,[47] *Venables and Thompson v News Group Newspapers Ltd*,[48] and *A v B plc*.[49] The judgments in these cases are

---

[43] One possible qualification is that Commonwealth authority exists for the judicial development of public law damages remedies for human rights violations by public authorities, including courts (*Maharaj v A-G of Trinidad and Tobago (No 2)* [1979] AC 385, applied in *Simpson v A-G (Baigent's Case)* [1994] 3 NZLR 667). There would not appear to be Parliamentary support for the development of such remedies in English law (HL Deb, November 24 1997, vol 583, cols 856–7; HC Deb, May 20 1998, vol 312, col 979), but absence of legislative support did not act as a bar to courts in the Commonwealth cases. It might yet also be possible to argue for the development of such remedies by analogy with EC law (see further N Bamforth, 'The Application of the Human Rights Act 1998 to Public Authorities and Private Bodies' (1999) 58 CLJ 159). It should be stressed that these possibilities remain tentative, however.

[44] For an accurate summary of his position, see Hunt, n 39 above, 424, 441–2.

[45] ibid, 425.   [46] ibid, 434–5.   [47] [2001] QB 697.   [48] [2001] 2 WLR 1038.

[49] [2002] 3 WLR 542.

not identical in their approach. However, the clear majority offer support for the notions that Convention rights can be used in common law litigation involving private parties, and—more tentatively—that they can be used when interpreting existing common law causes of action and remedies. It is not yet clear whether they can also be used to create new causes of action, but it should be noted that no court has yet gone down that path and that there are *dicta* in the *Venables and Thompson* case against it.[50] It is thus clear that Sir Richard Buxton's argument has not been vindicated in these cases any more than it was in the context of s 3. The present cases also employ, in practice, a more gradual approach than that advocated by Sir William Wade, even if the courts have not yet pronounced upon whether they can create new causes of action. Furthermore, no settled view has yet emerged concerning the significance (if any) of the inclusion of courts and tribunals as public authorities under s 6 of the 1998 Act.

In *Douglas and Zeta-Jones v Hello! Ltd*, the defendant sought to have discharged an interim injunction obtained against it by the claimants, two internationally-famous film stars, preventing the publication in one of its magazines of unauthorized photographs of the claimants' wedding (the claimants having granted to a rival magazine the exclusive right to publish the wedding pictures) prior to the full hearing of the claimants' action for (*inter alia*) breach of confidence. The Court of Appeal declined to keep the injunction in force, but made clear that Articles 8 and 10 of the Convention could play a role in litigation between private parties concerning injunctions. The reasoning in the three judgments differed somewhat, and all three judges focused at some length on the role of s 12 of the Act (to be considered in the next section). Nonetheless, the case contains some significant observations about the role of Convention rights in cases involving only private parties.

Brooke LJ based his decision squarely on s 12.[51] However, his broader comments concerning the Act display a certain ambivalence about the context in which Convention rights might be deployed. Brooke LJ pointed out—seemingly in an echo of Sir Richard Buxton—that the Convention was primarily concerned to give individuals rights against the state (or, in the context of the 1998 Act, public authorities), that Article 8 could only legitimately be violated by a public authority, and that s 8 of the Act was concerned only with the power of the courts to award compensation for unlawful acts of public authorities which were incompatible with Convention rights.[52] The Act gave courts no power to order one private party to compensate another for breach of their Convention rights.[53]

---

[50] Text to n 67, below.   [51] [2001] QB 697, para [95].

[52] ibid, paras [81]–[82]. The only other dictum in the case law to this effect was delivered by Sir Richard Buxton himself: see *Home Office v Wainwright* [2001] EWCA Civ 2081, para [74].

[53] [2001] QB 697, para 81.

However, Brooke LJ acknowledged that Article 8 sometimes placed the state under a positive duty to prevent a rights violation by a private actor and to compensate the claimant in the event of such a violation, a factor which domestic judges might take into account in the future when developing the common law.[54] In an apparent departure from Sir Richard Buxton, Brooke LJ then suggested that the Act involved a dilemma instead of certainty:[55]

> On the one hand, art 8(1) . . . appears to create a right, exercisable against all the world, to respect for private and family life. On the other hand, art 8(2) . . ., s 8 of the Human Rights Act, and the general philosophy of both the convention and the Act (namely that these rights are enforceable only against public authorities), all appear to water down the value of the right created by art 8(1).

Despite this last assertion, Brooke LJ was content for Articles 8 and 10 to be considered, under the ambit of s 12 of the Act, when deciding whether the injunction should be maintained in force—an approach which is surely inconsistent with Sir Richard Buxton's extra-judicial views.

Sedley LJ suggested that 'equity and the common law'[56] could now recognize a right to privacy 'grounded in the equitable doctrine of breach of confidence',[57] and without the need to 'construct an artificial relationship of confidentiality between intruder and victim.'[58] This conclusion—later qualified in *Home Office v Wainwright*[59] and *A v B plc*[60]—is of less concern here than Sedley LJ's fall-back position based on the 1998 Act. Like the other two judges, much of his reasoning rested on s 12, which he began by characterizing as a basis distinct from the common law for giving some support to privacy.[61] Sedley LJ made some interesting observations concerning the role of courts under the Act. He suggested, for example, that whatever the position at common law concerning privacy, the Act required domestic courts to give 'appropriate effect' to Article 8.[62] Convention rights now ran 'in a single channel' with the common law since 'by virtue of s[ections] 2 and 6' of the Act, courts 'must . . . take into account' the Strasbourg case law and 'themselves act compatibly with' Convention rights.[63] Sedley LJ was clear that, if the common law did not—contrary to his earlier conclusion—itself recognize a right to privacy, such a right could still be recognized due to the Act. It would be 'precisely the kind of incremental change for which the Act is designed: one which without undermining the measure of certainty which is necessary to all law gives substance and effect to s[ection] 6.'[64] Interestingly, Sedley LJ also suggested that, in the absence of s 12, s 6 would have required the court to

---

[54] ibid, paras [83]–[91]. [55] ibid, para [82]. [56] ibid, para [111].
[57] ibid, para [125]. [58] ibid, para [126]. [59] n 52 above. [60] n 49 above.
[61] [2001] QB 697, para [111]. [62] ibid, para [111]. [63] ibid, para [111].
[64] ibid, para [129].

give effect to the Article 10 right to freedom of expression (subject, as the right was, to qualification by competing Article 8 rights).[65]

Sedley LJ therefore clearly accepted that the Act could stimulate the development of common law rights (and, by implication, remedies, given the subject-matter of the case) through interpretation. How far he felt that the court had jurisdiction to go is, however, unclear. For one thing, despite concluding that s 6 mandated the recognition of a right to privacy, he officially declined to decide whether on a more general basis it merely required the courts' procedures to be Convention-compliant, or whether it required 'the law applied by the courts, save where primary legislation plainly says otherwise, to give effect to . . . Convention principles.'[66] Given his specific conclusion concerning privacy, as well as his citation of Murray Hunt's article (which, as we have seen, supports an interpretation-based approach due to the obligation apparently placed on courts by s 6), it would seem likely that Sedley LJ might support the second, substantive interpretation of s 6. If so, however, this would still not tell us how far he believed s 6 permitted courts to develop the law (including remedies) in a substantive sense. For, while Sedley LJ spoke of the recognition of a right to privacy as an 'incremental change'—implying something for which a relatively solid foundation already existed—he suggested that the Act would only need to be invoked if the recognition of privacy was 'not simply a modern restatement of the scope of a known protection but a legal innovation.'[67]

Keene LJ began by focusing on s 12, given that the case concerned a remedy—the injunction—which would impact upon freedom of expression. Having ruled that the appropriate standard for the claimant to meet in order to keep an interim injunction in force was whether they were likely to establish at trial that publication should not be allowed (rather than being awarded damages for loss suffered), Keene LJ applied this test in determining whether an injunction could lie when the claimants' cause of action was breach of confidence. Keene LJ appears, therefore, to have been openly running the two things together, unlike Sedley LJ, who treated the Human Rights Act argument essentially as a fall-back if his argument based on the common law failed. These two approaches are rather different: Keene LJ seemed happy to approach the problem as one of the availability or otherwise of a remedy, without engaging in lengthy speculation about the nature of the underlying rights. For Sedley LJ, by contrast, the rights were the key to the availability of the remedy. In relation to s 6 itself, Keene LJ was inconclusive. He noted that:[68]

---

[65] ibid, para [137].   [66] ibid, para [128].   [67] ibid, para [129].
[68] ibid, para [166].

[s]ince the coming into force of the Human Rights Act 1998, the courts as a public authority cannot act in a way which is incompatible with a Convention right:
section 6(1). That arguably includes their activity in interpreting and developing
the common law, even where no public authority is a party to the litigation.
Whether this extends to creating a new cause of action between private persons
and bodies is more controversial, since to do so would appear to circumvent the
restrictions (placed on proceedings and remedies by sections 7(1) and 8(1)).

Despite this uncertainty, it is submitted that Keene LJ was in fact using an
approach based on interpretation rather than on the direct creation of any
new cause of action: for this seems clear from his suggestion that the case
could be resolved by recognizing that breach of confidence had been
expanded due to the court's obligation to take account of Convention
jurisprudence, so that it might now protect a claimant's privacy even
where they did not have a confidential relationship with the defendant. It
was, Keene LJ hinted, largely a matter of labelling whether any resulting
remedy was described as being for breach of confidence or for breach of
privacy.[69]

What is clear from *Douglas and Zeta-Jones v Hello! Ltd* is that all three
judges were happy to give effect to Convention rights when determining
whether the injunction should be maintained. This clearly suggests,
despite Brooke LJ's apparent misgivings, that (at least) Articles 8 and 10
may be invoked in litigation where both litigants are private parties. In
that sense, all three judgments might be said to mark a defeat for the extra-
judicial stance advocated by Sir Richard Buxton. In relation to the broader
role of Convention rights in private litigation, however, the case is less
definitive, given that Sedley and Keene LJJ sought to avoid reaching any
definite conclusions concerning the ambit of s 6. However, it can be noted
that both judges were (or, in Sedley LJ's case, would have been in the
absence of s 12) happy to treat s 6 as imposing an obligation on courts at
least to interpret the common law in the light of Convention rights. In that
sense, the *Douglas and Zeta-Jones* case provides no support in terms of
precedent for the view that s 6 enables the courts directly to create new
causes of action in litigation between private parties, and it seems clear—
from the role played by Convention rights in the judges' reasoning concerning the possibility of granting an injunction—that the Court of Appeal
was happy in *Douglas and Zeta-Jones* for the relevant Convention rights to
influence the remedial side of the case.

Shortly after the *Douglas and Zeta-Jones* case, direct authority *against* the
view that s 6 might have full 'horizontal effect' appeared in Butler-Sloss P's
judgment in *Venables and Thompson v News Group Newspapers Ltd*.[70] In this
case, the claimants were asking the court to maintain in force injunctions

---

[69] ibid, para [166].   [70] [2001] 2 WLR 1038.

preventing the defendant newspapers from publishing information which might reveal their new identities or whereabouts after their release from prison. In upholding their claim based on breach of confidence rather than direct use of Convention rights, Butler-Sloss P asserted that Convention rights could not be enforced directly against the newspapers as private bodies, but noted that the court was bound by s 6 to act compatibly with Convention rights. She suggested that this:[71]

> obligation on the court does not seem to me to encompass the creation of a free-standing cause of action based directly upon the articles of the convention. . . . The duty on the court, in my view, is to act compatibly with convention rights in adjudicating upon existing common law causes of action, and that includes a positive as well as a negative obligation.

Furthermore, although not containing a conclusive view on the issue, the Court of Appeal's judgment in *A v B plc* seems also to support an approach which is confined to interpretation. Giving the judgment of the court, Lord Woolf CJ observed that s 6(1) required the court not to act in a way which was incompatible with a Convention right. He suggested that, in this case, '(t)he court is able to achieve this by absorbing the rights which art[icle]s 8 and 10 protect into the long-established action for breach of confidence. This involves giving a new strength and breadth to the action so that it accommodates the requirements of those articles.'[72] In consequence, it was 'most unlikely that any purpose will be served by a judge seeking to decide whether there exists a new cause of action in tort which protects privacy.'[73] In most situations, the reinterpreted action for breach of confidence would provide the necessary remedy.

The decision in *A v B plc* left unresolved the question of whether a fully-fledged right to privacy will emerge, quite apart from the question whether much territory would remain for such a right to occupy even if it did. For Sedley LJ's assertions about privacy in the *Douglas and Zeta-Jones* case dealt with a subject-matter which would fall within the scope of breach of confidence, as interpreted by Lord Woolf CJ in *A v B plc* (even if an injunction would not be forthcoming on the facts). What is particularly interesting about both cases, however, is the courts' reluctance to acknowledge that s 6 empowers them to create new causes of action, as Wade's theory would require. Instead—and despite the many uncertainties which still exist in the case law—the courts seem content with the view that they can develop the common law (including both causes of action and remedies) through interpretation, even where both parties are private litigants. Whether this will be the case for all time remains uncertain, but it seems clear for the moment that the full, s 6-driven 'horizontal effect'

---

[71] ibid, para [27].   [72] ibid, para [4].   [73] ibid, para [11](vi).

envisaged by Wade has not materialized. Whether this is an acceptable position is, of course, a question which can only be answered by considering the arguments for and against each of the rival theories discussed at the start of this section of the paper.

(c) Section 12

Section 12 of the 1998 Act specifies that where a court is 'considering whether to grant any relief which, if granted, might affect the exercise of the Convention right to freedom of expression', the court 'must have particular regard to the importance' of that right, and 'where the proceedings relate to material which the respondent claims, or which appears to the court, to be journalistic, literary or artistic material' to any relevant privacy codes. As Sedley LJ noted in the case of *Douglas and Zeta-Jones*, s 12 'puts beyond question the direct applicability of at least one article of the convention as between one private party to litigation and another.'[74] The remedy in relation to which s 12 was important in both the *Douglas and Zeta-Jones* case and *A v B plc* was an interim injunction to prevent the publication of material which arguably violated the claimants' Article 8 rights.

In the case of *Douglas and Zeta-Jones*, Brooke and Sedley LJJ employed analogous approaches to s 12. Brooke LJ noted that the Press Complaints Commission Code of Practice—which constituted a relevant code within s 12—gave particular weight to privacy, especially where a suitable public interest argument could not be produced to defend the publication in question.[75] This mirrored the drafting of Article 10, which allowed expression to be restricted in the interest of the Article 8 right to respect for private life. Section 12, coupled with the Code, provided the ground rules by which the court could weigh up the competing claims of privacy and expression,[76] and the effect of s 12 was that a publisher which flouted the Code 'is likely in those circumstances to have its claim to an entitlement to freedom of expression trumped by Article 10(2) considerations of privacy.'[77] In similar vein, Sedley LJ noted that since Article 10 is a 'qualified' right, the protection offered to freedom of expression by s 12 must be similarly qualified: thus, '[e]verything will ultimately depend on the proper balance between privacy and publicity in the situation facing the court'.[78] In applying s 12, 'the reputations and rights of others—not only but not least their Convention rights—are as material as the defendant's right of free

---

[74] [2001] QB 697, para [133]. And, as Sedley LJ went on to suggest (para [134]), whenever Article 10 is in issue—due to s 12—the drafting of Article 10(2) requires other Convention rights to be weighed against it. All might therefore have a role to play in purely private litigation.

[75] ibid, paras [92]–[94].   [76] ibid, para [95].   [77] ibid, para [94].
[78] ibid, para [135].

expression.'[79] The appropriate balance between the two rights was to be determined principally by using the proportionality standard. Interestingly, Sedley LJ suggested that s 12 had to be interpreted in this way both because of its 'inherent logic'[80] and because the interpretative obligation placed on courts by section 3 of the Act applied when a court was interpreting the 1998 Act itself. To give freedom of expression a priority which it did not enjoy under the Convention would be to violate s 3.[81] Keene LJ also relied upon s 3 to similar effect, and reached analogous conclusions about the 'qualified' role of Article 10 in relation to s 12 of the 1998 Act.[82] It should be noted that the Court of Appeal employed a broadly similar approach in *A v B plc* (the details of which need not be noted here) where Lord Woolf CJ laid down a series of criteria to be taken into account by courts when applying s 12.[83]

2. THE SUBSTANTIVE IMPACT OF CONVENTION RIGHTS

We have seen that some 'horizontal effect' is given to Article 10 of the Convention (and to such other rights as offset it) when s 12 of the 1998 Act comes into play in the area of remedies which may affect freedom of expression. In addition, courts are charged with interpreting statutory causes of action and remedies, so far as it is possible to do so, so as to give effect to Convention rights under s 3, and appear to have determined— whatever the correct interpretation of s 6—that they can interpret the common law compatibly with Convention rights so far as there are no conflicting statutory provisions and without creating new causes of action.

It would seem that the substantive Convention rights which are likely to be of greatest relevance in the context of private law litigation, at least in the area of remedies, are Articles 6, 8, and 10, and Article 1 of the First Protocol. Articles 8 and 10, together with Article 1 of the First Protocol, may be described as 'qualified' rights in that—as Richard Clayton and Hugh Tomlinson suggest—a public authority may prima facie justifiably restrict them 'by identifying specific objectives which make the restriction legitimate.'[84] When distinguishing between permissible and impermissible prima facie violations of such rights, the Court of Human Rights uses

---

[79] ibid, para [136].   [80] ibid, para [135].

[81] Keene LJ refused to speculate about the priority generally accorded by s 12 to competing Convention rights, but was clear that freedom of expression had to be balanced against the protection of private life when determining whether an injunction should be granted.

[82] [2001] QB 697, paras [149]–[150].

[83] [2002] QB 542. For further discussion of s 12 in relation to injunctions, see *Imutran Ltd v Uncaged Campaigns Ltd* [2001] 2 All ER 385.

[84] n 8 above, para 6.123; see also paras 6.90 and 6.91.

some form of proportionality test. In consequence, domestic courts have also been applying such a test in cases involving arguable violations of these rights. Article 6 is slightly more complicated, in that the Strasbourg Court has treated it as containing both 'qualified' and 'unqualified' elements. A right is said to be 'unqualified' where the claimant can establish a breach of it merely by showing, on the balance of probabilities, that the public authority failed to comply with its requirements: as Clayton and Tomlinson suggest, there is 'no obligation upon the court to examine whether the interference [with] the . . . right can be *justified* by the public authority.'[85] In consequence, domestic courts have been somewhat variable in their treatment of Article 6. The operation of these four Convention rights, and in particular the role of the proportionality test, will be considered in this section of the chapter. It will also be necessary to consider the 'discretionary area of judgment':[86] effectively, a degree of leeway which courts are prepared to offer public authorities when (at least, in the private law context) determining whether legislation which arguably violates Convention rights should be the subject of a declaration of incompatibility. Both the proportionality test and the 'discretionary area' are new elements in private law litigation.

(a) 'Qualified' rights: Article 8, Article 10, and Article 1 of the First Protocol

The structure of Articles 8 and 10 is similar. The first paragraph of each Article sets out a prima facie right, while the circumstances in which that right may justifiably be restricted are set out in the second paragraph. Restrictions must be 'prescribed by law'—that is, have a sufficiently clear basis in national law—and 'necessary in a democratic society' in the interest of a specified goal (examples, set out in Articles 8(2) and 10(2), include the protection of public safety, the prevention of disorder or crime, the protection of health or morals, and the protection of the rights of others).[87] In establishing whether an interference is necessary, the Court of Human Rights examines two logically distinct but in practice related issues, namely proportionality and the 'margin of appreciation' (to be discussed below in the context of the 'discretionary area of judgment').[88] The intensity of proportionality-based scrutiny—and hence the test employed by the Court—varies according to the nature of the right in question, the

---

[85] ibid, para 6.88.   [86] *R v DPP, ex p Kebilene* [2000] 2 AC 326.

[87] Clayton and Tomlinson, n 8 above, para 6.91.

[88] The logical distinction between proportionality and the margin of appreciation is explained in D Feldman, 'Proportionality and the Human Rights Act 1998', in E Ellis (ed) *The Principle of Proportionality in the Laws of Europe* (1999) 118, 124–7. In practice, however, the Court of Human Rights tends not to make the distinction explicit.

degree to which it has been violated, the consequences of the violation, and the sensitivity of the goal advanced as a justification for the violation. The reason for this is straightforward. Considered in the abstract, the meaning of proportionality seems relatively self-evident: the court is being asked to decide whether a restriction imposed on a right went beyond what was necessary, or reasonably necessary, in pursuit of a legitimate counter veiling goal.[89] In practice, however, this definition tells us nothing about *how* tight the relationship between the restriction and the goal must be. This is a question for the Strasbourg Court (and now for domestic courts), and the differing nature of the various Convention rights and the many contexts in which they can arise almost inevitably means that any answer varies in practice depending upon the factors mentioned. The price which must be paid for this sensitivity to circumstances is a measure of uncertainty in the case law.

The differing nature of the Convention rights is a factor which is particularly important when dealing with Article 1 of the First Protocol. This Article is drafted more loosely than Articles 8 and 10, and contains no mention of a measure needing to be 'necessary in a democratic society'. Instead, it stipulates that a person shall not be deprived of their possessions 'except in the public interest and subject to the conditions provided for by law . . .', and includes the express proviso that the state may enforce 'such laws as it deems necessary to control the use of property in accordance with the general interest or to secure the payment of taxes or other contributions or penalties'. In consequence, the Court of Human Rights has openly employed a looser proportionality test when dealing with this Article than when dealing with Articles 8 and 10.[90] The differing nature of these tests will be considered in the paragraphs below.

The most well-known formulation of proportionality, in relation to Article 10, can be found in *Handyside v UK*. Here, the Strasbourg Court sought to define what was 'necessary in a democratic society' by noting that 'whilst the adjective "necessary" . . . is not synonymous with "indispensable", neither has it the flexibility of such expressions as "admissible", "ordinary", "useful", "reasonable" or "desirable".'[91] In consequence, every restriction on freedom of expression 'must be proportionate to the legitimate [Convention] aim pursued'.[92] The Court built upon this reasoning in *Sunday Times v UK*, where it suggested that '[i]t must . . . be

---

[89] See, eg, Clayton and Tomlinson, n 8 above, para 6.40: there must be 'a reasonable relationship between a particular objective to be achieved and the means used to achieve that objective'; A Lester and D Pannick, *The Law of Human Rights* (1999), para 3.10: '[c]entral to the principle of a "fair balance" is the doctrine of proportionality. . . . There must be a "reasonable relationship of proportionality between the means employed and the legitimate objectives pursued".'

[90] Clayton and Tomlinson, n 8 above, paras 6. 45, 18.26, 18.76–81.

[91] (1976) 1 EHRR 737, para [48].   [92] ibid, para [49].

decided whether the "interference" complained of corresponded to a "pressing social need", whether it was "proportionate to the legitimate aim pursued", whether the reasons given by the national authorities to justify it are "relevant and sufficient" . . .'.[93] In the context of Article 8, a similar formulation was used in *Smith v UK*, where the Court asserted that an interference would only be deemed 'necessary' if it answered 'a pressing social need and, in particular, is proportionate to the legitimate aim pursued.'[94]

It is clear from the case law concerning Articles 8 and 10 that the 'necessity'-based proportionality test has been applied with variable intensity by the Court. This becomes clear from *Dudgeon v UK*, where the Court was required to consider whether the criminalization of private, consenting sexual acts between adults of the same sex violated Article 8. In relation to proportionality, the Court stated that since consenting sexual activity was 'a *most intimate* aspect of private life . . . there must exist *particularly serious* reasons before interferences on the part of public authorities can be legitimate.'[95] By implication, more mundane reasons might suffice if the subject-matter was less sensitive. Furthermore, the Court's definition of a 'democratic society' can affect the intensity of the proportionality standard. For the Court observed in *Handyside v UK*, and reiterated in *Dudgeon v UK* and *Smith v UK*, that a democratic society demands 'pluralism, tolerance and broadmindedness' towards unpopular causes, and that this was an important factor to be considered when evaluating what was 'necessary' in such a society.[96] In other words, policy considerations of this type are sometimes in-built within the proportionality test.

The drafting of particular Convention rights is also sometimes used by the Court as a basis for explaining how the proportionality standard is to operate. In *Handyside v UK*, when deciding whether a restriction on freedom of expression was 'necessary', the Court stated that it could not overlook the 'duties and responsibilities' which Article 10 specifically stated were owed by those exercising the right to freedom of expression.[97] More generally, the rather different drafting of Article 1 of the First Protocol has led to the adoption by the Court of a looser proportionality test in this context. Rather than demanding that a restriction is shown to be 'necessary', the Court merely requires a public authority to show that a 'fair balance' was struck between the general interest of the community and the fundamental rights of the individual,[98] something which requires

---

[93] (1979) 2 EHRR 245, para [62], citing *Handyside v UK*, n 91 above, paras [48]–[50].
[94] (2000) 29 EHRR 493, para [87].   [95] (1981) 4 EHRR 149, para [52] (emphasis added).
[96] n 91 above, para [49]; *Dudgeon v UK*, n 95 above, paras [52]–[53] ; *Smith v UK*, n 94 above, para [87]. See further Clayton and Tomlinson, n 8 above, paras 6.124–124A.
[97] n 91 above, para [49].
[98] *Sporrong v Sweden* (1983) 5 EHRR 35, para [69]; *Beyeler v Italy* (application 33202/96) para [107].

a 'reasonable relationship of proportionality between the means employed and the aim sought to be realised.'[99] That this is a looser test than that employed in the context of Articles 8 and 10 can be seen by considering *James v UK*, a case where the Court accepted that the compulsory transfer of the fee simple title of property to tenants under the provisions of the Leasehold Reform Act 1967, passed the fair balance test.[100] The Court suggested that under Article 1 of the First Protocol, public authorities were not required to prove that their measures met a strict necessity standard, and that the availability of alternative, less restrictive solutions did not in itself render the legislation unjustified. Rather, the availability of other solutions:[101]

> constitutes one factor, along with others, relevant for determining whether the means chosen could be regarded as reasonable and suited to achieving the legitimate aim being pursued. . . . Provided the legislature remained within these bounds, it is not for the Court to say whether the legislation represented the best solution for dealing with the problem or whether the legislative discretion could have been exercised in another way.

An obvious contrast can be drawn between the cases of *James* and *Smith*,[102] where the possibility that less restrictive measures could have been applied appears to have been crucial to the Court's finding that the government's measures *were* disproportionate in the circumstances.

It will be suggested below that proportionality is now being applied by domestic courts in disputes between private parties. This being so, it is important for courts to appreciate the context-dependent nature of proportionality if the principle is to be applied coherently when assessing the legitimacy of prima facie violations of 'qualified' Convention rights. How far this has been the case to date will be considered further below.

(b) Article 6

Article 6(1) stipulates that: 'In the determination of his civil rights and obligations or of any criminal charge against him, everyone is entitled to a fair and public hearing within a reasonable time by an independent and impartial tribunal established by law.' The general Article 6(1) right to a fair hearing is 'unqualified'; however, many of the specific rights contained within Article 6 are 'qualified'.[103] It is clear from the House of

---

[99] *Beyeler v Italy*, n 98 above, para [114].   [100] (1986) 8 EHRR 123.

[101] ibid, para [51]. See also the Court's discussion of compensation payable for compulsorily acquired property: *Lithgow v UK* (1986) 8 EHRR 329, para [121]; *Holy Monasteries v Greece* (1995) 20 EHRR 1, para [70]; *James v UK*, n 100 above, paras [54]–[57].

[102] n 94 above.

[103] *Brown v Stott*, n 9 above, 836 (Lord Bingham), 840–1 (Lord Steyn), 851 (Lord Hope), 859–60 (Lord Clyde), 861–2 (Rt Hon Ian Kirkwood).

Lords' decisions in the *Brown, A* and *Lambert* cases[104] that a proportionality test must be employed in determining whether an apparent restriction of a 'qualified' element of Article 6 is legitimate, an issue which will usually arise on appeal from a criminal trial. By contrast, *R (Alconbury) v Secretary of State for the Environment, Transport and the Regions*[105] suggests that Article 6(1) does not require courts to deploy a proportionality test in judicial review where a person's civil rights are at stake in a specialist field such as planning, and that whether a decision-making procedure is found to comply with Article 6 will depend upon all the circumstances. According to Lord Slynn, Article 6(1) required 'sufficient review of the legality of decisions and of the procedures followed',[106] 'sufficiency' being a context-dependent notion. Lord Clyde emphasized the context-based character of Article 6(1) by observing that 'in some circumstances a breach in one respect can be overcome by the existence of a sufficient opportunity for appeal or review',[107] and that not every stage of the decision-making process need comply with the requirements of Article 6(1), so long as sufficient opportunities existed for appeal or review.[108] Whether sufficient opportunities for appeal existed would again depend upon the context:[109] a more exhaustive procedure might, for example, be required to satisfy Article 6(1) when the legitimacy of disciplinary proceedings was in issue.

In cases involving the determination of arguable private law rights, specific Article 6 protections for litigants which will come into play include an effective right of access to a court, the right to equality of arms before the court, a 'qualified' right to legal assistance, a right to a hearing within a reasonable time, the right to an independent and impartial tribunal established by law, and the right to a public hearing and public pronouncement of judgment.[110] As will be seen below, questions concerning Article 6 may come into play in private law disputes before domestic courts both in relation to procedure at the hearing itself, and in relation to the background rules which control the court's discretion when determining the case.

(c) The 'discretionary area of judgment'

The notion of the 'margin of appreciation' is an intrinsic, if controversial, aspect of the Strasbourg Court's jurisprudence, particularly in cases

---

[104] nn 9, 15 and 16 above.   [105] [2001] 2 WLR 1389.
[106] ibid, para [49] (Lord Slynn). cf, however, the more general analysis offered, in the public law context, in J Herberg, A Le Sueur, and J Mulcahy, 'Determining Civil Rights and Obligations', in J Jowell and J Cooper (eds), *Understanding Human Rights Principles* (2001) 102
[107] [2001] 2 WLR 1389, para [152].   [108] ibid, para [152].   [109] ibid, para [154].
[110] See, generally, Clayton and Tomlinson, n 8 above, ch 11.

involving 'qualified' rights.[111] The Court suggested in *Handyside v UK* that '[b]y reason of their direct and continuous contact with the vital forces of their countries, State authorities are in principle in a better position than the international judge to give an opinion on the exact content of these requirements as well as on the "necessity" of a "restriction" or "penalty" intended to meet them'.[112] National governments therefore retain a 'margin of appreciation' when making the initial assessment of the need for an interference with a Convention right, although the Court reserves to itself the role of making a final judgment as to whether the reasons cited for the interference were sufficient.[113] The generosity of the 'margin' varies according to the aim and magnitude of the interference and the nature of the Convention right affected by it.[114] Lord Hope accepted, obiter, in *R v DPP, ex p Kebilene* that the Strasbourg 'margin' could not play a direct part in domestic law: for, while it was 'an integral part of the supervisory jurisdiction which is exercised over state conduct by the international court', there was no gap between the international and national levels when domestic courts determined Human Rights Act cases.[115] An international principle of deference was therefore conceptually inapplicable at national level. However, Lord Hope suggested that an equivalent domestic principle—the 'discretionary area of judgment'—should instead be employed: where the executive or the legislature had to make difficult policy choices between the rights of the individual and the needs of society, '[i]n some circumstances it will be appropriate for the courts to recognise that there is an area of judgment within which the judiciary will defer, on democratic grounds, to the considered opinion of the elected body or person whose act or decision is said to be incompatible with the Convention'.[116]

It is thus necessary to consider this principle alongside proportionality when considering how courts give effect to Convention rights. In the *Kebilene* case, Lord Hope was—perhaps inevitably—able to offer only loose indications concerning the criteria to be used when calculating the appropriate degree of deference. It would, he suggested, be 'easier for such an area of judgment to be recognised where the Convention itself requires a balance to be struck'—ie, where a 'qualified' right was in issue—'much less so where the right is stated in terms which are unqualified. It will be easier for it to be recognised where the issues

---

[111] For general analysis, see Grosz, Beatson, and Duffy, n 8 above, 114-5, 173; Clayton and Tomlinson, n 7 above, paras 6.31–9.

[112] n 91 above, para [48].

[113] *Handyside v UK* n 91 above, para [48]; *Smith v UK*, n 94 above, para [88].

[114] *Handyside v UK*, n 91 above, paras [48]–[49]; *Sunday Times v UK*, n 93 above, para [59]; *Dudgeon v UK*, n 95 above, para [52].

[115] n 86 above, 993. See also Grosz, Beatson, and Duffy, n 8 above, 19-20; Clayton and Tomlinson, n 8 above, paras 6.37-9.

[116] n 86 above, 994.

involve questions of social or economic policy, much less so where the rights are of high constitutional importance or are of a kind where the courts are especially well placed to assess the need for protection.'[117] The operation of the 'discretionary area', like that of the Strasbourg 'margin of appreciation', thus appears to vary according to the right in issue. Its role will also depend upon the nature of the case. In litigation against a public authority, the 'discretionary area' can be used both when assessing the legality of executive action under s 6 of the Act, and when determining whether a declaration of incompatibility should be issued concerning legislation relied upon by the respondent as providing a lawful basis for its action. In private law litigation, by contrast, use of the 'discretionary area' is logically confined to assessments of the Convention-compatibility of legislation on which either party has relied.[118] A good example of this is provided in *Wilson v First County Trust (No 2)*, where the Court of Appeal had to determine whether a declaration of incompatibility should be issued concerning s 127(3) of the Consumer Credit Act 1974. Morritt V-C accepted that the 1974 Act was concerned with issues of social policy, and as such fell within the 'discretionary area'. However, while the court had to show deference to Parliament and to the executive, this did not entail unquestioning acceptance of their determinations: '[i]t is one thing', Morritt V-C suggested, 'to accept the need to defer to an opinion which can be seen to be the product of reasoned consideration based on policy; it is quite another thing to be required to accept, without question, an opinion for which no reason of policy is advanced'.[119] For the moment, the 'discretionary area' thus forms a relevant—if somewhat ambiguous—factor in private law cases in which Convention rights are invoked.

3. SOME PRIVATE LAW EXAMPLES[120]

It has been suggested that there are numerous uncertainties surrounding the exact requirements of the substantive Convention rights (not least due to the proportionality standard in 'qualified' rights and the 'discretionary area of judgment'—both new factors in private law litigation), quite apart

---

[117] ibid; Lord Hope reiterated the point concerning 'qualified' rights in *R v A*, n 15 above, para [58]. See further *B v Secretary of State for the Home Dept* [2000] 2 CMLR 1086, 1093–4 (Sedley LJ); *R v Secretary of State for the Home Dept, ex p Isiko* [2001] 1 FCR 633, 648 (Schiemann LJ); *Brown v Stott*, n 9 above, 843; *R v A*, n 15 above, para [36] (Lord Steyn).

[118] See further *R (on the application of International Transport Roth GmbH) v Secretary of State for the Home Dept)* [2002] EWCA Civ 158, Laws LJ (dissenting).

[119] n 30 above, para [33].

[120] See, generally, H Beale and N Pittam, 'The Impact of the Human Rights Act 1998 on English Tort and Contract Law', ch 7 in D Friedmann and D Barak-Erez (eds), *Human Rights in Private Law* (2001).

from the broader difficulties surrounding the range of circumstances in which such rights can be relied upon in litigation involving only private parties. Space precludes a full examination of every situation in which Convention rights are likely to pose questions for the private law litigator. However, the points made in previous sections may perhaps be usefully be illustrated by considering two examples.[121]

The first—and perhaps, to date, the clearest—example of the role of Convention rights in private law litigation is provided in *Wilson (No 2)*. The claimant had in January 1999 signed a loan agreement with the defendant pawnbroker, with her car pledged as security. Litigation arose, and when the Court of Appeal first heard the case—as *Wilson v First County Trust (No 1)*[122]—it ruled that the loan did not constitute a properly executed regulated agreement as defined in s 61(1)(a) of the 1974 Act. Section 65(1) of the Act stipulated that an improperly executed agreement could only be enforced against the debtor on an order of the court. However, s 127(3) specified that in order for this to happen, a document had first to exist, signed by the debtor and containing all the prescribed terms of the agreement. Unfortunately, one consequence of the Court's ruling that the agreement which existed was improperly executed was that there were no other documents in existence which could satisfy 127(3). The credit agreement was thus unenforceable against the claimant, as was the security provided by her. In consequence, the claimant could keep the money she had borrowed and demand the return of her car. The issue in the case of *Wilson (No 2)* was whether this outcome—caused by ss 65(1) and 127(3) of the Consumer Credit Act—violated the creditor's Article 6 right alongside Article 1 of the First Protocol.

Morritt V-C concluded that the creditor's rights were violated. In reaching this conclusion, he suggested that s 127(3) was hard to explain. For example, a court could dismiss applications for the enforcement of agreements which were improperly executed because they fell within other parts of s 127 only if it was just to do so, something which required consideration of the culpability of the creditor and the potential prejudice to the debtor. By contrast, no such calculation was permitted under s 127(3): the rule that no enforcement order could be made in the absence of the stipulated document was absolute. Section 127(3) excluded any consideration of the behaviour of the owner, turning instead on a mechanistic approach which focused only on whether the document contained all the prescribed terms. This clearly raised in acute form the question of whether

---

[121] For a more complete list, see Clayton and Tomlinson, n 8 above, paras 11.313-8, 12.160-4, 15.254, 18.102.

[122] [2001] QB 407.

s 127(3) was proportionate. Morritt V-C accepted that the 1974 Act was concerned with issues of social policy, and as such fell within Lord Hope's 'discretionary area of judgment' from *R v DPP, ex p Kebilene*.[123] However, as we have already seen, he felt that this did not excuse the production of reasoned statements of policy if the section was to be explained. It was necessary for the court to identify the issue of social policy which the legislation sought to address, and the thinking which led to it being dealt with as it was. Morritt V-C found that neither the White Paper which preceded the 1974 Act nor the Parliamentary debates which accompanied its passage provided any real indication why Parliament might have chosen to distinguish so sharply between the power of a court to enforce agreements falling within s 127(3) and agreements which were improperly executed for other reasons. While the policy goal behind s 127(3)—promoting formality in commercial transactions—was perfectly legitimate, the means used to achieve it (namely the inflexible prohibition contained in s 127(3))—was disproportionate. The policy could instead have been achieved by giving the court power to determine from case to case whether the agreement in question should be enforced. An absolute bar was excessive. A declaration of incompatibility should thus be issued concerning s 127(3).

As previously indicated, the case of *Wilson (No 2)* is clearly an example of ss 3 and 4 of the 1998 Act in operation—and, as indicated above, the Court of Appeal's reasoning concerning s 3 is readily defensible. Unfortunately, a weaker aspect of the reasoning—from the Strasbourg standpoint, at least—was that Morritt V-C simply assumed that the *same* proportionality inquiry would suffice for Article 6 and for Article 1 of the First Protocol. As we have already seen, the Strasbourg case law concerning these two rights employs neither the same proportionality test, nor even the same interpretation of each proportionality test in relation to every case concerning one of the two Articles. So long as domestic courts do not offer a lower level of protection to litigants—for example, by employing a harsher proportionality test than the Strasbourg Court—then this divergence need not generate problems of a Convention nature; however, it will detract still further from any quest for commercial certainty in domestic law. It is therefore to be hoped that domestic courts will become clearer about which proportionality standards they are employing.

A second useful example of the potential reach of Article 6 is provided by freezing orders (formerly known as *Mareva* injunctions) and search orders (formerly known *as Anton Piller* orders).[124] As Richard Clayton and

---

[123] n 86 above.
[124] See, generally, R Bradgate, *Commercial Law* (3rd edn, 2000) 873–6; DJ Hayton, *Hayton and Marshall: Commentary and Cases on the Law of Trusts and Equitable Remedies* (11th edn, 2001), ch 11.

Hugh Tomlinson have suggested, the coming into force of the Act means that the granting of freezing orders 'will be affected' by Article 6 where the order in question does not include a proviso allowing for payment for legal advice out of the frozen moneys.[125] For it would appear that the right to have effective access to a court, guaranteed by Article 6, may arguably be violated without such a proviso. This issue was not taken up by the Court of Appeal in its recent decision in *Motorola Credit Corp v Uzan*,[126] but it should be noted that the defendants' interest in privacy—presumably a parallel interest to the Article 8 right to respect for private life—was discussed at some length by the Court in determining whether to make an order. Given the existence of a statutory basis for freezing orders in the Supreme Court Act 1981, it would seem likely that any reinterpretation of previous case law will be effected via s 3 of the Human Rights Act 1998. Search orders were challenged before the Court of Human Rights in *Chappell v UK*[127] and were found not to constitute a disproportionate intrusion upon a litigant's Article 8 right provided that their use was accompanied by adequate safeguards and so long as they were not used oppressively. United Kingdom courts retain a discretion, under s 2 of the Human Rights Act 1998, to depart from Strasbourg case law (subject, of course, to the litigant's right to appeal to the Court of Human Rights), but—unless they are prepared to go beyond the position as approved at Strasbourg level—it would seem likely that search orders can continue to be used so long as appropriate safeguards are maintained.

It would therefore seem that unless a satisfactory explanation for the provisions of an existing remedy cannot be found from the standpoint of the proportionality test, the remedy in question is likely to survive Human Rights Act scrutiny. It will nonetheless be important for courts to apply relevant proportionality-based scrutiny clearly and accurately. In the context of discretionary remedies, this will require the inquiry to commence by identifying the requirements of the Convention right in issue, before proceeding to examine the nature of the justification advanced for restricting the right and the question whether that justification is in fact proportionate to the policy goal which underpins the restriction. As Clayton and Tomlinson suggest, 'when granting an injunction . . . the court must not interfere with a private litigant's right to privacy, freedom of expression or freedom of assembly without proper justification.'[128] Whatever the outcome in individual cases, this seems likely to require courts to engage—as in the *Wilson (No 2)* case—in a more explicitly policy-based inquiry than characteristically took place prior to the coming into force of the 1998 Act.

---

[125] Clayton and Tomlinson, n 8 above, para 11.315A.
[126] [2002] EWCA Civ. 989; The Times, 10th July 2002.   [127] (1990) 12 EHRR 1.
[128] n 8 above, para 5.82.

4. CONCLUSION

Any attempt to evaluate the likely impact of the Human Rights Act 1998 on private law remedies must, as this chapter has done, focus on questions of method ('will Convention rights impact on private law litigation, and if so how and to what extent?') and substance ('if they do impact, how considerable will that impact be?'). It has been suggested here that the major mechanism by which Convention rights will affect private law is interpretation, whether of existing statutory provisions or common law rules—including, where appropriate, remedies. However, courts have not—and, absent a complete change of stance, seem unlikely to—decide that they have the power to create entirely new causes of action so as to give effect to Convention rights. In litigation between private parties, courts will apply Convention rights within these parameters, and might in particular choose to make use of Article 6 to make judgments concerning the rules surrounding the case. Clearly, a court's primary concern should, in the post-Human Rights Act period, be to give priority to Convention rights save where conflicting primary legislation requires otherwise. It is nonetheless to be hoped that they do so mindful of the subtleties of novel (in private law) standards such as proportionality and the 'discretionary area of judgment'. By doing this, it is to be hoped that adequate weight can be given to the need for commercial certainty.

20

Private Law Remedies and the Human Rights Act 1998: Defining the Limits of Interpretation

ANDREW HENDERSON[1]

In Chapter 19 Nicholas Bamforth makes a persuasive case that the major mechanism, under the Human Rights Act 1998 ('the 1998 Act'), by which Convention rights will affect private law is interpretation, whether of existing statutory provisions or common law rules—including, where appropriate, remedies.

The following can be added: When meeting the horizontal 'literal argument',[2] it is important to focus, as Bamforth does, on the observation that it is implausible to talk of courts being placed under a legally enforceable duty by the 1998 Act, in support of which he cites the remarks of Lord Clyde in *R v Lambert*.[3] It may however be preferable to think of the courts as being under a *constitutional* duty, ie as a matter of practice the courts are under a duty to act in a manner that is compatible with Convention rights. The courts may be said to be bound by a constitutional convention akin to, albeit not as robust as, the practice of following the rules of precedent, 'one of those conventions which are so significant a feature of the British constitution . . .'[4] The following points should be noted:

- Even in the absence of the Human Rights Act 1998 the judicial practice of acting compatibly with Convention rights, by interpreting ambiguous legislation, developing the common law, and exercising judicial discretions consistently with the Convention, has developed over the last decade, at least.[5]
- As is the case with any 'breach' of the rules of precedent, the appropriate redress for a judicial decision which is incompatible with

---

[1] Associate Solicitor, Norton Rose. I am grateful for the comments made by the various participants at the Oxford Norton Rose colloquium. The errors contained in this paper remain mine alone. Many of the observations in this paper were first made in 'Operation of the constitution between private actors: the inevitable consequences of section 35(3) and the dilemma of conflicting rights' (1995) *De Rebus: The Attorneys Journal of South Africa* 439 ('Conflicting Rights') and 'Do to your neighbours as we, the people, would have them do to you' (1997) *De Rebus: The Attorneys Journal of South Africa* 345 ('Neighbours').

[2] See Sir William Wade, 'Human Rights and the Judiciary' [1998] EHRLR 520 and 'Horizons of Horizontality' (2000) 116 LQR 217.

[3] [2001] 3 WLR 206, HL.

[4] *R v Knuller (Publishing, Printing and Promotions) Ltd* [1973] AC 435 at 484.

[5] See, in particular, M Beloff and H Mountfield, 'Unconventional Behaviour? Judicial Uses of the European Convention in England and Wales' [1996] EHRLR 467.

Convention rights is an appeal to a higher court which, as Sir Richard Buxton points out,[6] is not a remedy, or intervention by Parliament in the form of legislative amendment.

- The notion of redress lacking legal force is a key theme of the 1998 Act. Indeed, the 1998 Act's most innovative creation, the declaration of incompatibility in s 4, falls into this category. The 1998 Act denies the courts the power to give an applicant a legally enforceable remedy, leaving that instead to Parliament.[7] Moreover, the courts have no power to ensure that new Acts of Parliament are certified in terms of s 19 of the 1998 Act, enforcement being a matter for Parliament alone.[8]

Constitutional niceties aside, it should be noted that in a typical City litigation practice the Human Rights Act and Convention rights issues seldom arise. Where they do, it is generally in the context of the relations which clients have with regulators performing public functions.[9] Moreover, in relation to interim remedies such as search orders (formerly *Anton Pillar* orders) and interim injunctions, the impact of Convention rights was felt even before the advent of the 1998 Act.[10] Although the cases show that the 1998 Act has had some effect in disputes involving private parties, ie where the defendant was not subject to s 6,[11] the small number of reported cases would tend to suggest that the 1998 Act's impact in the realm of private law remedies has been limited.

This highlights the fact that the 1998 Act is most effective where a claimant can rely on s 6 against a private defendant, ie where the defendant to a claim, as opposed to the court charged with adjudicating the claim as Bamforth makes much of the focus of his paper, is the 'public authority' to which s 6 refers. At first glance, this would appear to be impractical since s 6 is confined to 'public law' disputes. Notwithstanding this public law aspect, s 6 was relied on in the context of a dispute between two private parties in *Marcic v Thames Water Utilities Ltd*.[12] Importantly, the defendant in the *Marcic* case was not acting in a regulatory role imposing duties on individuals, which typically gives rise to the types of issues

---

[6] 'The Human Rights Act and Private Law' (2000) 116 LQR 116.

[7] Human Rights Act 1998, s 10.

[8] See N Bamforth, 'Parliamentary Sovereignty and the Human Rights Act' [1998] PL 572.

[9] In particular, the Financial Services Authority exercising power under the Financial Services and Markets Act 2000.

[10] See, eg, *Chappell v UK* (1990) 12 EHRR 1 and *The Observer and Guardian v UK* (1992) 14 EHRR 153.

[11] *Douglas and Zeta-Jones v Hello! Ltd* [2001] QB 697; *Venables and Thompson v News Group Newspapers Ltd* [2001] 1 All ER 908; *A v B plc* [2002] 2 All ER 545; and *Campbell v MGN Ltd* The Times, 29 March 2002 (QBD) and The Times, 16 October 2002 (CA).

[12] [2002] QB 929, CA. The decision of Judge Richard Havery QC sitting in the Technology and Construction Court is reported as part of the judgment of the Court of Appeal ([2002] EWCA Civ 64). Leave to appeal to the House of Lords has been granted. The decision is noted by B Parker, 'A Continued Nuisance' [2002] CLJ 260.

decided in the context of s 6. Instead it was the entity charged with discharging the statutory function of water and sewage undertaker. The facts which gave rise to the liability at issue could just as easily have arisen outside the statutory context.

Using the *Marcic* case as an illustration, this paper highlights briefly a number of discrete points arising in the context of a claim for damages. It goes on to highlight the issue of exclusionary clauses which is germane to the question of the type of interpretation under the 1998 Act. It concludes with the observation that, given the absence of Article 13 in Sch 1 of the 1998 Act, the effects of the 1998 Act in creating new remedies may continue to be limited in practice, the development of existing common law remedies being the preferred route for the vindication of the types of interests protected by Convention rights.

1. *MARCIC V THAMES WATER UTILITIES LTD*: FACTS AND DECISION

The facts in the *Marcic* case are as follows: the claimant's property was seriously affected by flooding. The defendant was a statutory water and sewerage undertaker for the purposes of the relevant statutes.[13] Heavy rainfall led to back flow of foul water from the defendant's sewer system on to the claimant's property reaching as far as his house. Experts agreed that only major surface water drainage works would alleviate significantly the risk of further flooding.[14] The defendant refused to carry out the necessary works and the claimant brought proceedings in the Technology and Construction Court claiming that the flooding constituted a nuisance, for which the defendant was liable both at common law and under the 1998 Act. In particular, he alleged breaches of Article 8 and Article 1 of the First Protocol.

The court rejected the common law claim, holding that the effect of the authorities was that a statutory drainage undertaker was not liable to a person in its area who suffered damage by flooding where the claim was based on a failure on the part of the undertaker to undertake works to fulfil its statutory duty of drainage of the area.[15] It accepted, however, that the defendant's failure to carry out works to bring to an end the repeated flooding of the claimant's property constituted an interference with the exercise of the claimant's Convention rights.

---

[13] The Water Act 1989 and the Water Industry Act 1991.
[14] The cost of the works was in the region of £200,000.
[15] It made no difference for the court whether the cause of action was nuisance, the principle in *Rylands v Fletcher* (1868) LR 3 HL 330, or breach of statutory duty. The policy set out in s 94 of the Water Industry Act 1991 excluded any common law duty, cf *Stovin v Wise* [1996] AC 92.

There does not appear to have been any issue that the acts of the defendant were in principle subject to s 6 of the 1998 Act because, in terms of s 6(6), an act includes a failure to act. Moreover, the court drew support from the decisions of the European Court of Human Rights and the European Commission of Human Rights that an act, without justification, which gives rise to a nuisance could infringe Article 8 and Article 1 of the First Protocol.[16]

As to the question of whether the infringement was justifiable, the court observed that the defendant's argument that a body, such as the defendant, had more specialist expertise than the court in assessing the issue of proportionality was 'powerful'.[17] It held that it was nevertheless required to make the assessment, albeit giving the defendant a wide margin of discretion. The assessment required the court to decide whether the defendant had struck a fair balance between the competing interests of the claimant and of the defendant's other customers, allowing the defendant that margin. The court found that the defendant had provided insufficient evidence to show that the system of priorities used by the defendant fell within its margin of discretion. The defendant therefore failed to provide a justification for the infringement. The court appears also to have reached this conclusion after a consideration of the following factors: the claimant had suffered increased frequent flooding at his property for nine years; the defendant knew about that flooding since it occurred; nothing had been done about the flooding (other than steps taken by the claimant amounting to £16,000); and, under the present system of priorities, there was no prospect of the defendant doing anything to remedy the situation. The defendant was therefore liable in damages from 2 October 2000, the date on which the 1998 Act came fully into force, with the court determining the quantum of damages at a later hearing.[18]

At the later hearing the court held that the claimant was entitled to damages for future infringements of his rights in substitution for an injunction.[19] The court observed that it was not premature to award damages, nor was it wrong to award damages for future infringement of rights under the 1998 Act on the basis of a finding that the defendant did not intend to carry out the works necessary to remedy the nuisance.[20] It was

---

[16] His honour cited *Baggs v UK* (1985) 9 EHRR 235 (noise from Heathrow airport); *S v France* (1990) 65 DR 250 (presence of a nuclear power station); *Lopez Ostra v Spain* (1994) 20 EHRR 277 (fumes and smells emanating from a waste treatment plant); and *Guerra v Italy* (1998) 26 EHRR 357 (toxic emissions from a factory).

[17] [2002] QB 929, para [72].

[18] *Marcic v Thames Water Utilities (No 2)* [2002] QB 1003.

[19] Under the provisions of s 50 of the Supreme Court Act 1981.

[20] The court observed that its holding in the first judgment that there should be no mandatory injunction did not mean that the proposed schemes were impracticable. The refusal of a mandatory injunction was an exercise of discretion. The judgment on liability should be amended to clarify the position: an injunction was refused because it would have to specify

irrelevant that the common law would not award damages for future wrongs. The measure of damages would be the difference between the value of the property as it would be if and when works necessary to prevent the flooding were completed and its actual value. If the completion date was in the future when the damages were awarded, an appropriate discount should be made. The court concluded that the claim in relation to inconvenience, distress, and vexation arising out of the flooding would be reflected in the value of the house and no additional sum should be awarded in respect of it.

The Court of Appeal refused to disturb the finding of the first instance court on the claim under the 1998 Act. The Court observed, however, that a common law right to damages displaced any right that the claimant would otherwise have had under the 1998 Act. In this respect their Lordships, reversing the decision at first instance, held that the defendant had breached its common law duties to the claimant not to damage his property. The defendant could not establish that the breach of its duty was an inevitable consequence of the exercise of its statutory powers under the Water Industry Act1991. The claimant's common law claim would therefore succeed without the need for the question of relief under the 1998 Act to be considered.

2. SUBSTANTIVE ASPECTS

The *Marcic* case highlights a number of issues that are useful when considering Convention rights issues generally:

* The ongoing nature of the defendant's breach meant that there was no issue as to limitation. However, it should be noted that the liability of the defendant under s 6 of the 1998 Act brings into play s 7 of the 1998 Act. In this regard, anyone who seeks to rely on 1998 Act will need to be mindful of the one-year limitation period in s 7(5).[21] Section 7(5) only applies where proceedings are brought against the public authority pursuant to s 7(1)(a) and not where Convention rights are otherwise relied on in any legal proceedings pursuant to s 7(1)(b).[22]

the works precisely and the specification was a matter of engineering expertise which was not before the court, and because performance of any injunction would require the co-operation of third parties, albeit that the defendant had powers of compulsory purchase of land.

  [21] In such circumstances, its effect is the opposite to that in the context of judicial review. See D Nichol, 'Limitation Periods under the Human Rights Act 1998 and Judicial Review' (1999) 115 LQR 216.

  [22] Section 7(1) provides textual support for an interpretation based approach. If the Human Rights Act 1998 only envisaged a strictly vertical operation, s 7(1)(b) would be unnecessary.

- The court acknowledged the defendant's argument regarding the potential non-justiciablity of the subject matter of the dispute. Arguments relating to non-justiciablity and discretionary areas of judgment may carry more weight where the defendant is a private person rather than a public body. The court, itself bound to act in a manner that is compatible with Convention rights, will need to acknowledge a defendant's right to privacy and property by broadening the defendant's discretionary area of judgment.[23]

- The court emphasized that the burden lies on the defendant to provide the justification for the infringement.[24] The finding that the defendant had provided insufficient evidence with regard to its system of priorities, an important factor in determining whether the defendant had remained within its discretionary area of judgment, is significant. It suggests that a defendant who is a private person will not simply be able to rely on abstract arguments governing the breadth of discretionary area of judgment to defeat any claim based on Convention rights. The defendant will have to come to court armed not only with reasons as to why it has a broad the discretionary area of judgment but with evidence showing why the particular act complained of falls within that area of judgment.[25]

- The court identified certain factors which go to the seriousness of the breach. These included the length of time for which the breach persisted, the defendant's knowledge of the breach, and the fact that there was no immediate prospect of the defendant doing anything about the breach. This is useful in respect of gathering evidence to indicate whether a breach is or is not justified. It is useful also in its identification of the role of the defendant's state of mind in assessing whether or not a breach is justified. Finally, it creates a role for an enquiry as to whether, as a matter of fact, the defendant will be able or willing to remedy its breach. These factors, familiar perhaps to those that deal with common law claims in tort or contract, are thus brought into play in the novel context of the 1998 Act.

- In the *Marcic* case the claimant was awarded damages. However, it should be noted that the power of the courts to award relief under s 8 is discretionary and damages are not recoverable as of right.[26] Anyone seeking to rely on the 1998 Act against a defendant that is subject to s 6 will need to be mindful of this as the common law claim would appear to provide a better of guarantee of actual recovery.

---

[23] See Henderson, 'Neighbours', above n 1, 347–8.   [24] [2002] QB 929, para [103].

[25] More guidance from the court in the *Marcic* case as to what further evidence was required would have been useful.

[26] For discussion, see R Clayton and H Tomlinson, *The Law of Human Rights* (2000) 1414–20.

- In the decision at first instance, the measure of damages necessary to afford 'just satisfaction' under s 8(3) of the 1998 Act was adjudged at the same level as that in respect of a common law nuisance claim.[27] The measure of damages was held to be the difference between the value of the reinstated property and its actual value. Interestingly, although no reference was made to common law authority in support of this approach, no reference was made to European authorities either.[28]

3. SECTION 6: A SUPERIOR SOURCE OF INTERPRETATION?

Perhaps unintentionally, the *Marcic* case highlights the shortcomings of s 3(1) of the Human Rights Act 1998 in the context of private law remedies. One of the issues raised by the defendant related to the absence of an enforcement order made by the Secretary of State, or Director under the Water Industry Act 1991. The defendant's statutory duties under the Water Industry Act 1991 could only be enforced after an enforcement order had been made under s 18(8). An enforcement order was required for any remedy other than 'those for which express provision is made by or under any enactment and those that are available in respect of that act or omission otherwise than by virtue of its constituting such a contravention.' Counsel for the defendant appears to have argued that this did not include remedies under the 1998 Act, interpretation of the Water Industry Act 1991 being the starting point. Counsel for the claimant argued the opposite, submitting that the 1998 Act was the starting point. The court did not address this issue in detail holding simply that the starting point was immaterial; the Water Industry Act 1991 had been passed before the Human Rights Act 1998 and section 18(8) could not be interpreted so as to prohibit the bringing of the claimant's claim under the 1998 Act.[29]

Such a conclusion is hardly controversial, which appears to explain its very brief, if not unsatisfactory, treatment by the court. This aspect of the decision highlights, however, an important aspect of the role of interpretation and a difficulty with working out the proper role of the 1998 Act. At first glance, it would appear surprising that the court did not make reference to s 3(1) of the 1998 Act which would remove the need for worry about which came first, the 1998 Act, or the Water Industry Act 1991.

Without reference to s 3(1), but remaining within the Human Rights Act matrix, the court's treatment of the arguments raised by the defendant in the *Marcic* case can be properly analysed as follows: the Water Industry

---

[27] See generally, *McGregor on Damages* (16th edn) 965–71 and 972–4.
[28] Such as *Lopez Ostra v Spain* (1994) 20 EHRR 277 cited in the first *Marcic* decision in relation to liability.
[29] [2002] QB 929, paras [62]–[65].

Act 1991 must be read subject to the provisions of the 1998 Act which is a later enactment. If the 1991 Act cannot be read subject to the provisions of the 1998 Act, the provisions of the Water Industry Act must yield to the Human Rights Act in terms of the common law rule that a later act of Parliament overrides an earlier Act.[30] Section 6(1) of the 1998 Act places the defendant under a duty to act in a manner that is compatible with the claimant's Convention rights, including Article 8 and Article 1 of the First Protocol. If the defendant breaches the duty in s 6(1) of the 1998 Act, the court is entitled to award the claimant damages in terms of s 8 of the that Act. Note that the Water Industry Act 1991 is being interpreted in a manner, in the first instance, that is compatible *with the Human Rights Act 1998*, and the remedies provided by it, as opposed to those provided by the Convention.[31]

Turning to s 3(1) of the 1998 Act itself, the analysis would begin as follows: the Water Industry Act 1991 must be read, where possible, in a manner which is compatible with Convention rights. In terms of the Water Industry Act, properly interpreted, the defendant is under a statutory duty not to act in a manner that is incompatible with the claimant's Convention rights. The analysis therefore remains within the boundaries of the Water Industry Act 1991, although s 3(1) of the 1998 Act has a role to play in redefining those boundaries by reference to Convention rights, such as Article 8 and Article 1 of the First Protocol.

The difficulty is that, given the focus on the Water Industry Act 1991, any remedy in respect of the breach of Article 8 and Article 1 of the First Protocol would be subject to s 18(8). Section 18(8) would of course be subject to attack on the basis that it was incompatible with the right of access to the courts guaranteed by Article 6.[32] A declaration of incompatibility would, however, have been of little use to the claimant in the *Marcic* case, whose main complaint was that he had suffered financial loss as a result of the breach of his Convention rights.

4. CONCLUSION: THE ABSENCE OF ARTICLE 13—WHAT EFFECT THE 'IRREMOVABLE SPECTACLES'?

A more fundamental shortcoming of s 3(1), which operates even in the absence of an exclusionary clause, relates to the Convention rights to

---

[30] See F Bennion, *Statutory Interpretation* (2002), 155–61.

[31] The existence of the remedies under the 1998 Act is of course premised on a breach of Convention rights.

[32] This would appear to have been a possible outcome in the *Marcic* case were it not for the fact that s 18(8) was not held to preclude remedies under the 1998 Act: see para [65].

which s 3(1) would direct a court. In this regard it is significant that Article13 is not included in Sch 1 to the 1998 Act and is not therefore referable via s 3(1).

Article 13 declares: 'Everyone whose rights and freedoms as set forth in this Convention are violated shall have an effective remedy before a national authority notwithstanding that the violation has been committed by persons acting in an official capacity.'[33] Article 13 is not a free-standing right. It feeds off the other Convention rights and is only brought into play when there is an arguable case that one of those other Convention rights has been violated.[34] It can be contrasted with Article 6(1), which is included in Sch 1, which applies to disputes about civil rights and obligations and criminal charges rather than Convention rights.[35]

In the debates preceding the enactment of the 1998 Act, the Lord Chancellor made the following comments regarding the omission of Article 13: 'The Courts would be bound to ask themselves what was intended beyond the existing scheme of remedies set out in the Bill. It might lead them to fashion remedies other than the Clause 8 remedies, which we regard as sufficient and clear.'[36] Whilst it is doubtful whether these statements could be given the full *Pepper v Hart* treatment, they do support an argument that the intentional exclusion of Article 13 indicates that any awards of damages granted *under the 1998 Act* are confined to s 8. Article 13 may be used to interpret s 8, a source of remedy, consistently with the Convention.[37] However, Article 13, not being a Convention right listed in Sch 1, may not itself be the source of a remedy or allow the creation of a remedy in a domestic court, at least where reliance is placed on s 3(1) of the 1998 Act. Rather, it would extend the liability for acts performed pursuant to legislation, where the legislation itself provides a remedy in respect of those acts, as the Water Industry Act 1991 in the *Marcic* case would have, but for s 18(8).

As far as s 6 is concerned, in so far as it governs the acts of the *courts*, the comments regarding s 3 and Article 13 apply with as much force, which gives rise to a difficulty. The requirements of s 6 mean that the process of relying on non-constitutional statutes or the common law will necessarily

---

[33] For discussion of Article 13, see Clayton and Tomlinson above n 26, 1471–8.

[34] See *Silver v UK* (1983) 5 EHRR 347, para [113].

[35] See S Grosz, J Beatson, and P Duffy, *Human Rights: The 1998 Act and the European Convention* (2000) 220. Moreover, the European Commission on Human Rights has taken the view that Article 13 does not guarantee a remedy in connection with a violation of Article 6 (*Pizetti v Italy* (1993) Series A No 257–C).

[36] HL Deb, 18 November 1997, col 472. The Lord Chancellor seems to have indicated in later remarks that the courts could have regard to Article 13 when interpreting s 8: '. . . the courts may have regard to article 13. In particular, they may wish to do so when considering the very ample provisions of clause 8(1).' (HL Deb, 18 November 1997, col 475.)

[37] In terms of the common law: see Beloff and Mountfield, above n 5.

involve the interpretation of Convention rights.[38] In this regard, s 6, as it applies to the courts, has had the effect of making the Convention rights like a pair of spectacles through which lawyers are required to view all legal rules, statutory and common law. Importantly, like prescription spectacles, s 6 has a corrective effect, allowing repugnant laws to be seen for what they are, thereby facilitating the judges' efforts in ensuring that all laws march in step with the Convention.

However, the difficulty is that s 6 is deficient because it does not allow the courts to 'view' statute and common law 'through' Article 13, thereby allowing the courts to supplement the law with new remedies. Any argument which advances the proposition that where there is a right the courts must create a remedy loses much force because Parliament has chosen to exclude expressly the one right which points most directly to the requirement that new remedies be created.[39] Instead, the courts will need to look to existing remedies and develop them accordingly. This approach is consistent with the approach taken in *Campbell v MGN*,[40] a case involving a consideration of the role of s 6(1) and Article 8 in determining the bounds of a cause of action for breach of confidence. In the *Campbell* case the award of £3,500 (£1,000 of which was in respect of aggravated damages) was made both for breach of confidentiality (the law being developed or inter-

---

[38] Given the development of the common law by the Court of Appeal in the *Marcic* case to produce a result similar to that arrived at by the trial judge relying on the Human Rights Act 1998, it is disappointing that the Court chose not to grapple with Convention right arguments at the 'common law' stage of their judgment. Instead by holding that the claimant's success in his common law claim meant that the question of relief under the 1998 Act did not need to be considered, the Court of Appeal in the *Marcic* case would appear to have endorsed a principle of constitutional practice which holds that a constitutional enactment should only be relied on as a last resort and that, where possible, a dispute should be resolved without recourse to that enactment: see *S v Mhlungu and ors* 1996 (3) SA 867 (CC). Kentridge AJ writing for a minority of the South African Constitutional Court remarked: 'I would lay it down as a general principle that where it is possible to decide any case, civil or criminal, without reaching a constitutional issue that is the course which must be followed.'(para 59). The majority did not disagree with him on this point. In the light of s 6 of the 1998 Act and similar provisions in other constitutional enactments, such as s 39(1) of the South African Constitution 1996, the principle can perhaps be better expressed as follows: where it is possible to decide a case without placing *direct* reliance on a constitutional enactment, that is the course to follow. (See A Henderson, 'Restoring Law and Order', unpublished PhD thesis, University of Cambridge, 1999, chapter 8.)

[39] Although s 2 of the 1998 Act requires the courts to take into consideration, amongst others, 'any' judgment of the European Court of Human Rights including those judgments dealing with Article 13, the focus of the 'determination' under s 2 remains the 'Convention rights, ie those rights in Sch 1 of the 1998 Act, cf Grosz, Beatson, and Duffy, above n 35. The case law governing Article 13 may therefore have an indirect effect (see Clayton and Tomlinson, above n 33, 1471). However it would be difficult to assert that reference to Article 13 case law permitted the creation of a remedy for breach of a Convention right. Moreover, as Grosz, Beatson, and Duffy appear to suggest (at 5), this may be of more relevance in the area of public law remedies. Finally, as mentioned above, Article 6(1) is an inappropriate alternative candidate for the creation of a remedy for breach of a Convention right.

[40] The Times, 29 March 2002. The decision was reversed in the Court of Appeal (The Times, 16 October 2002) but the issue of measure of damages was not dealt with.

preted compatibly with Article 8 of the Convention) and under the Data Protection Act 1998.

As many of the papers presented show, the common law has often advanced at a rapid pace without the need for recourse to Convention rights. It may now be the case that the mere fact that Parliament has chosen to give further effect to Convention rights means that higher standards are generally expected of the acts of public authorities and therefore the courts may be more willing to fashion remedies to keep government in check.[41] In the private law realm, however, practice would tend to suggest that the effects of the 1998 Act may not be so easily felt. Sight must not be lost of the fact that the common law has created the mechanisms for the protection of a vast array of private law rights and interests without recourse to the Convention.[42] So far, the Convention has gently nudged the courts in the direction of developing existing common law remedies. This, it is submitted, is the better course than the wholesale import of fresh remedies, or perhaps more accurately, novel principles of determining the type and extent of remedy. Leaving the courts to develop the familiar should have the effect of vindicating the new.

---

[41] Lord Mackay may have had this in mind in *Kuddus v Chief Constable of Leicestershire* [2002] 2 AC 122 when he commented (para [36]): 'Many statutory duties have been created and the Human Rights Act 1998 has been enacted which gives rise to claims of damages the principles of which may well affect the propriety of and the necessity for a power to award exemplary damages to be continued to be recognised in the law of England.' However, in the absence of argument on this point and in the light of Law Commission recommendations to the contrary, his Lordship did not develop the contents of these comments.

[42] See *Clerk and Lindsell on Torts* (18th edn) 14–23 for a list of the various private law interests protected by the law of tort, which the authors divide into personal interests, property interests, and economic interests. See also Mulcahy, *Human Rights and Civil Practice* (2000), 131–5 where she discusses 'common law constitutional rights' and Baker, *The Human Rights Act 1998: A Practitioner's Guide* (1998) 4–7 for a discussion of 'English law human rights'.

21

Private Law Remedies and the
Human Rights Act 1998: Review of Discussion

There was a wide-ranging discussion of the question whether s 6 of the Human Rights Act 1998 was capable of creating an independent cause of action. It was accepted that the decision of the Court of Appeal in the *Marcic* case[1] had not resolved this issue. In particular, to the extent that there was a cause of action under the 1998 Act against the defendant (as opposed to a common law claim for nuisance), this was because the defendant was undoubtedly a public authority. It could therefore have been liable for breach of statutory duty for its infringement of the claimant's Convention rights under Article 8 and Article 1, Protocol 1. Nick Bamforth argued that, to the extent that the first instance decision went any further than this, it should be seen as wrong. In the context of a claim against a private body, he reiterated his view that s 6 did not create any independent cause of action, but that it may be relied upon in the interpretation and 'development' of existing common law claims. It was in this context that the discussion was particularly wide-ranging.

Reference was made to the recent paper from the Law Commission, *Damages Under the Human Rights Act 1998*, Law Com No 266. Nick Bamforth pointed out that in the parliamentary debates which preceded the 1998 Act, the Lord Chancellor made it clear that s 7 in particular was not intended to affect the current law relating to the availability of damages and judicial review. As far as the Law Commission paper was concerned, he pointed out that it was really concerned with claims against public authorities where there is an underlying existing cause of action available in the form of breach of statutory duty. It was conspicuously non-committal so far as claims against private bodies are concerned.

It was then considered whether there is a role for the 1998 Act in circumstances where the common law provides a cause of action, but it may be argued that the remedy is in some way 'defective' (a situation analogous to that in *Ruxley v Forsyth*[2] was put forward as a possible example). In response, it was suggested that the recent developments in cases such as *Ruxley* and *Blake*,[3] which had been the subject of earlier sessions, allowed one to conclude that the current law as to remedies was not 'defective' so as to require recourse to the 1998 Act. To the extent that there were any failings, eg in awarding damages for future wrongs (considered

---

[1] [2002] QB 929.   [2] [1996] AC 344. See above Chapters 1 and 2.
[3] [2001] 1 AC 268. See above Chapters 10 and 11.

in the *Marcic (No 2)* case)[4] the solution might be found in adapting existing remedies (eg allowing common law damages to be awarded in respect of future wrongs without needing to resort to equitable damages in lieu of an injunction).

There was some brief discussion about the definition of a 'public authority'. It was pointed out that s 6 of the 1998 Act draws a distinction between a 'fully public authority' (eg central government departments, the police) whose every actions are subject to the 1998 Act and 'quasi public authorities' (possibly eg Railtrack) where it is necessary to draw a distinction between their public and private law functions. However, as far as 'public authority' itself is concerned, it was noted that no settled answer had yet been given by the courts—some had been content to rely on the definition applied in the context of judicial review proceedings, whereas others had implied that a wider meaning might be appropriate. It was felt that this issue would not be fully resolved until a decision of the House of Lords.

The session closed by considering the decision in *Wilson*[5] and conducting a survey of the practitioner audience to establish whether the 1998 Act might have any wider effect in the field of contract and commercial law generally. In particular, the audience was asked to consider whether there might be any analogous circumstances to those encountered in the *Wilson* case, ie confiscation of contractual rights without any apparent coherent policy basis. The suggestions which were made from the floor included the following: (a) avoidance of security for unregistered charges: it was felt that there was a sound policy basis for this requirement so that it was unlikely to fall foul of the 1998 Act; (b) unenforceable guarantees under the Statute of Frauds 1677; (c) the effect of illegality on the enforcement of legal or equitable rights; and (d) the void effect of transactions in contravention of s 151 of the Companies Act 1985.

---

[4] [2002] QB 1003.   [5] [2002] QB 74.

22

Conflict of Laws and Commercial Remedies

ADRIAN BRIGGS[1]

An examination of the private international law of commercial remedies may be thought to present little more than a problem of organization or of deciding where, if anywhere, dividing lines are to be drawn. To begin with, there can be no real analysis of remedies which does not first look at the choice of law rules for the various rights that give rise to them; and if one does that, one ends up looking at the whole of the commercial conflict of laws. The word limit for this paper, and the patience of a tolerant audience, will not allow for that. So let us start with what we know. At least as far as English law is concerned, the legal rules relating to remedies occupy a quiet backwater, where the dominant approach is simple and clear. Whether the remedy sought is interim or final, an English court applies its own law to define and describe the limits of the remedies which it will grant. This was, and probably is, seen to follow from the proposition that whereas legal rights are substantive, and substantive issues are governed by the *lex contractus*, or the *lex delicti*, or by the law with which the obligation to make amends or restitution has its closest and most significant connection, or by the *lex situs*, the nature of the remedies which can be had, and the availability of those remedies in the particular case, raises a procedural question. And procedural issues are governed by the *lex fori*. So if the contract is governed by German law, it will still (on this view)[2] be English law which decides whether a decree of specific performance, or an order that the defendant deliver alternative goods, or deliver to a different destination, and so on, will be granted. If a tort is governed by French law, though French law will determine which heads of damage are recoverable[3] in principle (for the definition of the heads of damage is in its very nature part of the definition of the duty placed on the tortfeasor by the *lex delicti*), English law will quantify them; English law will decide whether they should be fixed or provisional, ordered to be paid in a lump sum or

---

[1] Fellow and Tutor in Law, St Edmund Hall, Oxford; Barrister, Blackstone Chambers, Temple.

[2] This is without reference to the proposition that Article 10 of the Rome Convention on the Law Applicable to Contractual Obligations (Contracts (Applicable Law) Act 1990, Sch 1) has affected this rule.

[3] *Boys v Chaplin* [1971] AC 356 established this basic distinction as a matter of the common law conflict of laws. It is unaffected by the Private International Law (Miscellaneous Provisions) Act 1995: see s 14. For a recent example of the view that the particular kind of loss which it is wrong to cause is part of the very definition of the duty of care in the first place, see *Fairchild v Glenhaven Funeral Services Ltd* [2002] 3 WLR 89, HL, especially in the speech of Lord Hoffmann.

in instalments, open to alteration if the loss turns out to be more or less than predicted, liable to deduction on account of social security or death benefits,[4] and so on. If a dispute arises between shareholders in a foreign company, the determination of rights and duties as between the parties will be a matter for the *lex contractus,* but the order which the court may make will be selected from the palette of English law.[5]

It is with this distinction, and the defensibility of it, that this paper is mainly concerned. In looking at it, it will be necessary to treat final remedies separately from interim remedies; and the conclusion may be that though it is inevitable that interim remedies are going to be governed by English law, the truth for final remedies is otherwise. It will also be appropriate to examine the puzzling role of equity in private international law; for the operation of equity sometimes seems to involve jurisdiction and remedy, but with no intervening component of substance.

Even so, if the thumbnail sketch in the opening paragraph represented the general approach of the common law, it is clear that it is no longer a sufficient headnote to the condition of English private international law in the twenty-first century. Legislation and scholarly consideration have each contributed to a reworking of some at least of the old assumptions. And some of the thinking can at first sight appear to be quite radical. To give a taste of it, one argument can be mentioned at the outset.[6] It proposes that the law which governs the remedial consequences of a violated right should be neither the *lex fori* (as English law may suggest it is) nor the *lex causae* (as a reformed view of English law may suggest it should be). Instead there should be developed a new and independent choice of law rule, owing little to the law which determined whether there was a right to relief. This choice of law would place its principal focus on the law of the place where the order will have its effect, which will often, though not invariably, be where the claimant is resident, or (in a commercial context) carries on business. The devil may lie in the detail, but the thinking behind this is that the remedy is meant to be most perfectly coherent, and what makes it so is to blend it into the landscape of the law of the place where it will take its effect. That is the best way to compensate the claimant or ameliorate the harm done when a right is violated. Often, it will be possible to say that the claimant's roots are in a particular society, and it is by reference to this—the expectations it makes, the levels of service it provides

---

[4] *Roerig v Valiant Trawlers Ltd* [2002] 1 WLR 2304, CA.

[5] This must be the conclusion from *Re Harrods (Buenos Aires) Ltd* [1992] Ch 72, CA, where it was accepted, apparently, that the English court (if it heard the case) would apply only English remedies to a proven claim of shareholder oppression, and that an Argentine court (if the case were stayed) would apply only remedies available as a matter of Argentine law.

[6] The doctoral thesis of Olivera Boskovic, of the University of Paris I (Sorbonne), to be published in the course of 2003 (LGDJ, Paris), deals with the analysis from the perspectives of French and common law systems, and inspires this part of the paper.

and does not provide—that compensation is most rationally assessed. Or to put it another way, the quantification of what must be paid to right the wrong is best calibrated by reference to the law of the society in which the victim has to live with the consequences of the wrongful act. In his Reply to this paper (Chapter 23 below), Mr Reed draws attention to the seeming injustice of awarding to the claimant in *Holmes v Bangladesh Biman Corp*[7] damages assessed in the Bangladeshi measure, and proposes that it would be more appropriate to award damages assessed on the basis of English law. He is right to do so, but the conclusion which one may more naturally draw is that this results from the fact that the claimant was an English resident, and not that English law was the *lex fori*.

Though such a change may not have instant appeal, it is cautionary to see how much of a difference this would and would not make to the state of English law. At present, English law draws a distinction which is located in roughly this place, between the law which determines whether there is a right to ground an order for relief, and the law which determines what, or how much, that relief is: it says that the second of these is governed by the *lex fori*. All this proposed alternative would do is to ask whether (for example) the computation of damages would not better be done by reference to the law of the place where the order is supposed to be effective, such as where the victim is supposed to be or to return to with the compensatory payment. Once one asks that question, the issue becomes more provocative. If English law already draws a distinction, or several distinctions, between right and remedy, it is not as novel as it first seems to ask whether that distinction could not be utilized in conjunction with different choice of law rules.

Though this may make some sense in particular in personal injury cases, it is less certain that it can be successfully generalized far beyond that territory; and it still supposes that a distinction for choice of law between right and remedy is defensible. Even so, it teaches a substantial lesson: that when looking for the appropriate law to govern remedies, there is much to be said for the view that there is a genuine choice of law to be made, and that the exclusive claim of English law to specify the remedies, and all the circumstances of their availability, is not self-evidently correct. It seems likely that the persistence of the *lex fori* in this area is a relic of an earlier time when much more of the conflict of laws was sorted out by recourse to the *lex fori*, and this part of it has remained behind as one of the last bastions. But it is generally accepted that the role of the *lex fori* in private international law is one which calls for careful scrutiny and painstaking justification. It may be disputed whether commercial litigants forum shop with an eye on final remedies (they may well do so with a thought to

---

[7] [1989] AC 1112.

interim remedies, though). But if they do, they should not be encouraged in their misbehaviour by primitive choice of law rules. If there is a better rule out there, it would be good to introduce it. A further incentive for this reconsideration may be seen in recent legislation, but also in a general awareness that to apply a rigid choice for English law when looking at remedies is not always appropriate even where it is tenable, and may not even be tenable at all.

So far as concerns interim remedies, it is as well to say a little now, and more later. In this area, the technique of the conflict of laws has been to concern itself with whether there is jurisdiction over the respondent to allow the making of the order, and then to make it or not in accordance with English rules. It follows that there is no power to order remedies not found in the English lexicon, but it is no formal bar to the making of orders against defendants, even if the trial will not take place in England. Though once upon a time such relief would not be granted if the trial were not taking place in England, all such limitations have in practice been removed by Orders made under Civil Jurisdiction and Judgments Act 1982, s 25. So an English court can order interim relief in aid of proceedings which will not take place in England, and the only formal limitation on its power is to ask whether the fact that the trial may not take place in England renders it inexpedient for the order to be made. More will be said about this later.

But for final remedies, the usual approach has been to consider that these are procedural, with the result that an English court cannot grant a remedy unknown to its own domestic law; cannot grant a remedy which it does have, such as specific performance, in circumstances where it would not be granted in a purely English case; cannot receive (because it would be irrelevant) evidence of how damages would be calculated in the courts whose law governs the substance of the case, and so forth.

The foundations of the rule, that procedure is a matter for the *lex fori,* is perhaps rather creaky.[8] It has been successively cut back by bold and clear-minded judicial endeavour within the law of remedies and beyond. For example, since 1975 judgments are no longer required to be given in sterling.[9] For another, entities of a kind which lack legal personality as a matter of English law have been allowed to sue in English courts.[10] The judges have been prepared, if not always then at least to a significant extent, to reconsider whether a provision of English law, muscling in as

---

[8] Ever since WW Cook, *The Logical and Legal Bases of the Conflict of Laws* (1942), pointed out the potential for damage if the characterization of issues as procedural is not kept under tight restriction, the identification of an issue as a procedural one has raised warning flags.

[9] *Miliangos v George Frank (Textiles) Ltd* [1976] AC 443; *Services Europe Atlantique Sud v Stockholms Rederiaktiebolag Svea, The Despina R* [1979] AC 685.

[10] *Bumper Development Corp v Metropolitan Police Commissioner* [1991] 1 WLR 1362, CA. The more conservative approach taken in *Kamouh v Associated Electrical Industries International Ltd* [1980] QB 199 illustrates the scope for judicial appreciation in this area.

the rule governing a procedural issue, ought not be sidelined. Whether this is done by altering the internal English rule, or by re-analysing the issue in question as a substantive one, matters rather less than does achieving the result. The rule that an English court applies the English law of remedies is no more deeply rooted than the distinction between substance and procedure, and it could be reconsidered if a court wanted to.

Moreover, the Rome Convention on the Law Applicable to Contractual Obligations contains a rule, and a pretty clear hint, that the encroachment of the *lex fori*, as remedial law, onto the territory of the *lex contractus* should now be restricted as far as reasonably possible.[11] What, then, is to prevent an English court from re-opening the proposition that remedies are exclusively a matter for it? More precisely, what is wrong with the proposition that the remedy which a court grants should be that provided for by the law which governs the substantive rights in the case, the *lex causae*?

There are obvious limits, though. In an extreme case, an English court could not be expected to make an order of a kind wholly foreign to domestic English law. So the colourful proposition that an English court could not make an order against a father that he constitute a dowry on behalf of his daughter will still hold;[12] and (no doubt) more alluring examples could be found. On the other hand, the extensive, even astonishing, powers of contractual variation and rewriting, given to an Australian court by the Trade Practices Act 1974, would be more novel, and perhaps too difficult, for application by an English court.[13] But orders of specific performance could conceivably be made in circumstances where English domestic law would not have considered it appropriate to grant such a remedy; damages could be ordered by reference to calculations and methods not part of English domestic law; applications for alteration to the quantum or other conditions of damages could be entertained even though there would be no right of return to court if the case were wholly English.[14] And so on.

Why would this not be the right thing to do? Doctrinal objections can be put on one side as unilluminating: the search is surely for the choice of law rule which best achieves the purposes of the conflict of laws. Rigid or historical classifications and rules on choice of law should not be preserved for reasons of doctrine, but because they work to produce the best possible answer. In a perspicacious commentary on the doctrine of characterization, Mance LJ has made it crystal clear that the rules are the servants of

---

[11] Contracts (Applicable Law) Act 1990, Sch 1, Art 10. See also Giuliano and Lagarde [1980] OJ C282/1 at 33.

[12] *Phrantzes v Argenti* [1960] 2 QB 19.

[13] All the more arguably so, given the real difficulty in controlling their exercise by appeal or review (at least without an increase in powers of judicial creativity).

[14] Though for jurisdictional aspects of this, see *Henderson v Jaouen* [2002] 1 WLR 2971, CA.

justice, and not the other way round. He accepted, with apparent calm, that a re-evaluation of traditional approaches to characterization would not necessarily be out of place in his court.[15]

Nor is there a need to justify the application of the *lex fori* as being less bad than the unknown alternative: this would be to follow the example of the child whose holding onto nurse was for fear of finding something worse.[16] If remedies were left to be governed by the *lex causae*, there would still be room for public policy, which would be needed but which would be available, to serve as a last resort to save a court from having to do that which it simply cannot countenance. There is no shortage of precedent for this shift from a choice of rule which institutionally selected the *lex fori* to one which allowed a foreign *lex causae* to govern, with public policy serving to guard against trouble. Limitation of actions,[17] and choice of law in tort,[18] have both moved from being issues where the *lex fori* applied in all its untrammelled glory, to issues where a foreign law may be applied subject to a defence of public policy when this seems just too much to bear. It has been done before, and it could be done again.

Is it necessary to wait until Parliament acts? Is it possible to remove the separate classification of remedies as procedural? Unless statute prevents it (and it does not), it is submitted that there is no need to do so; and it is the failure to do so which risks incoherence in adjudication and the threat of real difficulty. To the extent that statute has touched on the matter, there should be no insuperable problem. In relation to tort, the Private International Law (Miscellaneous Provisions) Act 1995 has been interpreted as leaving intact the rule that the availability of remedies and the content of same is governed by English law.[19] But the Court of Appeal in the case in question did not say, at least in terms, that the 1995 Act freezes the law in ice. It ought to be open to a court to conclude that the availability of remedies is a matter for the *lex delicti*, at least unless it is contrary to English public policy to implement this view in the individual case. In the context of contract claims, the encouragement from Article 10 of the Rome Convention is to see that the consequences of breach in general, and the assessment of damages in particular, are for the *lex contractus*. No reported case has yet had to grapple with what this actually means, but it appears to say that where a contract claim is governed by the Rome Convention, the *lex contractus* will apply as extensively as possible to the consequences of breach in general and the rules of law which govern the assessment of damages in particular. This is significant, for the Rome Convention is not

---

[15] *Raiffeisen Zentralbank Oesterreich AG v Five Star General Trading LLC* [2001] QB 825, CA, at [27].

[16] H Belloc, *Cautionary Tales.*   [17] Foreign Limitation Periods Act 1984.

[18] Private International Law (Miscellaneous Provisions) Act 1995, Pt III.

[19] *Roerig v Valiant Trawlers Ltd* [2002] 1 WLR 2304, CA.

limited to cases in which the *lex contractus* is the law of a member state of the EU: it applies whatever the applicable law, and applies its view that the *lex contractus* should apply to the extent possible to domestic laws from China to Peru.[20] If that is true in relation to contracts, it is difficult to see any rational reason to take a different approach (albeit that the source of the legal rule may be different) in relation to other forms of obligation.

The proposition that the courts cannot just do this themselves has looked pretty lame ever since the ancient rule that damages were awarded only in sterling was seen off by the House of Lords, which saw that dogmatic adherence to such a rule had become a bar to the proper functioning of the commercial courts. Moreover, the recent experience of the High Court of Australia has been that the reservation of the law of remedies to the *lex fori* under the guise of their rules which apply to procedural issues has to change. The Australian approach to statutory limitations and caps on damages in certain cases of personal injury was once[21] to see these as procedural issues, governed by the *lex fori*. But conscious of the distortion which would be brought about by having a foreign law determine existence and scope of liability, while the *lex fori* dealt with the assessment of damages, the High Court simply held that all rules dealing with quantum and limits on damages were to be seen as dealing with substantive issues, and were to be applied as part of the *lex causae*.[22] Though the High Court did later threaten to resile from the purity of this analysis,[23] it remains a shining light to those who would see the intrusion of the *lex fori* into the law of remedies as something which should not be encouraged any more than is strictly necessary.

This, then, is the thesis: that there should be no line which separates right from remedy in the conflict of laws, or, to put it another way, the remedial rules of the *lex causae* should apply in an English court unless it would be contrary to public policy to do so, at which point the nearest English equivalent should apply instead. To the argument that it is dangerous for an English court to be set free to fashion remedies invented by foreign laws, one need only say that the claim of the *lex causae* to be applied does not obviously stop once rights have been ascertained. To the proposition that an English court simply lacks the mechanism for making such orders, one answer would be that if the parties have contracted for a specific form of remedy, this could be decreed for specific performance. Under this umbrella, or with this mechanism, it may well be possible to order acts to be performed as if they had been promised to be done. Where they are the remedies specified by the *lex causae*, this will either be true or

---

[20] Article 2.   [21] *Stevens v Head* (1993) 176 CLR 433.
[22] *John Pfeiffer Pty Ltd v Rogerson* (2000) 203 CLR 503.
[23] *Regie Nationale des Usines Renault SA v Zhang* (2002) 187 ALR 1.

will be analogous to true. And the elimination of the line which separates right from remedy would have the advantage of negating the exercise in characterization which the existence of such a line requires to be undertaken.

It would also have the advantage of avoiding a much more difficult issue which may arise when proceedings are brought against a fraudster or someone who has dishonestly associated himself with a fraudster's scheme, and has been found liable as a result. One of several questions which may arise will be whether D can be held to be a constructive trustee of specific or unspecific assets which are now in his ownership. So far as can be seen, this is a difficult question within English domestic law, which has caused the judiciary to expend a lot of effort in trying to reconcile doctrinal purity with a desire to make effective orders. It has also drawn commentators to take up positions of extreme dogmatism, in an attempt to answer it.[24] The editors of Dicey and Morris[25] observe all this with suppressed alarm;[26] their attempt to deal with what might be mis-called 'choice of law for constructive trusts' is singularly unconvincing. It cannot be good for the rational development of the law for there to be, in here as well, a need to separate right from remedy as a precursor to the application of two or more distinct choice of law rules. Quite apart from the fact that the result of applying two rules to (what are held to be) two issues may be to produce a weird inconsistency of result, or (which is probably worse) to trigger an incidental question, it will almost certainly increase the chances of producing a result which no individual system of national law would have reached on its own. Now this is not conclusive proof that the system has let us down: in a case with significant international components to it, it may be small surprise that the solution is not drawn in its entirety from one as opposed to other systems of domestic law. But in this area, where the distinction between right and remedy, or between proprietary right and proprietary remedy, will not be identical across the systems of law, no good is done by applying one law to the right, and another to the remedy, where the underlying domestic laws are not in perfect harmony.

A related example of the problem may be seen when it is alleged that equitable liability lies on the defendant. There is a curious line of authority, discussed below,[27] to the effect that when a case would (if wholly domestic) be wholly governed by equitable principles (as distinct from a case where equity simply lends its remedies in support of a legal right), the

[24] There is just too much of it to make a rational selection.

[25] *The Conflict of Laws* (13th edn, 2000).

[26] The statement in para 34-028 that 'difficult questions may arise' is a significant understatement.

[27] But not predominantly English.

lex fori will apply all by itself. Australian cases have come to that conclusion: the recent and considered view of the authorities taken by the Full Court of the Federal Court[28] was that where fiduciary duties were concerned, an Australian court applied Australian law by itself, though taking some notice of other potentially relevant laws to the extent necessary to decide whether there was unconscionable conduct or not. The justification for this appears to be the view that equity has a system of remedies, which applies to anyone properly brought before the court, and that as remedies are a matter for the *lex fori*, Australian equity will apply as the chosen law. Nor is the position one which only Australian courts have adopted. When dealing with an application for an anti-suit injunction otherwise than on the ground that there is a breach of contract in suing in the foreign court, an English court simply applies English equity (that is to say, it applies a test of whether the actions to be restrained were vexatious or oppressive by the standards of English law).[29] It does not ask which law governs the substance of the claim for an injunction, and only after this has led to the conclusion that the applicant has a right go on to determine the appropriate remedy. At first sight this is a questionable result, which may be reached because of fallacious reasoning. If there were no rule that remedies were governed by the *lex fori*, it would be necessary to think again.

To put the point another way, if there is to be an elimination of the doctrinal choice of law which separates right from remedy, there will need to be a clearer certainty that the choice of law rules for substantive rights are themselves in good shape. In the case of equitable claims and remedies, it is far from clear that this is so.

The law on anti-suit injunctions is worth a little more thought, especially in the light of the decision of the Lords in *Airbus Industrie GIE v Patel*,[30] which also shines light on the relevance of the distinction between interim and final remedies. In that case, an anti-suit injunction was sought to restrain individuals who were taking proceedings in the courts of United States, in (as it must be assumed) accordance with the law of the United States. Now had it been alleged that they were breaking a contract, such as a jurisdiction agreement, the first line in the analysis would have been to identify the governing law of the contract, so as to see by reference to this whether the conduct was unlawful; if so, a question of remedy would then have arisen. If it were alleged that they were about to commit a tort, so that an injunction should be granted *quia timet*, it is reasonable to suppose that a choice of law rule would have been applied by reference to which to

---

[28] *Paramasivam v Flynn* (1998–9) 160 ALR 203, 214–18. Though there was a contradictory view from Tipping J in the New Zealand Court of Appeal in *Her Majesty's A-G for England and Wales v R* [2002] 2 NZLR 91, NZCA (29 November, 2001), at [28]–[30].
[29] *Airbus Industrie GIE v Patel* [1999] 1 AC 119.   [30] ibid.

decide if there was a tort which ought to be restrained. But where it is alleged that the nature of the wrong is that it is an inequitable act, conduct which is oppressive or vexatious or unconscionable, there is no reference to any law other than English equity to assess the foundation for the remedy.

But the solution adopted by Lord Goff of Chieveley was a revelation. He was well aware that it was inappropriate for an English court just to apply English law and equity without any consideration of the international dimension of the dispute. The response of a conflicts lawyer might have been to say that this was where a choice of law rule would be helpful: to point to the law to which reference needed to be made to identify the rightness or wrongness of the acts to be undertaken: some variant on the *lex loci delicti commissi* might have been expected.[31] But instead it was decided without public debate that English law, meaning English equity, was to be applied. Recognizing that this was inappropriate, and eschewing a choice of law solution, it was held that a connection was needed between England and the dispute before the order would be made. Not between English law and the dispute, but between England and the dispute.

This is apparently the way the English courts behave when it is submitted that English equity would recognize the cause of action and/or grant the remedy which the claimant is after. There is then apparently no question that a distinct choice of law is to be undertaken. When there is jurisdiction *in personam*, there is English equity, and that is that. In both instances, when equity is invoked, choice of law flies out of the window. Now while this may impose a proper limit on the application of English equity, it wholly fails to provide a mechanism for picking up and applying foreign law or foreign equity when the equivalent connection lies to that other country.

In Australia the courts have been open about it: in *Wimborne v National Commercial Bank*[32] and at first instance, at least, in *US Surgical Corp v Hospital Products International Pty Ltd*.[33] But even after twenty years to ponder the curious technique there, the Full Court of the Federal Court, in *Paramasivam v Flynn*,[34] came to the conclusion that the choice of law rule, if it is one, which conditions any argument for the application of equity was the *lex fori*. So for a very substantial area of rights and remedy, doctrine and discretion, the Australian *lex fori* applies by itself, with no other choice of law. The only reference to the foreignness in the story is to be found in the concession that if it is said to be inequitable to do *x*, and *x* was done in a for-

---

[31] A Briggs, 'The unrestrained reach of an anti-suit injunction: a pause for thought' [1997] LMCLQ 98.

[32] (1978) 5 BPR 11958 (NSW SC).

[33] [1982] 2 NSWLR 766, 797–8 (NSW SC); affd [1983] 2 NSWLR 157 (NSW CA); revd on different grounds (1984) 156 CLR 41.

[34] (1998–9) 160 ALR 203.

eign country, the law of that foreign country may be looked to to see whether it really was wrongful. In other words, the assessment of (un)conscionability takes some account of the argument that it was perfectly justifiable to act as was done where it was done; and that as a result it was not contrary to conscience for the respondent to be doing as he did. If this is all predicated on the proposition that equity is a remedial jurisdiction, and that remedies are determined by the *lex fori*, the rule has even more to answer for than it seemed. The tail is wagging a very large dog indeed.

Now in England, it is a fair bet that the Chancery Division spends a lot of its time dealing with chases for the proceeds of fraud. These may take the form of actions for the restitution of assets unjustly received; and suits for equitable relief against a fraudster, bribe-taker, constructive trustee, knowing receiver, dishonest assister, intermeddler, and the rest of the Chancery Division's rogues' gallery. What choice of law does a judge of the Chancery Division apply before he makes orders for such relief as *Snell*[35] allows? Less clearly than in Australia, perhaps, he still applies the *lex fori*. This was done in *Arab Monetary Fund v Hashim*,[36] and has been followed, so far as I can understand exactly what was done, in *Grupo Torras SA v Al Sabah*[37] and *Kuwait Oil Tanker SAK v Al Bader*.[38] Again, the only concession to foreign law is to look to it to see whether it would be inequitable to impose liability in all the circumstances. Admittedly there is a reference to foreignness, but not at the level of an organized choice of law rule. Given the enormous width of equitable liabilities, it is rather surprising that there is no regular reference to a choice of law rule to explain why it is right to apply English law, in this sense, to regulate what is going on.[39]

If this is right, a substantial part of English law as it regulates one branch of commercial activity is substantially free of the constraints of choice of law. There is a rudimentary sense of sufficiency of connection: a high level being required for an anti-suit injunction; virtually none for other forms of equitable relief. But there is no choice of law. It is not as if the judges who have come up with this did not have the mental acuity to see that there may have been something odd in what they were doing; and I suspect that the rule that remedies are for the *lex fori* has a lot to do with it, and therefore a lot to answer for. Where a court is being asked to grant a final remedy, it should derive this, in the first instance and in principle, from the *lex causae*. Where the claim is based on what may look (as a matter of domestic law) as equitable liability, *this lex causae* should not be English law.

---

[35] Snell's Equity (13th edn, 2000).　　　　[36] The Times, 11 October 1994.
[37] [2001] CLC 221, CA.　　　　　　　　　　[38] [2000] 2 All ER (Comm) 271, CA.
[39] A brilliant Oxford doctoral thesis by TM Yeo, now in the course of being prepared for publication, investigates the broader question of choice of law in relation to equitable claims and doctrines; it will be the first serious treatment of this most important topic in the common law legal system.

If it is possible to argue that the conflict of laws should now accept that final remedies ought to be defined and made available in accordance with the *lex causae*, and not by the *lex fori*, this will be motivated by the perception that the division is itself irrational and counter-productive: the imperative for consistency of reasoning and result ought to dictate this solution. All that is required is some confidence in the strength of substantive choice of law rules, and a preparedness to use the doctrine of public policy to protect the court from having to make unpalatable choices.

Turning now to look at interim remedies, it will be recalled that this is an area where English law also prevails; and that the approach to choice of law is that there is no approach to choice of law. Rather, the general limitation on the application of English law on interim remedies is that these will not be granted if the fact that the trial will be taking place outside England makes it 'inexpedient' to make the order. Actually, as a technique of limitation, it is not so far removed from the approach of Lord Goff in *Airbus v Patel*:[40] English law (equity) on anti-suit injunctions will be applied if the connection with England is strong enough to make it do so; and not otherwise; English interim remedies may be obtained unless it is not expedient for the court to grant them.

But inexpedience is a difficult concept, for what may seem expedient to an English court asked to grant relief against an alleged fraudster may not be seen in quite the same light by a foreign court (perhaps that in which the trial will take place) with a different sense of security of property. In *Credit Suisse Fides Trust SA v Cuoghi*,[41] a freezing order and ancillary disclosure order was made against a defendant to proceedings before the Swiss courts, it being accepted that a Swiss court had no power, at least before final judgment, to make such an order itself. The reported attitude of the Court of Appeal was that as the defendant was domiciled in England, and as there was no reason to suppose that the Swiss court would resent the assistance of the English courts, the order would be made.

With respect to those who thought differently, both these suppositions leave room for doubt. As to the first, this depends on accepting in all its force the proposition that as a *Mareva* injunction operates *in personam*, the limiting factor is where the respondent is domiciled or resident: if in England he should expect to be subject to the unlimited power of the court; if not, then even if his assets may be here, he should not be made subject to the order, for the order does not operate *in rem*. At once this exposes the curiosity of the view that anything jurisdictional follows from the character of the order to be made. If a foreign court—say the Swiss court—will not be able to make any order of attachment or seizure, on the basis that

40 [1999] 1 AC 119.   41 [1998] QB 818, CA.

the assets are in London, the English court will doubtless reconsider the scope of what is expedient, and may be tempted to make the order whenever the respondent is resident in England or has assets here: these may be different expediencies, but each can be defended. As to the second, it was hard to see how the Swiss court could have manifested any objection it may have had to the English order purportedly made in support of its proceedings. Anti-suit injunctions are not part of the Swiss procedural armoury, after all; and it is hard to see what else it could have done. The present writer can clearly recall standing before an audience of Swiss lawyers in the University of Zürich, telling them how the English court had considered that the Swiss judges would be grateful for the assistance rendered by their English brethren. It is fair to say that their faces ranged from incomprehension to horror, as the Swiss legal guarantee of security and privacy of property was swept aside in the Strand.

It is unlikely that a letter of (un)request would have been a possible response. There was a suggestion that it could refuse an application to enforce the order in Switzerland. That is certainly true. But it does not deal with the possibility of enforcement outside Switzerland under the Lugano Convention or the Brussels Convention (or now Council Regulation (EC) 44/2001): the order is, after all, a judgment from an English court, and the effect of the order is not to be limited to Switzerland.

Indeed, there is more than a little to be said for the view that it does not 'assist' a foreign court to make orders, the power to make which has been withheld from it by its own legislator, and which will necessarily affect the balance between the parties. In another context, and where the boot was on the other foot, English courts have come to realize, perhaps rather late, that the control of the procedural balance is more complex than it had seemed. There was no law on the point prior to 1987. But in *South Carolina Insurance Co v Assutantie Maatschappij 'De Zeven Provincien' NV*,[42] an application was made to a court in the United States for oral and documentary discovery in connection with proceedings before the English courts. An attempt to restrain this procedure by injunction was unsuccessful, though perhaps only because the application had been cut back to documentary discovery only by the time the case was before the Lords. The House of Lords noted that there was no general limitation on the manner in which a party acquired its evidence, and that there was no reason to interfere. But Australian courts have taken a markedly more assertive view, regarding such applications as having the potential, at least, to upset and contradict the procedural balance established by Australian law.[43] More recently

---

[42] [1987] AC 24.

[43] *Allstate Life Insurance Co v ANZ Banking Group Ltd* (1996) 64 FLR 61 (Aust Fed Ct); *National Australia Bank v Idoport* [2002] NSWSC 623 (10 July 2002).

still, some English authority has been found for the same conclusion;[44] and a principle may be beginning to emerge.

If, as Lord Hobhouse observed in *Turner v Grovit*,[45] the basis for an anti-suit injunction is that it may be made to protect the jurisdiction of the English court, or to prevent a wrongful act, there is much to be said for the view that a claimant who interim-forum shops his way around the globe, accumulating individual remedies as he goes, may have a striking impact on the course of English litigation. No-one in his right mind denies that a well-timed application for certain forms of interim relief can apply excruciating pressure on an opponent, and to do this in more places than one may tip the scales in a very marked way, and to a degree which no individual system would have specified. It ought to be, perhaps, that there is a presumption that any of these applications, unless positively sought in advance by judicial request, should be restricted to the court seised of the substantive action, and obtained only as part of the procedural balance struck by that individual legal system. In the fullness of time this may come to be accepted as normal; at the moment, the sense of free-for-all is unwelcome and unexpected. The proposition[46] that the English court should recognize its subsidiarity and reflect only the orders made in the court seised of the substantive dispute is a step in the right direction, but one which still has the potential to allow the applicant to oppress the respondent.

Does it follow from this that the view proposed above in relation to final remedies ought also to apply to interim remedies? Would it be correct to say that, for example, in a claim alleging breach of contract in which the contract is governed by German law, the English court should be prepared to award and not award interim relief, provisional and protective remedies, and so on, in accordance with German law? It is clear that the answer is no.

For one thing, the question of what law will govern the substantive rights and liabilities may be in dispute, and will therefore remain uncertain until trial. That being so, the actual or supposed *lex causae* offers a poor or unreliable basis for the granting of remedies which have to precede this in point of time. Of course, if we move to a procedure in which the choice of law issue is determined at a preliminary stage, as the High Court of Australia seems to contemplate,[47] this objection will recede. But we have

---

[44] *Bankers' Trust International plc v PT Dharmala Sakti Sejahtera* [1996] CLC 252; *Omega Group Holdings Ltd v Kozeny* [2002] CLC 132; *Glencore International AG v MetroTrading International Inc* [2002] EWCA Civ 524; [2002] CLC 1090 (18 April 2002).

[45] In his speech on the staying of proceedings pending a reference to the Court of Justice of the European Communities: [2002] 1 WLR 104, HL.

[46] *Ryan v Friction Dynamics Ltd* The Times, 14 June 2000; *State of Brunei Darussalam v Bolkiah:* The Times, 5 September 2001.

[47] *Regie Nationale des Usines Renault SA v Zhang* (2002) 187 ALR 1, at [73]–[74].

not got there yet. For another, there is an integrity about English trial and trial procedure which makes it appear important that English law determine the remedies which can and cannot be obtained along the path leading up to a trial in an English court. It is an entirely different matter once the substantive issues have been tried and adjudicated, so that we now know what the parties' rights and liabilities are: the argument from or for consistency is that the final remedy should fit seamlessly with the adjudicated right; and this will suppose that the *lex causae* supply, as far as possible, the whole of the remedy which will be granted to vindicate the right. And if this is correct, it would support the argument that an anti-suit injunction (at least where the foundation for the claim is not that there is a legal right not to be sued) should be granted in accordance with *English* law, and not foreign law, as if it were an interim remedy, even when ordered in final form. For it is not a remedy which follows from the adjudication of the substantive claim but seeks, as if it were an interim or interlocutory order, to regulate the course of the trial which will take place, or which should be taking place, in England. Lord Goff of Chieveley was, as ever, spot on. Where the trial is to take place outside England, it may be (just as the common law supposed) that an English court should not grant interim remedies at all. But if that abstention is not to happen, and an English court is to grant interim remedies contained in English procedural law, there is a critical need to do so in a way which has no adverse effect on the balance which is struck between the parties by the procedural law of the court seised of the dispute. This, if it can be done at all, will be very difficult.

The argument is therefore this. One of the pervasive problems of the conflict of laws, which works on the basis of classification of issues and ascription of rules for choice of law, is that there are seams. Contractual defences to tort claims furnish one such; questions of title to goods and the tortious refusal to respect that title are another. Each time a claim touches on two of these categories, a question necessarily arises whether the two rules can be made to work harmoniously and to produce a coherent result. The problem of joined-up adjudication is always with us. Now in the usual course, these are problems which just have to be dealt with. Where an alleged tortfeasor pleads a contractual defence to the claim, there is still[48] no real alternative to looking to two systems of law and hoping that they dovetail. Where a seller is alleged to have failed to transmit title to goods, there may be no alternative to looking to the laws which governed the acquisition of title as well as those which governed the contract of sale. Life is complicated, and only a child would suppose that a single claim had always to be governed by a single law. But the coherence of results is

---

[48] Though there are other points of view; and French law would be a good source for them.

conducive to the doing of practical justice and where lines of demarcation, or of characterization, can be eliminated without substantial cost, it is good that they should be. The line which separates right from final remedy is one which could usefully be eliminated, with the result that the *lex causae* would prevail generally; and where equitable claims and doctrines are concerned, some serious thinking-through of choice of law and its importance is now overdue. The granting of interim remedies should be governed by English law (if the trial will take place in England), but applications should take a very clear lead from the law of the court in which the trial will be taking place, if this is not England, but an order is still to be made. The coherence which this may tend to produce will be preferable to the rather archaic, or disjointed, current state of the law on commercial remedies.

23

Conflict of Laws and Commercial Remedies: Comment

PHILIP REED[1]

1. FINAL REMEDIES

Any useful criticism of the rules distinguishing between substantive and procedural remedies issues must take account of the fact that distinctions between legal systems as to remedies, and particularly as to the quantum of general damages, the law of remoteness of damage, and the availability of disclosure are representative of deep-seated cultural divides between the differing societies that those systems regulate. How much should a person be entitled to recover for the loss of an arm, the loss of the right to bear a child, the loss of a parent, or the loss of a reputation? The answers which society gives in Southern California are very different from the answers given in Bangladesh. One example may serve to illustrate.

In August 1984, Mr Geoffrey Holmes of Croydon died when the aircraft carrying him on an internal flight between Chittagong and Dhaka in Bangladesh crashed on landing. Most countries including the United Kingdom and Bangladesh have retained the right to set the value of limits applicable under the Warsaw Convention 1929 in the case of their own internal flights. Mr Holmes' widow discovered to her horror that the sum she was entitled to recover in respect of her husband's death was limited to 39,500 Bangladeshi takas, or £913. The equivalent limit in the United Kingdom would have been just under £84,000. Mrs Holmes' inevitable response was to engage in forum shopping, and hers is an example we might all do well to remember when we use that term with a curled lip. Her case gave rise to some interesting law[2] but brought her only £913 and a considerable degree of distress. How does a practitioner explain to Mrs Holmes that the death of her husband is valued at £913? Intellectually, it is no easier to explain to an aviation insurer that premium income on a liability policy which anticipated exposure in respect of domestic services in Bangladesh to liability limited to Bangladeshi levels now has to pay for Western-style of damages.

We are dealing with deep-seated legal and cultural divides as to the remedies which ought to be made available in certain circumstances and tinkering with our conflict of laws rules may not provide a comprehensive

---

[1] Partner, Norton Rose.   [2] *Holmes v Bangladesh Biman Corp* [1989] AC 1112.

answer. With that in mind let us now turn to the solutions suggested by Adrian Briggs' thesis (see Chapter 22 above).

The first possibility is that we should adopt an independent conflict of laws rule which determines the remedies according to the place where they take effect. This cannot be viewed as an improvement. It raises the spectre of the *lex fori*, the *lex causae*, and law of the remedy being different. Proving one set of foreign law principles by expert evidence is costly enough. Proving a second set will add enormously to the expense with no discernible benefit. It also increases the difficulty for the practitioner in the forum to advise on the likely outcome and hence to settle the case.

The second possibility is that the whole of the law of remedies should be governed by the *lex causae*. This proposal has a certain formal elegance, but it is hard to identify a situation in which it represents a real improvement over the present case. It is clear, but no more so than the current rule. Nor is it any more likely to avoid injustice or the disappointment of expectation. Furthermore, it gives rise to its own distinct problems. For example, what do we mean by the *lex causae* in cases of *dépeçage*, the process by which different elements of a cause of action may be governed by different systems of law?[3] It is doubtful whether such a provision would really discourage forum shopping.

It may be the case that Article 10(1) of the Rome Convention gives English law a steer in the direction of the use of the *lex causae* for all remedies issues arising from breach of contract, but the language of the provision is obscure and it appears to allow a carve out for procedural rules of the *lex fori*.

2. INTERIM REMEDIES

Similar conclusions may be drawn about any changes to conflict of law rules relating to interim remedies. The principal interim remedies with which we are concerned are freezing injunctions and search and seizure orders, or orders for the early disclosure of documents. Once again, we encounter entrenched views from different legal cultures. Is the interim disclosure of documents a vital tool for the furtherance of the interests of justice, without which the court can never get to the truth, as a common lawyer might believe, or is it an unwarranted intrusion on constitutionally-guaranteed rights to property and privacy, as a civilian lawyer might have it? One can readily understand the horror graphically portrayed in the expressions of the Zürich lawyers whom Adrian Briggs describes, but

---

[3] eg, for tort claims, see the Private International Law (Miscellaneous Provisions) Act 1995, s 12(1).

the question of what we do about it is more difficult. An obvious possibility is, in a case such as *Credit Suisse Fides Trust SA v Cuoghi*,[4] for the English court to make its order subject to the approval of the court in which the substantive proceedings were being conducted. But the question then arises, how would that court exercise the 'discretion' purportedly conferred upon it in those circumstances? It would either do so according to domestic law principles, in which case, *ex hypothesi*, it would refuse to sanction the order in question, or it would have to do so on some broader but as yet undefined basis.

It is perhaps noticeable that the drafters of Article 24 of the Brussels Convention (now Article 31 of Council Regulation (EC) 44/2001) fought shy of including limitations on the protective measures which might be granted thereunder, despite knowing, as they must have, that they were required in effect to reconcile common law and civilian approaches in this area.

3. EQUITY

It is clear from Adrian Briggs' paper (Chapter 22 above) that our rules of conflict of laws, in so far as they relate to equitable liabilities and equitable remedies, are rudimentary when compared to their common law counterparts. This is a matter of concern. However, one might question whether it is right to ascribe the crudeness of approach that one sees in cases such as *Paramasivam v Flynn*[5] to the rule providing that the procedural issues of remedies are to be governed by the *lex fori*. Equity has always been much more focused on remedies than the common law. In this connection, equity is perhaps far more in tune with the preoccupations of the client and thus of the practitioner than the common law. Furthermore, conflict of law rules, or the absence of them, is not the only area in which equitable principles relating to liabilities are less thoroughly delineated in the case law than those relating to common law liabilities.

One suspects that the matter is complicated by the preponderance of cases dealing with fraud. Fraud is not something which encourages the development of sophisticated conflict of law rules in relation to liabilities. So far as one is aware, the dishonest abstraction of funds from somebody else's bank account is something which gives rise to civil liability in every mature legal system. There is simply no reason to take a conflict point. But the remedies available in respect of fraud vary widely and may indeed be more extensive and sophisticated in the Chancery Division than in other parts of the world. Here the suggestion that the selection of remedies

---

[4] [1998] QB 818, CA.   [5] (1998–9) 160 ALR 203.

should be governed exclusively by the *lex causae* gives rise to difficulties. If one imagines a case where the fraudster, the victim, and the proceeds were all in England, yet the fraud and its planning had taken place in Ruritania, one would be led to a position where the fraudster would argue for Ruritanian law as the *lex causae* not because it gave him any defence on liability but because, for example, Ruritania has no equivalent to equitable tracing and accordingly he could not properly be deprived of his ill-gotten gains. Such a submission is an unattractive one to make and its acceptance would give rise to the kind of absurdity which conflict of law rules ought to avoid.

24
Conflict of Laws and Commercial Remedies: Review of Discussion

The initial discussion focused on the choice of law for equitable causes of action and considered the three options put forward in Adrian Briggs' paper (Chapter 22): (1) the *lex fori*, either on the basis that equity should be seen as an adjunct of procedure, or because equity operates *in personam* on the conscience of the defendant and the *lex fori* should therefore apply whenever the court has *in personam* jurisdiction (the 'Australian model'); (2) a set of new choice of law rules created and adapted specifically for claims in equity; (3) fitting equitable claims into existing categories for choice of law purposes.

Although option (1) was not dismissed as entirely unarguable, none of those taking part in the discussion felt that it could be sustained as a rational approach. It was also suggested that, if option (1) did represent the current approach of the courts, they were somewhat inconsistent in its application (eg in *Macmillan Inc v Bishopsgate Investment Trust Plc (No 3)*[1] the claim made therein for a constructive trust was not simply characterized as a claim in equity and determined according to the *lex fori*). The principal reason for rejecting option (1), namely that it seemed inappropriate to import the distinction between common law and equity into the realm of private international law, also led to support for option (3) over option (2). A number of examples were given as to how this approach would work, eg the characterization of dishonest assistance in a breach of trust as a tort (as may have happened in *Grupo Torras SA v Al-Sabah (No 5)*[2] although there seemed some residual uncertainty about the precise solution adopted by the courts in that case). It was pointed out by Adrian Briggs that option (3) is the approach which has recently been advocated in a thesis by Dr TM Yeo which it is hoped will be published in the near future.

Although in broad agreement with option (3), it was pointed out by Adrian Briggs that, in some areas, it may still nonetheless be appropriate for the courts to consider developing free-standing choice of law rules for equitable claims, eg in claims for anti-suit injunctions. At present, the English courts apply English law to determine the availability of such an injunction, but only if England is the natural forum (*Airbus v Patel*).[3] This solution, however, did not allow for the situation where the English courts may have jurisdiction over an application without being the natural

---

[1] [1996] 1 WLR 387.   [2] [2001] Lloyd's Rep Bank 36, CA.   [3] [1999] 1 AC 119.

forum, but in circumstances where the conduct of the respondent would be regarded as (actionably) wrongful, or an injunction would have been awarded by a closely connected foreign law. It was suggested that this 'gap' could be filled by a choice of law rule which allowed such foreign law to be applied in the English courts.

The discussion then moved to the law applicable to final remedies. There was widespread support for the position advocated in Adrian Briggs' paper that remedies should so far as reasonably possible be governed by the *lex causae* of the underlying cause of action, subject to the overriding control of public policy. Some doubt was expressed as to the proper role of public policy in this regard, but there was support for the view that, if foreign law on remedies was in some way unacceptable, it was appropriate for the English courts to articulate their reasons why this was so.

The prospect of applying the law of the place where the order is to take effect provoked further discussion, with examples based on the case of *Holmes v Bangladesh*[4] (as noted in Philip Reed's comment in Chapter 23) and the recent case of *Lubbe v Cape Plc (No 2)*.[5] While it was recognised that, for example, damages probably should be assessed on the basis of the place where the recipient has to survive on them, it was less clear how this could be achieved: (1) by adapting the normal choice of law rule (eg as in *Boys v Chaplin*);[6] (2) by employing an additional choice of law rule, but in what circumstances?; or (3) by adapting the domestic law of the underlying *lex causae*.

The discussion in relation to interim remedies perhaps exposed the greatest division of opinion between the academic and practitioner participants. The view taken by some of the practitioners was that there are sufficient safeguards in the exercise of the English courts' discretion whether to grant interim relief in support of foreign proceedings. In response, Adrian Briggs maintained his view that this may not always be sufficient to ensure that an appropriate 'balance' is maintained in the litigation as a whole; the view formed by practitioners was in that sense perhaps a little too concerned with the position of just one of the litigants.

---

[4] [1989] AC 1112.   [5] [2000] 1 WLR 1545.   [6] [1971] AC 356.

Index

account of profits
  amount recoverable 114–16
  arbitration 108, 109–10
  availability 93, 101–12
  Blake case 93, 95–119, 126–7, 133
  breach of confidence 100–1
  breach of contract 93–119, 125–30, 133
  breach of fiduciary duty 101, 103, 105
  causation 117
  causes of action 98
  circumstances of case 101, 102, 106–8
  confidential information 106
  discretionary remedies 100, 102, 103, 115, 116, 125
  disgorgement 113, 116
  dishonesty 111
  election 118–19
  enforcement 113
  equitable compensation 100, 101
  intention 107–8, 111
  irrecoverable amounts 97, 113
  justice of the case 114, 116
  last resort 105
  legitimate interest 102, 105–6, 109, 111–12, 126
  limitations 116–17
  measure of recovery 112–17, 118
  mitigation of profits 116
  multi-party litigation 119
  profit defined 112–14
  remedial inadequacy 101, 102–5, 111, 125–6
  terminology 98–101, 129
  third party deductions 113
  trade marks 107
  unjust enrichment 98
accounting for loss 43, 46, 47
agreed remedies
  bargaining power 197–8, 204
  contracts 191–219
  damages *see* **liquidated damages**
  forfeiture *see* **relief from forfeiture**
  freedom of contract 192
  limitations 192–217
  loss of bargain 200, 201–2, 211
  payments, contingencies 203
  penalties *see* **penalty clauses**
  performance incentive 192
  reasons 191–2
  risk allocation 192, 199, 204

bad bargains 5, 8, 27, 221
bank accounts
  authorized signatories 149–50
  cheques wrongfully dishonoured 31
  overdrafts 183
  tracing 149, 150, 183–4
banks
  bailment 150
  costs of borrowing 77, 78
  lending *see* **loans**
  mistake 140–3
  negligent property valuation *see* **valuer's negligence**
bargains
  bad bargains 5, 8, 27, 221
  bargaining power 197–8, 204, 212, 222
  consumer contracts 198
  good bargains 4, 27
  liquidated damages 197
  mistake 160–1
  unconscionability 212
borrowers
  covenants 77, 78
  creditworthiness 80
breach of confidence
  account of profits 100–1
  causes of action 240
  equitable compensation 28, 43, 44, 100
  equitable damages 44
  human rights 239
  injunctions 44, 238, 240, 241–2
  right to privacy 239, 241, 242
breach of contract
  account of profits 93–119, 125–30, 133
  cynical conduct 109, 126, 129, 130
  damages *see* **damages in contract**
  damages in contract 114
  deceitful conduct 109, 110
  defendant's gain 95
  duty of care 38, 39–40
  exemplary damages 93–4, 119, 121, 127
  injunctions 101, 102, 126
  minimum payment clauses 200–1
  obligations 5, 6, 109, 111
  penalty clauses 198, 200
  repudiatory 200, 202
  restitution 26, 97, 110–11, 112
  specific performance 101, 102, 126
  strict contractual duty 38, 39
  termination 192–3
  unjust enrichment 111, 130

breach of duty of care
Aneco case 60–3, 71, 83–6, 89
causation 60, 63, 68–9, 70, 72–3, 85
compensatory damages 55
Fairchild case 67–70, 74–5, 90
incorrect information 58
industrial disease 67–9
McGhee case 68, 69, 90
Platform Homes case 63–5, 71, 79–80, 89
risk 68, 69
SAAMCO cases 56–9, 63–5, 65–70, 71–2
scope *see* **scope of duty**
Tennessee Trailways case 59–60, 73
valuer's negligence 56–8, 63, 64, 67, 76, 81
breach of duty (fiduciary)
account of profits 101, 103, 105
bribes 158
equitable compensation 28, 43, 44, 45, 47, 100
exemplary damages 120–1
non-consensual substitution 156
professional negligence 43, 86–7
proprietary rights 148
shareholders' rights 223
skill and care 45
breach of duty (statutory) 37, 41
breach of trust 44, 46–7
bribes
breach of fiduciary duty 158
constructive trusts 182
property rights 156, 158
unconnected assets 174
Brussels Convention 283, 289

carriage of goods by sea 33
causation
account of profits 117
breach of duty 60, 63, 68–9, 70, 72–3, 85
breach of trust 44
but for test 68, 73
causal agent ignored 75
chain broken *see* **intervening causation**
deceit 7
duty distinguished 55, 59–62, 63, 66, 70
factual cause (*causa sine qua non*) 60, 66, 75
legal cause (*causa causans*) 60, 66, 73, 75
mesothelioma 67, 69
'mountaineer's knee' 59, 81, 89
proximate cause 73
public policy 59, 60, 66, 74
question of fact 66, 73–4
risk 75
suicide, police custody 75
thin-skull rule 69

unjust enrichment 150
valuer's negligence 56, 72
causes of action
account of profits 98
accrual 77, 78
breach of confidence 240
equitable compensation 44
exemplary damages 93, 119, 120, 122
human rights 227, 233, 236, 238, 241, 242, 269
unjust enrichment 130, 131, 148
change of position
anticipatory 138–9
good faith 156
reliance expenditure 136, 137
unjust enrichment 135–6, 137, 152, 156, 172
characterization
doctrine 275–6
cheques wrongfully dishonoured 31
choice of law
see also **conflict of laws**; *lex fori*
constructive trusts 278
doctrine 275
forum shopping 274
public policy 276, 277
rights/remedies 273
where order has effect 272–3
codes of conduct
insurance brokers 86
privacy 243
collateral security 38
companies, loss of amenity 25
compensatory damages
bad bargains 5, 8, 27
breach of duty 55
concurrent claims 4, 8, 35
consequential loss 5
contracts *see* **damages in contract**
contribution between defendants 68, 79
good bargains 4, 27
reparation 4
terminology 99
torts *see* **damages in tort**
compensatory damages assessment
central issues 3–19
conflict of laws 273, 287–90
defendant's gain 94–5
difficulty 109, 110, 125–6, 192
direct benefits of wrong 28
expense 191
forensic inquiry 109, 110
irrecoverable amounts 191
just and equitable reduction 65
limitations 27–48
nature of wrong 56, 58
quantification 68–9

remoteness in contract 28–36
rules 5–7
underlying purpose 3–4, 18, 27, 55
confidential information
see also **breach of confidence**
account of profits 106
conflict of laws
see also **choice of law**
commercial remedies 271–86
equity 278–80, 289–90, 291
fiduciary duty 279
final remedies 272, 274, 287–90, 292
fraud 278, 281, 289–90
interim remedies 272, 274, 282–5, 288–9
specific performance 274, 275, 277
torts 276, 279–80
conscience
equity 177, 179, 291
unconscionable *see* **unconscionability**
consent
manifestations 132, 133
non-consensual substitution 154, 155–6, 166
proprietary rights 154, 155–6, 166, 176–8
security interests 178
unjust enrichment 151, 152, 154–6, 159, 161, 163, 166, 174–5, 176–8
consequential loss
compensatory damages 5
damages in contract 13, 14, 22, 32
exclusion clauses 32, 49–52
limitations 27
loss of profit 50
normal loss distinguished 50–1
remoteness of damage 5, 6–7, 28-36
third party loss 14
consideration
failure *see* **failure of consideration**
good consideration exception 141–2
construction contracts
building contracts 14
defects liability 23
insurance 21
liquidated damages 196–7
public policy 23
tortious liability 21
constructive trusts
see also **trusts**
bribes 182
choice of law 278
equitable interests 160
fraud 278
innocent defendant 181
insolvency 173
proprietary rights 183
shareholders' rights 223
unconnected assets 182

consumer contracts
bargaining power 198
conditions 203
oppression 222
unfair terms 193, 196, 203
consumer credit
human rights 233, 251, 252–3
public policy 253
consumer surplus 11, 12, 19, 25
contracts
agreed remedies 191–219
breach *see* **breach of contract**
claims, choice 3–5
conditions 202, 203
construction law *see* **construction contracts**
consumers *see* **consumer contracts**
contractual task 84
damages *see* **damages in contract**
exclusion clauses *see* **exclusion of liability**
governing law 279
liability capped 21, 22
licences, third parties 164
obligations *see* **obligations**
penalties *see* **penalty clauses**
performance *see* **performance**
proprietary rights 174
'rewritten' 222
subject matter 106–7
termination *see* **termination of contract**
third party rights 24, 26
contributory negligence
breach of duty (statutory) 37, 41
categories of case 38–41
damages in contract 37–43, 54
equitable compensation 44, 45
fault 37
general limitation 28
just and equitable reduction 65
Law Commission 40–3, 54
loss actually incurred 63–4
proportionate defence 37, 54
risk 64
SAAMCO cases 63–5, 79–80
strict liability 37, 41
torts 37
uncertainty 40
valuer's negligence 63–5, 67, 79–80
conversion, strict liability 54
covenants
borrowers 77, 78
criminal law
enforcement 96
human rights 230, 248, 249

Crown
  fiduciary duty 96
  legitimate interest 106
  private law claims 97

damage
  see also **losses**
  mitigation of damage 37, 41, 43, 54
  physical damage 34, 79
  remoteness *see* **remoteness of damage**
damages
  compensatory *see* **compensatory damages**
  disgorgement 98, 99, 115
  equitable *see* **equitable damages**
  future wrongs 260–1, 269
  gain-based 98, 99, 101, 115
  human rights 235, 260–1, 263, 265, 266
  liquidated *see* **liquidated damages**
  nominal 23, 25, 99
  punitive *see* **exemplary damages**
  restitutionary 98, 99, 101, 115, 129
  terminology 99, 129
damages in contract
  breach of contract 114
  characterizing loss 8–17
  consequential loss 13, 14, 22, 28–36
  consumer surplus 11, 12, 19, 25
  contractual warranties 4
  contributory negligence 37–43, 54
  cost of cure 9–11, 18, 22
  difference in value 9, 18, 22
  disappointment 11, 13, 25
  distress 11, 13, 28
  duty of care 7–8, 13, 14, 38–9, 56
  expectation 3, 5, 8, 18, 27
  foreseeable losses 6, 29, 35, 36
  inconvenience 13
  intangible losses 5, 9, 19, 22
  loss of amenity 9, 11–14, 25
  penalty clauses compared 195
  performance interest 16–17, 18, 27
  promised result 7
  reasonableness 10
  remedial inadequacy 101, 102, 105, 109, 110
  remoteness of damage 5, 6, 22, 28–36
  sale of goods 25–6
  third party loss 9, 14–17
  tort compared 3–7, 28
  wasted expenditure 8
damages in tort
  contracts compared 3–7, 28-43
  culpability 6, 7
  deceit 5–6, 7
  disappointment 6
  exemplary damages 7, 119, 120

  foreseeable losses 6–7, 22
  inconvenience 6
  intangible losses 5, 6
  latent damage 22
  misrepresentation 4, 21, 27
  negative obligations 27
  out-of-pocket losses 3, 8
  reliance losses 3, 5, 6, 27
  remoteness of damage 5, 6–7, 22, 33, 34, 36, 53–4
deceit
  causation 7
  damages in tort 5–6, 7
  direct consequence 36
  dishonesty 36, 54
  limitations 46
  negative obligations 27
  remoteness of damage 53–4
defences
  bona fide purchase 150, 152
  negligence *see* **contributory negligence**
  proportionate defence 37, 54
  unjust enrichment 134, 135–9, 141–2, 147–8, 152, 172
deposits 207, 210–11
discretionary remedies
  account of profits 100, 102, 103, 115, 116, 125
  common law 46
  declarations of incompatibility 228, 230, 231, 232–3, 245, 251, 258, 264
  discretionary area of judgment 245, 249–51, 262
  injunctions 103, 130
  specific performance 103
disgorgement
  account of profits 113, 116
  damages 98, 99, 115
dishonest assistance 28, 43
dishonesty
  account of profits 111
  deceit 36, 54
distress 11, 13, 28
duty
  assumption 84–5
  breach *see* **breach of duty**
  causation distinguished 55, 59–62, 63, 66, 70
  public policy 60
  scope *see* **scope of duty**
  strict contractural duty 38, 39
duty of care
  damages in contract 7–8, 13, 14, 38, 39–40, 56
  economic loss 5
  implied obligation 56
  negligence 5, 38

reinsurance 38, 83
road traffic 60
third party loss 14
valuer's negligence 72

economic loss 5
election, account of profits 118–19
enforcement
 collateral security 38
 criminal law 96
 incompatible legislation 228
 statutory duties 263
 uncertainty 222
enrichment
 unjust *see* **unjust enrichment**
 valid contract 146, 147
 wrongful *see* **wrongful enrichment**
equitable compensation
 account of profits 100, 101
 breach of confidence 28, 43, 44, 100
 breach of duty of skill and care 45
 breach of fiduciary duty 28, 43, 44, 45, 47, 100
 breach of trust 46–7
 causes of action, choice 44
 contributory negligence 44, 45
 dishonest assistance 28, 43
 equitable wrongs 28, 43–7
 intervening causation 44
 limitations 28, 43–7
 remoteness of damage 44
equitable damages
 breach of confidence 44
 in lieu of injunction 270
equitable interests
 compound interest 164
 future property 176–7
 mere equity 160
 voidable 160
equity
 anti-suit injunctions 279, 282, 283, 284, 291
 conflict of laws 278–80, 289–90, 291
 conscience 177, 179, 291
 done what ought to be done 177, 180, 182
 in personam jurisdiction 280, 291
 lex fori 278–9, 280–1, 290, 291
 private international law 272
 recovery of payments 205
 relief from forfeiture 202, 209–10
 volunteers 181
estoppel
 contract for finality 137
 unjust enrichment 136–8, 186–7
European Contract Code 41
exclusion of liability
 consequential/indirect loss 32, 49, 51–2, 53

control 193
 lists 52, 53
exemplary damages
 breach of contract 93–4, 119, 121, 127
 breach of duty (fiduciary) 120–1
 causes of action 93, 119, 120, 122
 damages in tort 7, 119, 120
 independent actionable wrong 121
 misfeasance in public office 119
 oppression 120
 terminology 99
expectation, damages in contract 3, 5, 8, 18, 27
express trusts 158, 162, 163
extortionate credit bargains 222

failure of basis 144–7, 161, 162–3
failure of consideration
 recovery of payments 206, 208
 total/partial 206–7, 211
 unjust enrichment 144–6, 165
fault
 contributory negligence 37
 definition 37
 intervening causation 37, 41, 42–3, 54
 mitigation of damage 37, 41, 43, 54
 proprietary rights 164, 181
fiduciary duty
 breach *see* **breach of duty (fiduciary)**
 conflict of laws 279
 Crown 96
 obligations 101, 103, 105
 valuation 86–7
finance leases
 part performance 206
 relief from forfeiture 202, 214
foreseeable losses
 damages in contract 6, 29, 35, 36
 damages in tort 6–7, 22, 33
 negligence 6–7, 22, 34, 35
 public policy 59
 valuer's negligence 72
forfeiture *see* **relief from forfeiture**
forum shopping 273–4, 284, 287
franchising, goodwill 110, 126
fraud
 conflict of laws 278, 281, 289–90
 constructive trusts 278
 misrepresentation 6, 21, 58, 81
 wrongful enrichment 133
freedom of contract 192
freedom of expression 227, 238–41, 243–8
freezing orders
 human rights 253, 254
 in personam 282

gain
compensatory damages 94–5
gain-based damages 98, 99, 101, 115, 129
subtraction from claimant 99, 155
torts 100
wrongs 101
goodwill, franchising 110, 126
guarantees 207

hire-purchase agreements
minimum payment clauses 200–2, 203
part performance 206
relief from forfeiture 214
human rights
breach of confidence 239
causes of action 227, 233, 236, 238, 241, 242, 269
civil rights 248, 249
common law litigation 237–43
consumer credit 233, 251, 252–3
criminal law 230, 248, 249
failure to act 259, 260
incremental change 239, 240
limitation of actions 261
private law remedies 227–55
public policy 247
section 3 228–33, 244, 253, 254, 263–5
section 6 233–44, 251, 258–9, 260–1, 263–6, 269
section 12 238–9, 243–4
statutory interpretation 234–5, 236
uncertainty 233, 241, 246, 251
human rights (compatibility)
criminal statutes 230
declarations of incompatibility 228, 230, 231, 232–3, 245, 251, 258, 264
impermissible judicial legislation 229–30, 231, 232, 233
interpretative obligation 228, 229, 230, 233
judicial guidance 229
legislation 228–33
previous authority 232
reinterpretation 229
retrospective application 229, 230, 232, 263–4
uncertainty 233
human rights (Convention rights)
application 228–44
Art.6 227, 230, 244, 245, 248–55
Art.8 227, 238–41, 243–8, 254, 259, 260, 264, 269
Art.10 227, 238–41, 243–8
Art.13 259, 264–7
context-based 248
fair and public hearing 227, 230, 244, 245, 248–55

First Protocol 227, 244, 246–8, 252, 253, 259, 260, 264, 269
freedom of expression 227, 238–41, 243–8
freezing orders 253, 254
Marcic case 258–65
margin of appreciation 245, 249–51
planning 249
possessions 227, 244, 246–8, 252, 253, 259, 260, 264, 269
privacy 227, 238–41, 243–8, 254, 259, 260, 264, 269
private law examples 251–4, 270
proportionality 244, 245–9, 250, 253, 260
public authorities 234, 235, 236
qualified rights 244–9, 250, 251
remedies 259, 264–7
restrictions 245–8
search orders 253, 254, 258
substantive impact 244–51, 261–3
unqualified rights 245, 248, 250
violation 235, 238–9, 244–5, 246, 262
human rights (courts/tribunals)
appeals 257–8
constitutional duty 257
discretionary area of judgment 245, 249–51, 262
fair and public hearing 227, 230, 244, 245, 248–51, 254, 255
public authorities 234, 236–7
human rights (horizontal disputes)
authority against 241
causes of action 236, 237
remedies 235, 244
statutory interpretation 234, 235, 236
human rights (public authorities)
Convention rights 234, 235, 236
courts/tribunals 234, 236–7
damages 235, 260–1, 263, 265, 266
definition 235, 270
obligations 236, 237
rights violated 235, 238–9, 244–5, 262
vertical effect 234, 236

ignorance, unjust enrichment 151, 152, 155
impecuniosity 28
industrial diseases 67–9
injunctions
anti-suit injunctions 279, 282, 283, 284, 291
breach of confidence 44, 238, 240, 241–2
breach of contract 101, 102, 126
discretionary remedies 103, 130
freezing orders 253, 254, 282
search orders 253, 254, 258
insolvency
constructive trusts 173

mistake 175
order for sale 215
proprietary rights 177–8
protection of creditors 223
termination of contract 201
transaction at an undervalue 222
unjust enrichment 167, 172–3, 175
insurance
see also **reinsurance**
brokers 86
construction contracts 21
contingencies, recovery of payments 203
underwriting losses 34–5
intangible losses
damages in contract 5, 9, 19, 22
damages in tort 5, 6
negligence 6
interest rates
capped figure 78
commencement date 77–8
penalty clauses 198
statutory interest 76–8
interest swaps
closed swaps 164, 168
compound interest 164, 168
unjust enrichment 131, 164–6, 168
interim remedies
conflict of laws 272, 274, 282–5, 288–9
intervening causation
claimant's fault 37, 41, 42–3, 54
equitable compensation 44
general limitation 28
novus actus interveniens 89, 117

judicial review 249
jurisdiction, penalty clauses 198–205,
208–9

knowing assistance *see* **dishonest**
assistance

latent damage 22
Law Commission
contributory negligence 40–3, 54
human rights, damages 269
security interests 217, 218
legitimate interest 102, 105–6, 109, 111–12,
126
lex causae
remedial consequences 272, 276, 277–8,
281, 282, 284–5, 288, 290
substantive issues 275, 277
lex contractus
rights and duties 272
Rome Convention 275, 276–7
substantive issues 271
lex delicti 271, 276

lex fori
alternative unknown 276
compensatory damages assessment 273,
277
equity 278–9, 280–1, 290, 291
forum shopping 273–4
in personam jurisdiction 280, 291
procedure 271, 274, 277, 288, 289, 291
remedial consequences 272, 275, 279, 281,
282
lex loci delicti commissi 280
lex situs 271
liabilities
concurrent 39
contractual liability capped 21, 22
defects 23
exclusion clauses *see* **exclusion of**
liability
limits *see* **limitations**
tortious *see* **torts**
liens
beneficial interests 153, 167
equitable liens 178
operation of law 178
limitation of actions
human rights 261
negligence 22
torts 77
limitations
account of profits 116–17
compensatory damages assessment
27–48
consequential loss 27
deceit 46
equitable compensation 28, 43–7
types 28
liquidated damages
bargaining power 197
construction contracts 196–7
non-application of clause 198
risk allocation 195
shipbuilding contracts 198
loans
borrower's covenant 77, 78
consumer credit 233, 251, 252–3
costs of borrowing 77, 78
creditworthiness 80
syndicated agreements 198
valuer's negligence 57
loss of a chance 69, 70
loss of amenity 9, 11–14, 25
loss of profit
consequential loss 50
remoteness of damage 29–30,
32–4
losses
accounting for loss 43, 46, 47

losses (*cont*):
    actually incurred 63–4
    arising naturally 29, 30, 31, 49
    characterization 8–17
    consequential *see* **consequential loss**
    economic loss 5
    foreseeable *see* **foreseeable losses**
    genuine pre-estimate 192, 194, 199, 202
    indemnities 193
    indirect 32, 49, 51–2, 53
    intangible *see* **intangible losses**
    late delivery 49, 50
    loss of bargain 200, 201–2, 211
    normal/ordinary 50–1
    out-of-pocket 3, 8
    physical damage 34, 79
    possibility of loss 33
    reasonable contemplation 29, 30, 32, 35, 36
    recoverable, kinds/scope 5–6
    relevant, measurable loss 77
    reliance 3, 5, 6, 27
    remoteness *see* **remoteness of damage**
    scope of duty 55, 56, 57, 58, 62, 64, 66–7, 76, 80
    tangible 5
    third parties *see* **third party loss**
    types 29, 34–5
    underwriting 34–5
    use of money 28
Lugano Convention 283

margin of appreciation 245, 249–51
measure of recovery
    account of profits 112–17, 118
    choice 118
    expense saved 129
    restitution 99–100
medical negligence 69, 70
misfeasance in public office 119
misrepresentation
    damages in tort 4, 21, 27
    fraudulent 6, 21, 58, 81
    negative obligations 27
    negligence 27
mistake
    authority to pay 140, 141, 142, 143
    banks 140–3
    bargaining 160–1
    causative mistake 141
    donors 151
    essential elements 139
    good consideration exception 141–2
    insolvency 175
    mistake of law 145–6
    payment caused 139
    representations 138

    spontaneous mistake 160–1
    unjust enrichment 131, 133, 134–5, 138, 139–40, 151, 159, 172
mitigation of damage 37, 41, 43, 54
money
    unjust enrichment 183
    use, loss 28
mortgages 176

negligence
    claimants *see* **contributory negligence**
    duty of care 5, 38
    foreseeable losses 6–7, 22, 34, 35
    harm caused *see* **causation**
    incorrect information 57
    intangible losses 6
    limitation of actions 22
    limitations 59
    misrepresentation 27
    professional *see* **professional negligence**
    remoteness of damage 34, 35, 36
    sub-contractors 40
    unjust enrichment 135
    valuation *see* **valuer's negligence**
non-justiciability 262
nuisance, flooding 259, 260

obligations
    breach 5, 6, 109, 111
    certainty 21
    content 7–8
    conversion 19
    fiduciary duty 101, 103
    negative obligations 27
    perform or pay 19
    primary/secondary 199, 200
    proprietary rights 180–1
    restitution 157, 161
    rights *in personam* 154, 157
oppression
    consumer contracts 222
    exemplary damages 120
    formation of contract 221
    payment clauses 202
    penalty clauses 196, 197, 204, 218
    termination of contract 202

part performance
    finance leases 206
    hire-purchase agreements 206
    payments 207, 211–12
    test for relief 211–12
passing of property 150, 158, 159, 160, 161, 162
payments
    conditional 207
    contingencies 203

deposits 207, 210–11
detriment after payment 138
full performance 208
guarantees 207
instalments 206, 207, 208
minimum payment clauses 200–2, 203, 223
mistake *see* **mistake**
oppression 202
part performance 207, 211–12
pre-payments 208–10
retention 205
unconditional 207
payments (recovery)
contingencies 203
contractual provisions 207–8
equity 205
failure of consideration 206, 208
relief from forfeiture 205–12
restitution 205, 206–7
termination of contract 205–12
whether recoverable 207–8
penalty clauses
breach of contract 198, 200
clever drafting 200, 202, 204
commercial transactions 194, 196–8
damages in contract compared 195
genuine pre-estimate of loss 192, 194, 199, 202
in terrorem 194
interest rates 198
liquidated damages 195, 196–7
manifestly excessive 196, 204
not incorporated 193
oppression 196, 197, 204, 218
payments triggered 200, 201, 202, 203
penal bonds 194
penalty jurisdiction 198–205, 208–9
presumptions 195
problem areas 200–4
property transfer 195
rule against penalties 194–217
single lump sums 195
syndicated loan agreements 198
time of contracting 194
performance
conditional/unconditional 207
deposits 207
incentives 192
interest, damages in contract 16–17, 18, 27
part *see* **part performance**
perform or pay obligations 19
reduced performance 23, 26
specific *see* **specific performance**
Press Complaints Commission 243

privacy
breach of confidence 239, 241, 242
codes of conduct 243
common law 239
Convention rights 227, 238–41, 243–8, 254, 259, 260, 264, 269
freedom of expression 240, 243–4
sexuality 247
professional negligence
advice 57, 81, 84
breach of fiduciary duty 43, 86–7
medical negligence 69, 70
SAAMCO cases 81
valuation *see* **valuer's negligence**
profits
account *see* **account of profits**
loss *see* **loss of profit**
meaning 112–14
profit-stripping 100, 129
proportionality
defences, contributory negligence 37, 54
human rights 244, 245–9, 250, 253, 260
judicial review 249
proprietary rights
bare legal title 150
breach of duty (fiduciary) 148
consensual 176–8
contracts 174
fault 164, 181
fictitious persistence 153–4
formalities 177, 178, 179
identifiable asset 176, 179
indebitatus assumpsit 148, 172
insolvency 177–8
intention 176, 177
non-consensual substitution 154, 155–6, 166
objective manifestation of transaction 176, 177, 179
obligations 180–1
old/new assets 173–4
power to vest 150
priorities 167
recognised property 176
rights *in rem* 154
timing 164
traceable substitutes 157, 166, 167
tracing *see* **tracing**
unconnected assets 174, 182
unjust enrichment 134, 148–50, 152–69, 171–87
voidable title 150

Quistclose trusts 162

recovery
account of profits 97, 112–17, 118
double 78, 118
irrecoverable *see* **irrecoverable amounts**
measure *see* **measure of recovery**
payment *see* **payments (recovery)**
reinsurance
Bullen Treaty 61–3
duty of care 38, 83
fac/oblig treaty 61
quota share treaty 61
risk 61–2
reliance
expenditure 136, 137
interest 211
losses 3, 5, 6, 27
relief from forfeiture
agreed remedies 194, 205–17
contract allowed to continue 212–17
equity 202, 209–10
finance leases 202, 214
hire-purchase agreements 214
payments made 208–10
payments on termination, recovery
205–12
possessory rights 202, 208, 214
security argument 214–17, 223–4
tests 210–12
remedial inadequacy
account of profits 101, 102–5, 111, 125–6
circumstances of case 107
damages in contract 101, 102, 105, 109,
110
specific performance 104, 130
remedies
terminology 131
remoteness of damage
carriage of goods by sea 33
compensatory damages assessment
28–36
consequential loss 5, 6–7
damages in contract 5, 6, 22, 28–36
damages in tort 5, 6–7, 22, 33, 34, 36, 53–4
deceit 53–4
equitable compensation 44
general limitation 28
Hadley v Baxendale 29–34, 49, 50
loss of profit 29–30, 32–4
negligence 34, 35, 36
risk 34, 35, 53
shared knowledge 32
strict liability 54
trading loss 31
restitution
breach of contract 26, 97, 110–11, 112
measure of recovery 99–100
obligations 157, 161

recovery of payments 205, 206–7
Restatement of Restitution 138, 142, 143,
160
restitutionary damages 98, 99, 101, 115,
129
rights 133
ring-fencing 161, 162, 165, 167
terminology 99–100, 129
torts 101
unjust enrichment 131–69
resulting trusts 161, 163
retention of title 213
risk
breach of duty 68, 69
causation 75
contribution to harm 68, 74, 75
contributory negligence 64
loss of a chance 69, 70
medical negligence 69, 70
over-valuation 57
reinsurance 61–2
remoteness of damage 34, 35, 53
risk allocation
agreed remedies 192, 199, 204
commercial expectations 57, 82–6, 221
liquidated damages 195
Rome Convention 275, 276, 288

SAAMCO **cases**
breach of duty 56–9, 63–5, 65–70, 71–2
capped figure 78
contributory negligence 63–5, 79–80
Court of Appeal decision 55, 57, 58, 60,
62
in practice 71–87
litigation 56–9
outcomes 81–6
practical criticisms 76–81
professional negligence 81
scope of duty 55, 56, 57, 58, 62, 64, 76,
81–2, 89
statutory interest 76–8
wider implications 65–70
sale of goods
ascertainment 176
damages in contract 25–6
instalment payments 206
sale of land 210
scope of duty
commercial expectations 82
first question 55, 66–7, 70
losses 55, 56, 57, 58, 62, 64, 66–7, 76, 80
public policy 74
SAAMCO cases 55, 56, 57, 58, 62, 64, 76,
81–2, 89
terminology 73
Scottish Law Commission 196, 204

search orders 253, 254, 258
security interests
  collateral security 38
  non-consensual 178
  relief from forfeiture 214–17, 223–4
shareholders' rights 223
shipbuilding contracts 198, 207–8
specific performance
  breach of contract 101, 102, 126
  conflict of laws 274, 275, 277
  discretionary remedies 103
  remedial inadequacy 104, 130
  unavailable 103, 104
statutory interest 76–8
strict liability
  contributory negligence 37, 41
  remoteness of damage 54
  Rylands v Fletcher 41
  unjust enrichment 133, 135, 136
syndicated loan agreements 198

termination of contract
  breach of contract 192–3
  insolvency 201
  irrecoverable amounts 192, 193
  minimum payment clauses 200–2, 203
  oppression 202
  recovery of payments 205–12
  retention of payment 205
third parties
  account of profits 113
  breach of trust 44
  contractual licences 164
  rights, contracts 24, 26
third party loss
  building contracts 14
  collateral warranties 15, 16, 23
  consequential loss 14
  damages in contract 9, 14–17
  direct warranties 15
  duty of care 14
  narrower ground 14, 15, 23, 24
  performance interest 16–17, 18
  wider ground 14, 15, 16, 23, 25
torts
  burden of proof 74, 75
  choice 3–5
  claims
  conflict of laws 276, 279–80
  construction contracts 21
  contributory negligence 37
  damages *see* **damages in tort**
  deceit *see* **deceit**
  gain 100
  intention 5, 6, 7, 36
  limitation of actions 77
  negligence *see* **negligence**

restitution 101
uncertainty 21
unintentional 5, 6, 36
tracing
  bank accounts 149, 150, 183–4
  proprietary rights 153
  traceable substitutes 152, 153, 166, 167,
    182
trade marks 107
trusts
  accounting for loss 46, 47
  breach of trust 44, 46–7
  constructive *see* **constructive trusts**
  express 158, 162, 163
  Quistclose 162
  resulting 161, 163

unconscionability
  bargaining power 212
  general doctrine 221–3
  part performance payments 211–12
  payments made 209
  relief 193
  terminology 223
  unjust enrichment compared 132, 135
underwriting losses 34–5
UNIDROIT, Principles of International
  Commercial Contracts 41–2
unjust enrichment
  account of profits 98
  anticipatory disenrichment 138–9
  benefits in kind 134
  bona fide purchase 150, 152
  breach of contract 111, 130
  carelessness 133, 134–5
  causa data causa non secuta 144, 145
  causa debendi 148
  causation 150
  causes of action 130, 131, 148
  change of position 135–6, 137, 152, 156,
    172
  Chase Manhattan case 160–1, 173, 179, 186
  consent 151, 152, 154–6, 159, 161, 163,
    166, 174–5, 176–8
  contractual relationship 150
  corresponding loss 148
  court orders 131
  defective intent 159
  defences 134, 135–9, 141–2, 147–8, 152,
    172
  Derby case 134–8, 186–7
  Dextra case 138–40
  disenrichment 136
  disimpoverishment 147–8
  estoppel 136–8, 186–7
  expense of claimant 133, 134, 142–3, 148,
    149–50, 151–2

unjust enrichment (*cont*):
  failure of basis 144–7, 161, 162–3
  failure of consideration 144–6, 165
  failure of contractual reciprocation 145
  five-question analysis 133–64, 171–84
  Foskett case 153–6, 166, 174
  Goldcorp case 162, 165
  ignorance 151, 152, 155
  implied contract theory 132
  Independent Insurance case 140–3
  innocent defendants 134–5, 137
  insolvency 167, 172–3, 175
  interest swaps 131, 164–6, 168
  leapfrogging 150, 151
  Lipkin Gorman case 137, 148–53, 166, 173
  misdirected funds 131
  misprediction 139
  mistake 131, 133, 134–5, 138, 139–40, 151, 159, 172
  money 183
  negligence 135
  part performance payments 211
  personal rights 134, 157
  proprietary rights 134, 148–50, 152–69, 171–87
  restitution 131–69
  Roxborough case 132, 143–8
  skepticism 132, 169
  strict liability 133, 135, 136
  substitute assets 152, 157, 166, 167, 174, 175, 181, 182
  terminology 171
  undue influence 159
  unjustness 134–5, 139–40, 141–2, 144–7, 151, 159, 171–2
  Westdeutsche case 163, 164, 168, 179

use of money 28

valuer's negligence
  advice on loans 57
  breach of duty 56–8, 63, 64, 67, 76, 81
  causation 56, 72
  consequences 57
  contributory negligence 63–5, 67, 79–80
  duty of care 72
  foreseeable losses 72
  incorrect information 57, 63–5, 67, 83
  nstructions to valuer 58, 82
  no transaction 72, 77, 83
  pre-*SAAMCO* analysis 72
  successful transaction 72, 77

warranties
  collateral 15, 16, 23
  contractual 4
  direct 15
Warsaw Convention (1929) 287
wrongs
  acquisitive wrongs 158
  breach of duty 132
  deterrence 115
  direct benefit 28
  equitable 28, 43–7
  future wrongs 260–1, 269
  gain 101
  independent actionable wrong 121
  manifestations 132
  nature 56, 58
  restitutionary damages 115
  wrongful enrichment 133
  wrongful profits 109–10